SOVEREIGNTY

AT THE

EDGE

Macau

& the

Question of

Chineseness

Harvard East Asian Monographs 324

SOVEREIGNTY AT THE EDGE
Macau & the Question of Chineseness

Cathryn H. Clayton

Published by the Harvard University Asia Center
Distributed by Harvard University Press
Cambridge (Massachusetts) and London 2009

Printed in the United States of America

The Harvard University Asia Center publishes a monograph series and, in coordination with the Fairbank Center for Chinese Studies, the Korea Institute, the Reischauer Institute of Japanese Studies, and other faculties and institutes, administers research projects designed to further scholarly understanding of China, Japan, Vietnam, Korea, and other Asian countries. The Center also sponsors projects addressing multidisciplinary and regional issues in Asia.

Library of Congress Cataloging-in-Publication Data

Clayton, Cathryn H., 1966–

    Sovereignty at the edge : Macau & the question of Chineseness / Cathryn H. Clayton.

        p. cm. – (Harvard East Asian monographs ; 324)

    Includes bibliographical references and index.

    ISBN 978-0-674-03545-4 (cl : alk. paper)

      1. Chinese–China–Macau (Special Administrative Region)–Ethnic identity. 2. Chinese–China–Macau (Special Administrative Region)–Attitudes. 3. Ethnicity–China–Macau (Special Administrative Region) 4. Group identity–China–Macau (Special Administrative Region) 5. National characteristics, Chinese. 6. Macau (China : Special Administrative Region)–History–Transfer of Sovereignty from Portugal, 1999–Social aspects. I. Harvard University. Asia Center. II. Title.

    DS796.M29C43 2009

    951.26'06–dc22

2009039516

Index by the author

ʘ Printed on acid-free paper

Last figure below indicates year of this printing

18 17 16 15 14 13 12 11 10

For my parents, Jackie and Paul

For Luca, and for Thomas

Acknowledgments

This book is the result of a process that began long ago when I was a graduate student in the anthropology department at the University of California, Santa Cruz, and has continued through reconceptualizations and revisions in Macau, Boston, Torino, and Honolulu. In the course of its evolution into its present form, I have incurred many debts of many kinds—financial, intellectual, emotional, culinary—each indispensable in its own way. Although a full list of my benefactors over the years would be too long to include here, I wish to make mention of the following people and institutions who were instrumental in seeing this work (and its author) through the long process of its creation. Although they in no way should be held responsible for its shortcomings, they deserve a very large share of credit for its merits.

Gail Hershatter has been my most constant mentor ever since my first encounters with China as an undergraduate at Williams College; her commitment to me and to this project has been above and beyond the call of duty, and her sympathetic skepticism at key points along the way has been indispensable in saving me from myself. I have always been grateful for Anna Tsing's ability to see in my work far more than I am able to express and for her generosity in sharing that vision with me. And my graduate advisor, Lisa Rofel, helped shape my thinking about culture and power in ways too far-reaching for me to even articulate. Their close readings of earlier drafts of this manuscript were crucial to shaping its final form.

A three-year National Science Foundation Graduate Fellowship while I was at UC Santa Cruz allowed me to focus my time and energies on the conceptualization of this project. A summer FLAS funded my study of Cantonese at the Yale-in-China Center at the Chinese University of Hong Kong in the summer of 1997. The field research upon which this book is based was made possible with funding from the National Science Foundation, the Social Science Research Council, the Wenner Gren Foundation for Anthropological Research, and the Instituto Cultural de Macau. I would also like to thank the Committee for Scholarly Exchange with China for help in setting up research contacts at the Central Academy of Social Sciences and the First Historical Archive in Beijing. Finally, in 2003–4, an An Wang Postdoctoral Fellowship at Harvard University's Fairbank Center for East Asian Research allowed me the time, space, and intellectual environment to reconceptualize the dissertation.

The interlocutors and friends who enabled my fieldwork in Macau are too many to enumerate. I have long been gratified and inspired by their patience with my questions and their generosity with their time and information. Special thanks are due to Louella Cheng Chi Wai, who softened my landing in Hong Kong in 1997 and has been an unfailing source of support and friendship ever since; to Professor K. C. Fok, Cuc Kim Nguyen Fok, and Gary Ngai for the many kindnesses they extended to me and the many doors they opened for me when I first arrived in Macau; to my erstwhile colleagues at the Fundação Sino-Latina—Lita do Rosario, Yvonne Zhang, Florence Ho, Li Jian, and Anabela Monteiro—on whom I could always count for help, advice, and a good laugh; to Rui Simões—fellow fieldworker and frequent accomplice in the midday consumption of *mak-yuh beng*, a certain kind of fishcake, deep-fried and dipped in vinegar—whose humor lightened even the most frustrating days of fieldwork; and to the staff of the Museu de Macau and the Instituto Cultural, especially Ana Maria Catarino, Teresa Fu Barreto, and Carlos Moreno, for receiving me with openness, candor, and enthusiasm. I hope that my respect for their work is clear even when my analysis is critical.

Also deserving of special mention are Chan Meng Chak, Chan Wai Kan, Chen Meijuan and Chan Chak Chan, Chan Jileung, Margarida Cheung, Chiu Man Yin, Joe Chui, Rui and Inês Costa, Ho Sang Wong, Agnes Lam, Leong Iao Cheng, Carlos Marreiros, the Maryknoll sisters, João Nuno Riquito, Helena Rodrigues, Shirley Sam, Elizabeth Sinn, Sit Wing Tou, the late Rev. Carl Smith, Vong Chau Son, Wang Chun, and the students in the Macau Culture and Society course I taught at the Instituto Politécnico de Macau in the spring of 1998 and at the University of Macau from 2001 to 2005. To those of you (and others) who may recognize yourselves in these pages, I hope the shock is not too great to bear.

Over the years, various individuals have read, listened to, and commented on the manuscript in part or in its entirety. I thank the following people for their contributions: Ann Anagnost, Cherie Barkey, Steve Caton, Lynda Chapple, Tim Choy, John Clayton, Rob Culp, Virginia Domínguez, Lieba Faier, Judith Farquhar, Richard Handler, Shelley Drake Hawks, Cori Hayden, Michael Herzfeld, Engseng Ho, Lyn Jeffery, Jon Keesey, Eileen Otis, Alisa Puga, Annie Reinhardt, Carlos Rojas, Nina Schnall, Dan Segal, Shao Dan, Shen Hsiu-hua, Tim Simpson, Glenn Timmermans, and Paul Van Dyke.

I would also like to thank the two anonymous reviewers for the Harvard University Asia Center. Their comments provided encouragement as well as excellent suggestions for honing the argument of the book.

Finally, I would like to thank Luca Macchiarulo for his unswerving support and confidence in me and Thomas Clayton Macchiarulo for his giggles, which made the final months of revisions a happier, if slower, task. This book has been a part of our lives for as long as we have been a family, and I for one am looking forward to turning over a new page together.

C.H.C.

Contents

Maps and Figures

Notes on Conventions

The name "Macau" is often rendered "Macao" in English; in the years since the handover, the Special Administrative Region government has adopted the latter spelling as the official English name of the city. Nevertheless, as a matter of personal preference, I have chosen to use the Portuguese spelling throughout this book. However, the English version occasionally appears in quotations from English-language sources, and in these cases I have left the original spelling unchanged.

Somewhat more complicated is the problem of the romanization of Chinese words. Although Cantonese is the dialect spoken by more than 85 percent of Macau's population and is the principal spoken language in Hong Kong, most of Guangdong, and parts of Guangxi province, there are several different systems of romanization (I know of at least four). The Hong Kong and Macau governments, for example, have different systems, and because the Portuguese alphabet does not have the letters "w" or "y" or the hard "g" sound, the Macau system looks quite alien to anyone familiar with the Hong Kong system or with the *hanyu pinyin* system for romanizing Mandarin Chinese. For the purposes of this book, the problem has been alleviated by the ability to insert Chinese characters into the English text; where possible, I have simply included the Chinese characters rather than their romanizations. Where the Cantonese pronunciation is important to my argument, I have used the Yale romanization system. In the few cases in which quotations from Portuguese sources include Cantonese romanizations, I have left the

Portuguese transcription system unchanged. Finally, I use the *hanyu pinyin* in cases where the original quotation was spoken or written in Mandarin, as well as in transcribing terms or place-names (such as *te-se* or *Beijing*) commonly used in the PRC, even if they were originally uttered in Cantonese. In transcribing authors' names, I follow the authors' preferences where they are provided; otherwise, I use *hanyu pinyin*.

The inclusion of Chinese characters poses a problem of its own: for, although it is commonly supposed that Mandarin and Cantonese are spoken differently but written the same, this is not strictly true. Readers of Mandarin Chinese will notice the use of several characters not found in any Mandarin dictionary. These are standard characters for transcribing the sounds of spoken Cantonese into written form, used widely in the popular press in Hong Kong and Macau. A glossary of these characters, with Mandarin Chinese and English equivalents, is provided at the back. Unless otherwise noted, all translations from Chinese and Portuguese into English are mine. Interviews were conducted in Cantonese, Mandarin, English, or Portuguese, depending on the preference of the interviewee. Where I use direct quotes from interviews, I indicate explicitly or implicitly the language in which these interviews were conducted.

Finally, unless otherwise indicated, all the names in this study have been changed to protect informants' confidentiality. It is something of a fashion among many educated Macau and Hong Kong residents to be called by Portuguese or English first names; I have followed the conventions of my interviewees in assigning Chinese or Western-language pseudonyms. Because of Macau's small size and the political sensitivity of the topics under discussion, in some cases I have deemed it necessary to mask other markers of identity as well, such as age, occupation, and even gender.

The following abbreviations are used in the text and notes:

AMRB   *Aomen ribao* 澳門日報

CCP   Chinese Communist Party

DSEJ   Direcção dos Serviços de Educação e Juventude

ESLC   Escola Secundária Luso-Chinesa Luís Gonzaga Gomes

EU   European Union

FEER	*Far Eastern Economic Review*
ICM	Cultural Institute of Macau
JTM	*Jornal tribuna de Macau*
KMT	Kuomintang
MGTO	Macau Government Tourism Office
MOP	Macao pataca (currency)
PRC	People's Republic of China
SAR	Special Administrative Region
SCMP	*South China Morning Post*
SEZ	Special Economic Zone
STDM	Sociedade de Turismo e Diversões de Macau
UN	United Nations
UNESCO	United Nations Educational, Scientific and Cultural Organization

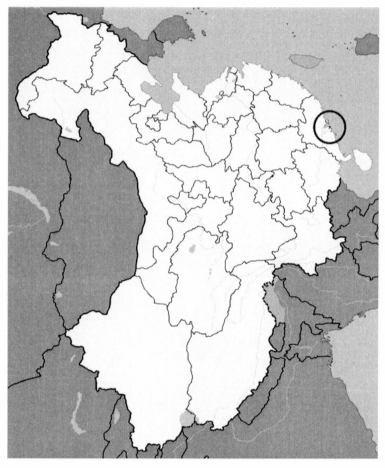

Map 1   The People's Republic of China showing the location of Macau.

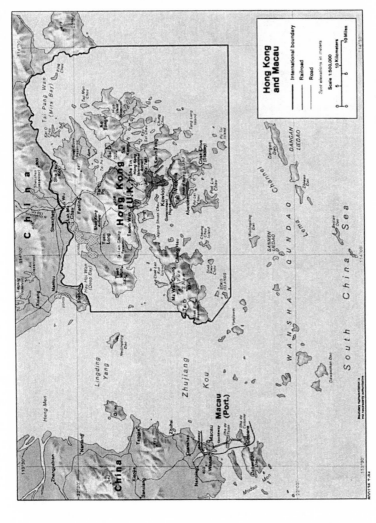

Map 2   Macau has just 2 percent of the total land area of neighboring Hong Kong (1984 map produced by the Central Intelligence Agency, courtesy University of Texas Libraries).

SOVEREIGNTY
AT THE
EDGE
Macau

& the

Question of

Chineseness

Introduction

What remains of the São Paulo Church stands atop a small hill near the geographic center of the Macau peninsula. If you approach it on foot from the city's main square below, the four-story buildings that hem in and hang over the narrow cobbled streets hide it from view until the very last moment; then, as you emerge from the shady labyrinth of shops and cafes and the press of shoppers and diners into the strong sun of the flagstone plaza, it surprises you. You knew it was there; you were, in fact, following the signs pointing in this direction; but you were not prepared for something quite this striking.

What remains of the São Paulo Church is its stone façade. The church, along with the seminary and fortress of which it formed a part, was built in the first two decades of the seventeenth century; in the thirty-fifth year of the nineteenth century, it burned to the ground and was never rebuilt. By the late 1990s, its four-story façade had come to be a monument in its own right. Look at the façade up close—run your hands along its cool granite surfaces; pose, as do hundreds of tourists every day, for a photograph in front of its main arch; listen to the tour guide explain how it was designed by Italian Jesuits and built by Japanese stonemasons; crane your neck upward to examine the bas-relief carvings (called a "sermon in stone")[1] that decorate each tier—and you will find a solid, coherent, tangible whole, analogous if not identical to a thousand other monuments in a hundred other cities. Walk through its portals to investigate the inside, however, and you will see that there *is* no inside; stand at the base of the long flight of stone steps leading up to it, and you

I

will see blue sky through its windows. The effect is probably unlike anything you have seen. This transparency, this unanticipated juxtaposition of stone and sky, of presence and absence, makes the monument unique.

Between 1990 and 1995, the Macau government spent approximately $23 million patacas (US$3 million) to restore this edifice.[2] The façade was cleaned, its foundation strengthened, the vegetation of neglect cleared away, and the ground behind it paved with stones in a way that marked the foundations of the nave, apse, and crypt; the original chapel annex was turned into a small gallery of Catholic sacred art from Macau, Timor, and Goa. With its restoration, the government officially adopted the São Paulo façade (also known as the São Paulo Ruins) as the city's icon. Throughout the 1990s, its image adorned the backs of coins, the dust jackets of books, the pages of tourist brochures; its silhouette was featured in television commercials advertising Macau as a weekend destination; miniature plaster casts of it were for sale in shops around the city and were given as gifts by government officials to visiting dignitaries. In 1998, when I asked a classroom of Macau Chinese middle-school students to draw a picture on the theme "My Macau," most of them sketched the São Paulo Ruins.

It is no coincidence that the Macau government took this monument as its *ex libris* during the long decade of the 1990s, also known as "the transition era"—an era in which Macau, a small city on the south China coast that had been governed by Portugal since the mid-sixteenth century, was preparing to be transferred from Portuguese to Chinese administration. This was also the era in which the city's Portuguese government mounted a massive campaign to convince the population, 95 percent of whom identified as Chinese, that they possessed a "unique cultural identity" which made them different from all other Chinese people—a difference resulting from the 450-year history not of Portuguese colonialism but of the existence of a deferential Portuguese state on sovereign Chinese soil. This project required a recasting of Macau's image: no longer would Macau be viewed, as it often was by its own residents and by observers around the world, as a colonial backwater, the last, far-flung colonial possession of a nation that was itself often figured as being on the margins of modern European civilization. The state would repeatedly remind the world of the city's true historical identity as a "four-century-old meeting-point between East and West," the earliest and most enduring site of amicable, respectful relations between Chinese and Portuguese people. No longer would it be portrayed, as it had been in countless gangster films both Chinese and American, as a cultural desert (文化沙漠) and a gambling town (賭城) whose culture was little more than the detritus of a mobile and materialistic population. To the contrary, it was an exemplar of the kind of tolerant, multicultural society that could result from a form of shared sovereignty unique in the modern world. No longer would Macau's residents be seen as abject colonial subjects corrupted by centuries of collaboration. Rather, they were bearers of a form of Chineseness at once more traditional and more cosmopolitan than any other—a form of subjectivity that could serve not only as a model for the rest of China but also as an inspiration for a globalizing world in which encounters between cultural others seemed increasingly to lead either to fundamentalisms and ethnic violence or to a destabilizing loss of cultural identity. Where the city had long been home to a series of communities divided by language, nationality, ethnicity, and ideology, the Portuguese government hoped to create a unified Macau identity fashioned around allegiance to the place, Macau, and to a particular understanding of the history that had made that place unique.

From one perspective, the São Paulo façade was an obvious choice for the emblem of this project: ancient, monumental, immediately identifiable and centrally located, an artifact of a once-mighty institution now sufficiently distanced from the material conditions of its production that its meaning could be powerfully reinterpreted. Both product and symbol of the cooperation between Europeans and Asians, it represented Macau's "glorious past," when the city had been a hub for commercial and cultural exchange between civilizations. The stone expressed wordlessly all the elements of the legacy the Portuguese state hoped to be remembered by.

It also expressed what this legacy could mean for the future. It may seem ironic that this last-minute attempt to monumentalize the history of Portuguese rule in Macau—in many ways a classic case of colonial nostalgia—gained the support of the staunchly anti-imperialist Chinese Communist Party. But this period of decolonization was also one of integration into the Chinese nation-state, which in turn was in the process of integrating itself into the world in new (capitalist) ways. The "one country, two systems" (一國兩制) formula, which Deng Xiaoping, the architect of China's economic reforms, had developed in order to facilitate the integration of Hong Kong and Macau into the People's Republic of China, both allowed and required Macau to maintain the political, economic, social, and cultural "system" that had evolved under Portuguese rule. If Macau's system could be defined as a harbinger of China's role in bringing about global harmony through the civilizing effects of international trade—rather than as the outcome of the exploitation, racism, and "national humiliation" (國恥) associated with colonialism—the São Paulo façade would be a proud symbol not just of the city's past but of the future of the nation and the world.

From a different perspective, however, this choice was high irony. A mere façade, a ruin, the burned-out remains of a former glory, a pile of stones that had lain untouched and crumbling for more than 150 years, until, just at the last minute, someone decided it should be patched up and polished and commodified—was this really the statement about Macau's culture and identity that the Portuguese wished to make? From this perspective, it reflected the transparency of the departing colonial state's last-ditch effort to whitewash the effects of its presence; indeed, some residents of Macau, both Chinese and Portuguese, suggested that the Portuguese wanted to leave a "cultural legacy" in Macau because in more than four hundred years of colonial rule they had left nothing else—not a robust economy, not a flourishing democracy, not a well-ordered society, not a well-educated populace. Others suggested that Beijing's acquiescence in making the ruins a symbol of Macau's unique system highlighted the incongruities of the CCP's claim that the one country, two systems formula was a "patriotic" measure, when in fact that formula was designed to maintain, in a form every bit as concrete as the ruin itself, the borders, institutions, and social distinctions begotten by colonialism. These ironies, pointed out to me on more than one occasion by long-term residents of Macau, were apparently lost on the state and on the tourists who came to be photographed in front of the ruin.

The state's transformation of the São Paulo façade from a decaying ruin into a symbol for the future paralleled its simultaneous attempt to bring Macau itself into existence in a new form: as a tangible, unified cultural whole, a system that would be both product and symbol of its own remarkable history; a place with a unique cultural identity that would provide not only a foundation for the city's continued prosperity but also a model for a multicultural world. The creation of this Macau involved more than the cleaning, patching, and polishing of the city and its history; it required a different way of imagining the world-scale processes that had brought the city into existence, as well as a different way of imagining both Macau's and China's relationship to the modern world. The leaders of the Portuguese state in Macau, in collaboration with certain members of the community and with the support of Beijing, managed to create a remarkably coherent vision of this new Macau and of the collective subject of the Macau people, defined by their sense of belonging to Macau and their pride in its history. But like the São Paulo façade, what you saw when you looked at this Macau depended on your perspective. From one angle—that found in world history books in China and elsewhere, which told an agonistic story of imperialists vs. nationalists, the march of progress, and the victory of secular modernity over the tyranny of sacred tradition—this vision of Macau looked like an ideological distortion of historical truth, a transparent attempt to paper over the ruinous effects of an illegitimate colonial power. But from a different angle, it called into question the truth claims of the modern anglocentric world order that had relegated both Portugal and China to its margins, and attempted to rescue from it a different and more subversive history. This book examines the work that went into making this Macau, its successes and its failures. It attempts to keep in focus both the tangible contours of its presence—the history of its construction, the way people interacted with it, and its place in the social, economic, and political landscapes of China and the world—and the thin blue sky visible through the gaping apertures in its structure, the absences it highlighted and the questions it provoked.

Sovereignty

One of the central questions this process provoked was that of sovereignty. Far away, in Tiananmen Square in Beijing, a huge clock counted down the days and seconds until December 20, 1999, when the People's Republic of China would resume administrative sovereignty over Macau. This event, called "the handover" in English and *huigui* 回歸, meaning "return," in Chinese, would end almost 450 years of Portuguese rule in Macau and the history of European imperialism in Asia. It is not surprising that such a momentous political transition would spark discussions about the interpretation of the past and its role in shaping the future. A similar phenomenon had occurred in the two other territories most closely analogous to Macau: Hong Kong and Taiwan. Both of these were, like Macau, capitalist economies with histories of colonial rule that had complicated political relationships with the PRC. In Hong Kong, which had been returned to Chinese control in 1997, the transition had provided the impetus for debates about the nature of local identities defined in contrast to the national and about the role of British colonialism in producing these identities (Abbas 1997, R. Chow 1998, Fung 2001, H. Siu 1996). And in Taiwan, the transition from dictatorship to democracy sparked a surge of interest in defining the cultural identity of the "Taiwan people," a surge that strained almost to the breaking point the island's relationship with China as well as with Chineseness (Melissa Brown 2004, Tu 1996, Weller 2001). But to a far greater extent than in Hong Kong or Taiwan, in Macau the transition process brought into question the meaning of sovereignty itself. What was "sovereignty" if Macau's past could be construed as "not colonial"? What had been the nature of the hundreds of years of Portuguese presence in Macau? Was the one country, two systems formula a completely new invention or the reiteration of an older, more fluid notion of sovereignty that had held sway in—indeed, that had allowed the city to attain—its moment of glory in the sixteenth and seventeenth centuries?

A settlement governed by the Portuguese had existed in Macau since around 1557. In April 1987, representatives of the governments of the People's Republic of China and the Republic of Portugal had signed the Sino-Portuguese Joint Declaration on the Question of Macau, stipulating that on December 20, 1999, the territory would become a Special Administrative Region (SAR) of the PRC. This declaration kicked off the long decade of the transition era: twelve years of change, uncertainty, and mounting (indeed, by the time I left in the autumn of 1999, almost paralyzing) anticipation. During this era, the 450,000 residents of Macau faced preparations for decolonization and the rollercoaster effects of an economy whose increasingly transnational linkages caused it to boom and then crash, entering a recession in 1994 that only worsened with the Asian financial crisis of 1998. But this was also a period in which the city was gearing up for integration into the PRC under the one country, two systems formula. This formula had three main principles: "no change for fifty years" (五十年不變), "Macau people ruling Macau" (澳人治澳), and "a high degree of autonomy" (高度自治). It was touted as a pragmatic way to quell fears about the forced integration of the capitalist economies of Hong Kong and Macau into the socialist system of the PRC and to ensure that they would continue to prosper despite their change in political status. As in Hong Kong, the specific implications of these policies were spelled out in Macau's Basic Law, which would act as the SAR's constitution. The effect was to impart to residents of the two cities the sense that, although the handovers were momentous occasions, marking the end of centuries of European colonialism in Asia and a step on the road toward the reunification of China, the only palpable change would be the replacement of European (colonial) officials with local (Chinese) talent. At the same time, however, the Chinese government repeatedly emphasized that the one country, two systems formula was a "historically unprecedented" policy and that great care would be required to ensure "continued stability and prosperity and a smooth transition."[3] Such caution was warranted, for in many ways the formula begged more questions than it answered: What precisely was it that would not change? Who exactly were the "Macau people"? How much autonomy would be enough? What would be the correct balance between emphasis on the one country and the two systems? What, after all, defined a "country"? And what made a system recognizably systematic? In this sense, the one country, two systems formula amounted to nothing less than an experiment in sovereignty.

The topic of sovereignty has burst back into the social sciences since the mid-1990s. While practical and philosophical debates have raged over whether formal nation-state sovereignty as we knew it should (or could) be defended, mourned, or finished off once and for all, a revitalized political anthropology has addressed the socio-cultural impact that various (and variously changing) practices of sovereign power have, especially on the lives of those whom they marginalize or exclude. In this book I build on the insights of this rich field, but I also propose a different approach: studying sovereignty not as a universal political theory or structure but as a mode of imagining power that becomes meaningful to people through its articulation to culturally and historically specific symbols, experiences, and desires. Recalling F. H. Hinsley's reminder that sovereignty is not a fact but a claim about how political power is or should be exercised (Hinsley 1966), I am interested in how these claims come to be meaningful to people in the everyday. I suggest that they do so through their articulation to cultural and historical experiences that do not translate easily across social and linguistic contexts. In this interpretive approach, I am inspired by Lisa Rofel's work on Chinese modernity, in which she focuses not on what modernity "is" and who has it but on how it is "imagined, pursued and experienced" differently across cultural and historical contexts (Rofel 1999: 3). As with modernity, sovereignty is "a story people tell themselves about themselves in relation to others" (Rofel 1999: 13; see also Geertz 1973).

To be clear: to say that sovereignty is a story is not to trivialize it or to deny the materiality of the institutions through which such power is exercised; it is, rather, to recall that these institutions themselves are the products of particular ways of thinking about power and its exercise that are in turn products of the human imagination. Sovereignty is a story about the nature of power that is far from being contained in a single, coherent plotline that has the same moral and the same denouement the world over. To the contrary, it is full of twists and contradictions, competing and tangential storylines, tellings and retellings, contingencies, surprises, and false beginnings and endings, as different narrators take up the tale for different purposes, using its language to express various experiences of domination and to effect various projects of power.

It is a story with life-and-death stakes. But these high stakes often obscure its nature as story; to my mind, this is one reason that social scientists have had such a hard time coming to terms with the question of sovereignty in the late twentieth century. In the interests of highlighting the difference this approach to sovereignty can make, I offer here my own story of the study of sovereignty. Much of the classical scholarship on sovereignty viewed it as a theory and practice of state power, defined as "supreme [or final or absolute] authority within a given territory or society" or simply as "supreme coercive power."[4] In the twentieth century, political scientists distinguished between two historical forms of sovereignty: in its premodern conception, sovereignty was concentrated in the body of the king, whose authority derived from his claim to a divine or hereditary mandate; at the edges of the realm, "borders were porous and indistinct, and sovereignties faded imperceptibly into one another." Supremacy was relative: sovereignty could be shared among two or more powers (B. Anderson 1991: 19; see also Thongchai 1994). By contrast, in the modern version, the authority of the state derives from its claim to represent the people it governs, and "state sovereignty is fully, flatly and evenly operative over each square centimetre of a legally demarcated territory" (B. Anderson 1991: 19). In this sense, modern sovereignty is an either-or proposition: a modern nation is either sovereign or subjugated; the state either has or loses the mandate of the people it represents; a citizen can stand either inside or outside the imaginary line (made very real by checkpoints, barbed wire, and men with guns) that marks the absolute spatial limit of the sovereign's power over her. The usual story is that modern sovereignty developed in Europe and spread around the world in response to European imperialism, eclipsing both the "premodern" form of sovereignty and other forms of political organization until, by the second half of the twentieth century, the idea that the source of the sovereign's legitimacy resided in "the people"—as expressed in the doctrine of national self-determination—had become fundamental to the practice of international politics. This story of sovereignty, in which the world is made of clearly bounded territories inhabited by peoples with a unified and continuous past and future who are the autonomous subjects of their own history, became the only legitimate form of recognition in the international political arena, the principal scale of economies, the proper subject of history, and the pre-eminent mode of organizing geopolitical space. It was also the ideal locus of culture, identity, and community (Handler 1988). As Michael Tsin (1999) demonstrates, in early twentieth-century China (as in other places at other times), it took an enormous amount of effort to convince people to believe in this story; but by the late twentieth century, it had become so commonsensical, in China as elsewhere, that it was difficult to think around it when talking or writing of the political.

In the 1990s, the possibility of thinking about politics without sovereignty was highlighted by two more or less contemporaneous influences. First, the relevance of the ideal of nation-state sovereignty was called into question by the acceleration of transnational movements of people, capital, and culture. Some theorists predicted the disintegration of nation-state sovereignty in the face of transnational institutions of capitalism (Camilleri and Falk 1992, Miyoshi 1993, Ōhmae 1990 and 1995, Horsman and Marshall 1994). State sovereignty, it seemed, was being replaced by the power of transnational corporations, institutions, and nongovernmental organizations; people began to speak of abstractions such as "the market" or "neoliberalism" as exercising a sovereign power of their own, defined now as a "supreme power over a set of people, things or places" (Latham 2000: 2). At the same time, it appeared to many that these political and economic transformations were engendering new modes of organizing space, culture, power, and community that would undermine the sovereign sensibility: diasporas, civilizations, cosmopolitanisms, localities, empires.[5] Others, however, endeavored to show that despite global reconfigurations, nation-state sovereignty was in no danger of disappearing: nation-states were managing to strengthen their power thanks precisely to those globalizing forces that appeared to be eroding it, and the logic and rhetoric of national sovereignty continued to haunt even those "displaced" economic and cultural

formations apparently challenging its limits (Basch et al. 1994, Helmreich 1992, Ong 1997, Sassen 1996).

Second, as the work of Michel Foucault gained influence in
North America, so did his emphasis on the need to move away from
studying the structures, institutions, and relationships—such as The
State or The Law—that most loudly proclaim themselves to be
about power. Sovereignty was, for Foucault, already dead, replaced
by a distinctly modern mode of exercising power he dubbed "biopower" (Foucault 1978). Biopower refers to relations of domination
and submission structuring those aspects of life that seem most distant from the centers of power: daily routines, forms of knowledge,
sexuality, and the "care of the self," even the very idea of a self capable of believing that it is a free, autonomous individual, standing
apart from state and society.[6] In this sense, Foucault was interested
in the creation of subjects: that is, how one becomes both "subject
to someone else by control and dependence, and tied to his own
identity by a conscience or self-knowledge" (Foucault in Dreyfus
1983: 212). Studies inspired by this approach have examined, among
other things, the techniques through which states or other "su-
premely powerful" institutions create citizens as governable, "normal" subjects, often in contradistinction to an array of deviants
(criminals, illegal immigrants, refugees, racial others, terrorists, radicals, and the insane).[7] Aihwa Ong, for example, in her ethnography
of Cambodian refugees in California, explores "the technologies of
government—that is, the policies, programs, codes and practices
(*unbounded by the concept of culture*) that attempt to instill in citizen-
subjects particular values . . . in a variety of domains" (Ong 2003: 6;
italics added).

Others have been inspired by Giorgio Agamben's rejection of the
distinction between sovereignty and biopower. Agamben (1998)
suggests that biopolitics, rather than being a distinctly modern mode
of power, has always been at the core of the exercise of sovereignty,
and that, conversely, the logic of sovereignty continues to structure
the practice of biopower, a fact that makes the study of sovereignty
more relevant than ever to understanding the intersections of politics and culture in contemporary life. Scholars inspired by this approach have shifted the focus of inquiry to the examination of how

the body and other forms of "bare life" have become targets for the exercise of sovereign power (see, e.g., Anagnost 2004 and Farquhar and Zhang 2005), and to situations of "*de facto* sovereignty" in which individuals and institutions do not seek legitimation in the law but simply act as sovereign by exercising their capacity to "protect or kill with impunity" (T. Hansen and Stepputat 2006: 296; see also Mbembe 2003).

The fact that compelling evidence can be mustered to show that sovereignty is both disappearing and proliferating, simultaneously diminishing and intensifying, suggests to me that when we attempt to define sovereignty as a universal, it disintegrates. If, for example, we define sovereignty as "the ability to kill, punish and discipline with impunity" (T. Hansen and Stepputat 2006), we see sovereign power everywhere: in the democratically elected government and the military dictator; in IMF policies and the petty gangster who gets away with murder; even in the schoolyard persecution of the geeky kid.[8] Yet we also see it nowhere: for what, after all, is impunity? It is a static and to my mind impoverished view of power relations that accepts at face value the claim implicit in the idea of impunity: that power is an all-or-nothing affair.[9]

Thus for all their contributions to our understanding of the permutations in the theories and practices of sovereignty, I find these approaches curiously unable to explain what I most want to understand: how, why, and when the modern story of sovereignty continues to be one that people want to keep telling and hearing, despite the violence that continues to be committed in its name. What does sovereignty mean to people—does it, in fact, mean the same thing to all people? What symbolic weight does sovereignty carry such that a wide variety of actors vie to use this language to claim legitimacy? How does this language exceed or escape the uses to which it is put? And what happens when people start imagining not just a different sovereign, but a different story of sovereignty?

In thinking about this set of questions, I find the Foucault-inspired approach to sovereignty too sterile: it sees sovereignty as a zero-sum game involving anonymous, rational structures and processes (the State, the Law, the Economy), abstract forces and ideologies ("capitalism," "the media," "neoliberalism," "globalization"), and the regulation of "flows" and "populations" rather than people. Roger Rouse (1995) has argued that the benefit of many studies of transnationalism is that they succeed in reconciling the best of marxist and post-structuralist analyses: they incorporate a focus on emergent cultural forms without losing sight of the role of capitalism. Yet it seems to me that many such studies also succeed in combining the weaknesses of both approaches. By reifying such structures as "the state" and "capitalism," they run the risk of imbuing abstractions with agency, intentionality, a unified will to power. By focusing on the techniques of governmentality through which states create subjects, they provide a mechanistic vision of the reproduction of power that leaves us no way of understanding the often surprising actions and interpretations of those subjects—some of whom are responsible for the formulation and execution of precisely the techniques in question.

Yet the second approach—which focuses on concentration camps, Rwandan refugees, Cambodian killing fields, US secret prisons, violence, terror, and brutality—I find equally limiting. Its appeal is understandable. It was precisely the violent and terrifying events of the twentieth century that led European and American intellectuals to reflect on the nature of sovereign power, and it is the violent and terrifying events of the early twenty-first century that have led many to despair of it. These representations of the surreal and traumatizing excesses of sovereign power provide an antidote to the language of rationality that pervades discussions of modern state power from Weber through Foucault but does so little to explain the irrational, destructive, and very uneconomical violence exercised by states otherwise considered thoroughly modern.[10] My fear, however, is that this approach reduces the study of subjectification to the study of victimization and the study of power to the study of injustice—both of which leave us unable to conceptualize of how anyone could ever consider modern sovereignty a legitimate, let alone desirable, mode of political organization.

Before calling for an end to sovereign thinking, then, I believe we must take a closer look at what is being thought, imagined, experienced, and changed when various agents (states, other institutions, or individuals) take up the story. Rather than defining what makes sovereignty sovereignty and then setting out to examine its effects in the world, I suggest that the question might better be studied ethnographically in ways that illuminate how a particular story of sovereignty becomes meaningful to the people in whose name it is exercised. This has two implications. First, we need to look at how particular sovereign projects mobilize symbolic resources (linguistic, aural, visual, textual) in order to make sovereignty matter—to shape the way people think about themselves, their past, and their future—as well as at how these projects might fail. And second, we cannot be content to study sovereignty as, in Ong's words, "unbounded by the concept of culture." We need, rather, to approach it as a story that, although it may be globally hegemonic in its contemporary usage, does not translate transparently across languages or social contexts.

In 1990s Macau there were no independence activists; the Portuguese were not fighting to maintain control of the city, nor was anyone challenging (overtly, at least) the PRC's right to assume sovereignty over it. In fact, the Portuguese state embarked on its project of creating the Macau people as a collective subject largely by denying that it ever had wielded full sovereignty over Macau. It attempted to demonstrate that the history of the Portuguese presence in Macau had been the history of a different kind of sovereignty, a shared sovereignty that did not fit the definition of supreme coercive power. Ironically, this situation made possible a conversation that questioned the nature, limits, and effects of sovereignty far more profoundly than a direct contest about sovereign power over Macau would have. The difficulty the state encountered in convincing Macau residents of their "unique cultural identity" draws attention to the kinds of work required to make any story of sovereignty compelling. It had to crosscut powerful notions of blood, language, territory, and state entailed in the usual story of modern sovereignty and replace them with a shared sense of belonging to the place, Macau, and all that it supposedly stood for: tolerance, hybridity, openness, and peaceful coexistence.

But "the state" in this instance, as in all instances, was not simply an "effect" or a set of technologies. It comprised actors who themselves had their own historically and culturally specific experiences of what sovereignty could and should mean.[11] A large number of Portuguese civil servants in Macau (including the last governor, General Vasco Joaquim Rocha Vieira) had come to Macau from Angola or Mozambique, and many had fought there, on the losing side, in the brutal wars of independence during the 1960s and 1970s. Other civil servants, born and raised in mainland China, had emigrated to Macau to escape the destructiveness of Maoist anti-imperialist revolution. Still others, born and raised in Macau, had never felt part of any nation-state and were suspicious of any state's claim on their loyalties. Meanwhile, a range of Macau Chinese intellectuals, both inside and outside state institutions, argued that although the Portuguese presence in Macau had been colonial, the form it had taken, rather than creating a hybrid culture, had allowed "traditional" Chinese culture to develop more "naturally," free from forcible intrusions by states (as in the PRC) or dilution by globalizing economic forces (as in Hong Kong).

Thus the narrative and physical sites in which the meaning of sovereignty was most fiercely contested during the transition era were precisely the points at which the meaning—or meaninglessness—of the collective subjectivity of Macau people was called into question. The exigencies of the transition to Chinese rule meant that these questions took on heightened political significance. But their significance was not only political. In this sense this book examines not just the immediate social and economic effects of the transfer of sovereignty from one state apparatus to another. Nor do I wish to confine the analysis to the "technologies" or methods through which either sovereign state (Chinese or Portuguese) tried to gain legitimacy in the eyes of the people it governed. Rather, I am proposing a study of colliding interests, histories, and theories of sovereignty and subjectivity: a study of the politics, possibilities, and *im*possibilities of collective subjectivity at the spatial, temporal, and conceptual edges of sovereignty.

Chineseness

The second question provoked by the edifice of Macau identity was that of Chineseness. What made China China, or Chinese people Chinese, such that the Chinese in Macau were "different"? I hesitate to pose this question, even though it was the structuring absence of the entire transition. I hesitate not because of its paralyzing un-answerability—after all, it is no less answerable than the question of what makes humans human, which animates anthropology—but be-cause, as we shall see, the way it is usually addressed tends to close down conversations and turn off audiences of all kinds.

The usual story is one in which the link between sovereignty and subjectivity can be keenly felt. It goes like this: the onslaught of Western modernity (which, in this story, can be pinpointed to 1842, when the British won the Opium War and forced the Qing dynasty to sign the Treaty of Nanjing, effectively bringing to an end that dynasty's status as the "highest or supreme power" in its own terri-tory) meant the end of traditional China, the slashing of ties to a historical-cultural ground, and the shattering of a monolithic and vaguely defined sense of Chineseness into the sharp-edged shards of identity—national, regional, ethnic, class identities—that informed the violence and upheavals of China's twentieth century, regrettable but necessary on the march toward modernization. Indeed, Western approaches to the study of China reflect this trend. Two generations ago, anthropologists worked with a conception of Chineseness as a set of cultural values and practices that structured the institutions of family, village, nation, and state and distinguished them as essen-tially Chinese. This approach mirrored Confucian ideologies in which being Chinese meant being part of a cosmological entity, *tianxia*, that encompassed the social, political, and moral order and was given unity by a singular state headed by the Son of Heaven. With the collapse of that state and the imperial ideology that under-pinned it emerged a sense of Chineseness as a modern national iden-tity, involving concerns with territorial integrity, sovereignty, and citizenship, informed by Social Darwinist ideas of competition and survival in a world in which national extinction was a real threat. During the Maoist era, when the Chinese Communist Party claimed its mandate as the representative of the "people's democratic dicta-torship," class-based concepts of the "national popular" came to dominate conceptions of Chineseness within the borders of the PRC (Shi 2003), and place-names such as "mainland China" and "Tai-wan" became imbued with a significance that was primarily political, rather than geographic, linguistic, or cultural. In recent years, the concept of "Greater China," and the work of authors such as Tu Weiming, Wang Gungwu, and Aihwa Ong, have definitively broken the link between the state and cultural identity and showed that Chinese communities existing outside the borders of a Chinese nation-state are no less "authentically" Chinese than those in the so-called heartland. Although these authors maintain a consciousness of the importance of the Chinese state as an institution that may legitimate itself by laying claim to various concepts of Chineseness (cf. Chun 1996a), they argue that in the end, this state and the territory under its control are but "one among many sites within and across which Chinese transnational practices are played out" (Ong and Nonini 1997: 12). On one hand, this approach has been crucial to understanding the possibilities of Chinese cultural difference within and across nation-states. On the other, however, the removal of the state from the discussion often works to strengthen the power given to culture and to non-state structures of autonomy: Chineseness at the turn of the twenty-first century is, in this formulation, about cultural formations that are, as often as not, beyond the state's reach. It begs the question of Chineseness by locating its coherence and recognizability in a set of cultural practices that may encompass a wide range of diversity, but whose status as "Chinese" is never interrogated. It is this that allows us to speak of Chinese transnationalism, Chinese modernity, and Chinese cosmopolitanism, as if everyone knows what "Chinese" means.

What does "Chinese" mean? When I have raised this question with my Chinese students and colleagues in Macau, many of them find the answer both obvious and inarticulable, something that only a foreigner would ever ask about and only a Chinese person could ever understand. It is a sentiment, a feeling, they say; it is a "sense of history," a "glow of fraternity" (Lee Kuan Yew, quoted in Ong 1999), a mode of being that simply lies beyond the realm of the analyzable. Many sinologists, especially in the social sciences, find the question too vague, too unwieldy—How does one study what is taken for granted? How does one measure sentiment?—and dangerously polarizing, for it seems to invite either essentialisms or deconstructions that are both empirically unsustainable and politically indefensible.[12]

Scholars who do not study China may find the question irrelevant or off-putting, not least because of the exceptionalism, obscurantism, and civilizational discourse it often provokes—the references to millennia worth of unbroken historical continuities and the conjuring of ageless and hermetically sealed systems of philosophical, sociopolitical, and ideological organization that make China the exception to any global theory and Chineseness fundamentally different from other conceptions of collective selves. Yet among many scholars who identify as Chinese, the question is a supercharged one: having been, at least since the early twentieth century, so closely identified with questions of patriotism, national humiliation, and despair over China's "predicament," some Chinese intellectuals find the question of what it means to be Chinese emotionally exhausting (see Link 1992; see also several contributions to Tu 1994b). Others feel trapped by the insistence that Chinese intellectuals must always address Chinese problems (C. T. Hsia 1999; see also Ang 2000, R. Chow 1998, Chun 1996b, and L. Lee 1994). Beginning with such a question would seem to doom any book to failure, since most people don't care, and others care too much.

But I will insist on posing this question, for I believe that ethnography is uniquely capable of providing the kind of answer that can open conversations across disciplines and areas. The question of Chineseness is of concern to others besides China scholars. The categories through which we have understood Chineseness and its transformation since the mid-nineteenth century are precisely the "universal" categories through which anthropologists and historians have constructed an understanding of how the world has come to be as it is in the early twenty-first century. These categories derive from or are informed by the modern story of sovereignty: national vs. transnational, colonial vs. post- (or neo-)colonial, local vs. global, emplaced vs. deterritorialized, traditional vs. (post-)modern. The prevalence and persuasiveness of these binaries as ways of understanding the forces transforming the world seem to grow with each economic downturn, each act of ethnic warfare. Insofar as these binaries are taken as solid footing for political action, this solidity is often illusory; insofar as they provide analytical coherence, this coherence often comes at the expense of understanding the historic-ity and cultural specificity of these categories themselves.

Although the presumed coherence of the category "Chinese" has been challenged in recent years by theorists such as Ien Ang, Rey Chow, and Allen Chun,[13] there has been little ethnographic work that takes up their challenge: "not to dispute the fact that Chinese-ness exists . . . but to investigate how this category operates in prac-tice, in different historical, geographical, political and cultural con-texts. . . . How and why is it that the category of Chineseness acquires its persistence and solidity?" (Ang 2001: 40). It is impossi-ble to address this challenge, however, simply by examining how purportedly universal categories or processes (such as "globalization" or "sovereignty") have affected articulations of Chineseness, for this again begs the question of precisely who is being affected (cf. Shi 2003). Rather, the task is to examine how certain categories of ex-perience (such as national sovereignty, colonialism, native-place ties) are identified as meaningful to or even constitutive of Chineseness at particular times and places, and thus how Chineseness—like any other form of collective subjectivity—becomes a possibility for some, an imperative for others, and an impossibility for the rest.

Examining how Macau was narrated as existing at the juncture of all these persistent binaries can provide insights into the limitations of the forms of collective subjectivity circumscribed by the assump-tions of modern sovereignty. One such form is that of identity itself, a term that (as we have seen) the Portuguese state used frequently to express the idea that Macau residents shared something that set them apart from all other Chinese people. It is little coincidence that, as Rogers Brubaker and Frederick Cooper have pointed out, the concept of identity rose to prominence in the social sciences during the middle years of the twentieth century, when the ideals of self-determination and national sovereignty were redrawing world maps. They argue that the concept of identity entails a sense not just of belonging or connectedness but of uniformity or sameness within the group, across space and through time, that distinguishes it from other similar groups separated by clearly demarcated boundary lines (Brubaker and Cooper 2000). Viewed in this way, it becomes clear that identity is not something that all people naturally have but a particular way of conceptualizing affinity and difference deeply influenced by the logic of national sovereignty. Significantly, Wang Gungwu (1988) has argued that Chineseness was never conceptualized as an "identity" until the twentieth century. Thus, on one hand, in suggesting that Macau residents had an identity setting them apart from all other Chinese people, the Portuguese state indirectly but no less effectively questioned their Chineseness; on the other hand, in challenging the usual story of modern sovereignty, it prompted some Macau residents to reject the very assertion that the term "identity" could give expression to their own sense of who they were, individually or collectively.

In some ways, of course, Macau is undeniably Chinese. Consisting of a tiny peninsula attached to the mainland, plus two of the dozens of islands scattered across the silty, salty waters along the coastline where the Pearl River meets the South China Sea, Macau is geographically as much a part of the Chinese subcontinent as the cities of Xiamen or Qingdao. By the time of the transition, its population numbered something under half a million people, nearly 60 percent of them born in the People's Republic of China. Over 95 percent of residents identified themselves in the census as "Chinese." Chinese had been one of the city's official languages since 1988 and was the native tongue of well over 90 percent of its inhabitants. By most standards, it would be difficult to make the case that Macau and its people were anything other than Chinese. Indeed, early in my fieldwork, when I explained my interest in exploring Macau's "difference" to a Western researcher who had recently concluded a study of Chinese religion in Macau, he told me sadly, "Macau Chinese are just Chinese. They are just Chinese who like to drink coffee." This intractable Chineseness of Macau residents, their apparent lack of interest in or understanding of what made them different, was a constant source of frustration for government officials and others engaged in the identitarian project in Macau, and it heightened their sense of the urgency of this task. They contrasted Macau "natives" with those in other Portuguese colonies (most notably in Africa), remarking that everywhere else the Portuguese had gone, they had managed to make Portuguese the *lingua franca* of the colonized peoples and to incorporate them more firmly into the Portuguese cultural universe. The difference, they would tell me, is in the culture. Chinese culture is "strong," whereas African culture is "weak"; Chinese culture is resistant to change and hybridization, and this is why Chinese people always live together and remain Chinese wherever in the world they go. As everyone knows, they would say, even those non-Chinese invaders who from time to time had managed to take control of China (Xianbei, Mongols, Manchus) ended up losing their own traditions and becoming "sinified." This understanding of the power of Chinese culture to draw everything into itself while remaining fundamentally unchanged was expressed by frustrated Portuguese administrators trying to drum up interest in Portuguese language and culture, as well as by Chinese residents proud of their "traditional" and "conservative" ways. Given this understanding of culture in general, and of Chinese culture in particular, Macau's transfer to Chinese sovereignty should not have made much of a difference. Indeed, as Ah Man, a Hong Kong–born man who had made Macau his home, told me, Macau was already so Chinese he didn't think anyone would even notice the handover: "I think we'll wake up one day and remember, 'Oh right—it was last week! Oh it was yesterday, oh, right!'"

In other ways, however, what became clear from my study was that the handover, which would integrate Macau for the first time ever into a Chinese nation-state, would make a difference. During the transition era one heard constant reminders of the precariousness of Macau's Chineseness. Although Chinese was an official language, it was a dialect (Cantonese) unintelligible to national leaders in Beijing. Approximately 30 percent of Macau's ethnic Chinese residents held Portuguese passports. Visas to enter Macau were difficult for mainlanders to obtain, and special permits were necessary for Macau residents to enter the PRC, where they were charged higher prices for state services than their mainland "compatriots." Although more than half the city's population had emigrated to Macau from mainland China, most had come because Macau provided an alternative to the conditions of poverty and political violence that had characterized life in many parts of China during the previous half-century. The question of what would happen to Macau after the handover, when it "became Chinese," was the subject of frequent and anxious conversation.

This ambivalent Chineseness was highlighted for me in the first ethnographic conversation I ever had about Macau. It occurred in California in February 1996, with a young woman (let us call her Susana) who identified herself as Macanese—a member of Macau's Eurasian community, many of whom have lived for generations in the United States, Canada, Brazil, Australia, and Portugal. When I told her I was investigating Macau's cultural identity, she told me that she thought Macanese culture was like a certain Macanese delicacy, which she described as "sort of like a wonton, but different." She felt this summed up the relationship of Macanese culture to Chineseness: the Macanese were sort-of Chinese, but different.

At first I appreciated this comment primarily in the spirit in which it had been uttered, as a metaphor of difference, and it stayed with me for the duration of my fieldwork. I had hastily scribbled down notes on our conversation but later discovered that I had neglected to write down the name of this "sort-of wonton." When I arrived in Macau I made a point of trying to find it, sampling as many wontonesque dishes as I could in restaurants around the city. I came across several variations on wontons in the noodle shops and dim sum restaurants of Macau (shrimp wontons, pork wontons, vegetarian ones; fried, steamed, boiled; in soup or dry, with noodles or without) and found one or two varieties that I had never heard of anywhere else—the black-pepper wonton, for example. Yet although each was different from the others, they were nonetheless wontons and listed as such on menus. As time passed and my search continued, I found myself beginning to contemplate the wonton itself, wondering less about the identity of the "sort-of wonton" and more about the category against which it was being defined. What made the Macanese "sort-of wonton" less completely "Chinese" than the *jiaozi*, the *baozi*, the *tangyuan*, the *shaomai*, or any other of the regional variations on dumplings that, although they are not wontons, share the undisputed right to be listed in the index of Chinese cuisine? It was not until I attended a going-away party for a Macanese friend during the last month of my fieldwork that I came across the *apabico* and knew that I had found it.[14] Although there are probably as many recipes for apabico as there are Macanese cooks, the one I sampled consisted, as far as I could tell, of a rice-flour skin filled with minced pork, mushrooms, and dried shrimp, shaped into a walnut-sized globe and steamed. With its thicker, chewier skin and saltier, heavier filling, the apabico I had certainly was different than your average wonton. But I found nothing intrinsic to the apabico that could answer my question: When does a wonton stop being a wonton and begin to be something else?

I do not mean to trivialize the complex and deeply felt senses of belonging and alterity that are at issue in discussions of Chineseness and Macaneseness by equating them with a choice of items on a Chinese fast-food menu. But I do think Susana's metaphor is instructive here. When I first arrived in Macau for preliminary research in the summer of 1996, I was immediately struck by the way that the discourse of the departing Portuguese government echoed that of my first informant: the state was trying to get the broad range of Chinese residents of Macau to think of themselves as "sort-of Chinese"—"Latin Chinese" was the phrase used in one publication (Macau Government Tourism and Information Bureau 1979)—whose quickly disappearing difference was the only thing that would guarantee the city's continued importance and economic viability in the region. But wherein lay this difference? The state suggested that it lay in their experience of the unique mode of sovereign power it had exercised for hundreds of years. But when I returned to Macau in 1997 and stayed for two years of fieldwork, I was able to hear, along with the state's noisy, self-congratulatory declarations about Macau's unique cultural identity, a more subtle conversation about the meaning of, and relationship among, sovereignty, history, and subjectivity, not simply in Macau but in the world: a conversation that was not only about the value of Macau's difference but also about what Chineseness meant and where its limits lay. Thus the sort-of wonton and the edifice of Macau identity together help us pose the question of Chineseness in a more palatable way: not by attempting to answer once and for all the question of what makes Chinese people Chinese, but by asking when, why, and in what forms the category of Chineseness becomes persuasive as an expression of community and commonality. In Macau on the eve of the handover, several different stories of sovereignty and Chineseness and the relationship between them were being told at the same time. These stories informed the attachments, decisions, and day-to-day lives of a wide range of Macau residents, and allowed different relationships between sovereignty and subjectivity to become thinkable even as they provided a sense of why, at times, it may not be desirable to think them.

Locations

The territory of Macau comprises a small peninsula and two islands (Taipa 氹仔 and Coloane 路環) on the western bank of the Pearl River Delta, along the coast of Guangdong, one of the southernmost provinces of the People's Republic of China (see Map 1). By most standards, Macau is tiny. As of 1998, it covered a land area of just under 24 square kilometers (about nine square miles), but most of its population lived on the 3.5-square-mile peninsula, whose length and breadth it was possible to cover in the space of an afternoon walk. With a total population of approximately 450,000, Macau had the highest population density in the world.

Until 1995, when the Macau International Airport opened, there were only two points of entry into the city: from the north, one could walk or drive across the border from the Zhuhai Special Economic Zone (SEZ); or from the east, one could make the trip from Hong Kong, a distance of some forty nautical miles.[15] The high-speed ferries and jetfoils that plied the route to Hong Kong day and night made the trip in about an hour; these boats, which delivered the vast majority of the seven or eight million tourists who visited the territory each year, were owned and operated by the Sociedade de Turismo e Diversões de Macau (STDM), the privately held company that also owned all the casinos that were the mainstay of Macau's economy.[16]

In the eyes of Beijing and the world, it seemed, Macau was little more than an afterthought to its larger, more prosperous, and better-known neighbor Hong Kong, which had preceded Macau in "returning" to Chinese rule on July 1, 1997. The similarities were obvious. Both Hong Kong and Macau were colonies of European powers located in southern China; both had capitalist economic systems based largely on their role as commercial entrepôts; both were relatively small, largely urban coastal enclaves; both had populations that were more than 95 percent ethnic Chinese and predominantly Cantonese speakers; both underwent "consensual decolonization" at roughly the same time; and both became special administrative regions (SARs) of the People's Republic of China, governed by the one country, two systems policy. In Macau as in Hong Kong, the specific implications of this policy were spelled out in detail in the Basic Law, which would act as a "mini-constitution" after the handover. In both cities, joint liaison groups composed of representatives from Beijing and London or Lisbon were set up to negotiate the specificities of the transition to Chinese rule. In this sense, the political transition in Macau was virtually an exact copy of the process in Hong Kong: it followed the same sequence of procedures; the Basic Laws of the two territories were, word for word, almost identical; and the mechanisms for choosing Macau's new chief executive, electing and appointing its legislature, "localizing" its civil service, and aligning its legal system with the constitution of the PRC were modeled closely on those developed for Hong Kong.

Yet, as several Macau residents involved in the transition process pointed out worriedly in the years before the handover, Macau was *not* Hong Kong. Economically, Macau had nowhere near Hong Kong's wealth, infrastructure, or potential for growth. With less than 2 percent of Hong Kong's total land area, and just 7 percent of Hong Kong's population, many economists argued, little Macau did not have the natural or human resources necessary to become an economic "dragon" (W. C. Ieong and Siu 1997).[17] Unlike the diversity that characterized Hong Kong's economic structure, Macau was heavily dependent on casino tourism: in 1997, nearly 60 percent of government tax revenues came from the gambling industry alone. Although Macau had enjoyed a boom in export-processing, manufacturing, and real estate in the 1980s, thanks in large part to cheap land and labor, the city's near-total dependence on Hong Kong and PRC capital meant that its growth spurt was short-lived; by 1996, in a region characterized by double-digit growth rates, Macau had the only economy to register negative growth. The financial crisis of 1998 only exacerbated this trend, as tourism from Hong Kong and southeast Asia slowed to a trickle. Whereas some people feared, or hoped, that the strength of Hong Kong's economy would lead to the "Hong Kong–ization" of China after 1997, in Macau the fear was that its economic weakness would cause Macau to be "swallowed up" by neighboring Zhuhai.[18] Liang Guangda, the mayor and Communist Party secretary of Zhuhai, was rumored to have boasted as much.

The political systems of the two cities also had little in common. Macau's legal system was based on European continental law, not British common law as in Hong Kong. In Hong Kong, the gradual process of localizing the bureaucracy had started after World War II, as ethnic Chinese were groomed to take top leadership positions in the government and Chinese was made an official language; in Macau this process began late, proceeded slowly, and proved cumbersome. Macau's political culture was characterized by a greater degree of bureaucratic corruption, lower levels of mass participation, and a stronger presence of "pro-Beijing" factions and civic organizations (such as neighborhood associations, the Chinese Chamber of Commerce, and the Federation of Labor Unions) than in Hong Kong (S. H. Lo 1995, H. S. Yee 2001). The fact that Beijing exercised far greater control over Macau than it did over Hong Kong was seldom disputed. The public's sense that the local government lacked any real economic or political autonomy was captured nicely in a joke I heard several times in the mid-1990s, in which the Portuguese governor was portrayed as sitting at a table with Stanley Ho (the Hong-Kong based billionaire head of STDM) on his right hand and the head of the New China News Agency (Xinhua she, the PRC's official representative in Macau) on his left: whenever the governor wanted to do anything, the joke went, he first turned to his right to ask Ho for the money and then to his left to ask Beijing for permission to spend it.

In terms of social structure, too, Macau was often compared unfavorably to Hong Kong. One young and politically well-connected ethnic Chinese businessman told me that the way that Macau's civic institutions had developed under Portuguese rule meant that political and economic power were not just linked but fused into a fossilized and unassailable conservatism: "There are no political parties in Macau," he said, "there's only the [Chinese] Chamber of Commerce.

New ideas in business are not tolerated, as the old men who are in charge see them as a challenge to the political status quo. If you want to innovate, you have to go to Hong Kong." Macau's smaller middle class, lower levels of education, more widespread "stepping-stone mentality" (A. H. Yee 1989), and larger proportion of recent immigrants (as of 1996, less than 40 percent of Macau's population had been born in Macau) were often cited as reasons that Macau did not have the dynamism or stability of Hong Kong:

> More than 50 percent of Macau's 400,000+ population are newcomers who have arrived from the mainland since 1978. Most of them have a low level of education. They know almost nothing about Macau, and identify themselves as Chung Kuo Yan (Chinese) rather than Ou Mun Yan (Macau-ese). Even among the old residents, many just regard Macau as a springboard to move overseas, to get better jobs and opportunities abroad. The sense of belonging here is much weaker than in Hong Kong where people are proud of being Heong Kong Yan (Hong Kongese). (Ngai 1999: 126n1)

For all these reasons, it seemed to some that the promise of one country, two systems, although intended to ensure Macau's autonomy and protect its "system," would simply demonstrate the extent to which Macau had, instead of a system, a chaotic jumble of differences that reflected the shortcomings of Portuguese colonialism. The problem was not just that it would be impossible to maintain Macau's "uniqueness" without more clearly defining, systematizing, and institutionalizing these differences; this impossibility also threatened to undermine the coherence and validity of the one country, two systems policy. For if Macau had no clearly identifiable system, on what basis could Macau people claim autonomy? Thus to a greater extent than in Hong Kong, the transition in Macau entailed a conversation about the significance of difference: the nature and extent of Macau's differences from the PRC as well as from Hong Kong, their loci, and their causes; which differences should be identified, celebrated, and preserved, and which were signs of "backwardness" and irrationality that needed to be overcome. Some people argued that the last thing Macau needed was more difference; rather, it should become as similar to Hong Kong as possible. Others argued that Macau's differences, properly identified, systematized, and harnessed for political and economic advantage, could and should form the foundation for the city's long-term autonomy, stability, and prosperity.

Among the proponents of the latter view, the loudest voice was that of the departing Macau Portuguese government.[19] According to the state, Macau residents—as well as the PRC and the rest of the world—needed more than anything else to become aware, as Governor Vasco Rocha Vieira put it in 1998, of "the uniqueness of the culture of Macau." They needed to understand that this culture was the result of "450 years of coexistence between communities that are different but that respect each other in the tolerance and acceptance of these differences."[20] References to Macau's "unique cultural identity" and its historic role as a "bridge between East and West" cropped up constantly in speeches and government publications. Guarantees of protection of the city's "cultural heritage" were included in the Basic Law and other legislation. The state built monuments to the "friendship between the Chinese and Portuguese people"; it published, or sponsored the publication of, hundreds of books and magazines exploring various aspects of Macau's culture and identity. It poured millions of dollars into projects that would institutionalize this identity: the restoration not just of the São Paulo Ruins but of dozens of historical buildings and monuments; the construction of ten new museums; the introduction of Macau history into the middle-school curriculum; the sponsorship of international conferences that were always televised on the evening news; and the staging of a staggering variety of cultural events (festivals of food, music, art, and film; performances of folk dance, fado, bullfighting, Chinese opera; competitions of fireworks displays, lion dancing, photography, calligraphy, children's dances; and, of course, the annual Macau Grand Prix). All these were taken as evidence of Macau's wealth of culture and its identity as a hybrid city that gave equal importance to "East" and "West." By mid-1998, the public sphere was so saturated with references to Macau's "unique cultural identity" and "crossroad of cultures" that a Portuguese acquaintance confessed to me, "If I hear the phrase *cruzamento de culturas* one more time, I think I'm going to puke."

At first glance, this may appear to be little more than what another Portuguese acquaintance called "anticipated nostalgia." As he put it, in 1987, when the Portuguese government realized its days in Macau were numbered, "they wanted to preserve something of the past, some legacy of the Portuguese presence in Macau that would endure beyond the handover." But the question of Macau's difference came to have a more than passing relevance to a larger set of individuals, groups, and civic institutions in Macau, across ethnic divides, who feared that the recent influx of mainland immigrants and capital, combined with the departure of the Portuguese and the city's absorption into the Chinese nation-state, would cause Macau to disappear into an undifferentiated "China." Although they often differed in how they defined what was unique about Macau, most agreed that if measures were not taken to instill in Macau people a stronger sense of their difference from mainlanders and Hong Kongers, Macau as they knew it would soon cease to exist.

Meanwhile, economists and planners (both Chinese and Portuguese) came to see cultural identity as the answer to Macau's economic woes. As a tiny territory with a shallow harbor, one of the highest population densities in the world, low levels of education, rising costs of land and labor, and no natural resources to speak of, it was generally believed that Macau could not compete with its neighbors (Hong Kong, Zhuhai, Shenzhen, and the rest of the Pearl River Delta) in any of the industries that allowed those regions to experience phenomenal economic growth: export-processing, shipping, international finance, the promise of high-tech. Put crudely, it seemed that the only way Macau could compete economically in the twenty-first century was to have something other regions did not have: and the only two things Macau had that its neighbors did not were a legal code that permitted casino gambling and its history of Portuguese rule. Because revenues from gambling already constituted such a significant proportion of the GDP, "culture" seemed to be the way to go (see, e.g., Chau 1999, Fang 1998, and Ngai 1995). If Macau could diversify into cultural tourism, the reasoning went, it could attract a wider tourist base and provide a corrective to the dangerous overdependence on gambling. If it could maintain its Portuguese flair after the departure of the actual Portuguese people, it could flourish (as it once had flourished) as an entrepôt, a bridge between China and "Latin-speaking countries" (southern Europe,

Latin America, and parts of Africa) that would provide an alternative to the Anglo-American focus of Hong Kong. Thus a variety of bureaucrats, developers, businessmen, and tourism industry leaders began to argue the need for "fusing cultural and economic interests by finding a lucrative way to preserve the unique essence of Macau's culture and history" (Ngai 1995). This was a strategy that gained support from Beijing, and by 1997, the phrase "Macau's unique cultural identity" had become every bit as ubiquitous as the image of the São Paulo Ruins. What this book examines are the volatile effects of the intersecting claims about sovereignty and Chineseness that underlay these attempts to systematize Macau's uniqueness under the seemingly sanitized sign of the Ruins.

The Story

Like the São Paulo Ruins, the structure of this book depends on the play between presence and absence. The massive and very public attempt to bring Macau into being as the site of a local identity that would be meaningful to all its residents is the stone from which the ethnography is fashioned; yet what makes this material remarkable is everything that wasn't there. Chapter 1 sets the scene with a brief account of how the history of Portuguese expansion in Asia, and of Portugal's and China's hazy and overlapping claims to sovereignty in Macau, provided the foundations for Macau's "system" as well as fodder for latter-day reinterpretations of this history. The attempt to create and instill in Macau residents a sense of their own unique identity did not take place in a vacuum: events and controversies that had nothing to do with debates about Macau's culture and history nonetheless shaped and colored public responses to the state's initiatives. Two such controversies are the subject of Chapters 2 and 3 of this book. The first centered on a wave of violence perpetrated by Chinese organized crime and on the Portuguese government's inability to combat its effects; the second was sparked by the Chinese government's attempt to define whether and how China's nationality law would apply to Macau residents. Although these were not fieldsites in the conventional sense, these topics were what everyone in my fieldsites was talking about when they were not trying to answer my questions—and sometimes when they were. But as I gradually discovered, they were more than just background noise; these controversies themselves were also debates about how a sovereign state should act, and how Chineseness should be defined. Although they were not intentionally engaging with the Portuguese state's assertions about its history of shared sovereignty and the unique hybrid identity that resulted, each provided a different perspective on the unintended yet very concrete effects that such a discourse could have.

My formal fieldsites were the institutions, places, or projects through which the Macau Portuguese state and a range of its interlocutors gave materiality to their vision of Macau as a bridge between East and West and of the history of Portuguese governance as the source of Macau's uniqueness. Four middle schools where the effort to introduce Macau history as a classroom subject highlighted the problems of what "the local" could mean in a place like Macau; the architectural heritage projects through which the state attempted to map its own version of Macau history across the city; and the Museum of Macau, where many Macau residents found their city's pasts represented in unexpectedly compelling ways: material from my interviews and encounters in these sites form the three central chapters of the book and provide the basis for discussions of scale-making, place-making, and value-making projects as sites for the articulation and contestation of sovereign claims. Chapter 7 draws together the themes and arguments of the previous six through an exploration of three alternative articulations of Macau's "uniqueness." Both the content of these alternatives and the ways they were suppressed, ignored, or overlooked as part of the public debates about Macau identity chisel out in finer detail some of the reasons why the emerging state orthodoxy on "Macau's unique identity" seemed at times to be falling on deaf ears. The discomfiting distance these individuals felt between "official" articulations of identity, nationality, and citizenship on one hand and their own daily experiences of belonging and alienation on the other suggest that forms of subjectivity structured by the precepts of modern sovereignty are unable to give expression to the fundamental ambivalence that lay at the heart of Macau Chineseness and, by extension, at the heart of all collective subjectivities. It also suggests that the idea of "flexible citizenship," in which individual subjectivities are shaped more by the forces of transnational capitalism than the moral-political affinities of national sovereignty, may be too quick to over-look the continuing power of these affinities in the lives of even the most flexible of citizens.

ONE

Sort-of Sovereignties

History at a Historic Moment

One often hears about the unique power of the Chinese past: the 5,000 years of civilization, its glory, its burden, its immense weight, which, even if one manages to hold it suspended for a moment, always crashes back down in place and moves inexorably along its own course. One often hears too, that in China, the writing of history is seen as a moral act. The historical record—as well as popular historical novels and films that romanticize the Chinese past—is full of references to orthodoxies and heterodoxies in understanding the past and to the unfortunate lot of scholars who dared commit historical heresies or break historical taboos.[1] These very words index the connection between history and sacred power, its centrality to the cosmological vision of Confucian order on which imperial claims to sovereignty rested. Although it may be summoned, twisted, or played with by individuals for political gain, the idea remains that history is an objective, omniscient phenomenon, ultimately external to the machinations of mortals, and it will eventually stand in impartial judgment of the injustices of the present (including that most unjust of injustices, the falsification of history). It is in this sense that history is often seen as that which defines the very "Chineseness of China": not simply because China has a long and complex history that all Chinese people share, but because Chinese people have a consciousness of the continuity and inescapable moral force of that history.[2]

Whether this is a positive or a negative thing is open to debate. In the 1980s, Chinese intellectuals concerned with what they saw as China's inability to move beyond feudalism envisioned China as trapped not only by its own history but by its own obsession with history; they condemned the "fixation on the past" as a timeless feature of Chineseness that had prevented the Chinese people from moving beyond the limitations of that history.[3] History was thus rendered not a "sign of the modern" (Dirks 1990) but the cause of China's perpetual incapacity to achieve modernity. By the early twenty-first century, this logic has been turned on its head: China's five millennia of history are often touted as evidence of the Chinese people's organic desire for unity; their consciousness of and rootedness in that past are what makes them so well equipped to take on the future as a fully sovereign nation, able to modernize and globalize without losing their soul.[4]

These broad assertions about the timeless importance of the Chinese past to the present and future depend, of course, on the elision of just how contentious that relationship has been. Plenty of other studies have drawn attention to the fact that the twentieth century witnessed an almost constant attempt to redefine the relationship between past and future. The iconoclasm of the May Fourth movement, the Kuomintang's (KMT) embrace of "tradition" in the service of modernization, the Maoist practice of "speaking bitterness," the "culture fever" of the 1980s, and the rediscovery and commodification of "tradition" in the 1990s all have entailed shifts in the interpretation of the meaning of past events and of the proper scale, subject, and significance of narratives about the past.[5] What bearing does, or should, the past have on present actions? What representational form—the written word, the spoken denunciation, the stone monument, the living museum—is best suited to make this relationship to the past come alive in the present? And what kind of subject, be it individual or collective, might emerge as the result of this mode of reflection on the past? These shifts index, among other things, changing ideas of sovereign power as a restorative or transformative force whose legitimacy derives from heaven or the masses or the market and of Chineseness as a form of subjectivity rooted in affinities with state or family or class. Throughout the twentieth century, the refashioning of narratives about the past and its relationship to the present was central to various projects of reform and revolution. This was not just a case of the history books being written by the victors (although a good deal of that took place as well), as much as it was that the past, thanks to its stature as the "great teacher" and "mirror for life," was a vital field through which victory could be effected (Ng and Wang 2005).

This particular metaphor of history as mirror may be specific to Confucian thought, but the idea that present-day sovereign claims are legitimized through reference to particular narratives about the past and its relationship to the present is hardly unique to China.[6] It may thus come as little surprise that history became a central concern in Macau's transition era—an era that was quite self-consciously narrated as a "historic moment." In this period, both the Chinese and the Portuguese states granted history a remarkable degree of agency: in the first paragraph of the Joint Declaration, the decision to "return" Macau to Chinese administration is characterized not as an end to Portuguese colonialism but as the solution to a "problem left by history" (歷史遺留下來的問題/*a questão . . . legada pelo passado*). For the Chinese state, how it was that history had bequeathed to the present such a sensitive problem had to be explained in ways that would clarify why the one country, two systems policy was the best possible solution to that problem. Meanwhile, the Macau Portuguese government's project of instilling in Macau residents the sense that their "uniqueness" resided in the history of its own presence in Macau meant that the correct understanding of that history was the foundation upon which Macau's future rested.

The crux of this project was what we might call (to continue in the Confucian vein) the rectification of names: the attempt (which Confucius saw as crucial to any project of governance) to fix the relationship between words and world, ensuring that words, with all their embedded meanings and connotations, were used accurately to describe reality, with all its inherent indeterminacy. As bureaucrats scrambled to figure out how best to effect the transition between administrations, Chinese and Portuguese historians scrambled over whether and how to use terms such as "colony," "autonomy," and "sovereignty" in understanding Macau's past. Thus, for example, in the late 1990s, I heard or read a wide range of assertions about Macau's relationship to colonialism. Some people declared that the political and social conditions in the city had all the hallmarks of a "classic colonial situation"; others claimed that Macau had "never been colonial in the strict sense of the term." Once or twice, I heard someone insinuate that the handover would represent little more than a change in colonizers; somewhat more common was the suggestion, either seriously or in jest, that in economic and cultural terms Macau was actually a colony of Hong Kong.

This was not mere semantic sleight-of-hand. The ways that different political actors in Macau defined colonialism—what it was, when it was, and whom it implicated—had profound connections to how they expressed the significance of Macau's "difference" from China and thus the significance of the city's impending transfer to Chinese sovereignty. In their debates, scholars drew not only on examples of the long history of partial, overlapping, and sometimes ambiguous sovereign claims and counterclaims but also on earlier attempts to rectify the names through which this history was narrated. Since the sometimes dramatic effects of these debates occupy the rest of this book, I want to set the stage by providing the contours of this history. I begin with a history of the names by which Macau has been called: names that both encode the complicated reality of the various sovereign claims over Macau and chart the unstable meanings of words such as "sovereignty" and "colonialism," "Portuguese" and "Chinese."

City of the Name of God of Macau in China, There Is None More Loyal

The Portuguese name of the city encapsulates in a few words the twentieth-century Portuguese view not just of Portugal's dominion over Macau but of the entire process of the creation of its empire in Asia: a mercantile enterprise dominated by the institution of the *Padroado Real*, which tied the political, economic, and missionary aims of the Portuguese crown and the Catholic church together into an ideologically and administratively coherent empire, centered in Lisbon, that stretched from Rio de Janeiro to Nagasaki.[7] In this view, the history of Macau began with the arrival of a small number of Portuguese trailblazers working in loyal service to god and king, who created a flourishing entrepôt on what had been barren land, and then tied that entrepôt—and with it, the whole of China—into the world's first truly global empire.

Recent scholarship has shown that the reality of Portuguese power in Asia was far more fractured and precarious than this story suggests; indeed, the fragility and sometimes outright absence of Portuguese crown control over the string of trade entrepôts that constituted the Estado da Índia has led some to ask in what sense the Portuguese empire could really be called an empire (or, for that matter, really Portuguese).[8] True enough, the Portuguese crown's initial goals in undertaking this ambitious enterprise were to dominate the lucrative spice trade with Asia and to forge political alliances with the Christian kingdoms believed to exist in east Africa and India— two goals aimed alike at crippling or destroying the powerful Muslim realms that controlled the overland trade routes between Asia and Europe and that had, until 1249, ruled all or part of Portugal itself. Yet the Portuguese explorers who set out from Lisbon in the late fifteenth century—among them the disaffected second sons of noble families, orphaned wards of the state, convicted criminals sentenced to exile, and Jews forced to convert to Christianity during the Inquisition (called *novos christãos*)—found themselves immediately dependent on African and Indian Ocean peoples and knowledges. Having only the vaguest notion of where precious spices such as pepper, cloves, and cinnamon came from, they brought samples so they could inquire at every port of call if anyone knew where such things could be found (Boxer 1969: 35). Despite their vaunted naval superiority, they relied heavily on Arab, Gujarati, Javanese, and Malayan maps, ship designs, navigators, pilots, and strategists—the very idea of capturing the Muslim-controlled port of Goa, for example, was suggested to Afonso de Albuquerque by Timayya, a Hindu privateer, who also offered his ships and men for the attack—as well as on local knowledge of trade routes, winds, and languages. Finding an already flourishing intra-Asian trade anchored at Hormuz and Malacca, they inserted themselves into this system by compromise where possible and by force where necessary. Seizing a series of strategically located port cities (notably Hormuz, Diu, Goa, and Malacca), they built fortresses and factories from which they attempted to monopolize the Indian Ocean trade, in part through direct trade with Asian merchants, and in part through the *cartaz* system by which they forced Asian traders to pay them for the right to ply long-established trade routes.

Yet this monopoly was never complete, as funding, manpower, and ships were in perennially short supply. Although Albuquerque once boasted that he could deliver control of the Asian trade to the king of Portugal with just four well-placed fortresses and a navy of 3,000 European-born men, upon reaching Asia those men who survived the voyage often deserted, preferring to enter the service of Asian rulers, join a religious order, or establish themselves as petty traders or pirates. In the early years, the Portuguese crown offered its male subjects in Asia economic incentives for marrying local women and thereby helping to establish a permanent Portuguese presence in the East. This meant that within a generation or two, although a tiny number of European Portuguese (known as *reinois*) dominated political and economic life in the administrative centers of Goa, Malacca, and Macau, they were always a minority who had to contend with far greater numbers of wealthy and well-connected Asian-born *mestiços* (not to mention Asians) whose interests were usually contrary to those of the crown.[9] But the *reinois*, too, often ended up working at cross purposes to the crown: rival embassies claiming to represent the king of Portugal fought among themselves to secure alliances with powerful kings, and the perquisites of an official post often included the right to prey on merchants, both Portuguese and Asian, whose cargoes would otherwise have been the source of substantial state revenues. By the late sixteenth century, cutthroat competition between far-flung, nominally Portuguese trading communities meant that even though individual merchants prospered immensely, each settlement was perpetually on the verge of bankruptcy. Political resistance to, and sometimes outright rebellion against, unpopular royal policies were often successful in asserting the will of the settlers over that of the king; only rarely and reluctantly would one settlement come to the aid of the crown in suppressing resistance in another. And although under the *padroado* the

Catholic church and religious orders provided theological justification for the endeavor, they, too, were often competing with the crown and private traders and one another for revenues from the intra-Asian trade. The Jesuits in Asia, for example, supported themselves through their investments in the trade in silk, sandalwood, cloth, pepper, and gems and profited from their role as financiers for the voyages of private merchants. For all these reasons, then, Portuguese expansion into Asia is best thought of not as an aspect of "the West's" domination of "the rest" but as the introduction of new and volatile elements into the series of shifting alliances and competitions among interest groups vying for power and profit in maritime Asia.[10]

This is not to deny the brutality of the Portuguese expansion. Several historians suggest that one of the new elements that the Portuguese introduced into the Indian Ocean trade (in the first few decades of the sixteenth century, at least) was the willingness to use violence as a first, rather than last, resort.[11] For example, Albuquerque's 1511 conquest of Malacca—a thriving city of well over 100,000 residents—entailed the slaughter of every Muslim within its walls and the repeopling of it with outsiders and Malays who swore allegiance to Portugal. Three days' plunder was the standard reward for soldiers' loyal service in sacking a city; temples and mosques were regularly razed to the ground, their land seized by religious orders, and their stones used to build churches on the spot. The destruction of any ship without a *cartaz*, and the massacre of all on board (especially if they happened to be Muslims), was common practice. But the presence of the Portuguese—their insatiable demand for "Christians and spices" and gold and silver and slaves, their well-armed and maneuverable ships, and their position as outsiders that enabled them to defy the laws and conventions others felt constrained to uphold—made possible the accumulation of new forms of wealth, the accrual of new forms of knowledge, the creation of new political alliances, and the establishment of new kinds of economies, all of which, for better or worse, altered the contours of the early modern world.

Macau was a key node in this process. Had Vasco da Gama made it to India eighty years before he did, it might not have been so. He might have met en route (in Calicut, Hormuz, or Mogadishu) Chinese ships under the command of Ming admiral Zheng He 鄭和, who led seven state-sponsored voyages across the Indian Ocean between 1405 and 1433, with fleets that would have dwarfed da Gama's in size, armaments, and the wealth of goods they contained. As it was, by 1513, when Jorge Alvares claimed the distinction of being the first Portuguese to sail into Chinese waters (aboard a Portuguese-owned, Pegu-built, Malay-crewed junk), the Ming had turned its focus away from maritime voyages; China was open to foreign trade but only through the tribute system, whereby foreigners wishing to engage in trade did so under the guise of paying tribute to the emperor and had to abide by restrictions on the frequency of their missions.

It was not until more than forty years after Alvares's arrival on the south China coast that a Portuguese settlement was established at Macau. In the intervening years, the Portuguese periodically petitioned the Ming court to allow them first to trade and then to settle more permanently on Chinese soil, but their embassies were refused and their ambassadors jailed when their actions led some Chinese officials to perceive them as unreasonable, untrustworthy, and dangerous.[12] Portuguese mariners sailed up and down the Chinese coast, illicitly conducting trade with willing local merchants from aboard ship or from small settlements on offshore islands.[13] They disguised themselves as Malay and Siamese traders and, at the encouragement of local merchants, smuggled their goods into port cities like Ningbo.[14] They allegedly established settlements—such as Liampo, near Shanghai, and Chincheu, which seems to refer to both Quanzhou and Zhangzhou in Fujian province—that were also allegedly sacked and burned to the ground by Chinese troops.[15] They skirmished with (and lost to) the Chinese navy at times, clashed with pirates at others, and sometimes joined forces with both.

The terms on which the Portuguese were finally allowed to settle in Macau is a question that has no definitive answer in the historical record. Eventually, opposition to their presence waned, as they proved themselves useful to both southern merchants, who profited from foreign trade, and the Ming court, which profited from the luxury goods and military technology they supplied. In either 1555 or 1557, probably by dint of verbal negotiations between Portuguese crown traders and local officials in Guangzhou rather than by imperial edict, permission was granted for them to settle at Macau. But unlike Hong Kong, whose transfer to British control in 1842 was clearly spelled out as a part of the treaty that ended the First Anglo-Chinese War, the details surrounding the earliest Portuguese settlement in Macau are lost or, more likely, were never recorded. To many historians, the haziness of this origin story is the origin of Macau's sovereignty problem.[16] To others, this haziness was the condition of possibility for the very existence of Macau.

Even the origins of the name "Macau" are unclear. By far the oldest and most common legend—one that the Jesuit scholar and missionary Matteo Ricci mentions in his journals in the late sixteenth century (Ricci 1953: 129)—is that when Portuguese mariners first anchored in the calm harbor to the west of the peninsula and inquired as to the name of the place, inhabitants told them it was called "Ah-Ma Bay" (阿媽澳, pronounced *ah-ma ngou*), or perhaps "Ah-Ma Pavilion" (阿媽閣, *ah-ma gok*), for the prominent temple to the goddess Mazu (nicknamed Ah-Ma) that graced the hillside overlooking the anchorage.[17] But others have suggested that the name derived from a rocky promontory on the eastern side of the peninsula known as "Mating Horse Rock" (馬交石), pronounced *mah gaau sehk* in Cantonese.[18]

Why Macau, rather than any of the other islands in the region? Chinese records suggest that the Ming considered Macau more defensible than the pirate-infested islands that surrounded it, since it was connected to the mainland by a narrow isthmus that could be easily closed off. But a legend that was far more popular during the transition era places the decision in the hands of divine powers and establishes a parallel between Chinese and Portuguese origin stories. Just as the Ah-Ma Temple, which gave Macau its Portuguese name, is believed to have been built by the grateful sailors of a ship from Fujian that got lost in a storm and was guided to the calm harbor at Macau by a vision of the goddess Mazu, so the first Portuguese in Macau are supposed to have been the crew of a shipwrecked Portuguese carrack who asked permission to come ashore at Macau to mend their ship and dry out their waterlogged cargo. The crew, grateful to the Virgin Mary who had guided them to this safe harbor, built a small chapel in her honor on top of the hill overlooking the harbor, directly above the Ah-Ma Temple, and never left.

Until recently, Portugal maintained that China had granted the territory of Macau to Portugal in gratitude for their help in ridding the area of the "Japanese pirates" then ravaging the southeast coast.[19] Legends persist that there once existed some tangible proof of the claim that Macau was Portuguese territory: the Jiajing emperor (r. 1521–67) had presented the Portuguese with a golden plaque (*chapa de ouro*), or perhaps an engraved stone tablet, or an illuminated scroll, thanking them for their military assistance and confirming the "solemn cession of the place," but all such evidence has been lost, through fire, shipwreck, or carelessness (Pires 1988: 113–14). In any case, in 1586, the viceroy of Portuguese India, acting on the orders of Lisbon and on the assumption that he, not the Chinese emperor, had jurisdiction over the settlement in Macau, granted it the status of a city. He christened it *Cidade do Nome de Deus na China* (City of the Name of God in China), reflecting the joint dominion of the Catholic church and the Portuguese crown. With this new status came the privilege of a high degree of autonomy: as residents of a city, rather than a mere settlement (*povoação*), the Portuguese at Macau were entitled to form a municipal council and elect their own council members, rather than being subject solely to the authority of the crown-appointed captain-major who passed through once or twice a year on his voyage to Japan (see L. G. Gomes 1997: 88 and Souza 1986).

But even before Macau became a city, its residents found themselves in a sort of one country, two systems situation. In 1580, a succession crisis in Portugal paved the way for Philip II of Spain to take over the Portuguese throne, uniting the Iberian peninsula under Habsburg rule. The terms of this unification would have sounded familiar to anyone in 1990s Macau: Philip II promised that no decision affecting Portuguese people or lands would be made without consulting the newly formed Conselho de Portugal, and that this council, as well as all the top juridical, military, and ecclesiastical positions dealing with Portugal, would be filled by Portuguese subjects. Thus, even though the Portuguese residents of Macau recognized Philip II as their king when news of his accession reached them in 1582, the Spanish flag never flew over the city. In other words, almost from the moment of its founding, Macau enjoyed a high degree of autonomy and self-governance (see Boyajian 1993, L. G. Gomes 1997, and Schaub 2001).

In 1640, Portugal regained its independence under the house of Bragança. Two years later, on a clear spring day following a night of thunderstorms that was subsequently understood to have been a portent of great joy, news of the restoration reached the residents of Macau, who celebrated with two full months of daily festivities: processions, bullfights, horse races, masses, masquerade balls, military parades, bonfires, music, and flags, involving not only the Portuguese residents but, according to one author, the Chinese, Japanese, Persians, and Dutch, as well as their slaves (Marques Moreira, in Boxer 1984: 150–59). That same year, King João IV of Portugal added to the city's name the honorific *Não há outra mais leal* (There is none more loyal), in recognition of the extraordinary allegiance to the Portuguese crown shown by the people of Macau.

In 1654, the city's whole name, *Macau, Cidade do Nome de Deus na China, Não Há Outra Mais Leal,* was engraved on a stone diptych embedded in the wall of the entrance to the city hall, seat of the Municipal Council (Senado da Câmara), a body of elected representatives that governed the Portuguese in Macau as a quasi-autonomous community. In 1810, the king of Portugal decreed that the name of the Municipal Council itself be changed to Leal Senado or "Loyal Senate"—a name that was also carved in stone on the façade of the senate building.[20] There the inscription remained, a monument to both Portugal's nominal authority and Macau's *de facto* autonomy, until midnight on December 19, 1999, when it was covered by a white cloth and replaced by a small trilingual plaque just above the door to the building that read "Provisional Municipal Council of Macau" (臨時澳門市政執行委員會 / *Câmara Municipal de Macau Provisória*).

Aomen

The opening line of Wen Yiduo's 1925 poem "Song of the Seven Sons" asks: "Don't you know 'Macau' is not my real name?" (你可知 "MACAU" 不是我的真姓? Wen 2000: 161). In the poem, Macau is personified as a child separated from its mother, yearning to be returned to her embrace and asking to be called by its "childhood pet name" (乳名), Aomen 澳門 (Portal of the Bay). According to Wen, the name Aomen must be restored to the city for its true history to be understood, and its true identity as one of seven Chinese cities occupied forcibly and unjustly by foreigners to be recognized. The poem's use of the name Aomen thus encapsulates the Chinese view of China's rightful claim to Macau, and the twentieth-century nationalist view that all the encounters between Europeans and Chinese in China, from the sixteenth through the early twentieth centuries, were part of a single escalating process of European imperialism and Chinese subjugation.

In fact, Aomen is but one of many Chinese names by which the peninsula and its surroundings have been known and appears to have come into use in the late Ming.[21] Prior to this, there was no single name for the place: the upper half of the peninsula was known by the name of its largest village, Mong Ha 望廈, and the lower half was most often referred to in official Chinese documents as a variant of Haojing'ao 蠔鏡澳 or 濠鏡澳, meaning either "Oyster Mirror Bay" or "Moat Mirror Bay."[22] Because it was the main harbor in Xiangshan county, it was also called Xiangshan Bay 香山澳.[23] In more poetic speech, the region was referred to by names that incorporated the word "lotus" (Lotus Flower Port, Lotus Sea), since the shape of the peninsula was thought to resemble a lotus bud "furled on its stalk like a divine flower."[24]

China has always denied that it ever ceded sovereignty over Macau and insisted that prior to the mid-nineteenth century, the Portuguese were allowed to remain in Macau only in exchange for an annual payment of 500 taels of silver. Anti-imperialist Chinese historians and colonialist Portuguese historians converged in characterizing these payments as "bribes": the Chinese suggested that they were pressed by the Portuguese on unscrupulous local officials whose greed led them to ignore the imperial edict forbidding the Portuguese from erecting any permanent structures on Chinese soil (Fei Chengkang 1988), whereas the Portuguese insinuated that they were extorted by unscrupulous local officials whose greed led them to ignore the imperial edict granting this land to the Portuguese (A. M. Pereira 1870, Jesus 1902).[25] In the Chinese version, the Portuguese "rented" (僦居, 租居), "seized" (侵占), "occupied" (盤據),

or "sneaked into" (混入) Macau; the so-called *chapa de ouro*, if it existed at all, was probably nothing more than a "proclamation (金劄) given to the Portuguese by Chinese officials, thanking and praising them for their aid in suppressing the Zhelin mutiny of 1564" (Tam 1994: 77, paraphrasing Dai Yixuan 1987; see also Chen 1996, Huang Hongzhao 1987, and Yin and Zhang 1992).[26] The Portuguese governors, judges, and other elected officials whom the Portuguese settlers at Macau viewed as symbols of their autonomy, note these historians, were awarded titles and ranks by the Chinese government: evidence that the Ming and Qing considered them an integral part of their state bureaucracy (Chang 1934: 101).

Recently, historians have found evidence that the Ming court in fact did sanction the Portuguese settlement in Macau and the payment of the ground rent, sometimes over the protests of southern officials who feared for national security.[27] This evidence became the basis for historian K. C. Fok's notion of the "Macau formula." According to Fok, this was a strategy (never articulated as formal policy) developed by the Ming for reconciling two contradictory imperatives: the need for a strong coastal defense and the profitability of foreign trade. The strategy was to allow the Portuguese "to have trade and no more," to confine their activities to "an area that could be confidently defended," and "to supervise the activities of the Western traders and control the treacherous elements from the interior" who might be inclined to conspire with the foreigners against the dynasty (Fok 1996: 222; 1991; and n.d.). Fok and everyone else agree that, at least for the first three hundred years of the Portuguese presence in Macau, Chinese people living both inside and outside the walled city of Macau were subjects of the Chinese emperor. The Portuguese were allowed to administer their own affairs and to run, under the watchful eye of the Chinese customs office, the foreign trade that sustained their city's economy, as long as they paid their ground rent and did not harm Chinese subjects or property. If they became too intractable, the Chinese government would simply close the border gate, cutting off their food and supplies, and starve them into submission.[28] In this view, the fact of Portuguese self-governance in Macau looks less like Portuguese colonialism than like the policy of "using foreigners to control foreigners" (以夷制夷)

that the Chinese state had implemented in its dealings with foreign groups on its borders, especially in the far west, periodically since the Eastern Han dynasty (25–220 C.E.).[29]

Thus the divergent histories of the establishment and growth of Macau encoded in the names "Macau" and "Aomen" suggest that the origins of the sovereignty "problem" lie not simply in the lack of documents but in twentieth-century historians' anachronistic attempt to discover, in the sixteenth century, the definitive answer to a question that was not asked or even formulated until the nineteenth century: Was the Portuguese settlement at Macau/Aomen an unwelcome incursion of European imperialists onto sovereign Chinese soil or the result of a long-standing Chinese policy for controlling foreign subjects residing in the Chinese imperium? That the answer to this question could be "both" is incommensurate with an either-or theory of sovereignty in which the world is divided into the colonizers and the colonized. The advent and spread of this theory in the nineteenth and twentieth centuries changed not only the way Macau historians approached their subject but also the course of events in Macau itself.

Colony

Of the various ways I heard the term "colonialism" used to describe the historical situation of Macau, by far the most common was the idea that Macau had been a colony of Portugal for precisely eighty years of its history: from 1887 until 1967.[30]

Beginning in 1842, with the conclusion of the Sino-British treaty that ended the First Opium War and ceded the territory of Hong Kong to Great Britain, the Portuguese government endeavored to get the Qing court to formally recognize what they considered a "*de facto* situation": Portuguese sovereignty over Macau (Saldanha 1996a: 48). Little came of these attempts until 1846, when a new governor, João Maria Ferreira do Amaral, arrived in Macau with orders from Lisbon to assert this sovereignty unilaterally. By 1849, Amaral had expelled the Chinese customs officials, declared Macau a free port (like Hong Kong), and extended Portugal's territorial claim far beyond the original city walls, up to its present-day border. He refused to recognize the authority of any Qing official within these new city limits and levied taxes on all Macau residents, Chinese and Portuguese alike. He met all attempts to resist these measures—attempts that included boycotts, strikes, and blockades on the part of Chinese residents and local Qing authorities and considerable backroom maneuvering on the part of longtime Portuguese and *mestiço* residents who felt that Amaral was pursuing the interests of the Portuguese state to the detriment of their own—with intransigence and the threat of violence, until the summer of 1849 when, after razing several Chinese tombstones to make way for a road to the new border gate, Amaral was assassinated by a small band of Chinese villagers just outside the city walls.

It was not until 1887, under pressure from Great Britain as well as Portugal, that the Qing signed the Sino-Portuguese Treaty of Friendship and Commerce, confirming the "perpetual occupation and government of Macau and its dependencies by Portugal, as any Portuguese possession."[31] According to Chinese sources, the treaty was never ratified by Beijing and thus was not a binding agreement; it was later classified as an "unequal treaty" on a par with those that gave rise to the treaty-port cities (such as Hong Kong, Shanghai, Ningbo, and Tianjin) in the mid-nineteenth century. Nonetheless, this formal definition of Macau as a "colonial territory" of Portugal, rather than as an "*establishment* tacitly tolerated by imperial munificence" (Saldanha 1996a: 50, italics in original), later came to be viewed as the moment when China "lost" Macau. Soon thereafter, and until around 1950, the Portuguese government formalized its view of Macau's status as its colony in a series of acts and laws that centralized and justified Lisbon's power over its shrunken imperial domain.[32]

By 1999, many people in Macau had come to view the denouement of the 123 Incident in 1967 as the moment when it was Portugal's turn to "lose" Macau. The 123 Incident is so named because on December 3, 1966 (12/3), Portuguese soldiers fired on a crowd of Macau Chinese residents protesting an earlier clash between police and a group of Taipa residents who had tried to renovate a school building without the proper permits. Eight Chinese residents of Macau were killed, and several dozen wounded. Inspired and partially backed by the ultra-leftist policies and leaders of the Cultural

Revolution in Guangzhou, a group of Macau residents presented the governor with a series of demands including not only a public apology, reparations to the injured parties, and a promise never to use force against the people of Macau again but also the expulsion from Macau of all organizations and individuals with ties to the KMT and the admission that the Portuguese state had committed a "crime" against the Chinese people. Over the next two months, as Governor Nobre de Carvalho tried to negotiate a middle ground between the adamantly anti-communist prime minister of Portugal, António de Oliveira Salazar, who insisted that the demands were unacceptable, and the equally adamant Chinese Communists, who insisted that their demands be met unconditionally, PRC gunboats circled the waters around Macau, and thousands of Macau residents fled to Hong Kong. In late January, leftists in Macau organized a boycott, encouraging Chinese residents to refuse to sell goods or provide services to any Portuguese or to employees of the government. Soon thereafter, Salazar allowed the governor the autonomy to decide his own course of action, and on January 29, 1967, Nobre de Carvalho, sitting at a table in the Chinese Chamber of Commerce under a portrait of Mao Zedong, publicly signed an "admission of guilt" and agreed to meet all the demands.

Most accounts of this incident term the governor's admission of guilt a "surrender" and suggest that Portuguese authority in Macau had become so weak that the administration was forced to more or less abjectly concede to any and all Chinese demands. Franco Nogueira, Salazar's minister of foreign affairs, reported that Salazar (still smarting from India's forcible repossession of Goa in 1961) was upset at what he perceived to be an irremediable loss of Portuguese sovereignty over Macau: "There still existed the outward signs of [our] sovereignty: the flag, the currency, some officials. But our effective sovereignty had dissolved. . . . We were no longer sovereigns: we were merely the administrators of a 'joint venture' (*condomínio*) under foreign supervision" (Nogueira 1986: 217).[33] In the following months and years, by most accounts, a Chinese "shadow government" arose in Macau with strong ties to the CCP, thus giving Beijing even greater control over Macau and obviating the need for an open confrontation with Portugal over the status of the territory—

a confrontation that the CCP, its hands full with the domestic problems of the Cultural Revolution, could ill afford (see Tam 1994, Santos 1998, and Castanheira 1999). Reinforcing the sense that Portugal had lost not just face but all real authority in Macau, Hong Kong people began calling Macau a "half-liberated area" (半解放地區).

Well before this crisis brought the question to a head, however, both the Portuguese and the Chinese governments had begun to insist that Macau was not a Portuguese colony. This was due largely to a change in the valence of the term "colony" after World War II. In Europe, the possession of overseas colonies was no longer viewed with pride as a badge of membership in the club of modern industrialized nations; rather, it came to be seen as a betrayal of the universal right to self-determination and thus a sign of hypocrisy, racism, and backwardness. With the establishment of the United Nations in 1945, all member-states that had colonial possessions were required under the terms of the UN Charter to work toward their eventual independence and to report back to the United Nations on the progress of this work.[34] "Colonies" were no longer defined simply as the overseas possessions of powerful countries, but as territories "whose peoples [had] not *yet* attained a full measure of self-government" (UN Charter Article 73; italics added). The implications of this definition—that self-determination and self-government were the normative goals for all territories and groups under foreign rule—was cause for concern to Portugal and China both.

In 1951, the Salazar government in Portugal passed an amendment striking the expression "colonial empire" from the Portuguese constitution and redefining Portugal's territories outside Europe as "overseas provinces" (*províncias ultramarinas*)—integral parts of "one state unified and indivisible" (*um estado uno e indivisível*) (Macqueen 1997: 11). To many scholars and anticolonial activists, this *was* mere semantic sleight-of-hand, performed expressly for the skeptical audience of the United Nations: legally redefining the boundaries of the Portuguese nation to include territories in Africa and Asia allowed Portugal to maintain both its UN membership and its claim to sovereignty over Macau, Goa, Angola, Mozambique, and its other colonies. The United Nations' skepticism was deepened by the fact that aside from the name, little else about Portugal's policies toward those regions changed.

Meanwhile, the new Chinese government formed in 1949—which had won legitimacy in large part through its dogged determination to regain the Chinese territory occupied by Japan in the 1930s and 1940s—made clear from the beginning that it considered Macau (as well as Hong Kong and Taiwan) to be an integral part of the Chinese nation that was being administered illegitimately and temporarily by a foreign government.[35] But it stopped short of accusing the Portuguese of colonialism, for calling Macau a colony would have implied that the city had the right to independence. Instead, the CCP made clear that its goal was reunification. But for years, it made no moves toward this goal. In 1949, when the People's Liberation Army (PLA) was preparing its "mopping up" campaign in Guangdong province, spokesmen assured Macau residents that the army would not cross the border into Macau (M. Fernandes 2006: 55). Throughout the 1950s, the CCP repeatedly assured Lisbon of its commitment to maintaining the status quo, while periodically reminding everyone that it still had the power, both literally and figuratively, to close the border gates: in 1955, for example, Beijing forced the Portuguese administration in Macau to cancel plans to celebrate the four-hundredth anniversary of the Portuguese presence on the peninsula and used the opportunity to remind the world that "Macau is Chinese territory" (M. Fernandes 2006: 70). Yet in 1965, when the CCP drew up a list of 23 colonial "targets for revolution" around the world, Macau and Hong Kong were expressly left off the list (Van Ness 1970, F. G. Pereira 1991: 271).

In 1972, within months of the PRC's admission to the United Nations, Chinese Ambassador Huang Hua presented a letter to the Special Committee on Colonialism arguing that Macau and Hong Kong should be called not colonies but "Chinese territory occupied by the British and Portuguese authorities" and that "the questions of Hong Kong and Macau . . . should be settled in an appropriate way when conditions are right."[36] Two years later, after its socialist revolution in 1974, Portugal divested itself of its colonies and on at least two (possibly three) separate occasions made known to the PRC its intention to "give back" Macau. After rumors that these negotiations were already under way caused panic on the Hong Kong stock market in 1975, China refused the offer, on the grounds that conditions were not yet right.[37] The political advantages of resuming full sovereignty over Macau did not yet outweigh the economic and strategic advantages of leaving the situation unresolved.

In 1979, when Portugal and the PRC established diplomatic ties, the two governments signed a secret agreement declaring Macau to be "Chinese territory under Portuguese administration." In legal terms, this agreement created a new category, a new kind of territory: neither colony nor sovereign state; a part of the PRC subject to the laws of another nation and a part of the Republic of Portugal living on borrowed territory. In fact, however, this change of legal status made little difference: it simply provided a legal framework that allowed the ambiguity to continue indefinitely. Ironically, Macau's new status remained a state secret until 1987, when negotiations for the city's return to Chinese administration began.

Sort-of Sovereignties

It is tempting here to conclude that, since China had the power to decide whether and for how long the Portuguese would remain in Macau, China "really" held supreme authority over Macau all along. The rest was just legalistic charades, since the Chinese state, for all its strident anti-imperialist rhetoric, was pragmatic enough to realize that having a foreign nation administer part of its territory could in fact work to its advantage. But rather than close the subject with the simple finality of this conclusion, I would like to take seriously the idea that the phrase "Chinese territory under Portuguese administration" was invented not to mask the truth of *de facto* Chinese sovereignty but to describe a condition of sort-of sovereignty in a world that could imagine no such thing. Doing so allows us to explore the new and sometimes surprising positions and juxtapositions opened by this assertion. Among the most ironic of these juxtapositions was the way that the Chinese government's insistence that the Portuguese presence in Macau was not exactly colonial created resonances with one of the foundational ideologies of Portuguese colonialism itself, thus further blurring the distinction between what could be called sovereignty and what subjugation.

The extolling of Macau as an example of cultural exchange, tolerance, and mutual respect—as well as the attempt to legitimize the exercise of sovereign power by questioning the meaning of sovereignty—will be familiar to anyone versed in the ideology of twentieth-century Portuguese colonialism. This ideology, which became known throughout the lusophone world by the name of "lusotropicalism," held that Portuguese expansion was an enterprise of racial and cultural mixing that was fundamentally more humane and progressive than its northern European counterparts. The term was coined by Gilberto Freyre, a Brazilian writer and social scientist who did graduate work at Columbia University, where he was profoundly influenced by Franz Boas.[38] His first book, *Casa-grande e senzala* (translated into English as *The Masters and the Slaves*), was published in 1933 in Brazil in a political and intellectual environment invigorated by a brand of postcolonial nationalism that rejected Brazilian attempts to imitate everything European in favor of political systems and theories that reflected "the uniqueness of Brazil." A crucial part of this uniqueness, according to both Brazilians and the Europeans who disdained them, derived from the long history of "miscegenation" between Portuguese colonizers, African slaves, and indigenous peoples. Freyre, in good Boasian style, rejected the tenets of Social Darwinism, separated race from culture, and located the source of the ills of Brazilian society not in the biology of race mixing, but in the "unhealthy relationship of master and slave under which it occurred" (Skidmore 1993: 192). According to Cláudia Castelo, Freyre was "the first author to popularize and legitimize the idea that Africans [and *índios*] had made a positive contribution to Brazilian society" (Castelo 1998: 18); to this day in Brazil, Freyre is celebrated for suggesting to Brazilians that "they no longer needed to see scandal and shame in their racial mixture; instead they could look to their art, literature, music, dance, in short to their culture to discover a richness and a vitality that were a result of the fusion of races and civilizations" (Bender 1978: 5).

More than just a theory of Brazilian history or national character, lusotropicalism involved a theory of Portuguese colonialism. The racial and cultural fusion that characterized Brazil, Freyre argued, was the result of the particular form of colonialism that the Portuguese had invented and practiced around the world. How could a nation so small and sparsely populated have colonized so much of the world? The answer, he believed, lay in the Portuguese people's ability, unique among Europeans, to tolerate difference. This ability, Freyre argued, was due to Portugal's history as a "border zone" between Africa and Europe: "Before the Arabs and the Berbers: the Capsians, the Phoenicians, and elements from more remote parts of Africa. Waves of semites and blacks . . . , breaking against those of the North" (Freyre 1966: 8). Although the contacts established in this border zone had more often than not taken the form of invasion, conquest, and enslavement, Freyre argued, the end result was that the inhabitants of the Portuguese nation were "a people existing indeterminately (*indefinido*) between Europe and Africa. Belonging intransigently neither to one nor to the other, but to both" (Freyre 1966: 6). This condition made them, unlike the "purer" northern Europeans, mobile, adaptable, and prone to "mixing." In addition, because the full effects of the industrial revolution did not reach Portugal until well into the twentieth century, "the Portuguese colonizer, basically poor and humble, did not have the exploitative motivations of his counterpart from the more industrialized countries of Europe. Consequently, he immediately entered into cordial relations with the non-European populations he met in the tropics."[39] Through the hybridization that resulted, Freyre argued, Portugal was the only European power to "accomplish the true work of colonization" (Freyre 1966: 18). Whereas northern Europeans were mere "exploiters" interested in colonial possessions only for economic gain, "the Portuguese colonizer of Brazil was the first among modern colonizers to shift the basis of tropical colonization away from the mere extraction of mineral, vegetable or animal wealth—gold, silver, wood, amber, ivory—toward the creation of local wealth" (Freyre 1966: 22). In material terms, then, Portugal had accomplished not merely a "kinder, gentler" form of colonialism, but indeed the only true mission of colonialism: the creation of a "modern society . . . with national characteristics and qualities of permanence" (Freyre 1966: 16).

In *Casa-grande e senzala*, Freyre limited his analysis to the history of Portuguese colonialism in Brazil. Later, however, as he read and traveled around the Portuguese empire, he extended his analysis to include the Portuguese territories in Africa and Asia as well and concluded that what the Portuguese had created was nothing short of a "Luso-tropical complex of civilization."[40] All the societies that resulted from Portuguese colonialism, Freyre argued, were unified and distinguished from the colonies of other European nations by characteristics of tolerance and hybridity, in which *mestiçagem* (mixing) had been an "active and creative force" in society (Freyre 1951: 43). Although materially impoverished, they exhibited a form of civilization more virtuous, more universalist, more cosmopolitan, than any other: a "civilization of the spirit." In a sense, then, lusotropicalism was a civilizational counterclaim, directed against (northern) Europe's attempt to appropriate the adjective "civilized" for itself alone. Gerald Bender argues that as the industrialized north came, in the late nineteenth and early twentieth centuries, to establish a hegemony in which nations were ranked in terms of their proximity to or distance from a universal standard of "modernity"— defined as a set of material conditions and epistemological assumptions that positioned industrialized Europe at the top of this hierarchy—"neither [Portugal nor Brazil] could measure up . . . they were desperately clinging to the bottom rungs of the ladder of western civilization" (Bender 1978: 6).

With the rise of António de Oliveira Salazar and the Estado Novo (New State)—the longest right-wing dictatorship in twentieth-century Europe[41]—lusotropicalism became not just a theory of Portuguese colonialism but simultaneously a denial of it and a justification for it. As Salazar and his supporters fought back against the United Nations' imperative to decolonize, they adopted aspects of Freyre's work to show that calling the Portuguese presence overseas "colonial" was not just a misnomer but an injustice to Portuguese, Africans, and Asians alike.

Franco Nogueira drew heavily on Freyre's characterization of the hybrid nature of Portuguese colonialism in his 1963 book, *The Third World*. In this book Nogueira defended the Portuguese presence in Africa by turning the tables on the United Nations, accusing the world's most powerful states of promoting the principle of self-determination for reasons of racism, hypocrisy, and naked self-interest in a world riven by the Cold War. For what, he asked, is a colony? He demolished the usual definition of a colony as a territory that is geographically, racially, and culturally distinct from the land of its central government, first by arguing that "in fact there is no pure race just as there is no closed culture . . . and in the end nations are inhabited by various races and include different cultures" (15), and second by asking why the United Nations considered Angola and Mozambique to be colonies, not provinces, of Portugal but considered Alaska and Hawaii to be states, not colonies, of the United States. He provided an alternative definition of colonialism, one that hinged not on cultural, racial, or geographic difference but on the nature of power relations: "A colony," he wrote, "can be said to exist when one people dominates another whom it considers to be inferior; . . . when there is economic and financial exploitation; . . . when a religion or culture is imposed on others; and when, finally, a political or ideological doctrine is forced upon other peoples for the aggrandizement of a country or group of countries" (Nogueira 1963: 90). In the case of Portugal and its overseas provinces, he continued, none of the above conditions applied: for, as Freyre's studies had proven, Portugal "alone practised the principle of multiracialism, which all now consider to be the most perfect and daring expression of human brotherhood and sociological progress" (Nogueira 1967: 148–49).[42] Rather, it was the United Nations that was guilty of imperialism, for the principle of sovereign self-determination it espoused was nothing more than a sham: "the new countries, no sooner enrolled in the United Nations as independent members, begin straightaway to lose their independence and to be submitted to . . . a colonialism that is infinitely harsher and more total than that from which they imagined they had freed themselves" (36–37).

What are we to make of Nogueira's analysis? In some respects, it is remarkably cutting edge: he deconstructed colonialism before deconstruction became an established mode of critique and subscribed to the view of neocolonialism espoused by leaders in the newly independent African states next door to Portugal's colonies—a view that has by now become a commonplace among critics of the postcolonial world order. In other respects, of course, it is irredeemably reactionary. Nogueira's critics have long since pointed out that his descriptions of multiracial brotherhood bore no resemblance to the reality of Portuguese rule in Africa and that lusotropicalism "gave expression to a myth that ignored the realities of racial arrogance, cultural genocide, human degradation, and exploitation" (Boxer 1963: xxiv).[43] But it proved to be a remarkably seductive myth: a romance of hybridity, a locus for imagining a different trajectory that the encounter between Europeans and their Others might have taken. As early as 1925, no less distinguished a figure than W. E. B. DuBois wrote: "between the Portuguese and the African and the near-African there is naturally no 'racial' antipathy—no accumulated historical hatreds, dislikes, despisings" (quoted in Bender 1978: xxii). The career of lusotropicalism in the half-century after its coining was so successful in creating a sense of the "difference" of Portuguese colonialism that even at the 1960 All-African Peoples' Conference, a fellow delegate from another part of Africa reportedly told Guinean revolutionary leader Amílcar Cabral, "Oh, it's different for you. No problem there—you're doing all right with the Portuguese" (quoted in Davidson 1969: 10). Within the next four years, Cabral and revolutionaries in the rest of lusophone Africa had become embroiled in struggles for independence that were, by the time they ended in 1974, among the longest and bloodiest in Africa.

By the 1990s, the Salazar regime, the African wars, and the idea that empire had been a justifiable and morally necessary project were, for most Portuguese, a distant and distasteful memory. Portugal's socialist revolution in 1974 had ended both the Salazar regime and the country's aspirations to empire. In Macau, the vast majority of residents had never heard of Salazar, let alone of Gilberto Freyre and his theories of the uniqueness of Portuguese colonialism. Yet the influence of lusotropicalism lingered.[44] Indeed, I heard the theory echoed almost verbatim by a Portuguese schoolteacher in Macau, who was concerned lest I fall into the fallacy of believing Macau to be just like Hong Kong. "The British conquered," she said. "We didn't. We are much softer. We didn't make colonies, we made children." She stopped and said it again, in Portuguese: "Não fizemos colônias, fizemos crianças. We mixed wherever we went. We'd send ships to various places, in Africa and the Americas and Asia, and our boys who went there would take native wives, and that's how the places were settled." This was the only good thing about the Portuguese, she joked, was that compared to most other white people, they were more tolerant of different races. Because they have mixed with so many kinds of people, there are many different-colored Portuguese. She would not be in the least surprised if there were a checkerboard Portuguese somewhere in the world, walking around plaid.

This was also the discursive ground on which Mário Soares, president of Portugal at the time of the 1987 Sino-Portuguese Joint Declaration, stood when he described the history of Sino-Portuguese relations as "a kinship of reciprocal discoveries, a creative and peaceful coexistence without parallel" and extolled Macau as "the historical symbol of, and the modern center for, this relationship" (Soares, quoted in ICM 1987: 5).[45] The terminology had changed: I never once heard the word "lusotropicalism" uttered in Macau, and "culture" had come to replace "race"; the official catchwords of 1990s Macau were "cultural tolerance," "cultural mixing," and, on occasion, "multiculturalism."[46] But the structure remained much the same. The emphasis on hybridity, tolerance, and mutual respect; the highlighting of "intangibles" in the face of economic stagnation and political corruption; the idea that "colonialism" was not the correct word to describe the situation in Macau; and the sense that Macau embodied an alternative to the hegemony of Anglo-American values and institutions, not just in neighboring Hong Kong but in the world, were all reminiscent of lusotropicalism.

The difference, of course, was that in 1990s Macau, the Portuguese state was not the only voice promoting this view. As China emerged from the era of high socialism and began to envision a future built on a reinvigorated role in international commerce, it too began looking for ways to legitimize this vision by way of the past. At a conference in Macau in 1998, the controversial scholar He Xin 何新 gave a keynote address in which he described Chinese civilization as the result of millennia of exchange and hybridization between cultures. For both China and Portugal, then, insofar as the history of the Portuguese presence in China could be made to fit this new understanding of both the past and the future, Macau could stand as a symbol, not of Portugal's backwardness and China's humiliation, but of an alternative (and superior) mode of sovereignty based on compromise, flexibility, and ambiguity rather than on unpragmatic notions of clarity and supremacy.

Thus despite its troubling history of ideological appropriations, I still find something useful in Freyre's notion of lusotropicalism—and, more cautiously, in Nogueira's deconstruction of twentieth-century conceptions of sovereignty. It is not necessary to accept their assertions of the moral superiority of Portuguese imperialism to see the value of their insistence that blanket terms such as "colonialism" and "sovereignty" conceal more than they explain. Although what many readers (including Nogueira) have taken from Freyre is his emphasis on race and *mestiçagem*, I would argue that what is most useful for understanding sovereignty and Chineseness in late twentieth-century Macau is his underlying argument about power: the need to examine how specific forms of power arise from and are thoroughly embedded in particular social and historical circumstances (in the case of Brazil, the racialized, sexualized master-slave relationship in rural landowning households) and how these forms create their own enduring, far-reaching effects. From the cursory glance at the history of Macau above, we may conclude that at its height, Portuguese imperialism in Asia did indeed operate through different assumptions about the value of ambivalence, and a greater reliance on the blurring of boundaries, than did the Anglo-American kinds of imperialism and notions of sovereignty that later supplanted it and made it appear to be an example of moral and political failure. I would argue that this grew out of not the Portuguese national character, as Freyre and many of his latter-day adherents would have it, but the contingencies of encounter in early modern Asia. Nonetheless, it did create its own enduring, often unexpected effects. It created the conditions of possibility for the new ideologies and practices of imperial expansion and anti-imperialist nationalism that came later, but its traces may still be found in the present day. In the rest of the book, I examine both the possibilities and the problems created by attempts to unearth those traces and forge them into the foundation for a different vision of the meaning and practice of sovereignty—a sort-of sovereignty that could serve as the basis for a better world—and thus a different way of being Chinese in the modern world.

TWO

Outlaw Tales

> There is no question that it harbors in its hidden places the riffraff of the world, the
> drunken ship masters, the flotsam of the sea, the derelicts, and more shameless,
> beautiful, savage women than any port in the world.
>   It is a hell.
>
> —Hendrik de Leeuw, *Cities of Sin* (1933)
> Chapter 4, "Macao—Brown Girls and Fantan"

I had never considered the *Wall Street Journal* to be a publication
given to sensationalism and hyperbole. Yet on February 26, 1998, it
ran an article describing Macau as "the most lawless six square miles
on earth" (Morrison 1998). Virtually every time Macau made headlines in the international press between 1996 and 1999, the story
featured some such exaggerated claim or a lurid description of violent crime: drive-up execution-style shootings in broad daylight; bodies found in locked cars with their hands cuffed to the steering wheel
and a bullet in the back of the head; severed body parts in sewers;
prison brawls ending in the beating deaths of inmates or guards;
bombs in cars and motorcycles strategically placed and timed to explode as a warning, but not kill. Such reports were not unfounded; as
the handover countdown clock ticked away in Beijing, the rate of
certain kinds of violent crime in Macau—or at least the visibility
with which these crimes were being committed—soared. But the
representation of Macau exclusively and gruesomely through its
crime vexed many Macau residents far more than the commission of
the crimes themselves.

Knowing that I was preparing a manuscript about Macau that
would eventually be published overseas, several informants urged me

not to mention the violence and to write instead about Macau's rich historical and cultural legacies, the opportunities for investment, the infrastructure development that promised to make the territory a first-rate tourist resort. I, too, constantly assured overseas friends and relatives that there was a lot more to Macau than what they read in the papers. I insisted, truthfully, that I felt safe walking alone down any street in Macau at any time of the day or night; that I could leave the door to the balcony of my apartment wide open all night long and still sleep soundly; that no one I knew had been murdered or stabbed or mugged. I did not interview gang members. I did not sniff out (as did the *Wall Street Journal* reporter) suspicious connections among Macau casino magnates, Beijing party politicos, and Washington campaign finance scandals. I was not interested in asking government officials or police superintendents for their analyses of the problem or their strategies for containing the violence. I assured my interlocutors that I did not intend to perpetuate the image of Macau as a gangster film cliché.

But in beginning to write about Macau, I realized that the very topic that my informants and I had tried to push so firmly to the margins of my research agenda was, in fact, crucial to understanding the questions that I had come to study. I realized that to ignore the rise of violent crime in the three years prior to the handover would be to neglect a significant aspect of the process of political transition. To disregard the ways Macau people talked about the problem of crime and its representation—their conspiracy theories, public protests, and private grumblings—would be to miss out on not only a major topic of public discourse but also an important locus for the ongoing debate about what Portuguese sovereignty had meant and why the handover would matter. To dismiss as sensationalistic the idiom of lawlessness and the ways the Hong Kong and international press represented Macau through its crimes would be to overlook the way these representations fit into a long history of narratives about Macau that have focused on images of seediness, disorder, and liminality—narratives that portray Macau under the Portuguese as a dangerous yet alluring city not just between civilizations but on the margins of civilization. In short, I realized that although I had not made it a fieldsite in the conventional sense, the crime wave in late

1990s Macau and the way everyone (the departing state and the incoming state, the international media, the alleged perpetrators, tourists, and innocent bystanders) positioned themselves in relation to it were central to my attempt to understand how and why the story of "sort-of sovereignty" that the Portuguese and Chinese states claimed was the basis for Macau's uniqueness was one that Macau residents did or did not find convincing. In this chapter, then, I embrace the image of Macau as gangster-film cliché, in part to demonstrate the extent to which sovereignty is a representational strategy that draws on fantasies, myths, and rhetorics that are often culturally specific and in part to read this image against the grain, asking why it gained such currency in transition-era Macau and what alternative "systems" and models of power it concealed.

Sovereignty and the State

One of the problems in attempting an ethnographic analysis of sovereignty is the difficulty of disentangling the study of sovereign power from that of the state. To my mind, this difficulty has two main dimensions. First, for a long time it was difficult to speak of sovereignty outside the state or state-like institutions such as the European Union or the World Trade Organization. Today, concepts such as "social sovereignty" (Latham 2000), "informal sovereignty" (T. Hansen and Stepputat 2006), and "shadow sovereigns" (Nordstrom 2000) have helped overcome that difficulty by demonstrating that the state is but one of many agents contributing to the maintenance (and contestation) of sovereign power. But these concepts do so at the risk of obscuring what is ethnographically distinct about the relationship between the state and sovereign power: the fact that, in many cases, the interdependence and interconnection between them is not just a theoretical stumbling block but an ethnographic fact. Despite the range of non-state institutions, extra-legal networks, market mechanisms, and forms of authority that may engage in practices that can be called sovereign, and that may even lay overt claim to sovereign power, rarely do they acquire the aura of legitimacy routinely ascribed (or prescribed) to states practicing or claiming the same. Yet to understand sovereignty as a "tentative and always emergent form of authority" (T. Hansen & Stepputat 2006), we must examine how the legitimacy of this form has become associated with some institutions more consistently and effectively than with others.

Second, it is still perhaps difficult to conceptualize of a modern state that operates on a different imaginary of power. The phenomenon that Aihwa Ong (2000) has identified as "graduated sovereignty," in which states parcel out control over certain populations and territories to corporations or other market institutions (as in export-processing zones in east and southeast Asia), is often cited as an example of the way that the state-sovereignty nexus is being realigned in a globalizing world. However, insofar as this realignment is effected through the policies, contracts, and other bureaucratic and legal practices that are the stuff of modern state sovereignty, it does not challenge the notion that it is the state's ultimate right to determine how its territory and people are governed. As Akhil Gupta notes, a definition of sovereignty that looks very much like the ideal to which liberal Western democracies aspire—which might be characterized as the legitimate and effective use of various kinds of force to ensure the well-being of its people, to control their movement, secure its borders, and suppress other groups contending for power within a given territory—is held up as a standard by which states around the world are measured as failed or successful, weak or strong; difference is not an option (Sharma and Gupta 2006: 10). This kind of sovereignty, then, is not just one imaginary of power among many; it carries a normative force. To understand the continuing appeal of sovereignty-speak, we must ask how this particular articulation of sovereignty comes to have such normalizing power.

The conflation between state and sovereignty may be further compounded by the similarities in two recent anthropological approaches to the study of each—approaches designed to address these very questions. First, a number of studies of the state and of sovereignty, inspired by the work of Judith Butler, emphasize the representational and performative nature of their object of inquiry: they argue that sovereignty, like the state, is the result of "reiterative and citational practice[s] by which discourse produces the effects that it names" (Butler 1993: 2). In other words, sovereign power is at least in part made real by the force of repeated assertions—both material and symbolic—of absolute authority, just as the idea that the state is a unitary entity standing impartially above the society it governs and having sole legitimate access to the various means (military, bureaucratic, symbolic) of imposing order on it, is made real through repeated assertions of the unbridgeable distance between state and society (T. Hansen and Stepputat 2001). These assertions necessarily draw on and reinforce norms, tropes, symbols, and narratives of power that, although they may be specific to one cultural or historical context, may well resonate across such contexts—and in the process become all the more compelling for their apparent universality. Such an approach puts representation at the center of any analysis of both states and sovereign power: rather than an ideological dressing-up of the timeless principle of violence that is the true essence of state sovereignty, representation is the means through which this principle is justified and comes to appear timeless. In this sense, the conflation of state and sovereignty is no accident: the idea of the sovereign's status as a unitary and solitary subject, always already transcendent, imbued with the capacity and will to make decisions alone and unobstructed, is reinforced by its association with states that willfully draw on this notion of sovereignty to naturalize their claims to legitimacy.

A second approach, inspired by the work of Giorgio Agamben, examines both states and sovereign power from the perspective of border regions, marginal populations, liminal sites, "states of exception," and "zones of indistinction"—phrases that Agamben uses to refer to spaces and conditions (such as concentration camps, death row, secret prisons, and overcomatose patients) in which the sovereign decides to suspend the laws and distinctions (such as between inside and outside, culture and nature, transgression and punishment, human and animal) that are fundamental to normal workings of the political and social order. These liminal or "threshold" spaces, he argues, are not exceptions to politics as usual, but in fact reveal the basic principle of sovereign power: the sovereign's paradoxical position of being both "inside" and "outside" the law, as one whose powers are defined by the law but who also has the power to suspend that law. In this sense, ethnographic studies of the margins of the state (such as those by the contributors to Das and Poole 2004) based on

Agamben's analysis of sovereignty examine how blurred distinctions between inside and outside, citizen and noncitizen, legal and illegal, are not examples of the breakdown of state control but in fact are necessary to the functioning of even the most rational-legal of state apparatuses. In so doing, they are extending one of the key insights of anthropology: the idea that marginality and liminality are both produced by and necessary to the production of centrality and normalcy.[1] For an ethnographic analysis of sovereignty, however, the second part of this anthropological argument—that what matters is not just the marginality of the margin but the specific ways in which marginality is imagined and inscribed on persons and spaces—is crucial. Concentration camp inmates, brain-dead patients, and bandits are all marginal figures that Agamben uses to make his point about the sovereign's power to decide life and death. But unlike the camp inmate or the brain-dead patient, whose liminality politicizes their bare existence while confirming the absolute power of the sovereign, the bandit lives a mythologized existence that threatens back. Precisely for this reason, the bandit, unlike the camp inmate, is a figure that evokes fascination and desire as well as fear and contempt. To understand both the force and the instability of claims to absolute authority, then, we must take as the object of our analysis the powerful mythologies of marginality through which individuals and institutions ground or contest such claims.

To do either of these things, we must also take into consideration the transnational culture of state sovereignty, in which hegemonic conceptions of sovereign power are shaped and reinforced not only by the discourses of and between individual states but also by films, television, and the news media; not only through straight political discourse but indirectly through evocative images and narrativized references to the perils of transgressing such norms. Stories about marginalized figures such as gangsters, pirates, vigilantes, and rogue states are unsettling yet captivating representations of what happens when individuals upset the distinctions necessary to the exercise of state sovereignty.

The various responses to the spike in violent crime in late 1990s Macau provides a unique point from which to tease out these strands of analysis. At a moment when the Portuguese state was trying to naturalize its claim to legitimacy by drawing on a notion of a liminal, sort-of sovereignty that made no claim to transcendence, the crime wave and the tropes through which it was represented constituted a very public threat to its authority: a threat that it met not with a swift demonstration of its absolute power but with a series of statements that Macau residents and the international press alike interpreted as signs of a failed sovereignty. In this context, the state's attempt to claim legitimacy on the basis of a different ideology of sovereignty was undermined by what appeared to be the intolerable legacy of that mode of power. Thus Macau's crime problem became a focal point not for debate about the potential virtues of alternative "systems" but for a renewed commitment on the part of a vast majority of Macau residents to the canonical concept of state sovereignty: the myth of a unitary power standing above and apart from society, wielding supreme authority over it. In what follows, I ask how Macau residents came to find this story of sovereignty not just plausible but necessary, despite the plentiful evidence of its status as myth.

Marginal Macau

Macau has often been portrayed as multiply marginal: the last, far-flung colonial possession of a nation itself often figured as being on the margins of a modern European civilization, it was until 1999 the last remaining European colony in post-colonial Asia; a city-state far from the centers of political and economic power in China, whose economy had long been based on activities that were illegal elsewhere. The one country, two systems formula seemed designed to ensure that even after the handover, Macau would continue to be a place where the normal rules did not apply.

During the transition era, as we have seen, the question of what this historical condition of marginality meant became an important locus for debates about the legacies of Portuguese rule, the significance of the handover, and the real-world possibilities for alternative imaginaries of power. Consider the *Wall Street Journal*'s depiction of Macau as "lawless." This was one rather literal way of narrating Macau's marginality as a dangerous exception to the rules, and it formed part of a long history of representations of the city that focus on the liminal, the criminal, and the illicit. An anthology published by Oxford University Press in 1997, called *Macao: Mysterious Decay and Romance*—a book about pirates, prostitutes, smugglers, spies, thieves, gamblers, ghosts, half-castes, opium addicts, barbarians, corpses, murderers, and Chinamen—is a compilation of some ways that visitors to Macau have written about the place since the seventeenth century. A series of adventures-in-real-life books published in the United States in the 1920s and 1930s, such as Aleko Lilius's *I Sailed with Chinese Pirates*, Crosbie Garstin's *The Dragon and the Lotus*, and Hendrik de Leeuw's lurid classic *Cities of Sin*, feature Macau as a haven for vice-mongers and degenerates as well as for contraband heroes. The list of such publications is long and includes not only the popular media but also official reports and academic analyses, in English as well as Chinese. Yet this representation is not a twentieth-century invention: even the *History of the Ming*—the official history of the Ming dynasty compiled by state historians in the early Qing—quotes several passages from seventeenth- and eighteenth-century documents describing Macau and its surroundings as "fertile ground for traitors and lowlifes" (而境澳亦蓄奸藪澤) (Chen 1996). As in the *Wall Street Journal* article, this idiom of lawlessness was sensationalized to entertain outsiders, even as it served as a way to condemn Macau as a den of iniquity and castigate the Portuguese as inefficient, irresponsible rulers without the wealth, ability, or moral fiber to run their colonies properly.

In fact, by reading accounts like these across time, it is possible to narrate the history of Macau under Portuguese rule as one long illicit existence, a single act of piracy sustained over 450 years. Soon after the Portuguese arrived in China in the late Ming, the emperor issued an edict prohibiting Chinese subjects from engaging in trade with Japan; so the Portuguese fought off the other pirates in the region and paid off local officials to allow them to set up a trading post in Macau that had a hazy relationship with Chinese imperial law. Continued bribery, their willingness to pay lip service to the emperor, and their occasional usefulness to the Chinese authorities were the only things that kept them from being expelled for nearly 300 years. But with the establishment of Hong Kong in 1842 (and the advent of steamships, which made Macau's shallow harbor obsolete), the city quickly lost its place in the world—a world that was in any case being rapidly redefined by the growing might of the British empire. Built as a city-fort, Macau had no natural resources, little land for agriculture, and no industry to speak of. The entire city and its social and political structure had been built around a single illicit activity—foreign trade—which had now been legalized and taken over by others. So to fill the gap, the Macau government simply turned to other forms of commerce that were illegal in neighboring regions. In 1850, gambling was legalized in Macau as a means to generate state revenue. Soon thereafter, the coolie trade (which involved sending Chinese laborers as indentured servants to South America and the West Indies, and whose resemblance to the slave trade was more than passing) grew to be a mainstay of the economy, until it was banned in 1894.[2] Opium was next: the government ran (or franchised) opium-processing factories and trading companies and sold licenses for opium dens until the drug was outlawed after World War II. Because Portugal did not sign the Bretton-Woods agreement, gold trading became a government monopoly in the 1950s and 1960s—a monopoly whose porous boundaries made rich men of many private traders. Then came casino tourism, which took off in the 1960 and 1970s. The 1980s and 1990s brought real estate speculation: the government reclaimed from the sea huge tracts of land and sold them for a tidy profit to investors from the mainland, who so overbuilt the place that even after the handover, more than 30,000 apartment units stood empty.

By the 1990s, this tale, which portrayed the Portuguese in Macau and all who profited with them as the rogues and demimondaines of the capitalist world system, was by far the dominant interpretation of Macau's history. Hardly the stuff of civic pride, it was often cited as the source of Macau's problems—isolation, backwardness, stagnation, corruption—which the city's impending incorporation into the PRC would fix by integrating the city more tightly into the administrative frameworks and commercial networks of the Chinese nation-state. But this was not the only way to narrate Macau's marginality. In a different view, the city's existence on the edges of nations, oceans, cultures, languages, economies, laws, and civilizations was not just what Macau had been built on: it was what had enabled the creation of the modern world system of capitalism, which had then proceeded to marginalize not just Macau but China and Portugal as well. In this view, Macau's position outside the conventions and laws that structured either Chinese or Portuguese society was precisely what allowed the city to become a major hub of world trade in Asia for over 300 years, anchoring trade routes that spanned the known world, and a center of culture and learning, home to Asia's first university. The *laissez-faire* policies of the Portuguese state and its "obedience" to the Chinese emperor were not signs of incompetence, weakness, and irresponsibility; they were precisely what had created a society more tolerant of difference than the mainland, more relaxed than Hong Kong, and more full of *renqing-wei* 人情味—human warmth and decency—than either. Macau's "system" was not an unsuccessful form of Hong Kong–style capitalism, it was the unique product of the Portuguese state's more fluid conception of sovereignty, one that refused the absolutist language of supremacy vs. submission, legality vs. lawlessness, and spoke instead in terms of pragmatism, negotiation, and compromise with powers deemed illicit by its neighbors. It was this form of sovereignty that had enabled the Portuguese to remain in China for over four hundred years and that had allowed Macau's economy to flourish, or at least survive, in periods when the regions around it were devastated by wars, invasions, embargoes, and forced evacuations. In this view, Macau was not a backwater but a model for a better world.

This was the story the Portuguese state embraced as it prepared to depart from Macau. The last Portuguese governor, Brigadier General Vasco Rocha Vieira, committed millions of dollars to the construction of museums, the publication of books, the production of films, and the sponsorship of research, with the hope of creating a countermythology of marginality that would tell of Macau as a city of culture, not sin; of hybridity, not lawlessness; of difference, not backwardness; and of charm, not decay: fertile ground not for lowlifes and traitors but for poets and revolutionaries, from Luís de Camões to Sun Yat-sen.[3]

The question that intrigues me here is not which of these narratives is more historically accurate but how the first came to be so globally dominant. Although much of the rest of the book is devoted to an analysis of how and with what consequences the state attempted to promote the second version, in this chapter I ask how Macau's marginality came to be so widely accepted as pathological rather than productive. How did the peculiar advantages of the "sort-of sovereignty" that the Macau government claimed to have practiced come to be seen as its greatest failures? Although the answers to these questions may seem self-evident given one glance at Macau's socioeconomic circumstances near the end of Portuguese rule, I argue that in fact a great deal of work went into ensuring that this narrative of Macau's past, and the form of sovereignty it purportedly demonstrated, were viewed as Macau's biggest problem rather than the basis of the "system" that deserved protection and cultivation as the foundation of post-handover Macau. The kind of work this process entailed was perhaps nowhere more evident than in the transnational representations of sovereigns and bandits in late 1990s Macau.

"It Has Never Been Like This"

On November 26, 1996, Lieutenant Colonel Manuel António Apolinário, head of the Macau government's Gambling Inspectorate, was shot in the head and neck by a motorcycle gunman as he got into his car outside his office on the Avenida da Praia Grande during the afternoon rush hour. In this rather spectacular way, violent crime became one of the most serious "problems" of the transition, perhaps the only problem that captured the attention of the international media in a sustained and systematic way. Apolinário survived, barely, but the city was shaken by the audacity of the attack, fearing what it might signify and who might be next. Indeed, the violence proliferated into 1997: shootings, stabbings, armed robberies, firebombs that ripped apart storefronts and ravaged automobiles, and arson attacks directed at motorbikes. With a few notable exceptions (Apolinário among them), the violence was not directed at government officials; most of the victims were young men, often described in newspaper accounts as having had "ties to casinos." But even when the victims were not government officials, the openness with which the violence was carried out—often in broad daylight, on main streets—seemed a deliberate, taunting provocation of the authorities.

The newspapers kept a running toll of annual homicide rates: 21 murders in 1996; 29 in 1997; 30 in 1998; 42 in 1999. The murders and shootings tended to come in clusters, sometimes as many as four or five in the space of three days, followed by a respite of a week or two. The brief reports in local papers of young male corpses being found in abandoned automobiles soon became a kind of grim monotony occasionally broken by more spectacular cases, such as the Molotov cocktail thrown into the grounds of the governor's residence, the Legislative Assemblyman who was beaten up by five young men as he left a lunch meeting downtown, or the two homemade bombs that exploded outside one of the city's newest hotels. A cluster of three high-profile shootings over six days in March 1998 put the problem squarely back on the front pages. On March 24, the third-highest official in the Gambling Inspectorate was shot dead at point-blank range as he walked with a friend along the plaza outside the Judiciary Police headquarters at lunchtime. Two days later, an officer of the Marine and Fiscal Police was killed in his car by a motorcycle gunman in the Rua do Campo during morning rush hour as he was taking his daughter to school (the daughter, in the back seat, was unharmed). Four days later, a Hong Kong tourist was shot in the face—the first time a tourist (and a woman) had been involved, let alone directly targeted, in any of the violence. Two weeks passed; then the chauffeur for the undersecretary for security was shot and killed as he left his house for work one early morning.

In late 1998, the violence began moving into Macau's prison: brawls in which guards and a score of inmates were critically injured, or one or two inmates beaten to death, began to happen regularly; attempts were made, sometimes successfully, on the lives of prison officials and guards newly recruited from Portugal and Nepal. By 1999, the forms and scope of crime had multiplied. Previously, the victims of shootings had been meticulously targeted, and the attacks carried out with precision; but in May 1999, for the first time, two passersby were critically injured in a streetside gun battle. Previously, the target of drive-up shootings had usually been the driver or passenger of a private car; in July 1999, for the first time, a motorcycle gunman shot and killed a passenger on a crowded public bus at eight o'clock in the morning. No longer was it only the children of the super-rich or the wives of mobsters who were the targets of kidnappings; now unemployed teenagers and illegal immigrants, it was said, emboldened by the apparent impunity with which these crimes were being committed, had taken to snatching any child in a middle-class neighborhood in hopes of netting a ransom of even just a few thousand patacas. Shortly before I left Macau in September 1999, a friend told me her parents' apartment on the eighteenth floor of an apartment building in the northern part of the city had been robbed in the early hours of that morning by three masked men who forced their way in the front door. The apartment she shared with her boyfriend had been robbed twice in the past year, she said; their downstairs neighbor's flat two times in just four months. "It's never been like this," her boyfriend, an instructor at the university, said quietly. "There's just no fear of the police, no fear of getting caught. It's never been this bad."

Despite the pathos of my friends' comments, it was not home burglaries that provoked the kind of hyperbole evident in the *Wall Street Journal*. Rather, it was a particular kind of violent crime, committed by a particular kind of criminal, that was being narrated so vividly in the international media and that was the focus of so much attention in Macau as well: crimes that were, or were said to have been, perpetrated by members of criminal syndicates—triads— who were either protecting their interests or exacting retribution for some kind of treachery. The term "triad" (黑社會, or "black societies," in Chinese) refers to a number of secret transnational associations whose main economic activities include a range of illicit businesses in virtually all the cities of the world with a significant Chinese population.[4] Defined by law in Macau, as in most countries where they operate, as criminal organizations, triad associations and membership in them are illegal.

But the triads, everyone knew, had an unshakable and indispensable presence in Macau. Although casino gambling was legal and run by a government-franchised monopoly—Stanley Ho's privately held STDM—it was commonly assumed, though hotly denied by STDM, that triads ran the day-to-day business of protection, loansharking, debt collection, money laundering, prostitution, drugrunning, human trafficking, and other racketeering activities, as well as the profitable enterprise of managing the high-stakes "VIP rooms" in STDM's ten casinos. In a city where over 60 percent of government tax revenue derived from casino-based tourism, some kind of truce, people surmised, must have existed between the government and the triad businessmen. This is why the 1996 attack on Apolinário was so disturbing: it came just after he had suggested tightening government control over the process by which casinos subcontracted out the management of VIP rooms. What shocked people was that the triads would strike so publicly at the state; what worried them was the implication that the truce might be unraveling into all-out war.

The mood, however, was not one of fear. Most people were not directly affected by the crimes and usually assumed that the victims had done something to warrant the attacks—belonged to a gang, borrowed from loansharks, tried to cut in on the triads' action. One cabbie held forth against his relatives in Hong Kong who had refused to set foot in Macau until the violence stopped, saying that he had told them what every Macau resident knows: "If you don't hang out in casinos, you won't get into trouble. Anyway, gambling is a bad habit." Although some families took precautions against kidnapping, most people did not change their patterns of movement; most were not afraid of random attacks, nor did they worry about going out at night or traveling to certain parts of town.

Rather, the mood was one of anger and frustration. These sentiments were directed not against the triads but against international media on one hand and the state on the other. In the Hong Kong papers, which are well known and often criticized for their sensationalism, each incident in Macau would be accompanied by a gory front-page photograph and stories with narrative structures reminiscent of the hyper-violent gangster films made popular by the likes of John Woo. The Hong Kong television news had a standard graphic representing "more violence in Macau"—a cartoon representation of the São Paulo Ruins with a little gun or a red-and-yellow explosion icon in front of it—that would appear in the space next to the news anchor's head whenever he or she introduced a story about the latest incident in Macau. These rhetorical and graphic depictions of Macau as a dangerous place and the predominance of stories about violent crime to the neglect of any other angle on Macau succeeded not only in selling more papers but also in keeping Hong Kong residents, who at the time constituted well over 70 percent of Macau's tourist base, away from Macau.[5] The University of Macau and the Macau Journalists Association held seminars about the proper role of mass media in society; they sent letters to the editors of Hong Kong papers protesting the sensationalism and implored the Macau government to respond.

But to little effect. The international media—*Newsweek, Asiaweek, Time, The Economist, The Far Eastern Economic Review*— picked up on the hyperbole and ran with it.[6] One story in *Newsweek*, entitled "Lords of the Cellblock: Lawlessness Is Spreading as Portugal's Lease Runs Out," begins with a description of an inmate staggering down the prison hallway holding a rag against his bloodied head and collapsing on the floor as guards smoke cigarettes and chat nearby. The journalist narrates the event as a witness—it had happened during his visit to the prison to interview the warden—and sets the reader up to expect a spectacular story of gang warfare, the Portuguese state's callous disregard for human life, and its inability to enforce discipline even inside its prisons. As it turned out, the inmate had been injured in an accident while working in the prison's auto repair training program and was rushed to the infirmary as soon as he caught the attention of the guards. Acknowledging this briefly, but undaunted by the disappointing mundanity of the accident, the author continued:

Isolated on a tiny island 1.5 kilometers off the coast, surrounded by 20-foot-high concrete walls, the dank, factorylike Central Prison reflects its society: like the rest of Macau, it is engulfed by lawlessness six months before the Portuguese colony is to be returned to China. Outside the walls, rival triad gangs explode car bombs, shoot each other and hurl grenades with abandon. (*Newsweek International Edition*, May 17, 1999: 15)

As crimes not directly traceable to triad activity began to proliferate, an article in the *Far Eastern Economic Review* suggested that there was "an even deeper problem: Macau's organized crime has degenerated into *disorganized* crime" (FEER, March 12, 1998: 26; italics in original). The implications were that the only thing worse than organized criminals were criminals who did not play by the rules and that Macau was so lawless it could not even properly organize its crime.

It was precisely this kind of synecdoche and hyperbole that the majority of Macau residents found to be the most vexing aspect of the violence. Triads operate in Hong Kong, Guangzhou, London, New York, Sydney, Vancouver, and elsewhere—and in point of fact, the per capita crime rate in Macau at the peak of the violence was far lower than that of these other cities—so why was Macau being singled out for such scorn? This was more than a question of pride; with stories such as these dominating international representations of Macau, tourists from around the world began staying away, and Macau's already sluggish economy worsened. In the first four months of 1998, the number of tourists entering Macau from Hong Kong dropped 31 percent from the previous year. The Japanese government listed Macau as a "dangerous" destination and warned its citizens to steer clear; the Asia-Pacific conference of the International Jaycees had been planned for 4,000 but only half that number showed up; even the US Navy forbade its sailors from taking R&R in Macau when their ships docked in Hong Kong.[7] As the crime rate surged, the economy crashed and people implored the government to respond: not only by taking stronger measures against the triads, but by doing something about the way Macau was being represented overseas; not because their sons and brothers were being murdered, but because the bad press was ruining everyone's livelihood.

"Pig Answers"

For many Macau residents as for much of the international media, the crime wave, the ailing economy, and the international representations of Macau as a lawless land were evidence of the illegitimacy of the Portuguese state in Macau. The bad press was at least partly the result of the government's apparent inability to, as John Searle put it in his description of performative speech, "bring about a fit between words and world" (Searle 1989). "The situation is under control," the chief of police or the undersecretary for security would say after each murder or robbery; that same afternoon there would be another jewelry store robbery in a downtown area during rush hour or a shooting the next day. In August 1997, after shootings in two of the territory's most popular hotel-casinos began to scare off tourists, the legislature passed a tougher anti-triad law; but by mid-1998 it became clear that the main effect of this law had been to turn the Central Prison into the new triad meeting hall. Adding to the public's exasperation was the sense that although the police kept mentioning the arrests they had made and the undercover operations they had in the works, they never seemed to solve any cases. In the spring of 1998, Stanley Ho himself suggested that Macau's problems had more to do with the Portuguese government's inability to perform the normal functions of a state than it did with the triads: "almost thirty people have died within eight months, and not even one case has been solved in four years" (quoted in T. M. Liu 2001: 206).[8]

In November 1997, a Chinese journalist of my acquaintance attended a press conference at which a spokesman for the Judiciary Police had fielded questions about the worsening situation. She was appalled by the responses he gave—which she called "pig answers" (豬答案) because of their stupidity—especially his responses to the charge that the Macau police were ineffectual in the face of these well-trained, well-armed, well-organized, and well-connected criminals. She told me:

He actually said, "The criminals must be afraid of the police still, because they always leave the crime scene before we arrive. If they weren't afraid of us, they wouldn't run away." He also said, "How can we catch these criminals? When we start working on solving a string of jewelry store hold-ups, they change tactics and start holding up restaurants instead. So how are we supposed to be able to catch them?" He actually said this at a press conference, can you believe it? How can you expect the public to have any confidence in this government?[9]

Chinese journalists were not the only ones chagrined by such "pig answers." One after another, Portuguese officials in Macau were quoted in local and international publications making what appeared to be ill-advised attempts at humor. A Portuguese-language paper in Macau reported that Afonso Camões, director of the Macau Government Information Bureau, had been immortalized in the *Washington Post*'s "Quote of the Day" for his observation, "It's true that we have problems with organized crime, but it's not exactly Chicago" (*Ponto final*, January 15, 1999).[10] But the most infamous statement came from Undersecretary for Security Manuel Monge, who tried to reassure the public by saying that law-abiding tourists and residents had nothing to worry about, since the triad hitmen were "professional killers who never miss their target." Although many residents either jokingly or seriously agreed with the sentiment of this statement and even admitted to using this logic with overseas friends and family nervous about visiting Macau, the fact that it had been uttered at a press conference by the highest-ranking security official in the territory was considered by everyone I spoke to as a sign of not just incompetence but irresponsibility. The state's refusal to even try to represent itself as a supreme power that would inevitably vanquish this challenge to its authority was seen as a sign of its premature abdication of sovereignty.

Aggravating the public's sense that the Portuguese government had forfeited its legitimacy was Macau's history of blurred boundaries between state and criminal. This blurring began with the public knowledge that without the revenues from activities run by triads, the government would collapse. The Chinese expression "soldiers and bandits are one family" (兵匪一家) was often invoked to explain the problem of policing such a small territory in which the bonds of blood and childhood friendship were stronger than the law.[11] It was taken as fact that the Macau police force was thoroughly infiltrated by the triads; how else could so many police raids on known triad headquarters fail to result in arrests?[12] Corruption at all levels of government was equally presupposed: in 1990, Governor Melancia had been forced to resign over alleged bribes he had received in connection with the construction of Macau's first airport, although his supporters said he was framed; many junior civil servants could somehow afford to drive flashy cars; and even Chinese residents who spoke no Portuguese knew that in Portugal, getting a government post in Macau was called "shaking the pataca tree" (*abanar a arvore das patacas*). The 1996 Legislative Assembly elections brought into the legislature several businessmen rumored to have triad connections who were accused of having bought their constituencies. One of them, Chan Kai Kit 陳繼杰, was indicted in Hong Kong in 1999 for involvement in a scheme that had defrauded Guangnan (Holdings) Limited, a Hong Kong–based investment firm run by the Guangdong provincial government, of over US$25 million. Chan disappeared into the mainland.

Bandits and Sovereigns

More than just an embarrassment and an economic disaster, however, the triad violence and the state's inability or unwillingness to respond to it became a site for contestations over the "sort-of sovereignty" that the Portuguese state was claiming to have invented. Two interviewees separately and spontaneously spoke of the triad problem as a direct result of the particular form that Portuguese colonialism had taken in Macau. Mario, a Macanese community leader who had been educated in Portugal and was active in Macau politics (but was not employed by the government), admitted that the attitude and actions of Portuguese officials in Macau were not helping matters. But the real triad problem, he told me, was a cultural one: "These secret societies have existed for a thousand years in China, they are a part of the Chinese society and way of life, especially in the south, and there's nothing we outsiders can do about it. We certainly can't eradicate them now!"

This resonated with the narrative the Portuguese state had been trying to construct about the nature and meaning of the Portuguese presence in Macau: it had been a kind of colonialism by invitation, a politically correct form of colonialism that compared favorably to the British next door, those true colonizers who imposed their political and cultural will on everyone they ruled. Unlike them, the Portuguese in Macau had a "softer" touch; they had not forced anyone to learn Portuguese and had allowed the Chinese in Macau the autonomy to create and run their own civic associations and institutions, which often fulfilled many functions that elsewhere would have been performed by the state. And this kinder, gentler mode of sovereignty was reflected, according to Mario, in Macau's kinder, gentler underworld. "The local triads—," he said,

usually in the past they would not kill. You know? They would prefer to talk things out. I've seen a lot of those American movies about Chicago in the 1920s, the mafia, they were always saying things like, "If you can make a friend, make a friend. Making a friend is better than making an enemy." You know? That's what the local guys are like. Only if they have no other option, if they can't talk, then they will bring out the guns. But these new ones, they get people from China who were trained by the Red Guards—

they are killers, professional killers. They ride motorcycles in over the border, do the job, and ride back into China in the same day. Give them 20,000 patacas and they will kill anybody. They are completely different from the Macau guys. Never has there been so much criminality in Macau, not since before World War I. Even in America they are advising tourists to stay away from Macau. The hotels are empty, the restaurants are empty, the shops—empty.[13]

For many in Macau, the Red Guards were, like the Cultural Revolution in general, the paramount sign of the destructive and dehumanizing excesses of the Chinese Communist Party's chosen mode of sovereign power—a totalizing imaginary of state power that demanded of its subjects the kind of fanaticism and blind obedience that would lead them to betray their own parents and take a sledgehammer to their own traditions. This form of sovereignty, Mario claimed, had produced a generation of ruthless criminals in mainland China—rogue criminals who were not bound by the axioms of underworld civility and who conceived of human life solely in terms of its exchange value. At base, Mario seemed to be saying, the triad problem in Macau did not call into question the legitimacy of Portugal's claim to have invented a kind of cultural-relativist colonialism in the past; rather, it drew attention to the dangers of Chinese (Communist) sovereignty and boded ill for Macau's future.

Mario was not the only one who traced the origins of the 1990s triad problem back to the Cultural Revolution. Ng Kuok Cheong 吳國昌, a Macau Chinese man who was an outspoken pro-democracy member of the Legislative Assembly, found the roots of the problem in what he considered the crux of contemporary political, social, and economic development in Macau in the past half-century: the 123 Incident in 1966–67. This incident, Ng felt, had been nothing less than a *coup d'état*, one that had left the Portuguese nominally in charge but placed *de facto* sovereignty over Macau in the hands of the Beijing government. According to another interviewee, Mr. Chan, a spokesman for the Macau Union of Neighborhood Associations (澳門街坊會聯合總會), one result of the 123 Incident was that these associations took on new importance in Macau, not simply due to the influence of the Chinese Communist Party (which set up neighborhood associations in every city in China, including

Macau) but because after its "defeat" the Portuguese government "abandoned and ignored" (放手唔理) all social welfare projects—from housing and education to sanitation and recreation—affecting the Chinese population in Macau.[14] Echoing Mario, Ng Kuok Cheong continued,

This meant that the triads were defined as a "Chinese" problem. They [Portuguese officials] would say, "That's something that is part of your society, what can we do about it?" Organized crime as we know it today was around in the 1960s, but was not particularly powerful. The triads could have been easy to control back then, but the Portuguese government never bothered to fight them. The Portuguese haven't lifted a finger to control the triads since they "lost" in 1967.[15]

According to Ng, then, the Portuguese state's response to the triads was evidence not of a different, "softer," and superior form of sovereignty but of an outright refusal to govern. Once again, the comparison was with the British in Hong Kong, who crushed a similar attempt to destabilize the colonial government there in 1967 and who in the 1970s appeared to have taken strong measures to keep the triad situation under control.[16] In contrast, Ng suggested, the people of Macau were suffering from impotent and incompetent colonialism. At least the British had made something of Hong Kong. At least the British had managed to keep the triads underground where they belonged, out of the public eye. Ng's comments evoked the kind of rueful tinge I heard in the comments of many Macau residents (including some Portuguese) critical of the Portuguese government in Macau. The difference between the "Asian tiger" Hong Kong and "stagnant backwater" Macau, between a city that was the envy of all Asia and one that was the butt of the world's jokes, was bad management. Being subjected to colonial rule is one thing, Ng seemed to be saying; being subjected to inept colonial rule is something altogether intolerable.

Such analyses of the "difference" (be it positive or negative) of Portuguese rule were often cast in ethnic terms. The Portuguese state and its interlocutors insisted that its "softer" mode of governance reflected an alternative conceptualization of sovereignty that in turn derived from the laid-back Portuguese national character, whereas critics maintained that the Macau government was inefficient, hyper-bureaucratic, incompetent, and irresponsible because that was just how the Portuguese were. But at the same time, these criticisms led to a de-emphasis on ethnic solidarity and anticolonial ideology in Macau people's desire to be "returned" to Chinese sovereignty. This desire, they suggested, had nothing to do with Chineseness. The Portuguese state was illegitimate neither because it was colonial nor because it was alien, but because it was failing to perform according to the normative definition of modern sovereignty. It was less a matter of patriotism or ethnic pride and more one of practicality that made the Macau Chinese want to *huigui*; they wanted to be governed by a rational, responsive, and responsible state—one that left no doubt as to who was in charge. To be clear: some Macau residents did voice classic anticolonial sentiments, and as the date neared, the handover was increasingly spoken about in the language of patriotism and the eager return to the "embrace of the motherland" (祖國的懷抱). But even those who felt the greatest antipathy toward the Chinese Communist Party and the most apprehension about becoming part of the People's Republic of China agreed that incorporation into China had to be better than Portuguese rule. The "pig answers" tipped the scales of ambivalence. People began to wish that the handover could be moved forward a few months.

Meanwhile, the PRC had lost no time in performing as the responsive, responsible state that the people of Macau needed. Officials from the Guangdong Public Security Bureau made repeated offers of assistance to the Portuguese government and gave repeated assurances that what was a losing battle for the Macau police would prove no problem for them after the handover. And Macau was surrounded by examples of exactly what this would mean. On one hand, the growing social unrest caused by Beijing's streamlining of the state-run industrial sector led the PRC to launch yet another in a series of highly publicized "Strike Hard" (嚴打) anti-crime campaigns in 1998, cracking down on various categories of illegal behavior. Television footage of trucks full of Chinese criminals being carted off to the execution grounds and reports of high-ranking officials being incarcerated or sentenced to death for graft and embezzlement provided Macau citizens with a vision of a righteous state in action. On the other hand, in Hong Kong in 1997, a high-ranking official of the New China News Agency, Beijing's *de facto* embassy in Hong Kong and Macau prior to the handover, admitted in a public forum that in the early 1980s he had met with Hong Kong triad leaders and had come to a secret agreement with them: "I told them if they did not disrupt Hong Kong's stability, we would not stop them from making money" (Dannen 1997: 19; see also T. M. Liu 2001: 115). This revelation fueled suspicions in the international media of a sinister global alliance between the triads and the Chinese Communist Party: the same publications that reveled in Macau's lawlessness quoted with alarm various high-ranking CCP officials as having said, "The triads are not all bad; some are patriotic."[17]

But in Macau, far from being evidence that the PRC government was just as "lawless" as Macau's, this combination of crackdown and collaboration was viewed as precisely what was needed. That Macau residents considered evidence of the complicity between sovereign and bandit a sign of legitimacy in the case of the CCP, and of illegitimacy in the case of the Portuguese, reveals the extent to which the Macau government's principal failure was representational. The real problem was not that the Portuguese state was complicit with the bandits—in fact, it seemed, it was not complicit enough, or at least not in the right way. The real problem was that the government's inability or refusal to maintain the myth of its own transcendence was making Macau *appear* lawless.[18] No one expected the Macau government to actually stop the triads; rather, what was wanted was for the government to make a good show of stopping the triads, sending them back underground to do their job quietly: providing tourists with the cash, sex, drugs, and other services they sought, which would keep them coming back and thus allow everyone else to make a living too. Indeed, in the autumn of 1998, when China announced its unilateral decision to place People's Liberation Army troops in Macau after the handover—a decision that contravened an informal agreement with Portugal and led to vehement protests from Lisbon—newspaper surveys among Chinese Macau residents revealed that many of them looked forward to the sight of armed PLA soldiers patrolling the streets, not because they would protect residents from harm or bring an end to triad activities, but because it would be a "psychological comfort" to the law-abiding (*AMRB*, October 17, 1998).

For most Macau residents, then, the problem with Macau's triad violence was that it had become "matter out of place" (Douglas 1966): the irruption into public view, and public discourse, of the liminal elements that everyone knew existed but on whose concealment everyone depended. The triad violence of the 1990s both physically and symbolically threatened the authority of the Portuguese state and the stability of the social and political order—an order all the more fragile for being in a moment of political transition. The "pig answers" given by the state, the incompetence, the corruption, the legislators on the lam, became evidence not just of the porousness between the categories of sovereign and bandit but of the Portuguese state's inability to draw a line between them in a way that was at all meaningful for Macau residents or for the world. This was one reason the Hong Kong and international media had singled Macau out for such scorn; and by doing so, they underscored the extent to which the Portuguese state itself had become a kind of matter out of place, a state marginalized in its own domain: it not only failed to protect and control the activities of its population but also appeared to refuse the very paradigm of absolutism and transcendence that legitimated the international norms and practices of sovereignty.

Mythologies of Marginality

What really thwarted the Portuguese state's attempt to resignify its own history of marginality, then, was not simply its inability to control triad violence but its inability to control the circulation of mythic symbols of triad power. As the police lost control of crime, the government lost control of the proliferating layers of discourse about it. Everyone was telling stories about triads, including the triads themselves. It seemed then—and seems even more so as I write this, re-reading what passed for factual articles clipped from newspapers at the time, and realizing how little I can say for sure about the situation—that the dominant modes of public knowledge and representation about the violence were rumor, speculation, assumption, and myth. Reading newspaper reports or talking with friends, it was (and is) impossible to pry apart the insinuations of corruption from their basis in fact or the boasts of young bravado from the mythologies they indexed. The official statements of police officers had to be winked at, and hearsay considered more reliable. Newspaper reports had to be taken to be as (in)accurate as the statements of their unnamed sources, and assertions of fact doubled back and read as strategic fictions. The fine, upstanding Gambling Inspector, they say, had been supplementing his government income by loansharking; and did you hear?—the car that the Maritime and Fiscal Police officer (that hardworking junior civil servant struggling to raise a family on a monthly salary of MOP $12,000 [US$1,500]) had been driving when he was shot was a Mercedes, and he had just bought his wife a BMW; the triads, they say, are fighting for a dwindling pie, they won't look the other way anymore; someone said that the tourist who was shot had just gambled away HK$800,000 (US$100,000) in an afternoon and had borrowed hundreds of thousands more from a loanshark; the bus passenger, they say, was "the wrong man," he was just a chef at the Hotel Lisboa who was returning home from the night shift. "Sources" close to the triads said the violence would end soon; "sources" close to the governor said the government had completely lost control. Estimates proliferated about how many members the triads had in Macau: one 14K triad leader was quoted as having said he had "10,000 soldiers at his command"—which, if taken literally, would place membership in that one triad organization alone at over 2 percent of the entire population of Macau—while police sources suggested the real number was well under 1,000. Even the real reasons for the sudden surge in violence were open to conjecture. Some said it was a triad turf war sparked by the opening of a new casino; others argued that it was due to the influx of Hong Kong triads after 1997; some suggested that the triads wanted "concessions" from the government and a say in the handover negotiations; still others believed that Beijing had sent thugs of its own down to stir up anti-Portuguese sentiment. Because none of the murderers was apprehended, the Judiciary Police, like the journalists and cab drivers, had their sources, their suspects, their assumptions, their allegations; they had, it seemed, secret sting operations that could only be alluded to, but that was all that they had. They could not create a convincing counternarrative of the Portuguese state as the source of law and order; they could only contribute to the imagining of illicit networks of information, influence, and power.

But the rumors circulating about the triads—about their motives, their histories, their powers, and their enemies—were not simply about crime. The triad stories were deeply rooted in a well-established and dynamic set of narratives and narrative structures: they drew on powerful mythologies of outlaws. Myth is, as Roland Barthes (1957, 1977) argued, a "type of speech," a form of second-order signification in which signs become the signifiers of something greater, and every word, image, or object is really about something else. Liisa Malkki suggests that myths are a "recasting and reinterpretation of [the world] in fundamentally moral terms . . . [they are] concerned with order in a fundamental, cosmological sense . . . with defining self in distinction to other, with good and evil" (Malkki 1995: 55). In this sense, the triads embodied mythologies of marginality far more powerful than anything the Portuguese state could conjure.

Like the mafia in the United States, the triads have long been fertile ground for mythologization. Secret societies and sworn brotherhoods have existed in China for at least as long as the legends of the *Outlaws of the Marsh* (水滸傳) and the *Romance of the Three Kingdoms* (三國演義). These epics are archetypal tales of loyalty, honor, and the quest for justice and are the main source of the *jianghu* 江湖 tradition that triads today still draw on—the small band of righteous outlaws joined together in loyal brotherhoods with strict moral codes that are defined against the decadence and corruption of state and society.

Although there is considerable dispute over the origins of contemporary triads, recent scholarship argues that they are rooted in the brotherhoods and secret societies that sprang up in southeastern China during another era of political transition, the late seventeenth century, as the new Qing dynasty tried to consolidate the sovereignty it had wrested from the Ming (see Murray 1994, Ownby 1996, and Ownby and Heidhues 1993). Dian Murray (1994) traces these roots to the massive social upheaval created by the Qing state's policy of coastal evacuation, implemented between 1660 and 1683. In an attempt to starve into submission the Ming loyalists who lingered in the islands off Fujian, the emperor ordered the entire population of the southeast coast to move dozens or even hundreds of miles inland.[19] Entire villages were made refugee, and the territorial disputes caused by their eventual resettlement led smaller lineage groups to band together to defend their interests, swearing brotherhood through rituals of drinking wine mixed with blood. What is certain is that in the mid-Qing, as the population explosion and rapid commercialization and urbanization of Fujian and Guangdong provinces caused further turmoil, young men displaced from villages took to sworn brotherhoods as sources of mutual aid and protection. Once these brotherhoods were formed, their flexibility allowed them to mobilize for a variety of goals, from protective to predatory to revolutionary. The Qing, which regarded them as both politically dangerous and ideologically heterodox, outlawed them, initiating a spiral of further marginalization, secrecy, and resistance (Murray 1994). In the twentieth century, secret societies have been interpreted by both Chinese and Western scholars as a kind of patriotic underground, either representing the mandate of the Han people to rise up against foreign oppression (be it Manchu or European), or as proto-revolutionaries in the vanguard of the inexorable forward march of peasant revolution.[20]

Yet, according to Barend ter Haar (1998), what united the triads of southeastern China and distinguished them from other sworn brotherhoods, mutual-aid organizations, pirate bands, and smuggling rings was their elaborate narrative lore and ritual practice: the foundation myths, initiation rites, hierarchies, esoteric jargon, and identifying gestures, the common surname (Hong 洪), and, above all, the political messianism that legitimated not one or another particular course of action but unspecified rebellion—be it in the form of opium smuggling, freeing a brother from prison, or participating in a nationalist revolution.[21] Haar observes that both emperors and triads drew on the ideology of the "mandate of heaven" that had, since the earliest eras of the Chinese empire, legitimated the rise and fall of rulers and dynasties. In this ideology, portents such as earthquakes and rainbows could, when properly interpreted, herald the end or beginning of a dynasty, and the possession of certain objects or the exhibition of certain behaviors could indicate that an individual possessed the divine right to govern. But it was only in their public interpretation that these symbols derived their power to legitimate (Haar 1998: 312). By distilling into a single, mystified mythology some of the most powerful signs, ideologies, rituals, and tropes of Chinese political, religious, social, and literary culture—not just the mandate of heaven but also Buddhist and Daoist deities, ancestor worship and family loyalty, blood covenants, and the *jianghu* heroes and legends of the *Romance of the Three Kingdoms*—the triads cre-ated "an alternative interpretation of history," in which their illicit activities were righteous and their status as outlaws a sign of loyalty to the true sovereign, be it the defeated Ming dynasty or an older, more messianic notion of the "True Ruler" who would bring about a perfect age. Haar argues that it was this lore that defined the triads as triads and allowed networks of displaced men to develop into co-hesive groups with a cultural and social identity that outlived their individual members, rather than gangs whose unity was contingent on particular economic or political goals (Haar 1998; see also Mak 2002: 34).

This lore, I would argue, was also a source of the triads' power to threaten established authority in the nineteenth century, to attract revolutionaries in the early twentieth, and to be considered patriots even in the twenty-first. This power, which by most accounts far ex-ceeded that of other religious groups or secret societies, derived not simply from the nature of their activities or their position in the economic and social structures of Chinese society but from their use of the central symbols of Chinese political, religious, and literary culture. For precisely the same reason, although the term "triad" has long connoted vice and criminality, it is also a powerful signifier of "Chineseness."[22] This is the source of their continuing appeal today; it is this that renders understandable the apparent paradox of a re-tired Hong Kong Supreme Court judge who, in the preface to a book that details his "disgust" with the activities and attitudes of the Hong Kong triads, explains that his "burning desire" to contribute to the study of "this mystic subject, the triads . . . come[s] from the Chineseness in me" (T. M. Liu 2001: 4).

For although it is unclear to outsiders how much today's triads have in common with their putative forebears—probably not the

messianism, perhaps not the extensive ritual practices, but certainly
the ideology of a protective brotherhood, the belief in their own historical roots, and the use of cryptic language and codes[23]—they are
certainly the bearers of the mythological legacy of a powerful liminality that can be mobilized into potent threats to established authority. To be sure, the triads are not the only heirs to this mythological legacy. The *jianghu* theme is a long-established and much
beloved part of Chinese popular culture, especially in Hong Kong
and Macau. One of the most widely read contemporary Chinese
novelists, Jin Yong 金庸, was a prominent Hong Kong journalist
who owes his fame to a series of historical martial arts novels about
the adventures of wandering swordsmen (and women) whose prowess derives as much from their virtue as from their skill. It was on
this legacy that Hong Kong newspapers drew in representing the
very real violence in Macau, and it was the centrality of this mythology of outlaw marginality to contemporary Chinese culture that
made it such a powerful mode of representation. Triad organizations
in Macau, Hong Kong, and Guangzhou, with their evocative names
(14K, Water House/水房, New Righteous Peace/新義安, the Big
Circle Boys/大圈仔) and colorful leading figures with even more
colorful nicknames—Broken Tooth Koi (崩牙駒), Superman (超人),
Big Spender (大富豪), Fatgirl (肥妹), and Cuttlefish Kid (墨魚
仔)—are well known in the papers for their ongoing battles with the
authorities. The legendary lives of these real-life criminals are themselves mythologized, as a whole genre of film and literature, often
funded by the triads themselves, has grown up around them, and images, characters, and Cantonese slang phrases from these films circu-
late widely in popular discourse.

One such film, and the man who funded it, was crucial to the
drama of triad violence in 1990s Macau and the resulting hyperbolic
representations of Macau as a lawless land. I relate the story here in
some detail, because the tale of the rise and fall of Broken Tooth Koi,
Macau's most famous gangster, illustrates how age-old narratives of
outlaw marginality, deeply embedded in Chinese literary and popular culture, made the triad problem such a potent challenge to Portuguese authority as well as to the revisionist tale of a liminal sovereignty the Portuguese state was trying to tell.

Broken Tooth Koi

On May 5, 1998, the personal car of Macau's chief of Judiciary Police, António Marques Baptista, exploded in his driveway. Early rumors had it that this was merely a warning; after all, if the triads had been aiming to kill the police chief, he would be dead. Later reports, however, alleged that the chief's life had been saved only by the vigilance of his sniffer dog, trained to bark at the smell of explosives. That same evening, the chief, who was nicknamed "Rambo," and his men burst into a private dining room in the Casino Lisboa and arrested Wan Kuok-koi 尹國駒, alias Broken Tooth Koi, the alleged head of the 14K triad in Macau and the man reputed to be at the root of all of Macau's triad troubles. Television footage of the arrest showed Broken Tooth—thickset, handsome, well dressed, and well groomed, broken teeth long since capped—being escorted into a police van with an expression on his face that can only be described as confident but slightly inconvenienced (see Fig. 1).

In the 1990s, it was difficult for Macau to escape the gangster film cliché when Broken Tooth Koi consciously and publicly lived out the fearless, cool embodiment of triad charisma. The international media ran extensive interviews with Broken Tooth, with full-color photographs of him in natty suits and expensive jewelry. A few weeks before his arrest, *Newsweek International* published one such interview, entitled "Lunch with Big Brother," which portrayed him precisely as a righteous outlaw facing down a corrupt and incompetent state. "There is no one left in Macau worth being afraid of," he told the reporter when she asked him if he were not afraid of admitting that he was the head of the 14K triad in Macau. She explained, "Wan refuses to call himself a godfather or even a gangster. He says he prefers to think of himself as 'a person who rights injustices.' He says a triad is nothing more than a brotherhood, people coming together to support one another" (*Newsweek International Edition*, April 6, 1998, pp. 14–15).

It was even more difficult to escape the gangster film rhetoric when Broken Tooth quite literally turned himself into a gangster film. Two days after Broken Tooth's arrest, the movie *Casino* 濠江風雲, starring Hong Kong heartthrob Simon Yam 任達華, was

Fig. 1 Broken Tooth Koi and his captor, Police Chief
António Marques Baptista, on the night of his arrest,
May 5, 1998 (photo courtesy *Macao Daily*).

scheduled to open in Hong Kong theaters. *Casino*'s executive producer, Henry Fong 方平, was quoted as saying that he had not been
surprised when Broken Tooth agreed to "lend his life story" to the
making of a film, but that he had been "astonished . . . when [Bro-
ken Tooth] agreed to a series of lengthy research meetings" and had
funded the bulk of production costs (*International Herald Tribune*,
June 11, 1998). Broken Tooth even loaned the filmmakers his pur-
ple Lamborghini.

The film was reputed to be a thinly fictionalized narrative of Broken Tooth's rise to power. The protagonist is also surnamed Wan
and nicknamed "Broken Tooth Giant" (崩牙巨, nearly homony-
mous in Cantonese with the real Broken Tooth's nickname). The
plot, like Broken Tooth's real-life fame, hinges on the international

media. A female journalist from Hong Kong feels compelled by Broken Tooth's charismatic notoriety to come to Macau and follow him around for a few days, interviewing him and his men so as to better understand their motivations and their code. Following all the conventions of *jianghu*, Broken Tooth is portrayed as filial and manly, loyal to his mother and to those who treat him with respect, but quicker, smarter, and more brutal than anyone who dares to cross him; a clean-living man whose only weaknesses are gambling and ambition; a fearless man who respects integrity even in the police chief who has sworn to bring him down. Although the reporter in the film chastises him repeatedly for jeopardizing the safety of the Macau people, she concludes her report by observing that Broken Tooth is a "hero in a troubled world,"[24] and that a hero is nothing but a man forced by this troubled world to lead an extraordinary life.

The making of the film was a sensational news item in itself: because the Macau government did not take kindly to the film's depiction of the city as a place whose streets were ruled by gangsters, it denied the crew's application for a filming license. So Broken Tooth took matters into his own hands, filming "wherever and whenever he wanted" (*International Herald Tribune*, June 11, 1998). For one scene, the crew blocked Macau's main bridge at dawn to film a procession of more than 200 cars carrying triads on their way to a pitched battle. For another, they filmed a triad brawl directly outside Macau police headquarters. The *Herald Tribune* article quoted Henry Fong as saying, "It was easy for us, very easy. . . . We just shot it and ran."

I do not know if Fong intended this as a pun, equating the usual shoot-and-run mode of triad assassinations with a kind of drive-by cultural production. But the way he made the film and the way he talked about making the film had their effect. The implication was not only that the Macau government had lost control of the violence and the international media's sensationalized representation of that violence, but also that it could not even prevent the production of such representations on its own streets. The film was banned in Macau.[25]

Rumor had it that this combination of filmic and journalistic statements may have contributed to Broken Tooth's arrest: he was getting too "high profile," too flamboyant, wielding the tools of

Fig. 2   A burned-out motorcycle on a side street in downtown Macau,
late 1998—a sign of triad revenge (photo by author, 1998).

mythmaking a little too brazenly. It was said that Broken Tooth may
not have been the kingpin he portrayed himself to be, but that simply by portraying himself so openly as a kingpin, he made himself a
convenient target for a state that was now desperate to portray itself
as capable of responding to the triads' challenge to its authority. In
an atmosphere so rife with visual and verbal second-order significa-
tions, in which everything must always be about something else,
Broken Tooth's arrest itself was a cause for endless speculation.

In the wake of his arrest, a wave of car and motorbike fires swept
the city. In two hours one night more than 50 vehicles across the
city were firebombed, allegedly by young 14K members indignant
over the capture of their leader (see Fig. 2).

A judge threw out allegations of attempted murder against Broken Tooth because there was no evidence linking him to the bomb
in the police chief's car, but he was charged with belonging to a
triad organization and violating an earlier parole ruling by entering a
casino. Broken Tooth sat in the Central Prison on Coloane island,
not far from his palatial home in Coloane Village, as deliberations
continued over exactly what else he could be charged with and

where he would stand trial—in Macau or in Portugal. For Broken Tooth Koi, "big brother" (大佬) of the Chinese underworld and heir to the mythos of the Chinese outlaw, was a Portuguese citizen.

Deprived of access to its larger-than-life protagonist, the international press forgot about Broken Tooth for almost a year. But his arrest did not end the violence or the rumors. Local newspapers were still filled with reports of bank robberies, kidnappings, killings, and revenge killings. Some appeared to be attempts to intimidate authorities: five months after Broken Tooth's arrest, in September 1998, a car bomb exploded in central Macau; twenty minutes later, just as the police and journalists had assembled to investigate, another bomb rigged to a motorcycle went off several feet away, injuring fifteen people, including one of the three officers who had arrested Broken Tooth. Meanwhile, the local press treated its readers to detailed accounts of the illicit luxury of Broken Tooth's prison cell, with its well-stocked refrigerator, expensive stereo system, and all-night karaoke parties; the dozens of mobile phones with which he managed to run his empire from the inside; and the secret meetings he called with "Rambo" in which Broken Tooth first tried to cut a deal for his early release and then threatened reprisals should his offer be refused. Later that fall, Broken Tooth's gambling buddy, the notorious Hong Kong gangster Cheung Tze-keung 張子強, alias Big Spender, was arrested, tried, and quickly executed in Guangzhou by PRC authorities for crimes he had committed in Hong Kong. The Hong Kong press and legal establishment were outraged at this contravention of Hong Kong's autonomy and took it as a sign of the advent of a "one country, one system" policy. But in Macau, most people considered it rough justice and took from it a quiet sense of anticipation. One Macau Chinese man, a manager in STDM whom I spoke with shortly after the demise of Big Spender, complained that, in contrast to Chinese law, the Portuguese criminal code was not suited to the "realities" of Macau because it lacked a death penalty: "The Portuguese government is too . . . ," he paused, searching for the right adjective in Cantonese but finally finding it in English, "*magnanimous*." People speculated that if Broken Tooth stood trial under the Portuguese administration, he would be acquitted; but if his trial were delayed until after the handover, he would be shot.

When the press came back to Broken Tooth, to cover his trial in the spring of 1999, the saga proved still more compelling than fiction. Amid a whole set of anxieties about the future of Macau's judicial system, Broken Tooth stood trial in March 1999 for two of the many charges against him. In his first trial, he was acquitted of the charge of criminal intimidation of a casino croupier, due to lack of evidence, despite the fact that the incident in question had been recorded by the casino's security cameras: the acquittal came when witness after witness took the stand and claimed to be unable to remember what had actually happened. The opening of his second and more important trial, in which he and nine other defendants would face the charge of belonging to a triad organization, was originally scheduled for April 27, 1999, but was delayed when several witnesses did not appear in court.[26] When this trial finally got under way in June, it was interrupted and again postponed by the sudden resignation of the presiding judge, Alberto Mendes, who returned immediately to Portugal. By September 1999, when I left Macau, Broken Tooth's trial had yet to begin. These periodic announcements of delays and acquittals were greeted with cynical smiles and did nothing to dispel the suspicions of foul play, corruption, and incompetence that fueled the public's anger about the violence. They simply substantiated Broken Tooth's boast that there was no one left to fear in Macau.

In the summer of 2000, when I returned to Macau for a six-week research trip, I spent days on the edge of my seat devouring stacks of Portuguese- and Chinese-language newspapers detailing the trial, which had finally commenced in October 1999. The Portuguese reports read like scripts for a prime-time television legal drama—or rather, like scripts that would have been rejected by the writers of a legal drama for being too overwrought. The trial had lasted a month, coming to a climax just three weeks before the handover. It had featured a head judge fresh from Portugal who made prejudiced statements about the "criminal natures" of the defendants and repeatedly interrupted and insulted Broken Tooth's defense lawyer, Pedro Redinha. The defense team filed motion after motion to get the judge dismissed for his indiscretion, but in vain; witness after witness took the stand to testify that Broken Tooth was a triad leader, but each one cracked under cross-examination. Apolinário, the ex–gambling inspector whose attempted murder had first catapulted triad violence into the headlines, returned to Macau from Portugal to testify against Broken Tooth, the man who had allegedly ordered his execution. Broken Tooth himself took the stand and denied ever having admitted that he was a gangster, as his mother and wife listened, tearful and anxious. Just as his lawyer asked him to explain how he had gained such notoriety as a gangster when he in fact was not one, a power failure suddenly plunged the whole courtroom into darkness and forced the session to be adjourned. Redinha, the primary defense counsel, quit the case in mid-trial, after the judge once again interrupted him and refused to let him follow a particular line of questioning; a series of young and inexperienced attorneys appointed by the court to replace him kept resigning one after the other, terrified of the repercussions Broken Tooth might exact if they failed to get him acquitted. After all testimony had finally been presented, the three judges retired to their chambers to watch the film *Casino*, which they deemed "nothing more than an autobiographical sketch of Wan Kuok Koi" (*Ponto final*, November 12, 1999).

The judges deliberated for almost two weeks before deciding the verdict: guilty. Broken Tooth was sentenced to the maximum of fifteen years in prison. When the verdict was announced in court, Broken Tooth jumped up on a table, shouting obscenities in Chinese and Portuguese and accusing the judges of having been bribed. When the judge announced that Broken Tooth's assets—some MOP $20 million—would be confiscated by the state, his family jumped up too, shouting and swearing in protest. One week after the trial ended, the Portuguese judge, who had been hired from Portugal to replace Alberto Mendes and was under contract to stay in Macau for a year, suddenly found a compelling reason to return immediately to Portugal. Four days before the handover, on December 15, Broken Tooth's lawyers filed an appeal with the United Nations Commission on Human Rights, claiming that Broken Tooth's arrest, detention, trial, and appeals had violated so many provisions of both Portuguese and international law that the guilty verdict was not justice, but its mockery.[27]

As the courtroom drama waxed, the Portuguese-language newspaper that covered the story in the greatest depth did not tell a story of an outlaw finally meeting due justice; rather, it cast him and his lawyers as the victims of a kangaroo court convened by a decadent colonial administration so desperate to make itself look competent that it was willing to disregard its own laws.[28] It depicted a condition of lawlessness more complete than anything the international media had mustered in all its mythologies: a condition in which truth is stranger than fiction, and fiction is taken as truth; in which the lines between life and myth, law and lawlessness, right and wrong, soldier and bandit, are hopelessly blurred, and in which everyone is touched with the brush of the outlaw.

But among the people of Macau, this critique of the state fell on deaf ears. No one supported Broken Tooth's appeal. No one spoke of a miscarriage of justice. Man-on-the-street interviews published after the sentencing indicated that many people thought Broken Tooth should have been shot or locked up for life and sentenced to hard labor. At that moment, the state and the vast majority of Macau residents were united in a single desire. The desire for an act that would draw the lines, arbitrarily or not, in a way that would restore absolute authority to the state and send the triads back to the margins where they belonged, was more urgent than the empty promise of the "rule of law," more necessary, and more possible, than the hairsplitting attempt to prove the real difference between sovereigns and bandits.

Two weeks after the sentencing, the Hong Kong daily newspaper *The South China Morning Post* ran a long article based on an interview with João Guedes, a retired police detective turned journalist who had written a book on Chinese secret societies.[29] The article concluded that Broken Tooth was no underworld kingpin, but "nothing more than a common gangster suffering from megalomania and delusions of criminal grandeur [who had] simply usurped traditional triad names to gain respectability in the underworld" (SCMP, December 12, 1999, p. 10). By dissociating Broken Tooth from the mythologies of triad glamour and influence, this story reduced him to a petty crook, no more threatening to the social order than a common pickpocket. The state had taken away his freedom and his ill-gotten gains, and the media had closed off his access to the mythologies of power through which it had once catapulted him into the headlines. Only then was his fall complete.

Conclusion

One night in the spring of 1998, I stood in front of the class on Macau culture and society that I had been invited to teach at the Macau Polytechnic Institute, and suggested to my students (Chinese, Portuguese, Macanese, and Goans, all of them natives or long-term residents of Macau) how it might be possible for them to take a special interest, even pride, in the history of their city: by understanding this history not as one long story of mismanagement, corruption, decay, and stagnation but rather as a kind of challenge to modern, rationalist, capitalist conceptions of the proper functions of states and indeed to the very idea that true state sovereignty in the modern sense was either possible or desirable. What if, indeed, Macau's "difference" really did consist in an alternative way of thinking about the nature of states and the limits of sovereignty? Wasn't it just possible? The entire class objected vociferously, reminding me of the "backwardness" that had accompanied the practice of Portuguese rule in Macau—the poverty, the stagnation, the ignorance, the injustice—and the ridicule and opprobrium heaped on the city and its residents by the international media as a result. If Macau's difference was something to be celebrated, it certainly could not be that. Sort-of sovereignty was not an alternative way of thinking about power; it was a lame excuse for a state too weak to fulfill the requirements of "real" sovereignty. Outside the classroom, too, many people I talked to told me that to the extent that the history of Portuguese sovereignty had made Macau "different," that difference was nothing more than a kind of broken-down-ness, something that needed to be overcome, not perpetuated. What Macau needed was a state that could clearly demarcate the boundaries between sovereign and outlaw and then act like the modern sovereign power that it was.

This chapter has examined the kind of representational work that it took for Macau residents to come to this conclusion. For, as tempting as it might be to view this conclusion as commonsensical, given the very real problems Macau faced in the late 1990s and the very real dissatisfaction residents felt with their government's inability to address these problems, to do so would be to stop short of the unique contribution that ethnography can make to the study of sovereignty: inquiring how common sense comes to seem either common or sensible (Herzfeld 2001: 1). It would also be to accept at face value the assertion that there is only one way for a state to be sovereign in the modern world. What riled Macau residents was the state's inefficacy, both real and representational. But, just as the crime rates were far higher in plenty of other cities that were not ridiculed as thoroughly as Macau, so too do poverty, ignorance, and injustice form parts of the legacies of other states that do not claim to be working from an alternative mode of sovereign power. In other words, Macau residents did not necessarily have problems with the idea of a form of sovereignty based on compromise, flexibility, and ambiguity *per se*; yet the fact that the state that was attempting to claim legitimacy on the basis of these principles was, at the same time, proving itself incapable of ensuring basic public security made that claim starkly unconvincing.

Two things become clear when we examine the interrelationship of sovereignty and the state with regard to the 1990s triad violence. First is the extent to which sovereignty is, more than just a structure or set of technologies, a performative whose normative force derives from its appearance of being an abstract, universalizable ideal against which states, individuals, even whole cultures, can be measured and found wanting, but which in fact must be constantly reiterated through appeals to mythologies of power that are themselves profoundly cultural. To be clear: I do not mean to suggest that different notions of sovereignty "belong" to different cultures that are static and mutually exclusive systems of thought. In fact, my point is precisely that, like culture, they are dynamic, interconnected, and constantly in motion. This is why the gangster-film cliché was such a compelling mode for representing Macau in China as well as among the readers of English-language publications like *Newsweek*. It drew on time-honored Chinese mythologies of marginality as well as on transnational imaginaries of the legitimacy and illegitimacy of power, providing audiences in China, Hong Kong, and abroad with the frisson of pleasure that comes from questioning fleetingly when a bandit is a bandit, and when a sovereign, and why. The long history of fixation on all that was seedy, illicit, and decadent about Macau, and the constant association of the city with this liminal, criminal group, the triads, was a way of representing Macau as a kind of "matter out of place"—a pathological exception that reinscribed the hegemony and legitimacy of modern state sovereignty.

Second is the observation that although it may be possible to imagine alternative forms of sovereignty, it may not always be desirable. In describing how tiny Macau had been central to so many world-historical processes, the state was claiming legitimacy on precisely the grounds that the international media found to be its principal failure—it was attempting, like the triads that undermined it, to draw authority from an alternative interpretation of events and to derive power from alternative mythologies of marginality. In doing so, it crossed the line into illegitimacy: it played straight into the long-standing triad narrative of corrupt government officials whose refusal to act in the name of justice justifies rebellion, a narrative all the more compelling because it drew on historical, political, and legendary figures familiar to and beloved even by schoolchildren. These ready-made narrative structures for a thrilling tale of outlaw marginality made the state's claim to sort-of sovereignty appear in this moment as its converse: an intolerable, anarchic liminality. To be sure, there were other moments and contexts in which this claim was far more appealing, and these are moments that I explore in later chapters. But these tales of criminality, incompetence, decadence, and Macau's utter marginality to the modern world order also formed a powerful narrative about the meaning and legacy of Portuguese rule, one that would take enormous effort to overturn.

THREE

The Nonexistent Macanese

And you know, when you say to a Chinese, "You, being a Chinese, are not a Chinese," they don't believe you.

— N.R., a Portuguese lawyer in Macau

The young Portuguese lawyer looked at me from time to time over the hornrims of his spectacles and spoke as deliberately and authoritatively as if he were the law itself. His name was Nuno; it was early January 1999, and we were sitting in his office in downtown Macau as he explained what the new Resolution on Nationality, which had been issued by the National People's Congress in Beijing a few weeks before, would mean for the Macanese community after the handover.[1] The Macanese were Macau's small population of Eurasians, whom my very first informant, a young Macanese woman, had referred to as "sort-of Chinese." The Resolution was the final word on whether and how they and the other residents of Macau would be defined as national subjects of the PRC, and it had ignited a blaze of opinions, accusations, and insinuations in the press and among representatives of the Portuguese government as well as my friends and acquaintances. Because the controversy derived in part from a multiplicity of interpretations and misinterpretations of the text of the Resolution, I had asked Nuno, an adviser to the Portuguese government in matters concerning nationality law, to clarify for me precisely what it would mean. He was walking me point by point through the Resolution, explaining what the series of brief and ostensibly simple normative statements "really" meant. I was entranced by his authoritativeness and his grasp of the proofs, precedents, and philosophies

99

that fortified it. Reassured by his ability to lay bare the true meaning of the law, I trod eagerly in his footsteps as he swashbuckled for me a path of clarity through the ambiguities, elisions, and hidden implications lurking within the apparently straightforward language of the law. But then he made an observation that shook me out of my spell: he said, almost offhandedly, "We cannot define the Macanese legally. The Macanese legally do not exist."

This chapter arises from the multiple questions this simple statement provoked. What did it mean that these people who viewed themselves as the *filhos da terra*—the sons and daughters of this so-called lawless land, and the only true "natives" of Macau—could claim no collective existence in the law? Why had their legal definition, among all the other policy decisions and structural problems facing Macau during the transition era, touched off such controversy? Why had I, like so many others in Macau at the time, looked to the law to answer, interpret, and resolve all the unanswerable, multivalent, insoluble questions that the transition to Chinese rule had provoked? And how and for whom would it be possible to be defined, legally or otherwise, as "sort-of" Chinese?

As I sought answers to these questions, I realized that just as the public discourse about Macau's lawlessness had been an important site for contesting the meaning and legacy of Portuguese rule and of sovereign power more broadly, the public discourse about nationality law was a site in which these experiences and imaginaries of sovereignty were linked explicitly to debates about the meaning and limits of Chineseness. The law promised all the "bright lines and clear taxonomies" that many residents felt Macau needed in order to gain some semblance of respectability in the world and get its economy back on track.[2] The law would systematize the messiness of the everyday, making it legible and thus governable by the state (James Scott 1998). The key provision of the Resolution, which gave each Macanese person the right to choose whether or not he or she wanted to be considered a Chinese national, promised to put an end to the indefinability of the Macanese as a group by translating their "sort-of Chineseness" into the either-or terms of modern national sovereignty. As Patricia Williams points out, it is this capacity to decide the undecidable and to make sensible categories out of a jumble of conflicting possibilities and loosely associated contingencies that makes the law an object of desire. But, as Veena Das (2004) notes and as the controversy over Macanese nationality made evident, despite its apparent clarity, the power of the law to affect the daily lives of those it governs while appearing to remain impartial in fact depends on its illegibility—on the ways it is misread, misapprehended, and misused by the general public as well as by those charged with enforcing it. In attempting to clarify where the limits of Chineseness lay, however, the Resolution begged the question of what made certain claims to Chineseness legitimate and others impossible. It highlighted the extent to which Chineseness is not simply a matter of blood and territory and cultural practice but of politics and performativity as well. And in this sense, the law's apparent clarity simply created more confusion; the Resolution and the conflicting interpretations it enabled simply exacerbated the alienation, anxiety, and suspicion the law had set out to diminish. This chapter is therefore an ethnography not of the law as it was formulated in conference rooms, practiced in courtrooms, or taught in classrooms, but as a kind of public culture—a "zone of cultural debate" that blurs distinctions between official and popular, "traditional" and contemporary, and in this case between legal and extra-legal notions of Chineseness (Appadurai and Breckenridge 1988: 6).[3]

Before the Law

For the people who called themselves Macanese ("Macaense" in Portuguese), their legal non-existence had not presented a problem until the transition era. In fact, it was precisely their indefinability in law and in language that was the key to understanding the Macanese sense of who they were—and the Chinese and Portuguese sense of who they, respectively, were not. Although outsiders often assumed that the term "Macanese" referred to all 450,000 residents of Macau, to those who knew Macau it denoted a group that in the 1990s amounted to only a few thousand people—precisely how many no one could say, since there was no formal definition by which to create statistics about them, but estimates ranged between 3,000 and 10,000 persons (for various estimates, see H. S. Yee 1997,

Pina-Cabral 2002, and Xu Jieshun and Tang 2000). "Macanese" was most commonly understood to refer to the offspring of Portuguese men and Chinese women in Macau. But members of the oldest Macanese families traced their roots to the Eurasian population that had resulted from liaisons between Portuguese and the Africans, Indians, and Southeast Asians they had encountered along the sea route from Europe to Asia. By the late twentieth century, the term also denoted ethnic Chinese who were raised to be culturally Portuguese and, less frequently, to ethnic Portuguese born and raised in Macau.

It would appear, therefore, that the defining characteristic of a Macanese was some kind of affiliation with Portugal. However, although many Macanese did consider themselves the "Portuguese of the Orient," many others did not speak Portuguese, had never been to Portugal, and harbored no small degree of animosity toward "arrogant" metropolitans who often disdained them as "not-quite" Portuguese. Still others had no Portuguese ancestry whatever, but traced their genealogies to marriages between Chinese, Goans, Italians, Spanish, British, Filipinos, and Timorese. (One large and prominent "local-born Portuguese" family, for example, was actually of Peruvian-Chinese ancestry. The great-grandfather had emigrated to Peru from Guangdong province in the late nineteenth century, and there he had married and had children with a Peruvian woman; eventually he moved the whole family to Macau.) Perhaps, then, it was a connection to Macau, by birth or by choice, that was the necessary and sufficient condition to be Macanese? Yet due to waves of out-migration in the late nineteenth and mid-twentieth centuries, there were substantial numbers of Macanese born and raised in Canada, the United States, Australia, Brazil, and Portugal who had never set foot in Macau. Also, as we shall see, the half-hearted attempt to re-signify "Macanese" to include all residents of the city met with resistance from Macanese and Chinese residents alike.

Anthropologists João de Pina-Cabral and Nelson Lourenço (1993) have described three "vectors" of Macanese identity—language (Portuguese), religion (Catholicism), and "phenotypic appearance" (Eurasian)—any one or more of which could form the basis of an individual's identity as a Macanese (Pina-Cabral and Lourenço 1993:

22, Pina-Cabral 2002).[4] But others have disputed this characterization and emphasized instead the Chineseness of the Macanese: as one Macanese author pointed out, in the 1990s, young Macanese preferred to speak Cantonese and English rather than Portuguese; they practiced *fengshui* as often as Catholic rituals, and tended to marry Chinese rather than Portuguese or Macanese spouses (Marreiros 1994). I interviewed one young man, a Macau native living in California who was spending his vacation in his hometown, for well over an hour without realizing that he identified as Macanese; based on his "phenotypic appearance," his Chinese surname, and the fact that our interview was conducted in English and Cantonese, I assumed he was Chinese. It was only when I asked him what he thought about the controversy over the nationality of the Macanese, that he responded, "Well, I am Macanese myself," and then quickly added, "but I still consider myself Chinese, more Chinese than anything else."

Most Chinese in Macau, however, did not consider the Macanese as a group to be Chinese: partly because, despite their native fluency in spoken Cantonese, most Macanese could not read or write Chinese; partly because of the strong patrilineal principle and the perception that most Macanese traced their Portugueseness to a male ancestor; and partly because their historical status as intermediaries between the Portuguese state and Chinese residents had created a sense of the Macanese as a distinct colonial caste. This status was evident in their near-total domination, in the nineteenth and twentieth centuries, of mid-level civil service positions and occupations such as law, banking, accountancy, and translation. Although it could not serve as the only defining characteristic of Macaneseness—there were prominent Portuguese-speaking ethnic Chinese government officials who did not identify as Macanese, and plenty of Macanese employed in the private sector—their "white collar" class position and association with the Portuguese colonial government were crucial to the meaning of Macaneseness (at least in Macau) during the late twentieth century. It also arguably set them apart from prominent Eurasian families in Hong Kong and Shanghai (such as the Ho Tung clan, to which Stanley Ho belonged), who had made names for themselves in private enterprise and who were

thus able to distance themselves somewhat from the colonial administrations of these cities.[5] Although by the 1990s relations between most Macanese and Chinese residents of Macau were amicable, I heard plenty of stories of the high-handed, discriminatory, and
racist actions of previous generations of Macanese civil servants toward Chinese residents. And the common Chinese origin myth of
the Macanese—that they were the offspring of illiterate Portuguese
sailors and "flower-boat" prostitutes (so named because they lived on
boats moored in the harbors of south China's coastal cities)—gave
the Macanese a distinctly low-class image among many local Chinese, making their position of relative privilege vis-à-vis the Portuguese administration all the more galling. Indeed, the Chinese term
for "Macanese" encoded this sense of their fundamental alienness
and association with the Portuguese regime: *touh saang pou yahn*
土生葡人, or "local-born Portuguese," was used to denote everyone
who identified as Macanese, even those who had nothing "Portuguese" about them. One lawyer of my acquaintance who had attended Portuguese schools in Macau and spoke fluent Portuguese
and Cantonese (but could not read Chinese), told me in Cantonese
that although he was 100 percent ethnic Chinese, other Chinese
people referred to him as a "local-born Portuguese."[6]

Thus the question "Who are the Macanese?" could not be answered definitively in genetic, geographical, national, linguistic, political, or religious terms.[7] As most Macanese saw it, this indefinability was a point of pride and the very basis of their difference both
from the Chinese and from the Portuguese. This became especially
clear to me in March 1999, when the Macau government, in an attempt to foster the continued vitality of Macanese culture and
community, sponsored the third "Encontro das Comunidades Macaenses." The Encontro brought to Macau nearly 1,400 Macanese of a
half-dozen or more nationalities for a week of banquets, receptions,
concerts, dances, plays, seminars, and nostalgic encounters: high
school classmates were reunited after forty years' separation; parents
introduced their grown children to relatives they had never met;
strangers from opposite ends of the earth discovered their parents or
sisters had been distant cousins or childhood friends. In the Sé Cathedral, a mass was said in *patuá macaense*, the nearly extinct Portu-

guese-based creole peppered with terms, cadences, and grammatical structures from Chinese, Malay, and Indian dialects. Lavish feasts featured *cozinha macaense*, the cuisine known for endless family variations on intricate recipes (like the apabico) and epitomized by the legendary *chá gordo*, a high tea featuring rich cakes, puddings, and savories whose seasonings (curry, lemon, chili, cumin, turmeric, cardamom, olive oil, soy sauce, Worcestershire sauce, coconut, almond, chocolate) and names (*aluar, bebinca, chau-chau péle, minchi, lacassá, bají*) reflected influences from south China, Portugal, India, England, Ceylon, Malaysia, and Timor (see A. Amaro 1988 and Batalha 1977). But even in the midst of these reunions and festivities—even though the Macau government had expressly designed this event to cultivate a transnational sense of Macanese identity and affinity with Portugal that would flourish long after the handover—I heard obstinate refusals of any attempt to define the Macanese. At a meeting I attended with representatives of all the "comunidades" at the Encontro, the president of a Macanese association in North America insisted (in English) that "there is no Macanese identity. There's no common denominator. There are more differences among us than similarities."

The lawyer Nuno, a fan of Wittgenstein, explained this phenomenon by way of analogy:

How do you speak about the knight in a chess game? You cannot speak about the knight. Whatever you say about the knight, you say nothing. No, you can speak about the history and symbolism, no, but I'm asking how do you speak about the knight as a piece in a game of chess? You cannot speak about it. You can only show how it moves. You cannot make a narrative speech about it. You can only show how it works. And this is inherent to games, to the game concept. No rule of a game, no piece of a game can be explained, because it doesn't have a real existence, it has a functional existence. And the Macanese, and the cultural identity of Macau, is very much so. . . . I know a Macanese if I see one. You know, I can catch his behavior under different perspectives—his relation with China, his relation with Portuguese culture, his relation with the local government, so on and so on. But does that give me, at the end of the day, a definition? It does not.[8]

The meaning of "the Macanese," Nuno argued, could only be described, never defined. Just as the meaning of a chess piece cannot be explained to someone who does not already understand the rules of chess, explaining the meaning of "the Macanese" presumed an understanding of the historical contexts and social relations (namely, those created by the existence of a Portuguese state on Chinese soil) that had made the name meaningful in the first place. Their complexity was irreducible; their groupness could not be spoken about in the abstract, as a rule or law, but only as a collection of exceptions to other rules and other laws.

But in contrast to chess, these exceptions and the rules they indexed had the potential to be understood in a multiplicity of often contradictory ways. For some, the term "Macanese" invoked racial ideologies (both Portuguese and Chinese) of purity, contamination, and betrayal; for others, it mapped the ethnic contours of colonial structures of class and privilege. To at least one Chinese author, it served as a warning of the social and moral disequilibrium wrought by "a culture without roots,"[9] and to others it embodied the very definition of the quintessential hybrid Macau subject—the kind of subjectivity the Macau government was so fervently trying to promote—firmly rooted in the spaces "in-between."[10] To utter the word "Macanese," then, was to speak the complex and contested history of the Portuguese presence in Asia and to pronounce judgment upon the condition of liminality it had created in Macau. In the transition era, as we have seen, this liminality had to be recuperated, its power harnessed to the sovereign projects of both the Chinese and the Portuguese states. Given that law is the language in which sovereign power speaks, the Macanese had to be defined in the law.

The Force of Law

The 1990s was a period in which the law was summoned as a kind of magic potion that would cure Macau's ills: the enforcement of criminal law would restore order to society and regain the respect of the world; adherence to the Basic Law would ensure that Macau's distinctive "system" would be identified and safeguarded, that the rights and interests of the Macanese community would be protected, and that Macau's position as an inalienable part of China would be secure.[11] But the implementation of law in Macau had ramifications for the entire Chinese nation as well, for it was through the rule of law that both Macau and China would be legitimized in the eyes of the world as wholly modern societies, ready for full participation in global markets.

The Chinese Communist Party is often viewed in the West as perpetually incapable of implementing the rule of law, largely because it insists that the interests of state sovereignty take precedence over the law.[12] This insistence becomes more comprehensible when one considers that it is informed by an interpretation of China's modern history as profoundly shaped by the experience of imperialist subjugation and by the keen recognition that the colonization of Hong Kong and much of the rest of the country by the European powers and the Japanese in the nineteenth and early twentieth centuries had been conducted through a series of treaties, leaseholds, and international agreements. Given this history, the CCP long viewed the West's insistence that China implement the "rule of law" as little more than a smokescreen for continued imperialism.[13]

But beginning in the early 1990s, the CCP began to assert its legitimacy as much on its commitment to the rule of law as on its anti-imperialist revolutionary legacy.[14] This shift was spurred by the fact that, as Pittman Potter (1994) has noted, in the years following the Cultural Revolution, three of the PRC's new legitimating goals—integration into the capitalist world economy, the eradication of bureaucratic corruption, and peaceful reunification with Taiwan—necessitated at least the appearance of a commitment to the rule of law. Thus the political and historical imperatives for China's experiment in sovereignty in Macau required a series of clear-cut definitions: although nothing about Macau's second "system" would be allowed to contravene the Chinese constitution, which was the ultimate expression of that sovereignty, Beijing had to be scrupulous in abiding by its legal guarantees to uphold and protect that second system. The question of whether the Macanese could be considered Chinese nationals needed to be clarified not only to ensure that the Chinese state could assert full sovereignty over all Chinese people in Chinese territory and protect the rights of all its citizens, but also to demonstrate to the world its commitment to and capacity for adhering to the rule of law. For China in the late 1990s, legally defining the Macanese was a matter of national interest.[15]

But Chinese nationality law, like most nationality laws worldwide, had no place for a group defined primarily by its mixedness. The world-system of nation-states (Duara 1993) depends on the universality of laws defining which groups and individuals are subject to each state's power and detailing the criteria by which such definitions should be made: usually through a combination of the legal principles of *jus sanguinis* (law of blood), which ascribes nationality to people who can demonstrate that one or both of their parents were nationals, and *jus soli* (law of soil), which grants membership to those who can demonstrate that they were born in national territory (Brubaker 1992). It has been noted that the Chinese state has a penchant for overextending the principle of *jus sanguinis*—that is, for viewing everyone in the world who is of Chinese descent (*xuetong*/血統, literally "bloodline") as potential or actual national subjects (see Duara 1997 and Louie 2004). Indeed, the first Chinese nationality law, promulgated in 1909 as part of the reforms intended to transform the Qing empire into a modern nation, codified *xuetong* as the only valid basis for an individual's right to claim Chinese citizenship. Although the ideology of transnational ethnocultural unity expressed in the concept of *xuetong* is often characterized as a holdover from an ancient imperial mode of sovereignty based on Confucian assumptions about the unity of lineage, state, and civilization, Chinese states have not always viewed this bond as a sufficient basis for making sovereign claims on Chinese people outside the political boundaries of China.[16] Nevertheless, this "myth of consanguinity" (R. Chow 1993: 24) powerfully informs commonsense notions of Chineseness today, both inside the PRC and elsewhere. At a luncheon I attended early in my fieldwork in Macau, for example, a woman at my table was especially surprised at my ability to speak Chinese, for, she exclaimed, "You don't look like you have even one drop of Chinese blood in you!" (看來你一點中國血統也沒有!).[17] Thus, as Ien Ang points out, for many Chinese, *xuetong* acts as the limit point of Chineseness: that substance without which it makes no sense to claim to be Chinese, and with which it becomes impossible to escape being defined as Chinese.

Despite the prevalence of the concept of *xuetong* in everyday understandings of Chineseness, it was not codified in the Nationality

Law passed by the PRC in 1980. This law adopted a combination of *jus soli* and *jus sanguinis* criteria for determining Chinese nationals: persons who were "born in China" (在中國) and who had at least one parent who was a Chinese national (中國公民) are considered Chinese nationals; but persons "born abroad" (在國外) and who acquired foreign nationality by birth are not considered Chinese nationals, even if both parents are Chinese nationals. Thus, as is the case with most nationality laws worldwide, the definition of a Chinese national depended on the ability to make clean distinctions between historically constant sovereign territories ("inside" or "outside" China) and their subjects (Chinese nationals or not). Chinese nationality, not unlike *xuetong*, was an either-or proposition: the 1980 law expressly stated that the PRC did not recognize dual nationality.

But given Macau's history of hazy sovereignty, this law clearly required some interpretation. Was Macau "abroad"? What was the legal meaning of its ambiguous status as a "Chinese territory under Portuguese administration"? How would the "foreign" parentage and passports of the Macanese affect their eligibility for Chinese citizenship? The answer to this question would also have ramifications for the 130,000 ethnic Chinese residents of Macau who had Portuguese passports by virtue of their birth in what Portugal had historically defined as Portuguese territory: for if they were also defined as foreigners because they held foreign nationality by birth, what would that do to China's sovereign claim over the people and territory of Macau? Thus although the question "Who is a Macanese?" had long been a topic of debate within Macanese communities where membership had its privileges, during the transition period the question "Who are the Macanese?" took on a far broader salience. And although this question was often phrased in terms of being, it was effectively a question of becoming: of what and who the Macanese *could be*. What could the term "Macanese" be made to mean, and to whom? In terms of *xuetong*, the Macanese should have been Chinese, but in social and historical terms they clearly had never been; could they be Chinese or not, and why? In this sense, the controversy over Macanese nationality played out a larger controversy over the politics of potentiality—the struggle over what it would mean to envision possibilities where others saw givens, to see contingency where others saw necessity.[18] This controversy went straight to the heart of deeply felt but often barely articulated senses of self and other. It highlighted the extent to which the definition of Chineseness, in Macau at least, had less to do with blood than with politics. In so doing, it called into question the bright lines and clear taxonomies that the law promised and that Macau residents so keenly desired.

Potentializing the Macanese

The paradoxical politics of potentiality first caught my attention almost as soon as I arrived in Macau, as I tried to map out the social terrain I would be inhabiting. Most people I talked to, most books I read, told me that the population of Macau could be divided rather cleanly into three somewhat mutually antagonistic categories: Chinese, Portuguese, Macanese. But in the mid-1990s, the Macau government made a half-hearted attempt to resignify "Macanese" as a category that would include everyone born in Macau, regardless of ethnicity, language, religion, or nationality. It was an attempt, in other words, to give the name "Macanese" to the particular form of collective subjectivity the state was trying to promote in its final years. Although middle-aged Macanese informants told me stories from their youth of widespread discrimination, denigration, and exclusion of the Macanese by metropolitan Portuguese living in Macau, by the 1990s, the Portuguese state looked to the Macanese as both symbol and product of the legacy of Portuguese governance in Asia and of its potential to overcome the racialized and nationalistic understandings of community that had kept Macau's residents divided against one another. Some Portuguese officials began referring to all the people of Macau as "Macanese." The initiative was not limited to the government; a well-known Macau Chinese columnist published an article in a Portuguese-language newspaper (the article had been translated from Chinese by the editors) whose Portuguese title read "Primeiro, sou Macaense" (First, I am Macanese), in which she argued that everyone who felt a sense of belonging to Macau, regardless of their ethnicity, nationality, or place of birth, should define themselves first as Macanese and only then as Chinese, Portuguese, local-born, or anything else (Lam 1998).[19]

This initiative toward a more inclusive definition of the term "Macanese" was embraced by some Eurasians as a welcome effort to give their community the recognition it deserved and to foster a pan-ethnic commitment to the place, Macau, which they felt was their only real homeland. This was especially true of a new civic organization, Macau Sempre (根在澳門, literally "Roots in Macau"), launched in 1996. As Mario, one of the founders of Macau Sempre, explained to me, "We welcome anyone who is interested in, and committed to, making Macau a better place—anyone who has lived here and wants to stay here and help develop Macau culture and society, regardless of their ethnicity. After all, this is the true definition of a Macanese." The trilingual statutes of the organization stated that one of its primary objectives was "the promotion of macanese culture" (*cultura macaense*)—"macanese" conspicuously lowercased and defined as a "unique . . . intercultural way of living."[20] In this view, to redefine "Macanese" would be to extend to all the rest of Macau's residents the capacity to be defined not by blood, passports, or accidents of birth, but by their own decision, their dedication to the place Macau. In Mario's view, recognizing that every Macau resident had the potential to be Macanese was a way of ensuring that the Macanese would continue to be a vital part of Macau's future, making their indefinability the model for a broader, more inclusive Macau identity. Without this resignification, Mario feared, in post-handover Macau the Macanese community risked becoming irrelevant, and, in terms of both population and political influence, dwindling away to extinction.

But not everyone shared Mario's enthusiastic vision of the multi-ethnic potential of the term Macanese. Over lunch one afternoon a few months after my first interview with Mario, Pedro and I continued the rambling interview that we had begun in his accounting office two hours before. Earlier, Pedro, who styled himself an alternative voice of the Macanese people, had taken great pains to define the "true Macanese" as those "old Macau families" who had been in Macau for several generations and who had thus lost any real attachment to Portugal—unlike the "recent" or "first generation" Macanese (and here he singled out Mario as an example) whose fathers were Portuguese and who therefore had relatives, friends, property, and often several years' residence in Portugal. I asked Pedro what he thought about this current attempt to redefine the term "Macanese" and received a spirited response:

> Let's put it this way: How would you like it if one day I decided to start calling myself "Cathryn Clayton"? Eh? You wouldn't like it, right? That's your name, that's what people have called you your whole life, it is who you are. It has nothing to do with me! If I want to call myself something other than "Pedro," I should think up something new, I shouldn't just take your name. "Macanese" is "Macanese"—it already means something, it already has a history. When someone says "Macanese," I know more or less what to expect. I can understand that these politicians want a general name for everyone born in Macau, to encourage solidarity and all that, but why do they have to choose "Macanese" for that job?[21]

Pedro insinuated that this attempt to redefine "Macanese" was not only a peremptory appropriation of a well-defined and autonomous Macanese identity but also a direct attack on their already precarious interests as a group. Where Mario saw the potential for redefining the term Macanese in a way that would affirm their condition of "in-betweenness" and emphasize its value for the future of all Macau people, Pedro saw the dehistoricization of "Macanese" as an act that would strip it of a past or meaning of its own, valuable only insofar as it could be made to mean something else. The potential that Mario understood as creative and necessary for the future of the Macanese, Pedro saw as destructive of everything that made the Macanese who and what they already were.[22]

The politics of potentiality became controversial among the Macanese because Macau's transition to Chinese sovereignty promised to alter the sociopolitical conditions of Portuguese rule that had always given meaning to their existence as a group. But these were also the conditions that had long contributed to Macau Chinese residents' sense of their own Chineseness, defined partly in opposition to the alienness of the Macanese and of the Portuguese regime. The Resolution on Nationality, which explained that each individual Macanese person would have the right to choose whether he or she wished to be considered a Chinese national or not, assumed that the Macanese had the potential to become Chinese—an assumption that ran counter to the sensibilities, honed over centuries of Portuguese rule, of Macanese and Chinese residents alike.

Nationalizing the Macanese

Nuno continued his explanation. From the point of view of the Chinese nationality law that would govern Macau after December 20, 1999, he told me, the problem presented by the Macanese was not that they could not be defined but rather that they could be defined in too many ways: many of them qualified for both Chinese and Portuguese nationality. But whereas Portuguese nationality law was silent on the question of dual nationality, as we have seen, the PRC rejected the possibility that a person could have more than one nationality.

For this reason, ever since the Sino-Portuguese Joint Declaration was signed in 1987, the question of how the Macanese who wished to stay in Macau after 1999 would be defined as national subjects had been a confusing and anxiety-producing one for many Macanese. Until this point, national belonging had simply not been a question that impinged much on the lives of most Macanese: regardless of their nationality, their status as permanent Macau residents entitled them to live and work in Macau, to participate in the political life of their hometown, and to move freely in and out of Macau and Hong Kong—thus allowing them, *de facto*, many (though by no means all) of the social, cultural, and even legal rights and advantages of dual nationals.[23] But as the handover approached, the fears multiplied: some Macanese I talked to feared that the PRC would insist that they were, by virtue of their Chinese *xuetong*, Chinese nationals and thus subject to the same laws (read: the same restrictions on religious activity and free speech, the same onerous visa requirements for travel abroad) as any other Chinese citizen. Others feared the opposite: that by virtue of their mixedness, the Chinese government would consider them "foreigners" and exclude them from full political participation in the SAR (for example, making them by definition ineligible to hold high-ranking civil service positions, which would be open only to Chinese citizens). Still others feared that, de-spite Beijing's promises to the contrary, they would be treated as "tainted," second-class citizens because of their association with the colonial *ancien régime*. "It's not that we don't like the Chinese," ex-plained the members of one Macanese family to me, quietly, after making some dark jokes about what would become of them and of Macau after "the Chinese" took over. "After all, we all have Chinese blood, we're part Chinese too. We love China. It's just that the Communists can't be trusted. Even the Chinese don't trust them. They promise one thing and then turn around and do the other." Given the options, to some Macanese the prospect of inclusion was every bit as dismaying as that of exclusion, and in the early 1990s they began making preparations to leave Macau permanently, for Portugal, Canada, the United States, Australia, wherever they had family and decent prospects for the future.

Some of this anxiety was no different than that exhibited by many Hong Kong Chinese who acquired passports from second or third countries prior to the 1997 handover (see Ong 1999 and K. Mitchell 1997). Some of it clearly stemmed from a deep mistrust of the Chinese Communist Party that prevailed in the Macanese community partly as a result of the experiences of the Shanghai Macanese, who in the late nineteenth century had established a community in that city, complete with Portuguese-language news-papers, schools, and clubs, but had been forced to leave in 1949 along with the rest of Shanghai's "foreign" community. But the tenor of the controversy made it clear that this was not simply a question of economic calculations, political rights, or ideological an-tipathies; for most of the Macanese I spoke with, it was an ethical, deeply emotional question about the meaning of nationality. And although Macaneseness could not be reduced to Portugueseness, many of them felt that the latter was an inalienable part of what it meant to be Macanese. For them, holding a Portuguese passport was primarily a symbol of cultural belonging rather than of membership in a political-juridical order; similarly, holding a Chinese passport would mean claiming, in a broader sense, to be Chinese. One Maca-nese woman, Gabriela, expressed in a newspaper interview the sen-timent that many other Macanese had conveyed to me:

I could never manage, culturally, to feel that I am Chinese, even though I can understand the Chinese way of being and have no problem in accepting Chinese values. But it so happens that, since childhood, I have been taught at home that I am Portuguese, and people will not abandon their values simply because Macau is no longer a territory under Portuguese administration.[24]

Indeed, many Macanese were also nationals of third countries such as Australia or the United States; the fact that their passion in discussing this issue was undiminished suggests that the controversy was not as much about the legal rights of nationality as it was about what it would mean to so publicly claim or disavow their own Chineseness.

But the few thousand Macau residents who identified as Macanese were not the only ones affected by this question. Approximately 130,000 Macau residents—nearly 30 percent of the total population—could claim Portuguese nationality. The vast majority of these were ethnic Chinese who had no meaningful ties to Portugal but had become eligible for Portuguese citizenship simply because Portugal had, for the greater part of the twentieth century, insisted that the city in which they were born was Portuguese territory. The Portuguese state pointed to the fact that it granted full legal citizenship to any and all of the 130,000 who asked for it as evidence of the benign, responsible, and morally superior character of Portuguese rule in Macau, especially compared to the British in Hong Kong.[25] But given that most of these people were also eligible for Chinese nationality (by virtue of their birth in what China defined as Chinese territory, or by having one parent who was a Chinese citizen), they wondered if they would find their Chineseness compromised by their foreign nationality. If they wished to, or had to, be defined as Chinese, would that mean forfeiting their EU passports and the *de facto* dual nationality rights they enjoyed?

As early as 1987, Prime Minister Aníbal Cavaco Silva of Portugal addressed these fears by reassuring Macau's residents that "whoever is Portuguese now or becomes Portuguese before 1999 will have the right to remain Portuguese in the future and so will their children and grandchildren" (quoted in S. H. Lo 1995: 22). In 1994, prompted by a visit from Cavaco Silva, China's Premier Li Peng asserted the obverse, that the Macanese would not be "forced to become Chinese" after 1999 (Cui 1998, Ortet 1998). But the nationality question was not resolved in concrete terms until a scant year before the handover and only after contentious and highly publicized negotiations. Far more than a diplomatic sticking point, it was a question of potentiality: the question of who "we" could be, or, perhaps more troublingly, who could be "us."

A Clarification

On December 29, 1998, the National People's Congress of the PRC approved a resolution intended to answer, once and for all, the nationality question in Macau. The Resolution on Nationality was not new legislation; it was an official "clarification" of how the existing nationality law of the PRC would apply to all of Macau's 450,000 residents. The fact that Beijing would offer such an explanation was nothing special in itself; in 1996 a homologous clarification had been issued regarding the residents of Hong Kong. But the Macau Resolution differed from that of Hong Kong in ways that held special significance for the Macanese. The first paragraph of the Resolution addressed the crux of everyone's apprehension:[26]

1. All Macau residents who are of Chinese descent (*xuetong*) and who were born in Chinese territory (including Macau), as well as all others who qualify for Chinese nationality under the provisions of the Nationality Law of the PRC, whether or not they hold Portuguese travel or identification documents, are Chinese nationals.

All residents of the Macau SAR who are of Chinese descent and are also of Portuguese descent may, in accordance with their own wishes, choose either Chinese nationality or Portuguese nationality (國籍). Once this choice has been made, they will no longer hold the other nationality. Such Macau residents shall, prior to making this choice, be entitled to the rights stipulated by the Basic Law of Macau, except those that depend on nationality.

Chinese-language newspapers in Macau reported that PRC authorities considered this a just, even "generous" (寬鬆), response to the exceptional situation of the Macanese. After all, the Anglo-Chinese population of Hong Kong had been given no such choice in 1997; they, like all other residents of Hong Kong with Chinese ancestry, had been automatically considered Chinese nationals. China's Vice Premier Qian Qichen was reported as saying that the Resolution "takes fully into consideration the history and reality of Macau and protects the interests of all parties involved" (Cui 1998). That the Resolution did not contravene the Chinese constitution was proven by the precedent of an almost identical policy that the PRC had adopted toward Chinese dual nationals in Indonesia in the 1950s (see T. Hsia and Haun 1976). That it protected the interests of the Macanese community was clear because the impetus for this "generosity" had come from the Macanese themselves: it was a direct response to pressure from Portuguese and Macanese lobbyists who had visited Beijing in the early 1990s.

But the announcement of the Resolution was met with confusion and incomprehension by many Portuguese and Macanese residents of Macau. So much confusion, in fact, that the day the Resolution was made public, the two main sources of Portuguese-language news in Macau ran stories that drew two contradictory conclusions from the first paragraph: the evening news on the only Portuguese-language television station in town opened with the assertion that the Resolution meant that "the Macanese will become Chinese on December 20, 1999," whereas the Portuguese wire service Lusa reported that "the Macanese will be considered Portuguese citizens after the transfer of the administration to China." When the local Portuguese papers published the full text of the Resolution so that readers could come to their own conclusions, the Portuguese-language media quickly filled with questions, accusations, protests, impassioned denunciations, and demands for clarifications of the clarification. Exactly how and when was the "choice" to be made? What would be the status of Macanese who chose not to exercise their right to choose, or who did not make a choice right away— would the Chinese government consider them Portuguese, Chinese, or even stateless? And exactly what would that line "they will no longer hold the other nationality" mean? The fears and suspicions of previous years were replayed; spokesmen for the Portuguese government reiterated their view that anyone who had been Portuguese on December 19 would continue to be Portuguese on December 20. An editorial in the *Jornal tribuna de Macau* (whose editor was Portuguese, not Macanese) commented that the NPC's interpretation of the nationality law "adds nothing new" to the nationality issue, and that its ambiguity served only to "rekindle doubts as to the citizenship of residents with Portuguese ancestry" (*Jornal tribuna de Macau*, December 30, 1998, p. 4). Three weeks later, the same paper ran an editorial criticizing Beijing for its ambiguousness ("What does this decision mean? No one knows exactly; it depends on your interpretation") and pointing out that the Resolution had succeeded only in polarizing the Macanese and Portuguese communities. The upshot, the editorial concluded, was that "the Macanese must wait for an act of grace (*um acto piedoso*) from Beijing to be accepted in this land where they were born Portuguese" (J. Silva 1999). The sense was that the Resolution clarified nothing but the Chinese government's "intransigence" and "arrogance," its undemocratic disrespect of the rights and desires of the people, and its equivocating, authoritarian disregard for the rule of law.

One afternoon a few weeks later, I was having a drink with Jade, a Macau Chinese friend who had worked for several years as a journalist. She told me that the only thing she found puzzling about the Resolution was that it was controversial at all. She had been in the newsroom of the television station when the press release containing the text of the Resolution came in and had been thoroughly bewildered by the reaction of the Portuguese and Macanese journalists. "They got really emotional about it," she said, mimicking their consternation, "They said, 'I am Portuguese! How can I be Portuguese until I go to sleep on December 19, and wake up Chinese the next morning?'" She had tried to explain to them that it really wasn't such a big deal: if they didn't want to be Chinese, they could just not do anything and they would still be Portuguese. "And anyway," she added to me, "they are being given a choice, right? The whole point is that no one is forcing them to take Chinese citizenship. The logic is very simple. But they just didn't get it, and so when they broadcast their reports about the Resolution, they broadcast their confusion and got everyone else confused as well." And indeed, the sense that the Portuguese press had blown the issue out of all proportion and that the Macanese were missing the point and overreacting to the Chinese government's good-faith attempt to do justice to their unique situation was far more common in the Chinese-language press, which reiterated, in articles published over the course of the next several weeks, the PRC's "generosity" and "flexibility" in acknowledging the Macanese potential to be either Chinese or Portuguese and allowing them a remarkable degree of autonomy and "individual freedom" in deciding what they would like to be.[27]

According to at least some Macanese, however, the most troubling and confusing aspect of the Resolution was precisely the prospect of having to choose. This was spelled out in a letter to the editor that, contrary to usual practice, *Ponto final* published in mid-January 1999. The letter, written and signed by a Macanese woman named Esperança Cunha, was published under the headline "Nationality: Why Choose?," and read, in part, as follows:

No one in the world is as lucky as we are. Imagine, I am Portuguese until the clock strikes midnight on December 19, 1999—and in the next second, on December 20, I will have the greatest opportunity of my life: that of being able to choose nationalities. Funny, isn't it? I always thought that this could only happen to the rich and famous or in the films of Walt Disney. It's so amusing. It is as if they came and told me that I am of another race. I can dislike this comment and even feel offended by it. But that would be indisputably better than being told I must choose between white and black, when in truth I am white. This is a fact. In other words, it is my identity. The idea of allowing us to choose seems like a nice one, but why must we do so? I was born with one nationality and I grew up and was educated accordingly. Or is this all just because I decided to stay?   (E. Cunha 1999)[28]

As striking as the racial rhetoric is here, the point I wish to make is not simply the extent to which nationality is understood in racial terms.[29] Rather, what strikes me is the similarity between Esperança's lament and Pedro's: just as Pedro understood the effort to make the term "Macanese" more inclusive as an attempt to drain it of history and significance, so Esperança and other Macanese who identified as "Portuguese of the Orient" were upset because something they regarded as a natural and social fact—their Portugueseness—was now being redefined as one of two equally valid possibilities. In his reaction to the Resolution, Mario made it clear that what he found disconcerting was not the question of what choice to make—he swore he would never renounce his Portuguese nationality—but rather the idea of being required to make a choice about an issue in which there was no choice to be made: as he put it, "having to choose [to be] something that we already are causes great confusion for everyone." From their perspective, they were not and never could be Chinese, and Beijing's decision that each of them be *required* to exercise their right to choose nationalities was not generous—it was nonsensical, perverse, and somewhat menacing.

The link that Esperança drew between choosing nationalities and choosing races calls to mind the question posed by Virginia Domín-guez in her classic study of legally defining racial identity in Louisi-ana: "How, after all, can we possibly conceive of freedom of choice if we take identities as givens? And if there is really no choice, how are we to interpret the legal granting of 'choice'?" (Domínguez 1994: 4). In this case, Esperança interpreted it as a sign of the illegitimacy of a sovereign power that would demand such an impossible choice of its subjects. After petitioning the powers that be for an adequate solu-tion to the "unequaled sense of emptiness" created by the Resolution, she concludes, "There's a saying that goes, 'God writes law (*direito*) in crooked lines.' . . . I would like to ask, who *in this world* wrote all this in such crooked lines?" (italics added). There is a play on words here, or at least an ambiguity of expression: *direito*, which means both "law" and "right," also means the opposite of *torto*, "crooked." God writes straight in crooked lines, God writes law in crooked lines: in either case, Esperança seems to be saying, God may be entitled to communicate his will in paradoxical terms that confuse, mystify, and demand impossible choices of humanity, but the Chinese govern-ment is not. For Esperança, the suggestion that, after a lifetime of identifying (and being identified by others) as Portuguese, she now had the potential to be either Chinese or Portuguese, and the power to decide for herself which one she would be was not a gesture of multicultural inclusiveness but a shibboleth, a test of loyalty to the new sovereign that all Macanese who refused to leave their home-town would have to pass ("is this just because I decided to stay?"). Being presented with an impossible choice, in her view, simply served as a sign that an earthly sovereign had overstepped its bounds by partaking of a mode of sovereignty to which it was not entitled, ripping away its façade of impartiality and generosity to reveal itself as self-serving, arrogant, and unjust.

Speaking of the Macanese

As the controversy gathered steam—the accusations multiplying, the anxieties mounting, the whimpers of wounded collective selves echoing through the Portuguese public sphere—I made my visit to Nuno. I had originally asked him, several weeks earlier, for an interview because I knew he had made a broad comparative study of nationality law and was working as a consultant on nationality issues for the Macau Portuguese government. But by this time what I, too, wanted was a clarification: all melodrama and ideology aside, now, what did the Resolution really mean? Objectively speaking, in strict legal terms, how should it be read? As a sign of a capricious, self-serving sovereign power or of a well-intentioned sovereign state with a firm commitment to the rule of law, attempting to do justice to the unique situation of the Macanese? Who, in the end, was being unreasonable: the Chinese state in presenting such a choice or the Macanese in being outraged by it? And what could account for the difference in interpretation?

From Nuno's perspective, of course, the answer was that everyone was being unreasonable. On one hand, he said, the Macanese anxiety about "choice" was entirely unfounded. The "right of option" was not an existential decision; it was a strategic positioning. The Macanese had simply been given the right to tell the Chinese government how they wished to be treated by the Chinese government while living in territory over which the Chinese government had jurisdiction. Indeed, Nuno explained to me, the "choice" was not even a choice in the true sense of the word—although not for the reasons Esperança gave. For although Paragraph 1 of the Resolution stated that the Macanese would lose their Portuguese nationality if they opted for Chinese nationality, in fact the Chinese state does not have the authority to revoke a Portuguese passport or to force the

Portuguese government to do so. It is here that Paragraph 2 of the Resolution, which was a restatement of the policy first set out in the Sino-Portuguese Joint Declaration of 1987, becomes important:

2. All Chinese nationals of Macau who hold Portuguese travel documents shall, after the establishment of the Macau Special Administrative Region, be allowed to continue to use these documents to travel abroad, but shall not be entitled to Portuguese consular protection in the Macau SAR or in other parts of the People's Republic of China due to their possession of these documents.

The "Portuguese travel documents" referred to here are, of course, passports. Although Macanese who chose Chinese nationality would no longer be considered Portuguese nationals by the Chinese government, they (along with all the other Chinese in Macau who held Portuguese passports) would be allowed to keep their Portuguese passports and use them freely outside China. And since Portuguese law does not recognize a document that allows a person to travel as a Portuguese citizen without the rights of a Portuguese citizen, by virtue of these passports they would be considered Portuguese nationals by the Portuguese government—except while they were in Chinese territory. If they opted for Portuguese nationality, however, the Macanese would cease to be what, in the terms of the Resolution, they already were: a special category of Chinese nationals who were being granted the right (and duty) to legally affirm their status as such.[30]

Put simply, from a legal point of view, the Resolution was a *de jure* way for the PRC government to allow Macanese people who had Portuguese passports the *de facto* advantages of dual nationality—as long as they chose to adopt Chinese nationality. For although the PRC, like many other countries, does not recognize dual nationality, it does not forbid its citizens from having more than one passport.[31] The statement that upon choosing one nationality they would no longer hold the other, Nuno observed, amounted to nothing more than a reiteration of the Hague Convention of 1930 governing dual nationality worldwide, which prevents dual nationals from claiming protection from one state against the other state of which they are also citizens. In this sense, the Resolution did not force the Macanese to make an existential choice about their identity, or even to make a "choice" at all: rather, it offered them the opportunity to use the language of the Chinese law to preserve and even expand the rights they enjoyed by virtue of being legally undefined.

Rationally, legally, then, it should not have mattered to the Macanese; they should have chosen the Chinese passport. So why was the idea of opting for Chinese nationality anathema to so many of the people who would be affected by the Resolution? Originally I thought the problem was one of translation. What we had here, I thought, was a cultural and linguistic incommensurability in the understanding of nationality. In Chinese, the somewhat bureaucratic overtones of the term *guoji* (in which *guo* expresses a range of meanings that include "state," "country," and "nation," and the primary meaning of *ji* is "record," "register," or "book") do not carry the same romantic and ethical resonances of *nacionalidade*. The Portuguese meaning of *nacionalidade*, I surmised, meant that the Macanese and Portuguese who had been so upset by the ruling had experienced it as the obligation to affirm or disavow their Chineseness and thereby their Portugueseness—they were working from a "classical nineteenth-century nationalist" sensibility, in which passports are markers of "the alignment of habitus, culture, attachment, and exclusive political participation" (B. Anderson 1994: 324). And since, for decades or even centuries, Macanese habitus had been aligned more often with Portugal than with China, the idea of adopting a Chinese passport just because the Portuguese were no longer in power smacked of apostasy. In contrast, I hypothesized, my friend Jade and others like her—including the Chinese newspapers and even the PRC government—who viewed the Resolution as a commonsensical solution to the nationality question were working from a "flexible" view of passports as markers more of an "align[ment] toward world market conditions than toward the moral meaning of citizenship" (Ong 1999: 119). This would resonate with what the Macanese had told me about their objections to the Resolution and would explain why their objections were not shared or even comprehended by many Chinese residents of Macau. It would fit with the view that Chineseness is a matter of *xuetong* and culture that cannot be altered by government-issued documents. It would also tally with the prevalent image of the Cantonese as the quintessential "flexible citizens," for whom holding multiple passports was simply a strategic response to political and economic instability (Ong 1999).

But it soon became clear that the problem was more than a translingual one, just as the choice did have more than legal implications. In the summer of 2000, when I returned to Macau, a colleague told me the sad tale of the lone Macanese man (so the story went) who had opted to "become Chinese"—a story of choice that underscored the impossibility of choosing.³² Even though he said he had done so to demonstrate his loyalty to the territory of Macau regardless of who was in charge, she said, he was ostracized by other Macanese and "even by the Chinese," who considered him an opportunist and a traitor to his own people. Clearly, then, the nationality of the Macanese did matter deeply, and not only to the Macanese. The underlying assumption through most of the public commentary on the law in both Portuguese and Chinese was that, given the right to choose, the Macanese would, as a matter of course, choose Portuguese nationality and thus, according to the terms of the Resolution, lose their claim to Chinese nationality. The inevitability of this choice was built right into their Chinese name, *touh saang pou yahn*, "local-born Portuguese." In this case, assumptions about the congruence of blood, nationality, culture, and passport identity dovetailed with the maximizing logic of multiple passport holders: for, given the option, who wouldn't choose an EU passport over a Chinese one? But the apparently universal rationality of holding multiple passports was thrown into question by the prospect of a "local-born Portuguese" choosing Chinese nationality. For, in terms of world market conditions, what strategic advantages could a PRC passport afford? In this sense, the perceived undesirability of PRC passports heightened the moral meaning of Chinese nationality. A foreign passport may be a strategic choice, but a Chinese passport is just who you are. In an article published a few months prior to the Resolution, journalist Cui Zhitao interpreted the anxiety of the Macanese in precisely this way. He proposed that because the Macanese had been born in Macau, which had always been Chinese territory, any Macanese who did not exercise his or her right to choose nationalities should, for the purposes of the law, be considered Chinese by default. He continued, with a hint of petulance, "If they don't want to be Chinese people (中國人) even for one second, they can very well go ahead and choose Portuguese nationality right away" (Cui 1998). This comment recast the choice as one between Portuguese nationality and nationalized Chinese personhood.[33] In other words, it is the difference between choosing to have Portuguese nationality and choosing to be a Chinese person.

Although Nuno was technically correct that the Resolution on Nationality did not present the Macanese with an existential choice so much as a bureaucratic end-run around the legal prohibition on dual nationality, the sociohistorical context into which the Resolution was published ensured that it was experienced, by Macanese and Chinese residents both, as a referendum on the Chineseness of the Macanese. The Resolution and its language of choice foregrounded the principle of national sovereignty that underpinned the whole premise of transferring Macau from one nation to another; in the either-or rhetoric of us and them, colonizers and colonized, Chinese or other, there was no room for "sort-of Chinese" people or for a nuanced consideration of the sort-of sovereign conditions that had given rise to their community. The law could not take history into consideration; as a result, its assertion that the Macanese had the potential to become Chinese people (or not) was experienced by many Macanese as an erasure of all that made them who they were; it would define them instead either as foreigners in their own land or as no different from any of the other 1.3 billion Chinese nationals. At the same time, from the perspective of many Chinese residents in Macau, in suggesting the Macanese could become Chinese by the stroke of a pen, the Resolution erased the long history of Macanese association with alien rule as well as the structural racism and sometimes outright bigotry that had characterized their relationship with Chinese communities in Macau. Thus the Resolution caught the Macanese in a paradox of potentiality: the legal sanctioning of their potential to become Chinese served as a reminder of their alienness and a denial of the possibility that they could ever legitimately be Chinese. This denial had nothing to do with blood or territory; it had everything to do with the nature and legacy of the Portuguese presence in Macau.

Blood and Belonging

The controversy did not end there. The definition of Macanese implicit in the law did have everything to do with blood, and it was here that, in Nuno's eyes, the Chinese government was also being unreasonable. The fact was that the Resolution did not grant just anyone the right to choose nationalities. Although the word "Macanese" does not appear anywhere in the text of the Resolution, it was clear that the right to choose was to be extended only to those Macau residents who were both "of Chinese descent and also of Portuguese descent." As Cui Zhitao explained it in Macau's most widely read Chinese newspaper, the question of descent was the only reason the nationality issue had even come up in the first place: "being descendants of Portuguese people (葡萄牙人後裔), . . . most [Macanese] want to retain Portuguese nationality. It was in response to this strong desire that, in 1994, Li Peng declared they would not be forced to adopt Chinese nationality" (Cui 1998). This statement not only legitimizes the Chinese state's decision to grant the Macanese the right to choose as a rational response to the heartfelt desires of the people but also naturalizes the decision to grant the Macanese, and only the Macanese, this right: the reason the Macanese want, and should have the right, to be considered Portuguese is not mere cultural affinity or historical contingency; it is because Portuguese blood flows in their veins. The Resolution thus implicitly defines the Macanese as Chinese people with extra—Portuguese—blood. This definition, which excluded hundreds of people who identified as Macanese and thousands of ethnic Chinese who had valid Portuguese passports, was a source of even greater concern for the Macanese community and the Portuguese authorities.

During the negotiations over this Resolution, the Portuguese representatives to the Joint Liaison Group (where the Resolution was drafted) had tried to insist that the "right to choose" be given to anyone who qualified as a dual national—not only those few thousand who had Portuguese *xuetong*, but any of those 130,000 Macau residents who had or were eligible for Portuguese passports (see also Chio 1999: 95). The Handover Preparatory Committee[34] did not agree to this demand but did include in its revision of the Resolution a clause stating that everyone who qualified as both a Chinese and a Portuguese national but was not of Portuguese descent could apply to renounce his or her Chinese nationality under the terms of Article 11 of the Nationality Law of the PRC. This clause, Nuno emphasized, would have been nothing more than a "statutory reminder"—it was not new legislation; it simply reminded Chinese nationals in Macau of their existing rights under the Chinese constitution. But this proposed clause was voted down by the National People's Congress in Beijing. So although the Resolution indicates that Chinese citizens with Portuguese passports shall be allowed to keep their foreign passports as "travel documents," this simply means that China would no longer recognize these foreign passports as markers of foreign nationality; it says nothing about whether or how they might renounce their Chinese nationality. Mario, who had earlier expressed his confusion at having to choose to be what he already was, later told me of his concern that Macanese who did not have Portuguese "blood" would be denied even this choice. Two days before Chinese New Year's, in mid-February 1999, I met with him to discuss an unrelated issue, a research project we had been asked to consult on. But before long, he turned the conversation to the effects of the Nationality Law:

The ones I worry about especially are those who are ethnically Chinese but who have studied in Portuguese schools, speak Portuguese, have spent time in Portugal, maybe they married a Portuguese or a Macanese. They are not many—maybe 300 people, and if you include their families there are, let's say, 800 of them. But they are as Portuguese as I am! Some of them even served in the Portuguese army during the wars in Africa! Yet it's very, very difficult to get Beijing to admit that these people could be Portuguese.

It is always dangerous to try to interpret silence or to explain the refusal to say something that could have been said, but it seems to me that the Chinese authorities' reluctance to include in the Resolution either the right of all dual nationals to choose their nationality, or even the clause reminding all Macau residents of their right to renounce Chinese nationality, reveals that the Macanese were not the only ones uncomfortable with the prospect of this "freedom of choice." As much as some Macanese were baffled when confronted with the simultaneous legal possibility and social impossibility of choosing nationalities, so the men and women of the National People's Congress balked when confronted with the legal possibility and political impossibility of granting that choice to all Chinese people. Rationally, legally, it should not have mattered to the Chinese state: including that clause in the Resolution would not have contravened the Chinese constitution; indeed, it could only have reinscribed the sovereignty of that constitution by reminding all Macau residents that they, too, were now subject to its rule. But given the basic tenets of popular sovereignty—and given the possibility that this Resolution would be used as a model for incorporating into the Chinese nation-state another territory full of Chinese people (namely, Taiwan) who might have ambivalent feelings about becoming PRC nationals—the idea of reminding everyone that people who are "already" Chinese have, at every moment, the potential to (or not to) *become* Chinese must have seemed just as absurd as the right to choose nationalities seemed to the Macanese. A statutory reminder that Chineseness was in fact a choice that 1.3 billion people made every day that they did not decide to renounce their Chinese nationality must have seemed not just nonsensical but dangerous: an abdication of the state's sovereign claim to represent and safeguard the interests of the Chinese people.

But it is here that the politics of potentiality had their most paradoxical effects. For, in the final irony that Nuno pointed out to me, although the Resolution granted the "right to choose" only to individuals of both Chinese and Portuguese descent, any legal distinction between such people and Chinese people with Portuguese passports was meaningless. For, as we have seen, despite the pervasiveness of the idea, *xuetong* is not a legal concept. The *jus sanguinis* criterion adopted in the 1980 Nationality Law of the PRC was that of filiation (proof that at least one parent was a Chinese national), not the more ambiguous concept of descent.[35] Yet the word *xuetong* was right there in the first line of the 1998 Resolution. "But," asked Nuno, "how are you going to define the Macanese for the purposes of this Resolution, if it states that a Macanese is someone of Portuguese and Chinese 'descent'? Are you going to run a DNA test? Or is it going to be by the length of your eyes, or the amount of hair on your legs? There is no legal proof of 'descent.' None!" And in the end, he said, *this* was the difference that the Resolution made to the status of the Macanese: it did not define them out of existence but defined them into existence in a way that was meaningless in the context of Chinese law. If they could produce no legal proof of their Portuguese "blood"—which *ipso facto* they could not, since no such thing exists—the Macanese would lose their right to choose, and the state would treat them like any other Chinese national (and vice versa: if they could not prove their Chinese blood, they would be treated like any other foreigner). By legally defining the Macanese as Chinese nationals who also had Portuguese *xuetong*, then, the Resolution invalidated the very distinction between Macanese and Chinese that it appeared to confirm. As such, Nuno warned, the Resolution—which was supposed to ensure that the exceptional situation of the Macanese community would be protected and preserved—was actually a "time bomb for the extinction of the Macanese."

The fact was, however, that in Macau, almost no one but Nuno seemed to recognize the emptiness of the Resolution. The apparently straightforward language of the text, combined with the power of extra-legal ideas about *xuetong* and the conflation of legal and cultural Chineseness, meant that the Resolution made perfect (though troubling) sense to the majority of people it would affect. And of the few who did recognize its emptiness, even fewer found it problematic. The only other person I spoke with who found the alegality of the Resolution ironic was Jade. As she put it, "I could walk in and say that I was born in Macau, and so were my parents, and that my grandmother was the daughter of my great-grandfather's concubine, who was Portuguese but died in childbirth at home, and so in fact I have Portuguese blood even though I have no documents to show it. You know, I could just lie. No one would be able to prove anything either way." But she ultimately dismissed this problem, as well as the Portuguese government's apprehension about the rights—and the Chinese state's concern about the loyalties—of Macau Chinese people like herself: "It's us they're worried about, we who are ethnic Chinese but have Portuguese passports because we were born here. What would happen if all 130,000 of us decided to become Portuguese and move to Portugal? They don't need to worry, though," she laughed, "I for one would certainly never *choose* to be Portuguese!"

Conclusion

Every time I have related this story to friends or colleagues, the first question they have asked in some way or another has been, "So in the end, what happened?" By this, they have meant, variously, How was the controversy resolved? How many Macanese chose Chinese nationality? How did their choice affect their lives, their identities, their cohesion as a group? I have never been able to answer these questions. The only thing I can say is that there was no resolution. No repercussions. After a while, people simply stopped talking about it.

This is because the controversy was not about the juridical effects of the law. From a legal standpoint, the Resolution resolved nothing. It made no new law, created no new policy, altered no existing statute. It was intended to do nothing but explain a law that already existed; it did not define the Macanese in any consequential way, nor did it grant or deny them any special rights. They, like every other national of the People's Republic of China, would have the right to adopt or renounce Chinese nationality. It did not even present them with a deadline for making their choice.

Rather, the controversy was about the locus and limits of Chineseness, limits that are usually framed in terms of *xuetong* and culture but in this case were clearly inseparable from experiences of Portuguese colonialism. The public debates about the nationality status of the Macanese revealed how Macau's sort-of colonial history shaped the way that Macau residents thought about what Chineseness could or could not mean. The Macanese as a group were "sort-of Chinese" not simply because of their mixed *xuetong* but because of the role they had played as intermediaries between the Chinese residents of Macau and the Portuguese administration. The Resolution highlighted the potential for the Macanese to be either Chinese or Portuguese based on their mixed blood, while ignoring the historical conditions that made that choice all but impossible. And given the fragile position of the Macanese as "Portuguese of the Orient"—products of the colonial system who feared that Macau's transfer from Portuguese to Chinese sovereignty would spell the end of their existence as a group—this impossible choice functioned only to deepen their suspicion of their future sovereign and to make Chineseness all the more impossible as a position from which they might speak. At the same time, by implying that only the Macanese had this potential, and only because of their mixed *xuetong*, the Resolution appeared to give the Macanese special treatment that yet again set them apart from "real" Chinese. In refusing to mention that the right of any Chinese national to adopt or renounce Chinese nationality was written into the Constitution of the PRC, the Resolution denied the dizzying thought that all Chinese are "sort-of Chinese" and reinforced the lines of division between Chinese and Macanese communities that it had intended to soften. Ironically, it also confirmed the suspicions of skeptics like Nuno who believed that the CCP had no real commitment to the rule of law but was simply manipulating the language of law to further its own grip on power.

It was the one aspect of the Resolution that was not at all controversial, the definition of Portuguese passports as travel documents rather than markers of nationality, that had perhaps the most concrete and paradoxical effects. By requiring the Macanese to choose either Portuguese or Chinese nationality, the Chinese state reinforced the universality of the modern, nation-state mode of sovereignty, with its either-or rhetoric, its strictly patrolled borders, its ideologies of belonging based on congruities of blood, territory, culture, and state. But by doing so in a way that would allow them to maintain the rights of dual citizenship—in effect, by defining some passports as "more equal" than others—it challenged the epistemological foundations of that system. This epistemological challenge had very real effects. In the fall of 2003, almost five full years after the Resolution on Nationality had passed and four years after the handover, I was helping four of my brightest students at the University of Macau through the paperwork necessary for them to study at a university in the United States the following semester. They had given their information (name, age, sex, nationality, place of birth, and so on) to the Study Abroad coordinator at the US university, who had entered this information on the visa application forms the students would need to take to the US consulate in Hong Kong to apply for their visas. As they were preparing the materials they would need to give the consular officer in Hong Kong, they stopped by my office to ask if it would matter that the application forms they had received back from the United States listed their nationality as Chinese, even though they all had Portuguese passports. I asked how the mistake had occurred, and they insisted that there had been no mistake: they had accurately reported to the man who filled out the form that their nationality was Chinese. "Look," they told me, "it says so on our ID cards." They were perplexed at my insistence that they had given the "wrong" information; I was stunned that they did not realize that a consular officer anywhere in the world would view a Portuguese passport as evidence of Portuguese nationality. And of course, in our bewilderment, we were all right: a passport is, after all, a travel document, which has only secondarily come to function as a marker of nationality. But in emphasizing this distinction, the Resolution, which was an attempt to set aside questions of cultural citizenship and to parse the definition of Chineseness into the terms of *jus soli* and *jus sanguinis* recognized by international law, ended up deepening the conflation of legal and cultural Chineseness and, for my students at least, creating more confusion than clarity about the norms and practices of international law.

Finally, the Resolution intensified the suspicion that, despite all the promises of the one country, two systems formula, there would be no space for the local in the post-handover order of things. The people who considered themselves Macau's only real "locals" could not be defined or protected or even represented in the law if they did not choose to identify with a place outside Macau. In the next chapter I examine the politics surrounding one attempt to create and sustain a sense of locality that would connect Macau residents to their city's past and through that past to the globe, by emphasizing the vital role Macau had played in shaping the history of the modern world.

FOUR

Educating Locals

Civilization consists in giving something a name which is unsuitable, and then
dreaming about the result.

—Fernando Pessoa, *The Book of Disquiet*

When I arrived in Macau in the fall of 1997, I came with a plan to
understand how the Macau government would convince Macau
residents that the city's history of "sort-of sovereignty" should have a
direct impact on how they (Chinese, Portuguese, and Macanese
alike) thought about themselves as "Macau people." Knowing that
schools are important sites for the production of hegemony[1] and that
the study of history in China as elsewhere has long been an important way of shaping national and cultural identities[2]—and knowing
too, from preliminary research, that the Macau government had
made education reform one of its priorities in the 1990s—I intended
to find two schools of comparable educational quality, one state-run
and the other private, where Macau history was taught. I would interview teachers, students, and administrators, read textbooks, and
sit in on classes where I could listen to lectures and discussions on
colonialism, nationalism, and the relevance of Macau's past to the
students' futures. At the end of a semester, I would emerge with a far
clearer picture of how the state conceptualized Macau's past and its
relation to the present, as well as of how this view was taken up or
challenged in classrooms by the people whose lives it was intended
to transform.

My plan began to unravel almost immediately. One evening
shortly after my arrival, Wai, an acquaintance who had been born

133

and raised in Macau but had moved to Hong Kong for university and work, graciously agreed to help me move some things into my apartment on the nineteenth floor of a thirty-four-story building in central Macau. After we'd finished, we stood out on my balcony, leaning on the railing, drinking beer and gazing at the city lights. He pointed to the school across the street and told me it was his alma mater. A private school, I knew, and one of the most prestigious in town. I asked if he had studied Macau history while he was there, and he responded—the first of many such responses I would receive in the coming months—"*Macau* history?" From the tone of his answer I understood the absurdity of my question. No, he had certainly never studied any such thing; couldn't remember that it had even been an option. But since he had been on the science track, he told me consolingly, maybe he just hadn't been paying attention. And anyway, that was well over ten years ago.

It did not take me long to discover that the problem was not Wai's inattention or his age. The Portuguese government of Macau had, for the better part of a decade, been pouring money and effort into educating everyone—students, tourists, bureaucrats, journalists, historians, anyone who would listen—about Macau's glorious history as a meeting place between East and West; yet as I began asking around which schools might be good candidates for my comparative study, I was met with puzzled looks and nervous laughter. No one could think of any two of Macau's 44 secondary schools in which Macau history was being taught in any systematic way.[3] In dozens of interviews I conducted and articles I read, the reaction of Wai and others like him was cited as one of the fundamental problems facing Macau in the 1990s. As Wu Zhiliang, a historian and director of the Macau Foundation (whose mission was to further research and education in Macau and about Macau, and which had been generously funded by the Macau government since its founding in 1984) put it, "There are no courses about the History of Macau . . . in the curriculum of Macau's primary and secondary schools. As a result, Macau people do not understand Macau, and naturally they do not have a sense of belonging" (Wu 1994: 119). Without a sense of belonging, the youth of Macau would not grow up to care about their city and work to make it prosper. Without a past, the city and its people would have no future.

And so my plan changed. Instead of comparing local history instruction in two schools, I tried to understand why Macau history was such an omnipresent topic in the public sphere and so thoroughly absent from the schools. Instead of examining how the youth of Macau took up or contested the state's idea of a Macau person, I began paying attention to the diversity of ways that people spoke about Macau as a locality. The one country, two systems formula and the legal guarantees it promised meant that the question of locality was inextricable from the question of what Macau's second "system" was. Did it have an ethnicity? Where did it end geographically, and when had its history begun? Wherein lay the systematicity of the system? And what were the implications of espousing this system as the basis for Macau's uniqueness? In practice, the absence of clear answers to these questions meant that, on one hand, there was a need to emphasize, in order to clarify, the characteristics of a distinctly local system, one that could be shown to have a legitimate and legitimizing past and to be clearly identifiable in the present and plausibly sustainable in the future. For, as a Macau Chinese educator of my acquaintance was fond of asking, "If we have no system, on what grounds can we expect to have any degree of autonomy?" On the other hand, too much emphasis on Macau's difference could undermine the very premise of a shared Chineseness that was the basis of the CCP's claim to sovereignty over Macau; the local could then represent a decentering of the paramount claim of the nation-state to the loyalties of its people and a mockery of the one country, two systems policy. These tricky politics ensured that the attempt to define "the local" in a way that accurately reflected the distinctiveness of Macau's sort-of sovereign, sort-of Chinese status would become one of the most urgent and most delicate projects of the transition era. In this chapter I examine the process of "localization" not just as a mechanism for transferring state power from one set of bureaucrats to another but as the attempt to assert Macau as a coherent system and subject of history and of a collective identity that transcended the "merely" local. The proposed introduction of Macau history into the middle-school curriculum was but one way in which debates about the definition of the local became explicitly linked to questions of how the history of Portuguese rule had or had not shaped how Macau people thought about themselves as Chinese. These abstract questions became immediately concrete as soon as teachers and administrators tried first to create a viable local history curriculum and then to get schools to adopt that curriculum in the classroom.

Imagined Disunities and the Politics of Localization

The problems that faced both the Portuguese and Chinese governments in their attempts to define Macau as a unitary system or locality were vividly reflected in the metaphors through which those residents spoke about their home.

On one hand, many people I spoke with felt that Macau's biggest problem was the complete lack of any sense of locality whatsoever.[4] One Macanese man educated in Europe likened Macau society to the Paris metro—an assemblage of tunnels and train lines traveling in different directions on different levels, sometimes running parallel but never meeting. Similarly, he said, Macau has "many different strata of social existence" that have little or nothing to do with one another and its residents have little sense of Macau as anything but a means to get to their own ends. A Portuguese journalist who had been living in Macau for nearly a decade said he thought of the Chinese and Portuguese in Macau as an elderly married couple sleeping on opposite sides of the same bed, who no longer touch and rarely speak, but each of whom has grown comfortable with and dependent on the presence of the other. A young ethnic Chinese man who had spent the first seven years of his life in Macau but had since moved to California told me, on a return visit, that Macau reminded him of a "petri dish": a tiny but fertile space into which all kinds of different organisms had been thrown, where each individual organism "keeps expanding upward and inward, and all their differences get intensified, magnified." Francisco, a (white) Portuguese man who had lived in Macau since leaving his hometown of Luanda, Angola, in the early 1980s, gave me a visual metaphor for thinking about Macau history: he urged me not to envision Macau's past as a single unbroken sequence of 450 years, but rather as 450 years of four-year episodes—the term length for administrators, soldiers, and ships' captains who were sent to Macau or came to shake the pataca tree, each of whom transformed the place in his own image but left little that outlasted his tenure. And the image of Macau as a "stepping-stone," rather than a destination, for Chinese people seeking a better life outside China suggested that this mercenary view of the city was not limited to its colonial rulers.[5] Despite the differing and sometimes problematic politics of these metaphors, all conceive of Macau, both spatially and temporally, not as a unitary entity but as a ground on which disparate actors engage in unconnected activities. Rather than locality, they convey a sense of barely contained centrifuge.

On the other hand, some metaphors I heard did conceive of Macau as a coherent entity—one characterized by its utter marginality. Ah Man, an ethnic Chinese man in his early thirties who had been born in Hong Kong but had considered Macau his home since moving there as a teenager, told me what he appreciated about Macau was that "it's like having a rich relative, like having a supermodel sister"—its geographic, linguistic, and cultural proximity to Hong Kong meant that Macau residents could enjoy all the advantages of nearby wealth, fame, and glamour, without the pressures of life in the fast lane. But, he went on to say,

> Another metaphor I like to use [to describe Macau] is of a rapid-traveling brook. You know how water sort of forms eddies sometimes, and as the water rushes down the stream there might be little nooks, little places on the banks where the water runs into a sort of stagnant pool. I think Macau is one of those places. It's not a puddle far away from the stream—like maybe Laos, or places like Bhutan or Nepal—they are like puddles really far away. But Macau would be one of these little places where water sort of runs into a stagnant kind of pool, but is still part of the stream.[6]

These are metaphors of Macau as a hanger-on, a literal backwater; they envision "the local" as characterized primarily by its irrelevance to the places and processes that have shaped the modern world.

The project of creating a unified identity for all Macau residents was an attempt to transform these ways of thinking about the local. Rather than home to a haphazard and incoherent collection of cultural practices, Macau would be a clearly identifiable locality with its own unique characteristics. Rather than a stagnant pool on the margins of the rushing torrents of modernity, this locality would be seen

Fig. 3   On the flag of the Macau Special Administrative Region, a lotus flower
in full bloom rests on the stylized representation of a bridge.

as a cosmopolitan "bridge" that had first brought East and West together on equal terms. This metaphor of Macau as bridge was ubiquitous in official speeches and iconography and was even encoded
graphically on the post-handover SAR flag, which depicted the stylized image of a lotus flower in full bloom above the arch of a bridge
over rippled waters, under a canopy of five stars (see Fig. 3).

But the sensitive politics of this project were immediately evident
in the problem that was the hinge of the whole transition process:
the trifold problem of "localization" (*localização*/本地化).[7] Trifold,
because three aspects of the Macau polity had to be brought in line
with "the reality of Macau" (Ng Lam 1997: 16): the law (translating
the Portuguese legal code into Chinese and dropping or altering
provisions that did not conform to the Chinese constitution), the
language (implementing Chinese as one of the two official languages
of Macau), and the bureaucracy (replacing civil servants from Portugal with "local" employees). A problem, not only because of the
enormity of the task of training hundreds of administrators, lawyers,
translators, and judges, and of translating thousands of pages of legal
code,[8] but because suddenly the question of what, and who, would

count as "local" became a question of both political and practical survival: Who would get the civil service posts vacated by departing Portuguese bureaucrats? Who would pay the pensions of the departing civil servants? Under what circumstances, if any, might it be possible for a Portuguese person to be considered "local" and allowed to keep his or her job? Although the open questions inherent in the one country, two systems policy—questions of how to define Macau's system and its people and the extent of and limits to its autonomy—were usually interpreted in favor of Beijing, the opposite was clearly a possibility.[9] This instability made everyone tread lightly on the terrain of the "local."

The touchiness of this problem was illustrated by the comments of an acquaintance of mine, a young ethnic Chinese man who was affiliated with several "leftist" organizations in Macau (the labor union, neighborhood associations, and other groups with ties to the Chinese Communist Party). Over lunch with a few colleagues from the Internet startup company where he worked, he surprised me by admitting he thought that it might be good for Macau if some Macanese civil servants were allowed to stay on in their jobs. He observed that most people he knew thought "localization" should mean sinicization: replacing Portuguese and Macanese civil servants with ethnic Chinese who had been for so long prohibited, by law or by practice, from holding mid- and high-level government positions in Macau. He, however, believed the main criteria should be merit and commitment to Macau: as he put it, "some of the Macanese are hardworking, experienced, and good at what they do. They shouldn't be pushed out just because they are not Chinese." Of course, he continued, he could never say this publicly; he feared that his refusal to make the category "local" coterminous with the category "Chinese" would open him up to accusations of being unpatriotic or misinterpreting the one country, two systems policy. He believed that advocating a different conception of "locals"—one that put considerations of locality before those of ethnic nationalism—would have been political suicide.

For all these reasons, the almost constant debates about localization in the political arena tended to focus more on the need for localization and the sluggishness of localization and the practical concerns of localization rather than on a substantive discussion of the question that underpinned the whole endeavor: What could the "local" possibly mean in the context of late twentieth-century Macau?

Defining the Local

In other regions of the world, the process I have described above—of establishing a sense of collective identity and unity based on a shared history and belonging to a territorial unit—would be called nation-building. But in Macau, which had no prospect of becoming its own nation, we might very well call it a process of "local-building." The awkwardness of this turn of phrase highlights the extent to which we expect the local, unlike the national or the global, to be a self-evident locus for knowledge, politics, or collective subjectivity: an authentic core of reality rather than a social construction. But the politics of transition and sort-of sovereignty in Macau made it especially clear that the local, just as much as the global or the national, is a question of scale. As Anna Tsing puts it, scale

is the spatial dimensionality necessary for a particular kind of view, whether up close or from a distance, microscopic or planetary. . . . [S]cale is not just a neutral frame for viewing the world; scale must be brought into being: proposed, practiced, and evaded, as well as taken for granted. . . . Not all claims and commitments about scale are particularly effective. Links among varied scale-making projects can bring each project vitality and power. The specificity of these articulations and collaborations also limits the spread and play of scale-making projects, promising them only a tentative moment in a particular history.   (Tsing 2004: 58)

Scale-making projects, then, are about imagining, "*in order to see how [they] might succeed,*" social frames that are delimited, or limitless, in spatial terms (Tsing 2004: 57; italics added). They are about positing a spatial unit—be it a village, a city, a nation, a globe, a universe—as a sensible, feasible, even inevitable sphere for a given, more or less unified set of practices, histories, social relations, or subjectivities. Such projects are, of course, inextricable from the social contexts they are trying to transform: rather than simply superseding alternative scales of social life, they echo, appropriate, and collide with the practices and rhetorics of other scale-making projects, old and new. Their ability to compel us to think differently about the world or a corner of it depends on a combination of contingency and plain hard work.

What became evident in Macau in the 1990s was how much of the work necessary to conjuring this spatial dimensionality was temporal in nature. By this I mean two things. First, that in order to be successful even for a tentative moment, any scale-making project must conjure a spatial dimension with a past, present, and future. This is hardly a new observation: plenty of studies have shown how nations, for instance, create and then depend on narratives of historical continuity, simultaneously eternal and evolutionary, by projecting themselves backward into a distant ancestral past and forward into a limitless future (B. Anderson 1991, Duara 1995, Handler 1988).[10] Creating a local scale for Macau became problematic in this regard, since the whole point of the handover, the reason it was cause for celebration among many Chinese and dismay among many Portuguese, was that it was a deliberate historical break, an end to the very thing that had made Macau what it was for the past four hundred years. But, second, in order to make these temporalities convincing, scale-makers also impute to other spatial frames an association with particular morally charged pasts and futures. These associations then color our perceptions of what those other spatial commitments are commitments to—in other words, to turn the metaphor in a different direction, of what it is those scales are really weighing.

An example may help clarify. Much of the twentieth century in China has been spent in the creation of a national scale.[11] Sun Yatsen's famous early twentieth-century simile—"China is like a sheet of loose sand"—was both a complaint about the absence of national scale and a proposal that such a scale, rather than the imperial scale of dynasties, the civilizational scale of Confucian elites, or the regional scale of warlords, was the proper unit for a modern Chinese polity, economy, and identity. Yet the politics of national scale-making, in China as elsewhere, were never an either-or proposition. As Bryna Goodman has shown, in their efforts to create a national scale, Chinese nationalists alternately drew power from the networks and rhetorics of native-place regionalism by addressing them as transitional steps on the ladder toward an imminent national consciousness and repudiated them as outmoded remnants of the kind of grainy particularism they were trying to overcome (Goodman 1995a and 1995b; see also Duara 1995). Joseph Levenson once neatly summarized this shape-shifting quality of scale by arguing that China's communist revolutionaries, in relegating one form of cosmopolitanism—that of *tianxia*, or Confucian universalism—to the past, made it appear as little more than a sad and self-delusional provincialism; while in embracing the new cosmopolitanism of class consciousness, they envisioned the peasantry—whom the Confucians, Marxists, and Chinese nationalists had once dismissed as hopelessly provincial—as the basis for a revolution that would in future create not just a new China but a new world (Levenson 1967: 283). Envisioning China in order to see how it might succeed on a new, national scale depended not just on making strategic articulations among different scale-making projects but also on creating moral histories of scale.

Perhaps this story as Levenson tells it is too neat; yet a similar story could be told about 1990s China. Although the CCP's continued emphasis on territorial unity indicated that its commitment to the national scale remained strong, this commitment was articulated through new alignments with other social frames, which took on new histories. The global commitments of Marxism, Leninism, and Mao Zedong Thought once animated both the CCP's nationalist project of claiming leadership of the Third World and the Cold War nationalisms of the United States and Europe; but now, from the perspective of a different kind of globalism, these commitments appeared as evidence of Maoist China's "isolation" and the cause of its backwardness.[12] Meanwhile, new commitments to other regional and global scales, fostered by the Communist Party, proposed the nation not as an alternative to these scales but as the result of the productive interaction between them. As Tim Oakes (2000) has demonstrated, the central government mandate that provinces become self-sufficient in attracting foreign capital led to a new emphasis on the province as a scale for economies, cultures, and subjectivities, especially in China's interior where the opprobrium of "backwardness" could be countered by re-envisioning the province as the scale for the "ancient cultural continuities" that were the foundation for an authentically Chinese modernity. The coastal SEZs established in the mid-1980s as "exceptional" regions that were neither entirely socialist nor wholly capitalist, where foreign investment could be both encouraged and controlled, turned the localities of Shenzhen and Xiamen into models for a new and prosperous Chinese nation (G. Crane 1996). The phrase *aiguo aixiang* 愛國愛鄉, which translates loosely as "loving one's country, loving one's village,"[13] became a common term of praise for overseas Chinese who returned to or (more important) invested financially in their "home villages" and, as such, was a succinct and powerful way of articulating local, national, and transnational scales of Chineseness.[14] Such articulations both obscured other possible connections—making them appear to be the relics of a misguided past—and imputed to regional scales of various dimensions a newly invigorated role as the loci of China's national future.

The one country, two systems policy that was to guide the integration of Macau (and Hong Kong) into the Chinese nation-state was nothing if not a scale-making project. As a form of what Aihwa Ong has called "graduated sovereignty," it required the breaking up of the putatively homogeneous space of the nation and instead asked people to imagine a single sovereign power that would legitimately function differently in different spaces.[15] But in contrast to the Southeast Asian cases that Ong describes, the one country, two systems approach could not use ethnicity as a "sorting mechanism" to define the subjects of these different forms of governance, for central to its premise was the claim that it would enable the reunification of all Chinese territory and Chinese people under the protection of the Chinese state.[16] Rather, the criterion was history, or more precisely a particular spatialization of history: the idea that the historical experience of alien rule in Macau and Hong Kong had caused those cities to develop different socioeconomic "systems" from the mainland. Insofar as the Portuguese government's project of instilling in Macau residents a sense of their "unique cultural identity" coincided with the PRC's project of legitimating the SAR as a kind of recuperated exception to its rule, its attempts to create a local scale with which Macau residents could identify were welcome. But insofar as these attempts could also be read as the last-ditch effort by a lame-duck colonial government to shore up its influence and undermine Macau residents' sense of their own Chineseness—in other words, to draw a line of separation between *aiguo* and *aixiang*—they could also represent a continuation of colonialism by other means.

In what follows I show how the narratives of the glorious past and sorry decline of education in Macau, which circulated so widely in the public sphere during the transition era, trace a moral history of the local as it gets articulated and disarticulated from shifting civilizational, global, and national scales. In the last half of the chapter, I return to the question of why this or any other local history narrative was absent from the curriculum of Macau's middle schools and explore how the problem of scale was entangled in the temporal and spatial politics of transition and sort-of sovereignty.

Civilizing the Local

The transition to Chinese administration sparked a burst of research and writing about the history of education in Macau, funded by the Macau government, the Portuguese government, the Chinese government, and private or semi-private foundations, that resulted in museum exhibitions, international conferences, scholarly monographs and edited volumes, and doctoral dissertations.[17] General historical works on Macau virtually never failed to include at least a chapter on the history of education.[18] To be sure, the involvement of such organizations as the Commission for the Portuguese Discoveries, which published a number of sourcebooks for the history of education in Macau, indicated that the Portuguese state was interested in the topic from a public relations angle; but books in Chinese such as *On the Historical Significance of Macau's Colégio de São Paulo* (Liu 1994b) by Liu Xianbing, head of the Macau Chinese Education Association and an outspoken critic of Portuguese rule, suggested that there was more at stake here than the ideological concerns of the Portuguese state. Even those authors who wrote most scathingly of the Macau Portuguese state's dismal record of educating its populace almost always began by extolling the "glorious past of Macau education" (K. C. Tang 1998: 222; see also Bray and Hui 1991, Feng 1999, and A. H. Yee 1990). The political commitments of these narratives aside, what interests me is the extent to which, taken together, they trace a history of the local in relation to changing moral and spatial frameworks of civilization.

Gail Hershatter and Anna Tsing (2005) have suggested that "civilizational thinking" involves the "creation of legacies that not only set standards but also define a cultural space." The notion of civilization both differentiates a civil self (individual or collective) from a barbarian other and has come to distinguish differently civilized selves and others in a way that, although not as strictly territorial as the nation-state, is often understood in spatialized terms.[19] In Macau—as in Hong Kong, Shanghai, Singapore, and countless other cities in the 1990s—the spatial, civil, and culturally distinctive qualities of civilization were neatly captured in the phrase "East meets West" and in the image of Macau as a bridge (橋梁) or a "meeting point" (交匯點) between East and West. As a scale-making project, the East-meets-West rhetoric in Macau accomplished several things simultaneously: it divided the world into just two cultural spaces, thus suggesting that these were equal to each other and superior to other spaces (such as the South); it erased the violence that attended the various "meetings" of these civilizations; it asserted China's regional hegemony by implying, more often than not, that China was coterminous with "the East"; and it allowed Macau to claim status as a "world city" by association with other cities from Istanbul to Tokyo to San Francisco where a similar rhetoric was used to narrate in a positive vein the legacies of various histories of capitalist expansion. In this sense, the East-meets-West story about Macau's past proposed a different way of thinking about the changing relationship between the local and other spatial frames. For in this story, civilization is hemispheric, not global, in scale. But, as we shall see, it also bears a complicated relationship of interdependence with and antagonism to the categories of the local, the national, and the global.[20]

Histories of education in Macau were key to articulating a civilizational scale, not just because of the special position education holds in civilizational thinking as both conduit for civilizing influences and sign of the attainment of civilization but also because Macau could claim the distinction of having been home to "Asia's

first Western-style university." To an even greater degree than political or economic histories of Macau, the history of education in
Macau formed a cautionary tale about how the spatial, cultural, and
temporal definitions of civilization could shift, leaving behind (literally "savaging") localities that had once been at the forefront of civilization. In this sense, it could be read as a critique of Portuguese colonialism and as an explanation of the present-day "Macau realities"
that made reform and localization so urgent and so difficult to implement. Conversely, however, this tale could be read as a history of
the shifting significance of the local and provide readers in the
1990s with examples of the dangers of thinking too small.

The tale usually began with some variant of the following story:
"Four hundred years ago, missionaries in Macau established the first
university in the Far East, where they trained hundreds of missionaries; [since then], education in Macau has made an enormous contribution to the cultural exchange between East and West" (Feng 1999:
4). More often than not, the first chapter of this "local" history begins in Spain in 1540, with the founding of the Jesuit order by Ignatius Loyola (1492–1556) and the Jesuits' commitment to intellectual
rigor and missionary zeal. Sometimes the narrative starts in Rome in
1494, with the ratification of the Treaty of Tordesillas, in which
Pope Alexander VI for the first time divided the world (outside
Europe) between Spain and Portugal and created the *padroado*, thus
setting the terms for the Jesuits' arrival in East Asia. Or again it
might open on the island of São João (上川島), some forty miles
west of Macau, in 1553, some four years before the establishment of
Macau, with the death of the Jesuit Francis Xavier, whose vision of
the potential for Christianity in China inspired the scope and style
of the missions to come. It would certainly sketch the hazy origins of
St. Paul's College (Seminário or Colégio de São Paulo), which began as a school attached to the Jesuit residence, possibly as early as
1565 but probably not until 1572.[21] It would focus on Alessandro
Valignano, Michele Ruggieri, and Matteo Ricci, the first men to
recognize "Macau's importance not only as a trading post but also as
a bridge into China" (Feng 1999: 56) and among the first to suggest
that the road to the Christianization of China lay not in conquest
but in accommodation, the sinicization of Christianity and of the

missionaries who taught it, and the free exchange of knowledge and ideas. Through their efforts, in 1594, St. Paul's College was expanded into a university, a place where European priests—including Niccolò Longobardi, Adam Schall von Bell, and Ferdinand Verbiest, all of whom later served in the Imperial Observatory at the request of the court in Beijing—could study the languages and customs of China, and where Asian converts (such as the poet and painter Wu Li) could learn what they would need to understand, administer, and propagate Catholicism.[22] Supported by the crown, by the contributions of local merchants, and by the Jesuits' own investments in the silk trade with Japan,[23] the university had a library of more than 4,200 volumes, an archive, a printing press, a pharmacy, and an astronomical observatory; it offered classes in mathematics, physics, astronomy, medicine, music, philosophy, theology, rhetoric, Latin, and Chinese and soon became, according to author Feng Zengjun (1999: 60), "a Macau-centered hub of Asian culture" (澳門爲中心的亞洲文化中心). In addition, the Jesuits opened a second school, the Seminário de São José, to train Chinese novitiates and secular clergy in the fields of theology, calligraphy, Latin, science, and mathematics. But this school also admitted local lay students, which (according to Feng at least) was one of the first steps in China toward a public system of education and reflected the Jesuits' commitment to "teach all comers" (the words of Ricci, quoted in A. Ross 1994: 121). The work of the Jesuits caught the attention of the Shunzhi and Kangxi emperors, both of whom decreed that all new arrivals from Europe wishing to enter China "must first go to Macau to study the Chinese language."[24] But according to Feng, these schools also had a more lasting impact, for they "propelled the development of Asian science and technology. The modernization of Chinese science and technology is indivisible from the activities of these missionaries" (Feng 1999: 60).

Circulating in the 1990s, narratives that extolled the early glories of education in Macau framed this local history in terms of very contemporary preoccupations in China: the potential for Sino-Western relations on an equal footing, the advantages to be gained from trade and "opening up," the deep historical roots of Chinese science and technology, and the desire for China to be recognized as the center of an alternative (and possibly more enlightened) form of civilization. These narratives conjure an era prior to China's "national humiliation," prior to "Anglophone hegemony" (Ptak 1998), in which Macau held the promise of a cosmopolitan modernity that might have been. They leave implicit the contrast with what really was, at least according to standard histories of China—the violence and degradation that accompanied China's wrenching and still-incomplete transition to modernity.

The local history of education here is a history of extralocal imperatives and influences. It is a local history insofar as it is about educational institutions in the territory of Macau, but everything that one might usually think of as "local"—indigenous cultural practices, hybrid cultural forms, distinctive regional variations on a cultural mainstream—is excluded. What makes "Macau education" valuable in these narratives is not that it managed to protect a local "system" against the onslaught of distant people and ideas but that it was the conduit for a series of civilizational encounters that would alter the course of world history. It conjures "Macau" as a spatial unit that becomes meaningful only at the moment the local becomes completely aligned with (one might even say effaced by) a civilizational scale. This is the logic of the metaphor of Macau as a bridge, for a bridge is meaningful only when it leads somewhere else.

But the story continues. In the eighteenth century, the growing political and ideological influence of the Jesuits in China and in Europe began to be viewed as a dangerous trend, and the authorities turned against them. The accommodationist policies of Ricci and Valignano, which had been the basis for the São Paulo Seminary's status as a "center of Asian culture," sparked the Rites Controversy, which divided the church all the way up to the Vatican and ended badly for the Jesuits when a series of papal decrees in the early 1700s made the practice of the Confucian rites by Catholics grounds for excommunication.[25] In response, in 1721, the Kangxi emperor, who had been sympathetic to Jesuit missionaries in the Riccian mold, expelled European Christians from China.[26] In 1759, the Marquês de Pombal, a Portuguese reformer noted for his Enlightenment ideals and his distrust of the Jesuit order, found a pretext to expel the Jesuits from Portugal and all its territories. In 1762, when this news finally reached Macau, the Jesuits were banished from Macau as well, and the Jesuit schools ceased to function.

With the decline of the influence of the Catholic church in Europe, the expulsion of the Jesuits, and the bumpy road toward the secularization of the Portuguese state, the history of education in Macau becomes a series of petitions to the king for adequate funds and qualified teachers; indignant letters decrying the sorry state of schools and teachers; proposed reforms that were never implemented; and reports of schools being founded, then changing hands, then being converted to orphanages or granaries or crumbling hotels. Resurfacing every few decades in the century between 1760 and 1860 is the complaint that someone or something has dealt a "mortal blow" to education in Macau. By 1860, it—and civilization along with it—seemed finally to be dead. That year, a Portuguese-language newspaper in Macau ran an editorial warning that Macau was "well on its way to fulfilling the augury . . . made some twenty years ago by a Lisbon newspaper, which prophesied that [due to its near total lack of educational facilities], Macau would soon be *reduced to a land of savages*" (L. Ferreira, in Aresta et al. 1997: 17; italics in original). As for the São Paulo Seminary, that hub for the free exchange of ideas, it was abandoned by the departing Jesuits in 1762, burned to the ground in 1835, and was never rebuilt.

The view from Macau, in this narrative at least, was that the promise held out by the Jesuits of an enlightened road toward a transcultural, cosmopolitan civility achieved through education, mutual respect, and the open exchange of ideas had been thoroughly trampled by the process of secularization and the redefinition of "civilization" to coincide with the cultural space delineated by Enlightenment (and industrial) modernity. No longer is the imperative for education in Macau generated by the encounter of civilizations; no longer are Macau's prospective students the intellectual elite of Asia and Europe, destined for careers in the courts of distant emperors. Throughout the nineteenth century, as both China and Portugal became increasingly peripheral to a world system now centered on the industrialized nations of northern Europe, Macau's "local" became separable from, and thus irrelevant to, world affairs. A different West came into a different kind of contact with another

East, and Macau became a *mere* locality, a bridge to nowhere. To the extent that it draws attention to the global conditions that brought about the decline of education in Macau, this narrative forms a criticism not so much of Portuguese imperialism as of the condition of (Anglo-American) capitalist modernity that relegated both China and Portugal to the margins of world history.

Finally, just after the turn of the twentieth century, education once again became a matter of urgent concern as both China and Portugal experienced republican revolutions (Portugal in 1910, China in 1911). In both places, revolutionaries and the new governments they established acted on the assumption that mass education was essential to the task of transforming decaying empires into modern sovereign nations.[27] Both proposed that one of the key functions of modern states was to educate its citizens and that one of the key purposes of educational institutions was the cultivation of national culture, national language, and patriotism.[28] The discussion about education in Macau thus turned to the question of who was a citizen and what kind of education a citizen should receive. In 1908, for example, the secretary general of the province of Macau wrote a report to Lisbon in which he argued that the government had no responsibility to provide education for the vast majority of Macau residents, since "numerically, the residents are almost entirely Chinese, and as such are intransigent in the maintenance of their habits, customs, and traditions, to the extent that to this day no other race has been able to dissolve or dispense with their civilization" (Mansilha in Aresta et al. 1997: 56). Once civilization was realigned with national culture and sovereignty, civilizational difference became an obstacle to, rather than a building block of, a meaningful local scale.

In 1914, a special commission was convened by the Leal Senado to address what it perceived as a crisis of *desnacionalização*, or the loss of Macau's Portuguese character. A national *liceu* had finally been established in 1893 but limped along with enrollments of only about a dozen students. At the same time, privately run schools proliferated virtually without regulation, making Macau's education system disorganized, redundant, inefficient, and poor in quality. The commission argued that in order for Macau to regain its Portugueseness, education had to be made to be locally relevant. This, they suggested, was the problem with the Liceu, which had been established "without any attention to the conditions of life here" (in Aresta et al. 1997: 77). The Liceu's European subjects of study—Latin, history, Portuguese literature, philosophy, mathematics—were useless for most Macau residents, who would never go to university or to Europe and who instead needed to study accounting, English, stenography, and Chinese so that they could find work in Asia's commercial cities. The Liceu's expectation that young people would stay in school for most of their teenage years was a burden heavier than most Macau families could bear. The commission thus proposed that the Liceu and all other state-run schools in Macau be closed and replaced by one Portuguese-language primary school for boys and one for girls, several bilingual (Chinese/Portuguese) primary schools for Chinese children, and a single vocational school for all Macau students at the secondary level. In rebuttal to the Portuguese state's attempt to fold Macau into (paraphrasing Benedict Anderson) the homogeneous, empty space of the nation, the commission suggested that the only way to shore up the diminishing Portuguese national character of Macau would be to acknowledge and accommodate local differences and the uneven, heterogeneous cultural spaces they engendered.

In a series of passionate newspaper editorials, Manuel da Silva Mendes, a Portuguese teacher and writer who spent most of his adult life in Macau, refuted these recommendations. He agreed with the commission's assessment of the problems of education in Macau and praised it for making "special consideration of local conditions," which were in fact different from those of Portugal (Mendes 1996: 29). But, he argued, by insisting on defending this difference, the commission was making a grave error: it was defining the local in opposition to civilization itself. In suggesting that the Liceu should be replaced by a commercial school to teach typing, accounting, and shorthand, it was advocating technical instruction rather than education; yet education was, now more than ever, the yardstick by which civilization was measured:

Today, anyone who does not know something of geography, who has no knowledge of the history of humanity, who is ignorant of the fundamentals of the so-called natural sciences, who cannot follow the general lines of a map or a sketch, is not simply an ignorant person, but an uneducated person. . . . In countries at a more advanced level of civilization, everyone is required to be educated at least until the age of fourteen or sixteen. (Mendes 1996: 30)

The form of localization envisioned by the commission, he suggested, would be little more than a descent into provincialism and could only hasten the process of *desnacionalização* by further alienating Macau residents from meaningful inclusion in the Portuguese nation and further distancing Macau from the "civilized" world. Instead, Mendes proposed to reverse the process of *desnacionalização* and barbarization of Macau through a different kind of localization: adjusting the course offerings and schedule of the Liceu, opening state-run schools to educate Macau's Chinese residents, and teaching everyone—Chinese, Macanese, and Portuguese alike—correct Portuguese, as well as the history, geography, French, mathematics, and sciences necessary for an individual or society to claim membership in the modern civilized world. According to Silva Mendes, only this alignment of locality, nation, and civilization would allow Macau to prosper in the long term.

In the end, neither set of recommendations was implemented. The Liceu, which served primarily Portuguese and Macanese students, remained intact as the only state-run secondary school in Macau until 1985 (when a state-run bilingual middle school was opened), and the education of the majority of Macau's Chinese and Macanese residents was left to various civic associations.[29] But in this history of local education one hears more than a story of early glory and modern decline—a story as familiar to students of Portuguese imperialism as to those of modern Chinese history. One hears an alternative moral history of civilization that creates, if only implicitly, a gap in the ideologies of progress and uniformity embraced by modern nation-states. Contrary to nationalist histories, this story does not place full blame for the demise of education (and thus civilization) in Macau at the feet of Portuguese imperialism; in fact, it was Portuguese expansion that enabled the "meeting" of East and West and the exchange of civilizations in the first place. Rather, it is the decline of empires and the advent of nationalist thinking, with its insistence on unitary standards and its Eurocentric definition of civilization, that made it impossible to think of the local, in all its heterogeneity, as a meaningful scale for educational policies let alone for a collective subjectivity.

The part of these narratives most enthusiastically embraced by the Portuguese and Chinese states in the 1990s was, perhaps not surprisingly, not this subversive history of nationalism but the image of Macau (and thus China and Portugal) as early modern precursors to globalization—an image that fit well with the prevailing nationalist ideologies in both countries. Rather than an agonistic tale of imperialists vs. anti-imperialist nationalists, which would divide the population of Macau against itself and keep Macau mired in the antagonisms of the twentieth century, these narratives told of the glories of Macau's pre-national past and thereby posited it as a unified locality poised to reprise in the twenty-first century its original role as civilizing bridge in a globalizing world.

Localizing Education

These histories of education may have soft-pedaled the issue of sovereignty, but it was in the ostensibly tame sphere of education reform in the 1990s that questions about the coherence, scope, and significance of the local became explicitly linked to explosive debates about sovereignty, imperialism, and the relationship between Macau's past and its future. All the educators, administrators, alumni, and analysts I spoke with agreed that Macau's schools suffered from the same problem that my other interlocutors had identified as the city's biggest problem more generally: the lack of a local scale. Although the Joint Declaration promised that Macau would maintain complete autonomy over its educational system after the handover, in fact Macau's schools—often contrasted to Hong Kong's—were "not . . . a unified, distinctive education system, [but rather] an uncoordinated collection of institutions based on models in Portugal, the PRC, Taiwan, and Hong Kong" (Bray 1992: 328).[30] There was not and never had been a law guaranteeing free, compulsory, universal education. The only schools under the control of the Macau government were the *escolas oficiais*, or "official schools" (官校), which in 1993 accommodated less than 7 percent of the total student population (So Chiu Fai 1994). Nearly 94 percent of

Macau's students attended private schools, run by religious institutions (most notably the Catholic church), individuals, or civic organizations such as neighborhood associations, lineage associations, or the Federation of Labor Unions. These schools had pedagogical, administrative, financial, and often political orientations toward places outside Macau: for example, one school run by the Anglican church was a branch of a Hong Kong institution, a school run by the Federation of Labor Unions imported history textbooks from mainland China, and a prestigious Catholic girls' school followed a curriculum used in Taiwan. Prior to 1995, these private schools had "absolute freedom to devise their own curricula, recruit teachers, determine the conditions of service and the size of classes" (F. H. Tang and Morrison 1998: 250): although they had to be licensed by the state, they were not subject to state regulations on tuition, hours of instruction, graduation requirements, student discipline, teachers' salaries or qualifications, or any other aspect of their operation. Most schools imported educational models, curricular plans, and textbooks from—and prepared students to take university entrance examinations in—Hong Kong, the PRC, Taiwan, and other countries abroad, none of which had a stake or interest in the history of Macau.

This situation mitigated the influence that any state-sponsored curriculum could have, which meant that the problem was one of content as well as form: not only were there no educational policies or standards that would unify Macau's schools, but there was also no "local" content in the curricula these schools used. Graduates of Macau schools told me they regularly learned more about the history, geography, politics, and economy of Hong Kong than of Macau. All the many studies on Macau's diverse curricula found an "almost complete absence of references to Macau—which means, in practical terms, that the children of Macau are being educated without reference to the land where they were born or where they live" (Rosa 1991: 33).[31] According to some, the lack of local content in the curriculum was "demotivating" for students, since they did not have the opportunity to learn about "the histories and other features of their own societies" (Bray and Tang 1994: 37). Although not everyone agreed with Wu Zhiliang that this lack of localness posed a serious threat to the future of Macau, many analysts agreed that it contributed directly to the generally poor quality of education in the city (F. H. Tang and Morrison 1998: 251; see also Bray and Hui 1991 and Bray and Tang 1994).

Indeed, for most people, the shamefully poor quality of education in Macau was a far more pressing problem than the possibility that Macau students would graduate without a strong sense of belonging to their hometown.[32] With no government subsidies and no mandated limits on class sizes, as rents soared and the population swelled in the 1980s, classes became increasingly crowded, averaging around 50 students. With no regulations governing conditions of service, teachers in many schools were underqualified, underpaid, and overworked.[33] With no state funding for the publication of a Macau-centered curriculum, the tiny local market was dependent on imported textbooks.[34] With no required curriculum and no school-leaving examination, what exactly was a high school diploma proof of? And with no state-run university, Macau's brightest students—including the likes of my friend Wai—went elsewhere to pursue higher education, often never to return.[35]

There was indeed something very petri-dish-like in this total lack of uniformity in Macau's education system. But in contrast to the fertile productivity of a petri dish, in this era of localization, most people viewed the proliferation of differences in a field as important as education as a negative. It was attributed directly to the Portuguese state's neglect of education and taken as evidence of the colonial nature of that state. The word "colonial" was used to describe Portuguese rule more regularly and unquestioningly in analyses of education policy than in virtually any other context I encountered.[36] Echoing the historiographical comments of my friend Francisco, sociologist Albert H. Yee argued that the lack of coordination of Macau's educational system prior to the 1990s was due to the fact that "the colonial bureaucracy has been overhauled each time a new governor is appointed . . . [and] few Portuguese civil servants have developed real commitment to Macau" (Yee 1990: 69–70). Jorge Rangel, the undersecretary for education and youth affairs during the last decade of Portuguese administration (and, as a Macanese, the highest-ranking government official who was not from Portugal), suggested that the poor quality of education was a direct result of the "demagogic approaches, futile promises and constant policy changes by people whose tenure of service is too short to assure the necessary continuity and who impose imported models and experiences without the involvement of local institutions" (Rangel 1991: 322).[37] In these reformers' eyes, the disjointedness of Macau's history and the disaggregate character of Macau's "system" were not coincidental. They were signs of the Portuguese state's historical inability or unwillingness to adopt the spatial dimensionality necessary for the proper governance of Macau. As such, they were signs of that state's illegitimacy.

But in 1988, just one year after the Joint Declaration set the date for Macau's transfer to Chinese administration, the Macau government instituted a series of reforms intended to create "an education system with Macau characteristics" (具有澳門特色的學制) (Lei and Zheng 1991: 96).[38] Ironically, of course, once administrators began to try to systematize Macau's educational institutions, they discovered that "Macau characteristics" included precisely the *laissez-faire* policies that had been identified as the problem in the first place. By the early 1990s, Macau's private schools had come to enjoy a "high degree of autonomy" that they were loath to relinquish. Ironically, too, some commentators protested that these attempts to remedy the colonial lack of attention to local education amounted to little more than a final desperate push to effect true colonialism— a view that seemed to be borne out by the government's attempt to include in the reforms a policy that would financially reward schools that required their students to study Portuguese (J. Lo 1999, S. Ieong 1994).[39] But a more common reaction was summed up by one school administrator I spoke with, a Macanese man who had little sympathy for the Portuguese administration but who saw the need for educational reform. For him the problem with the state's last-minute efforts to create a local scale had more to do with the uncertainty of the future than with the failings of the past. When I asked him why there had been so much resistance to the reforms, he told me that it was not because schools feared intrusion by the Portuguese: "We all know the Portuguese thinking about education. It is quite open. But what the attitude will be in the future, no one knows. Some schools are afraid that there will be more interference with things like curriculum or finances. And so some schools, especially some Catholic schools, say 'keep your hands off.' They very much like their freedom." The project of making Macau the scale for a unitary system of education was caught up in the temporal politics of sort-of sovereignty.

In 1991, the Macau government passed the city's first education reform law. The law was carefully designed to maintain the flexibility of the system and the individual autonomy of the schools while creating a degree of administrative cohesion and expanding the state's supervisory role. The other main goal of the reforms, according to the principal of one of the state-run Chinese-medium schools, was to "create a curriculum, especially in history and geography, that would be *of* Macau and *for* Macau people" (澳門自己嘅, 畀澳門人嘅). To this end, the government's Task Force for Curricular Reform compiled a series of junior high school curriculum guidelines, among which was the *History Guidelines*: a 40-page booklet in Chinese that outlined the topics to be covered in history courses each year for Forms 1–3, as well as the approximate number of classroom hours and the educational objectives for each topic. The guidelines called for two years of Chinese history in Forms 1 and 2 (corresponding to grades 7–8 in the American system), to be followed by one year of world history in Form 3. A unit on Macau history was to be taught after the completion of world history.

One of the history teachers who had been part of the curriculum guidelines committee took it upon himself to draft a document called "The Essentials of Macau History" (澳門歷史綱要) which could be distributed to teachers as a rough guide for the unit on Macau history. Although this 34-page document—which presented, in sentence-outline form, twelve key topics in Macau history, followed by fourteen pages of hand-drawn historical maps and tables of geographic, topographic, and demographic statistics—did not have the formal imprimatur of the Macau government and circulated among teachers in photocopy form, it was to my knowledge the first Chinese-language history of Macau to be developed by and for Macau's middle-school teachers. The head of the history department in the only school I found that planned to teach Macau history that year suggested that because the "Essentials" had been developed in accordance with—and by the very same people who were responsible for—the curriculum guidelines, there would be "no conflict in perspective" and therefore no need for it to be formally approved by the Education Service before it could be used in a government school.

Indeed, there was little "conflict in perspective" between the "Essentials" and the historical narratives I had read or seen presented in the tourist brochures or the scholarly works being churned out in rapid succession in both Chinese and Portuguese. Like these other narratives, the "Essentials of Macau History" suggested that modern Macau resulted not from an act of imperialism, piracy, or corruption but from a kind of mercantile magnetism that drew together the representatives of two parallel civilizations. It confirms Macau's ancient and inalienable Chineseness, citing archaeological evidence unearthed at Hac Sa Beach in Coloane, which proved that the neolithic "ancestors of the Chinese people" had been living and working in Macau at least 6,000 years ago; it references textual sources proving that Macau had been part of the Chinese polity at least since the Qin dynasty 2,000 ago. It traces the roots of Macau's future status as a special administrative region back to the earliest periods of its history as a city: with the arrival of the Portuguese, it suggests, Macau became a "special region" (特殊地區) whose administration was subject to "special management," and it was this specialness that enabled Macau's Golden Age of commercial and cultural exchange in the sixteenth and seventeenth centuries. The text also dismisses any notion that the early Portuguese traders had been imperialists like the British and Dutch, noting that "the late Ming government certainly did not fear the Portuguese merchants . . . [and] the Portuguese obeyed the Chinese administration, a situation that lasted for about 300 years." Although this vocabulary of Portuguese subservience would scarcely have fit with either the nationalist Portuguese histories emphasizing the military prowess and glories of the Portuguese seaborne empire (such as A. M. Pereira 1870 or J. M. Pereira 1995) or the Chinese Marxist narratives that glossed the entire history of Europeans in China as colonialist (such as Fei Chengkang 1988), it echoed almost verbatim other histories of Macau as bridge that were saturating the public sphere in Macau. This "united front" on Macau history dealt with, or evaded, the question of sovereignty well enough to serve the interests of everyone involved. Like the histories of education circulating so widely outside Macau's classrooms, it conjured Macau as a forerunner to the late twentieth-century condition of global commerce that was transforming China as well as the world, thus placing Macau at the center of world history while reinforcing the globalist claims of that particular interpretation of history and that particular view of the globe.

Localizing History

Thus by the late 1990s, when I started asking about how Macau history was taught in the schools, the government had spent the better part of a decade making concerted efforts to introduce local history courses at the secondary level. It had reformed the education system to allow for greater consistency and had devised a curriculum to introduce Macau students to "their own" history. It had also come up with an interpretation of that history that proved broadly acceptable. But still, as one retired government official told me in late 1997, "The majority of schools do not offer courses in Macau history; there is still much promotion work to be done." The state's efforts had not gone unnoticed; he, and others, acknowledged that a great deal of "promotion work" had already been done. Yet something about this promotion was not convincing. Said one teacher at a prestigious private school, "The government has been talking about it for several years now but hasn't managed to make any progress. As soon as they start asking the schools for their input, the whole project comes to a standstill." I asked Ana Paula, a Portuguese woman who taught history at a Catholic school with a large Macanese enrollment and who had just completed a master's degree in Macau history at the University of Macau, if she ever had the chance to teach Macau history in her classroom. "No, never!" she exclaimed; it was not part of the curriculum, and she imagined that if she ever tried to introduce it on her own, she would be summarily fired.

Given Macau's non-system of education and its lame-duck administration, this could have been simply the inertia of bureaucratic reform speaking: there was no real incentive, from the bottom or the top or anywhere in between, to effect change among a collection of institutions each of which had its own entrenched procedures. And the looming horizon of the handover certainly fostered a wait-and-see approach. But even within the government's Education and Youth Services Division (or DSEJ, for Direcção dos Serviços de Educação e Juventude), there was no consensus about how actively the state should promote this local history curriculum. One DSEJ official I spoke with in the Office of Research and Support for Educational Reforms did not object to introducing students to Macau history but did object strenuously to the Macau Portuguese government's emphasis on the need to do so in order to create a "unique Macau identity." As he said, "We are Chinese. Macau is a part of China—the same way that, for example, the Algarve is part of Portugal, or that California is part of the United States. Are there classes about the history of the Algarve, or of California? Perhaps there are a few classes that relate these regions to the history of the nation as a whole, but even so, these courses are hardly a priority. This is how I explain it to people." Another DSEJ employee I interviewed, a young Macau Chinese man, believed the government was doing the right thing in actively advocating local history instruction, although he thought the particular narrative they were promoting smacked of colonial whitewashing. And a third, a Portuguese man who had spent years researching various aspects of the history of Macau, was an enthusiastic supporter of the initiative and made sure I left his office with as many books as I could carry (many of which were written, edited, or published by him or his department) on Macau history and education.

In many ways, the problems presented by teaching local history in Macau resembled the situation in Taiwan and Hong Kong.[40] Each of these places grappled with similar questions posed by its colonial history and its troubled relationship to the Chinese nation. Were Taiwan, Hong Kong, and Macau irrelevant when compared to the grand sweep of Chinese imperial and national history, or were they worthy loci of history and identification? If each of these localities derived its distinctiveness from its colonial history, could local students be taught to take pride in their locality without celebrating colonialism? Would too much emphasis on local identity detract from students' identification with the Chinese nation? In other words, was there only one (national) way to be Chinese, and was that way best learned in the classroom rather than in the homes and on the streets of the city?

But Macau differed from Hong Kong and Taiwan in two important respects. First, according to the educators I spoke with, Macau's market was too small to make the publication of textbooks a profitable venture; this made Macau marginal not just to the Chinese nation but also to the capitalist system of which it was supposed to be a product. Second, as we have seen, Macau could lay claim to a "glorious" past that predated the domination of the world by Europe and the nation-state form, and this provided fodder for a different and potentially far more troubling narrative about the nation's relationship to local and global scales.

When I began interviewing history teachers about the prospects of introducing local history into the curriculum, the problems caused by these tensions between competing scale-making projects became clear. In answering my questions about why the history of Macau was not taught at the secondary level, several teachers presented me with accounts of the history of Macau: why it was that the very source of Macau's uniqueness—the history of Portuguese administration—made the teaching of that history impossible or undesirable or both. Although the ideological thorns presented by this history had more or less been plucked clean by the narrative presented in the "Essentials," the practical legacies of Portugal's *laissez-faire* policies as well as the uncertain trajectories of transition meant that the significance of local history had to be measured not in its own right but on national, regional, and transnational scales—a situation that made local history simultaneously too irrelevant and too important to be taught in Macau's classrooms.

Escola Pui Ching (培正中學)

Pui Ching was the school that Wai and I had been looking at from the east-facing windows of my apartment. The school's administration was housed in a historical landmark building—a two-story mansion built in the late nineteenth century by Lou Kau 盧九, a wealthy merchant and scholar and friend of Sun Yat-sen—now painted a pastel green with white trim and sitting at an odd angle to the rectangular street grid that had grown up around it. Classrooms were located in a series of newer buildings, tall, functional, and concrete, that formed a kind of wall around the paved central courtyard. Behind the school, Mr. Lou's garden had been turned into a public park (called Lou Lim Ieoc Garden, after Lou's son who inherited the property in 1906); in front, one of the city's main east–west thoroughfares, now a perennially congested commercial district, connected Guia Hill to the Inner Harbor. On hot, sunny mornings I often stood out on my balcony watching uniformed children arranged in symmetrical lines in the shade of the classroom buildings, doing calisthenics in time to the eight-beat count intoned by the gym teacher through a loudspeaker powerfully enough to reach my ears above the jagged blare of rush hour traffic: "Yat! Yi! Saam! Sei! . . ." In the afternoons, dozens of Filipina domestic workers would gather outside the school gates ten minutes before classes let out, snatching a few moments to chat with their friends before picking up their charges. On most evenings, boys played basketball in the courtyard until the gates closed around ten o'clock.

Pui Ching had a reputation as one of the most prestigious, most competitive, and most expensive schools in Macau. Funded by the Baptist church, Macau's Pui Ching was affiliated with schools of the same name in Hong Kong and Guangzhou and followed a curriculum imported from Hong Kong.[41] It also had a reputation of having found creative ways to get students to learn about Macau history. I was told that if anyone could help me with my inquiries, it would be Wong Chao Son 黃就順 and Chan Jileung 陳子良, the geography and history teachers at Pui Ching, who were known for their dedication to teaching and writing about Macau's past.

Both these teachers told me, in separate interviews, that they believed the study of local history was desirable and important for Macau people of any age, since it would provide them with a more grounded sense of self and community and help them understand Macau's "system" and its new status as a special administrative region. But, they ruefully insisted, it could not be introduced in the classroom. Mr. Chan, the history teacher, gave two practical reasons. The first was that the students were already overworked; there was simply not enough time in the day to cover any more material. Pui Ching prided itself on the fact that over 90 percent of its graduates went on to university, but because there was only one university in Macau (which had been established only in the 1980s and was still outgrowing its reputation as a haven for the children of wealthy Hong Kongers unable to get into universities anywhere else), Mr. Chan's main task was to prepare students for university examinations abroad, none of which included questions on Macau history. This reason was given by all the teachers and administrators I interviewed and was confirmed by the weight of the backpacks that children lugged back and forth to school each day on the bus: there were many, many more important things to study. Knowledge of local history may have been valuable on a personal and civic level in Macau, but measured on a transnational scale of educational success and prestige, such knowledge was not just irrelevant, it was counterproductive: every classroom moment spent on Macau history threatened to shave points off students' exam scores. Their future and the school's would suffer.

The second reason Mr. Chan gave, however, pointed to quite the opposite conclusion: Macau history was not taught because it was too important. This was because the Portuguese and the Chinese "have always had different interpretations" of Macau history. There was far too much at stake in the interpretation of Macau's past, and far too little consensus on what that interpretation should be, for a textbook history to be written, much less used to teach young, impressionable minds. Mr. Chan knew whereof he spoke, since he was the author of the "Essentials of Macau History." Although the "Essentials" was little more than a rough and incomplete set of notes, he said he had no intention of expanding it for publication as a full textbook. "Whatever you write, someone is going to get angry. All that work and you just end up getting yourself into trouble," he said with a laugh. His colleague, the geography teacher Mr. Wong, agreed that one of the main obstacles to teaching local history was the lack of a textbook, and that this lack was due primarily to ideo-logical differences in the interpretation of Macau history: had the Ming emperor given Macau to the Portuguese in gratitude for their help in defeating the pirates that plagued the coastline, as the Portuguese had long maintained? Or had the marauding Portuguese bribed and bullied local officials into letting them stay, as the Chi-nese had it? Had the 1887 Treaty of Friendship and Commerce been a valid document legally granting Portugal sovereign rights over Macau, or had it been an "unequal treaty" that simply confirmed Portugal's imperialist intentions? And if they couldn't reach a consensus on these basic facts, how could they produce an entire curriculum?

Although it seemed to me that Mr. Chan's "Essentials of Macau History" had negotiated a way through this impasse, these two teachers clearly felt that longstanding ideological differences in the interpretation of Macau history presented an insurmountable obsta-cle to teaching it in Pui Ching classrooms, before or after the hand-over. There were no guarantees, after all, that the "united front" on Macau history would remain united after 1999. Nor, according to Mr. Chan, was teaching the controversy itself an option in middle school. It was appropriate in the continuing education courses he taught for adults, for example, and in that context he often did pre-sent such controversies to the class for debate. "But at the age of 15 or 16," he cautioned, "students' powers of judgment are not fully de-veloped; they need the guidance of the teacher." On one hand, then, measured on the transnational scale of university entrance examina-tions, local history was too trivial to merit class time. On the other hand, measured on nationalist scales in which local history was called on to justify competing sovereign claims, it was far too rele-vant to be left in the hands of students too immature to grasp the nuance and complexity of historical meaning-making. According to the Pui Ching teachers, at least, these "Macau realities"—that the Portuguese government had never bothered to establish a university in Macau, and that the ideological significance of its rule was open to question in ways that could, if misunderstood, threaten the basis for the PRC's claim to sovereignty over Macau—made the classroom instruction of Macau history doubly impossible.

Escola Secundária Luso-Chinesa
Luís Gonzaga Gomes (澳門高美士中葡中學)

Mr. Chan told me that if I was really interested in pursuing this question, I should inquire at the Escola Secundária Luso-Chinesa Luís Gonzaga Gomes (ESLC), where this year they were planning to teach Macau history as part of the normal curriculum for the first time.[42] The ESLC, established by the Macau government in 1985, was part of a small group of government schools whose language of instruction was Cantonese but which maintained an "emphasis" on Portuguese language and culture. This emphasis boiled down to six hours a week of compulsory Portuguese-language classes, which distinguished the curriculum of the ESLC from that of most private schools in which the compulsory foreign language was English, and Portuguese, if offered at all, was available as an elective for two or three hours per week. The other key difference was that the ESLC was, as a state-run school, free of charge. It tended therefore to draw students from Macau's lower socioeconomic classes, which meant it had a much higher percentage of "new immigrant" students than did private schools. It also had a reputation for underpaid and overworked teachers, scant resources, and relatively low college entrance rates (the principal told me that about 50 percent of graduates went on to some form of tertiary education).

The school was housed in a long, low, concrete building, also painted a light pastel green, and distinguished by the vaguely art-deco elements incorporated into its façade. It sat at the base of Guia Hill, facing west across a narrow, tree-lined, busy one-way street from Tap Seac Field (塔石球場), one of the city's main public outdoor soccer pitches. The young principal, Mr. Leung, told me that even in the state-run ESLC, they had until recently used textbooks and curricular plans imported from Hong Kong, because the Macau market was too small to justify the publication of a local curriculum. The ESLC, however, was the pilot school for many of the government's curricular reforms, which was why it had been chosen to teach the month-long unit on Macau history at the end of the World History course in Form 3, as per the curriculum guidelines.

He introduced me to Teacher Yu, the head of the history department, and left us to talk about the specifics.

Teacher Yu was a small, thin, fiftyish woman with short, carefully curled hair and large round eyeglasses, one of six history teachers in a school with nearly a thousand students. She was not particularly enthusiastic about teaching Macau history in her classes. Not only would it not help students on their college entrance or civil service exams, she said, it was also irrelevant to the goals of education in general, which were, as she put it, "to prepare young people to take up an active role in society." Like the Pui Ching teachers, she felt there was much more important material that needed to be covered. They were already falling behind in world history. She certainly would not be able to devote the entire last month of school to the unit on Macau; she would have to squeeze the Macau material into "whatever time we have left."

But to a greater extent than the Pui Ching teachers, the problem for Teacher Yu lay in how to define the subject of that history. On one hand, she clearly felt that "local" meant Chinese. This became apparent when it came to the question of textbooks. She mentioned that although they would be using the "Essentials of Macau History" outline, the teachers themselves would have a lot of work to do, browsing through old newspapers, books, and journals, clipping articles to compile readers and audiovisual materials to use in class. I had managed to obtain an old Portuguese-language Macau history textbook, already out of print, that had been published by the government in the mid-1980s, and asked if a translation of this couldn't serve as a basis for the course at ESLC. No, she replied; she knew of the book and believed it had been used at the Liceu; but the Liceu's curriculum, she said, "is not designed for local people . . . [it] is Portuguese-style, so they study more about Europe and Portuguese history." In contrast to the Pui Ching teachers, for whom the greatest problem was the debates over how to interpret the sovereignty question, for Ms. Yu the problem was that the Portuguese, although they were in Macau, were not of Macau; a history of Macau written by Portuguese people would be inappropriate because it was not local enough. But when I asked her if the Macau history unit would include anything about the history of the Macanese community, she said no. Despite the fact that most Macanese met almost any conceivable biographical or geographical criterion for being "of Macau," for Teacher Yu their questionable Chineseness put them outside the scope of the local.

But in that case, I wondered aloud, why was Macau history taught in Form 3, after World History, rather than in Forms 1 or 2, as part of Chinese history? Teacher Yu replied that it wouldn't be appropriate to teach it earlier, "because it's about world history, it's not about Chinese history. We teach Chinese history in Forms 1 and 2, but Macau history has always been categorized as part of world history. That's how it's arranged (係咁嘅編法)." To be sure, this was how it was arranged in the curriculum guidelines, in which "world history" referred essentially to "Western Civ," as well as some material on ancient India, the spread of Buddhism, and the Meiji Restoration in Japan. That Teacher Yu saw no contradiction between studying local history (defined as local by virtue of its Chineseness) as part of world history (defined as the history of that which is not Chinese) seemed to suggest the effectiveness of the bridge metaphor. Macau history provided a bridge between China and the West: the local was a way of articulating national and global scales.

This is not how Teacher Yu saw it, however. For her, the localness of Macau history was what made it irrelevant. Macau history "is a local subject (屬於一個本地嘅教材), really just a local thing," she told me. "We'll just introduce a little bit of material on Macau for the students to become acquainted with" (澳門啲資料只不過係介紹畀佢哋認識架嘛). When I asked her what she thought students would get out of studying this little bit of material, she said,

They will certainly be interested in it and feel close to it (對佢哋有親切感), since it is about Macau and they live in Macau, and they can go visit the sites they read about. It will be a tangible history, something that has a direct connection to their lives. Not like American history. American history has no relation to them whatsoever, but they still have to learn it.

For Teacher Yu, it was not, as the government hoped, that learning local history would provide students with the sense of belonging they lacked and which both they and the city would need in order to prosper; rather, the sense of belonging they already had would give them an interest in learning a few historical facts about their surroundings. In contrast to Mr. Chan's classroom, where local history signified too much, it seemed that at the ESLC, it had been at least rhetorically emptied of significance before being taught. It had the potential to challenge neither the categories through which modern history was taught nor the Chineseness of Macau people. "The local" was an afterthought, a curiosity, a good excuse for a field trip.

Liceu Nacional

The only person I encountered who vowed that Macau history was an unabashedly colonialist project that would never be taught in his classrooms was the principal of the Liceu Nacional, the only state-run Portuguese-language secondary school in town. This was where the sons and daughters of Macau's Portuguese civil servants were educated, along with those Macanese and Chinese students who hoped to pursue a university education in Portugal or who for other reasons wanted a Portuguese education.[43] As well as following the national curriculum used in Portugal, the Liceu, like such institutions elsewhere, reflected the conditions of advantage enjoyed by the Portuguese in Macau: housed in a sprawling downtown complex recently designed by one of Portugal's top architects, it had some of the best facilities of any school in town (it was the only school I knew of that had its own swimming pool) and was among the most expensive to maintain; the faculty received disproportionately high salaries and good benefits, including housing subsidies and annual trips back to Portugal; class sizes were smaller than average, and it had a high rate of graduates continuing on to university, mostly in Portugal or elsewhere in Europe.

But this was all about to change when I spoke with Jacques and Rogélia, the principal and vice-principal of the Liceu, in June 1998. Because Macau would no longer be under Portuguese administration, the Liceu Nacional would be privatized. In a few weeks it would close its doors for good, and in the fall its students and a carefully selected group of teachers would begin classes at a new school called the Escola Portuguesa, which, although funded partially by the Portuguese government, would collect tuition and otherwise function as a private school.[44] It would move to a smaller, more economical building, and the Liceu building would become the new central campus of the Macau Polytechnic Institute. The school's administration would be "localized": Jacques and Rogélia would return to Portugal, and the new principal would be Macanese. The process of privatization had been at the center of a controversy in the Macanese community the previous year, caused partly by the decision, made in Portugal, to move the only Portuguese-language secondary school in Macau to a building that could accommodate less than half the projected number of students who would need it.[45] But the decision was final, and the move was scheduled to begin as soon as possible after the end of exams. Meanwhile, in the still-cluttered offices of the outgoing administration, even though not a single item had been packed, even though everyone's time and energy were completely occupied with the usual year-end rush of exams and activities—and even though no one yet knew who would be the new principal, which teachers would be chosen to stay on in the fall, or whether the renovated building would even be ready in time for the start of classes ten weeks hence—I felt a breathless sense of anticipation that echoed and intensified the handover jitters outside.

I had read that, although the Liceu offered no courses on Macau history, in the early 1990s some of the history teachers had taken it upon themselves to introduce some elements of local history into their classes (J. Tan 1993). But the principal—a Portuguese man in early middle age who had been in Macau for just two years, whom everyone called Dr. Jacques—cut me off with an emphatic "no" almost before I could finish asking him if Macau history was taught at the Liceu. He, too, emphasized that there was not enough time in the already packed curriculum. The Liceu, he reminded me, was not a special case: just like any other school in Macau, it had to prepare its students for university studies abroad.

By way of explaining my first question, I mentioned that I had read this in a comparison of the history curricula in Macau and Hong Kong, where local history had been rather successfully introduced into the curriculum in the late 1980s, though not without controversy (J. Tan 1993; see also Vickers 2003). But once again Jacques interrupted, cautioning me not to make easy comparisons between the two cities. As he began to explain the folly of such comparisons, I soon realized he was telling me a comparative history of Sino-European relations and the by-now familiar story of Portuguese colonialism:

Hong Kong was a colony: the British said to the Chinese, "Despite what you say, this is ours and we will fight for it." By contrast, the Portuguese were tolerated because we helped the Chinese. There were pirates all around in these waters, they were a big problem all up and down the coast, and the Chinese had no navy, no ships. So when the Portuguese came with their big ships and artillery and drove the pirates out, the Chinese said, "You can stay." We were like partners. We were tolerated because our presence was good for the people in Macau. The same happened in Coloane many years later, there were pirates harassing the residents, and the Portuguese drove them out. And the same in São João Island, not far from here—you know, where St. Francis Xavier died?—the Portuguese had a settlement there for quite some time. The reason they left São João was that there was no more money to pay the guards. There was a garrison there, and a settlement and some guards guarding the place. But then Macau's Golden Age ended, and the population went down, there was no more money in the bank to pay the guards to stay there, so they all moved back to Macau. There was no money!—you see. That was the end of that settlement! [His tone here is ironic, wondering how pathetic, impoverished Portugal could ever have been mistaken for a colonial power.] The English created a colony in Hong Kong; but the Portuguese had no such pretensions in Macau.[46]

To a greater extent than anyone else I talked to, Dr. Jacques believed that local history meant colonial history and that any attempt to teach it in school would be a thoroughly ideological project, a colonization of consciousness. The British in Hong Kong had been colonizers, and that was why they had ensured that Hong Kong history was taught in schools. The absence of Macau history from Macau's schools was proof that the Portuguese had not been real colonialists. Similarly, because the British presence had been a colonial one, they had taught Hong Kong people to have a strong sense of identity as Hong Kongers, defined in clear opposition to mainland Chinese. When I mentioned that my interest in local history instruction was part of a larger project about the politics of cultural identity in transition-era Macau, Dr. Jacques responded forcefully: "If there is such a thing as a 'Macau citizen,' he has not been made in the schools." If a local identity could only be a colonial identity, the lack of such in Macau was evidence of the moral superiority of Portuguese colonialism, which Dr. Jacques said was "the result of our *brandos costumes*, our 'soft' customs." He reiterated this point more than once during the course of our hour-long conversation: "If there was cultural mixing in Macau, it was not the schools that produced it. It was the process of living together. There was no premeditation about producing a 'Macau citizen.'" Many people in Macau may well have a sort of "Macau consciousness," he allowed, in the sense that "they like this kind of living and feel comfortable here." But he stressed that this was something that had grown "naturally" from the experiences of daily life, the ties of blood and affect, rather than having been imposed forcibly and artificially by the state; and thus it was the opposite of colonial. Indeed, he suggested, far from being colonial policy, the Portuguese tendency toward mixing had been a resourceful strategy of adaptation on the part of individual Portuguese all over the world: "There are four million Portuguese living outside Portugal. How do they survive, how do they live for so long in so many places? It is because they have a tradition of mixing, a mingling philosophy." For Dr. Jacques, measured on Portuguese national/imperial scales in which Portuguese imperialism signified as morally superior to any other because it had been a "natural" process, teaching Macau history formally in the classroom was a denaturing act; it signified so powerfully as a colonial practice that the question could not even be broached.

Escola Portuguesa de Macau

But it was my interview with a senior administrator of the newly established Escola Portuguesa, a Macanese educator who had been born and raised in Macau and was trilingual in Cantonese, Portuguese, and English, that was perhaps the most revealing of what was at stake in teaching local history. In September 1998, the Liceu indeed became the Escola Portuguesa and moved from its original site to the building built for the Escola Comercial (a Portuguese-language middle school, established in 1878, by and for the Macanese community), which in turn ceased operation. I had heard that this localized new school, which would be administered and attended primarily by members of the Macanese community, would put a greater emphasis on teaching Macau history. A nodding acquaintance of mine was on the administrative staff and graciously granted me an interview on a busy winter afternoon.[47] I knew my interviewee to be a dedicated and thoughtful educator, and I had been looking forward to the interview, expecting a lively discussion of the politics of education, history, and localization and the significance and problems of teaching Macau history to students like these. I quote at length from the notes I wrote up after the interview.

I ask what some of the challenges of privatization had been. For example, I say, I remember last year when the decision was made to locate the school here, there was some controversy. How has that controversy played itself out, has it been resolved satisfactorily? What other issues have come up during the privatization process? Z replies that the "controversy" was simply that some people were saying that the Escola Comercial building would not be big enough to accommodate the needs of the Portuguese-speaking community. The decision was made in Portugal to locate the Escola Portuguesa in the old Escola Comercial building, rather than allowing it to continue in the Liceu building, which was very expensive to maintain; the number of students was projected to be 600. People were just concerned that this building could not accommodate 600 students, that was all. [I do not remember the controversy this way. I remember it being about language, belonging, and community, about faith in the future. About the Macanese feeling abandoned, sold down the river. I do not tell Z this.]

I ask, so, back to the question of Macau history. I've heard a lot of people talking about it, but when I mentioned it just now you looked rather . . . skeptical. We both laugh, and, looking off to the right toward the giant whiteboard on the wall, Z says with a small sigh, "I don't know. . . ." Long pause. I believe Z is thinking about how to respond, perhaps deciding how candid to be, so I don't speak. After ten seconds or so, Z looks back at me and asks, in a tone that is not hostile but simply matter-of-fact, "So what do you want to ask me?" My heart sinks as if I've failed a test. I say that I have heard many people talking about the need for a sense of belonging, or identity, in Macau, and how these people say that teaching Macau history is a good way to give kids this sense of belonging, because now many Macau kids know more about Hong Kong than they do about Macau. And I'd just like to know, unofficially now, what Z, as a person and not as an official of any institution, thinks about this topic. "Off the record?" Z laughs. "Off the record," I say, and put down the pen in my hand.

But it didn't matter that I had put down my pen and promised to keep our conversation off the record. It didn't matter that I was asking for a personal opinion, or that I had promised to disguise Z's identity, for Z said nothing substantial about the possibility of teaching Macau history in the future, either in the Escola Portuguesa or in any of Macau's schools. I pushed Z to say more, I asked the question in a different way, I asked a different question; but Z's resistance to discussing the issue was almost physically palpable, and Z brought the interview to an end shortly thereafter. Walking home, I cursed my inability to gain Z's trust and wrote off the interview as a waste of time. In writing it up, however, I realized that perhaps there was something to be learned from Z's refusal to speak and from the attempt to downplay everything, to empty everything—even controversies—of controversy. Perhaps, given the series of translocal imperatives that combined to create a radical uncertainty about the future status of the "local" (Would Lisbon continue to fund the school indefinitely, allowing Portuguese-speaking families to remain in Macau? Would the Macanese still be welcome in Macau after the handover? Would the incorporation of Macau into the PRC require a repudiation of the past and of everything Portuguese?), Z found it wisest to avoid the whole subject of formalized scale-making projects that promised to catapult "the local" to a position of paramount importance, but only for a moment. Perhaps, for Z, the "local" was simply a position so dangerous that it had to be formally erased in order to survive.

Taken together, the comments of these educators map out a number of potential significatory trajectories of the local through time and space. That the very idea of teaching local history would be so controversial suggests the volatility of the local in a place and time at the edges of sovereignty, in which conceptions of the local, the national, the global, and their interrelationships were open to contestation. In dissecting so painstakingly their comments, I do not mean to dismiss their practical reasons for not including Macau history in the curriculum: there was no time, no textbook, and no real imperative to teach it. Yet far from arguing simply that local history was too unimportant to be included in the curriculum, these teachers also suggested that the power of history as a scale-making practice made it a dangerous thing to experiment with. The same uncertainties of scale raised by the one country, two systems formula—questions about the future relationship of "locals" and the Chinese nation-state—that were making the localization of Macau's bureaucracy such a sensitive process were amplified in the realm of local history instruction. The delicate politics of nationalizing Macau meant that only when (as in the ESLC) the significance of Macau history could be contained, its relevance to the contemporary world diminished—only when local history could be presented as a set of curious facts about our surroundings, rather than constitutive of who we are—could it be taught.

Yet it was precisely this diminution that ensured the project would fail. In none of the schools was "Macau" firmly established as a frame of reference for either the classroom study of history or the collective identification of students. This was not simply a problem of local resistance to the ideological agenda of a lame-duck colonial government. It failed in part because of the inability to link up with other, more hegemonic ways of imagining globality, locality, and the relationship between them. Macau weighed next to nothing on scales that measured relevance in terms of the size of consumer markets, Taiwanese university entrance examination questions, or perceptions of what it took to be a productive member of a globalizing society. It failed also because of who was making the scale, when, and where. From the perspective of someone like Z, who planned to stay in Macau after the departure of the Portuguese, it must have seemed downright irresponsible for that state to try so hard to bring into being a "local" scale precisely at the moment when it lost any claim to or control over its future trajectory. Brought into existence at the last possible moment before the handover, by a state that had by now lost any claim to legitimacy, the "local" that the Macau Portuguese state attempted to promote as the proper subject of history and collective subjectivity seemed flimsy and transparent. It lacked opacity and weight, the gravitational pull of other scale-making projects that appear timeless and authorless: spatializing projects framed in terms of nations, markets, or civilizations.

Conclusion

What becomes clear from this analysis is that the transition to Chinese sovereignty made the task of envisioning Macau to see how it might succeed as a social frame for educational policies—as well as for history, for collective subjectivity, and for the ideological and practical purposes of one country, two systems—a difficult and dangerous one. These difficulties stemmed not just from the immediate practical politics of the transfer of sovereignty but from the precarious balance among multiple scale-making projects that overlapped in Macau and the contradictions in the way that the past was thought to matter to the future. The *laissez-faire* policies that had characterized Portuguese rule in Macau were hailed as that which made Macau unique and at the same time identified as that which was most in need of reform. A stronger focus on the local would remedy the problems caused by colonial neglect in the past but would also further marginalize Macau from the national, regional, and global networks so important to its future. The nationalist framework in which the handover was celebrated as the end of imperialism and a triumph of Chinese national unity sat uncomfortably with the civilizational framework in which Macau's cosmopolitan role as a historical "bridge" between East and West was acclaimed as its defining characteristic. The story of the illustrious career of education in early modern Macau was used to stoke the fires of both Chinese and Portuguese nationalism, but the story of its decline suggested that nationalism was Macau's problem rather than its savior. Attempts at "localization," then, in the school curriculum as elsewhere simply underlined the fact that Macau was a meeting place for several contradictory visions of what localness entailed: visions that were rooted in and given substance by their articulations to various other scale-making projects and civilizational dreams.

FIVE

Culture in Ruins

It is not down in any map; true places never are.

—Herman Melville, *Moby-Dick*

"We used to play soccer right there in the middle of Avenida Horta e Costa, do you believe it?" Mr. Lei asked me and his grown son and a number of their colleagues, as we each took up our bowls of sweet almond soup from the lazy Susan at the center of the large round restaurant table. A mutual acquaintance had suggested that I interview Mr. Lei, who was a prominent and politically active businessman; we had spent a congenial though not particularly enlightening (for either of us, I would wager) lunch hour discussing in very broad terms Macau and the transition, until, in the process of offering me a ride home, he discovered that I lived on the street where he had grown up. Suddenly Mr. Lei got specific. "It was a great place to play soccer—the street was nice and wide and there were almost no cars." He launched into a detailed description of what the neighborhood had been like in the early 1950s, when the broad avenue (which in the late 1990s was one of the two most traffic-clogged thoroughfares in the city) had echoed with the shouts of footballers rather than the honking blare of motor traffic, and when rows of two-story villas (now replaced by massive apartment blocks fronted by fast-food chains, drugstores, supermarkets, and clothing retailers), backed up against each other along narrow alleyways, had meant intimacy rather than overcrowding and had provided a child with plenty of playmates and places to play. It was a simple story, even banal, but in his tone there was an enthusiasm that had not animated our

176

earlier conversation, and it held me rapt as I tried to imagine the city I knew transformed in his memory.

By this time—it was late 1998—this kind of encounter was familiar to me. The overdetermined politics of transition were omnipresent, overshadowing every aspect of public life in Macau. Newspapers were running articles about contentious Joint Liaison Group negotiations, the slow pace of localization, and the grim implications of the crime wave. Radio call-in shows were getting calls from angry taxpayers wondering why the Portuguese were allowed to use Macau funds to pay for the pensions of civil servants retiring to Portugal. Schools had begun teaching children Mandarin Chinese and the principles behind the Basic Law. But when the people I spoke with were not speculating, fretting, or enthusing about the effects of the impending handover—or decrying the triads' effect on the economy—they often talked of the more open-ended process of urban change. During the two years of my fieldwork, at some point virtually every person I spoke with who had lived in or regularly visited Macau for more than a few years initiated a conversation about what the city was like "when I first came here" or "when I was a child," and how different it was now. Those who had little to say to me about the politics of the handover could usually, with little prompting, speak at length about the rapid and total transformation of the urban landscape. This transformation—in 1975, there were only seven buildings in the city taller than seven stories, whereas by 1995, the city was a maze of thirty-story high-rises—was something everyone could see happening around them. Although the change did not affect everyone equally, it did affect everyone, in ways that were often more tangible than the administrative, fiscal, and legal adjustments that attended the transition to Chinese administration.

The scale and rapidity of this change was by no means unique to Macau. Throughout the 1990s, cities, towns, and villages all over China, especially in the neighboring Pearl River Delta region, were experiencing similar or even more spectacular rates of urbanization and growth. In these places, such change could be an important locus for debates about the desirability and direction of development, the problems engendered by business-state clientelism, and the relationship of China's past to its future (L. Zhang 2006, O'Donnell

2001). But in Macau, because the capital financing the construction boom came largely from the unauthorized investment of state funds from mainland China, and because the Portuguese government was pouring millions of dollars into a variety of projects that encouraged residents to identify with Macau as a place defined in contrast to mainland China, the two processes fundamentally altering their social environment—the transfer of sovereignty and the transformation of the landscape—and how people spoke about them were hardly unrelated. Thinking about place and its transformation in transition-era Macau reveals how notions and practices of sovereignty inform even those aspects of social life that seem most distant from politics, such as the lived experience of one's physical environment. It provides an excellent way to rethink the relationship of the politics of place, sovereignty, and Chineseness.

Place, Sovereignty, Chineseness

Arturo Escobar, writing about the recent surge in anthropological studies of place and politics, defines a sense of place as the "experience of a particular location with some measure of groundedness (however, unstable), sense of boundaries (however, permeable), and connection to everyday life, even if its identity is constructed, traversed by power, and never fixed" (Escobar 2001: 140). In the field of Chinese studies, the question of place is more often approached in a form considered particularly Chinese: that of "native place," or the profound attachment to one's ancestral home. The importance of the sense of belonging or attachment to, or nostalgia for, one's ancestral home is evident in Chinese poetry and artwork; in the desires of Chinese sojourners in southeast Asia or the Americas to return to their homes to marry, retire, die, or be buried; in the facts that one of the first questions you might ask in getting to know a person is "Where are you from?" and that an instant bond often arises between two people who discover they are from the same place; and in the fact that, in the PRC, one's "place of origin" (籍貫), as distinct from place of birth or place of residence, is encoded on one's national identification card.[1] Native place often signifies in dialect and diet, accent and affect; it is said to reveal itself in congenital proclivities for business acumen, political savvy, violence, clannishness, and physical beauty.[2] It does reveal itself, and reproduce itself, in so-cial networks that reserve certain sectors of business in certain cities for people from particular regions (cf. Honig 1992, Goodman 1995a, Rowe 1984, and L. Zhang 2001).

In the scholarship on Chineseness, this attachment to place is of-ten considered a cultural phenomenon: one that is sometimes co-opted for political purposes but essentially exists outside of politics. Rootedness in the soil and the yearning for home are often treated, as they are often experienced, as ancient, essential, irreducible parts of what it means to be Chinese.[3] As anthropologist Fei Xiaotong (1991: 77) has written, the concept of *diyuan* 地緣, or "place ties," is an extension of *xueyuan* 血緣, or "blood ties"; thus, he argues, in traditional Chinese society, place bonds were simply "the spatial projection of the blood connection." In this understanding, political regimes may come and go, but the attachment to place and its social and cultural entailments are self-evident, eternal, and indissoluble. In short, native place implies not simply a grounded experience of a particular location but a lasting attachment—so lasting that it holds power even for those who have never set foot on the soil of their an-cestral home—to a particular location that carries with it a whole set of social, behavioral, even moral assumptions and imperatives.

This way of understanding the role of place in articulations of Chineseness does indeed demonstrate the "centrality of native place identity in Chinese conceptions of self and community" (Ho-nig 1992: 7); it has allowed historians and anthropologists to gain a more subtle understanding of the shifting lines of cohesion and divi-sion within Chinese society and of how the rhetoric and politics of nationalist movements have, at different historical moments, co-opted, bolstered, or been thwarted by native place ties and networks (Duara 1995, Goodman 1995b, Ho 1966, Honig 1992, S. Jones 1974). But the assumption that native place is simply a spatialized expression of other kinds of social bonds has meant that the ques-tion of how places become meaningful as *places*, in Escobar's sense, has gone largely unexamined. Rarely have studies of native place examined how the politics of sovereignty can shape affective attachments—or the lack thereof—to particular places, native or otherwise.

In fact, place and place-making have been key parts of the CCP's practice of sovereignty almost from its inception. Positioning itself as the party that led the Chinese people in their successful struggle to throw off the yoke of Western imperialism, the CCP made its own efforts to "place" colonialism (in treaty port cities, for example)[4] as well as revolution (the sanctification of Yan'an as the cradle of the revolution, the creation of Tian'anmen Square as icon and embodiment of the "dictatorship of the proletariat," the renaming of streets such that every city in China now has a "Liberation Road"). More recently, as the CCP has changed its legitimizing rhetoric to emphasize its role as the party that ushered China into a new era of modernity and ethnic nationalism, it has worked to emplace such apparently ungrounded concepts as "development" (in the SEZs that have transformed China's coasts) and "tradition" (in the restoration of certain sanctioned heritage sites and the iconography of the Yellow River and the Great Wall).[5] During more than two decades of reform and "opening up," millions of people both within and across Chinese borders have been displaced in the name of repositioning the Chinese state vis-à-vis international capital; ironically, although this process has transplanted populations and transfigured landscapes, little work has examined how these changes have altered, or been expressed through, changing senses of place.[6]

Anthropological scholarship on the politics of place-making outside China has had more to say about the politics of sovereignty and place. Indeed, a resurgence in the anthropological study of place over the past decade has been inspired by and interested in precisely the question of sovereignty and change. The deterritorialization of peoples and nations; the increasing porousness of national boundaries; the apparent plowing under of "local" lifeways by the bulldozer of globalization; the reconfiguration of physical and virtual space by new and more widely available technologies; and the new forms of "flexible sovereignty" (Ong 1999) through which states regulate the populations and territories at least nominally under their control: these are just a few of the phenomena that anthropologists and geographers argue have made the study of place so compelling in recent years. Ironically, however, to my mind, few of these approaches dig deeply enough into this relationship between place-making and sovereignty. Although concerned with power, these studies often make assumptions about how power works; although concerned with change, they often take for granted the meaning and implications of that change.

On one hand, they suggest, implicitly or explicitly, that the politics of place is a politics of sovereignty—that is, it is an attempt to create and maintain control over both the territory a group occupies and the narrative about how that group came to occupy it. This is not surprising, given that many such studies focus on polarized political situations in which the assertion of a sense of emplacement is necessarily articulated in terms of a sovereign claim.[7] But rarely do such studies examine how more mundane place-making practices may challenge the terms of this politics and the either-or assumptions about the meaning and practice of sovereignty. An ethnographic approach to how the work of place-making engages with and disengages from larger articulations of power will allow a more nuanced understanding of the politics of place.

On the other hand, although insistent that places are "always being made, always in process and in practice" (Raffles 2002: 183), rarely do studies of place-making focus on places that are undergoing rapid transformation. Studies of the politics of place that do deal with change often focus on the attempt to defend existing places from destruction at the hands of translocal forces, be they multinational corporations, national states, or a combination of the two (Escobar 2001, L. Zhang 2006). Other studies, primarily urban in character, concentrate more on questions of "space" rather than "place," exploring how planned changes to the urban landscape (such as metropolitanism or gentrification) reflect bourgeois, neoliberal, or colonial ideologies and strategies of "controlling and patrolling" inhabitants, or, conversely, how unplanned urban settlements challenge such state projects (M. Davis 1992, Rotenberg 2001, Chesluk 2004, T. Mitchell 1988, Smart 2001, L. Zhang 2001). Yet, on the whole, they do not examine how residents of these changing urban environments make places out of these transformed spaces. Indeed, the vast majority of studies of place-making (including, incidentally, all the contributions to Feld and Basso's influential edited volume *Senses of Place*) focus on rural places; and, as Clifford

Geertz (1996: 260) has noted, they often invoke but rarely investigate the "sense of fragility and change" that haunts even the strongest articulations of place-based sentiments. Taken together, then, the trend has been to reproduce (implicitly or explicitly) a dichotomy between "place" and "space" (or between "places" and "non-places)," in which the former is associated with the local, the rural, the indigenous, the traditional, and the disappearing, and the latter is associated with the global, capitalism, modernity, and the urban or suburban—in short, with all that *displaces* more authentic or feelingful sites or structures. These studies leave us with few theoretical tools to understand how the process of place-making continues even in a place, like Macau, that is no longer the place it was ten or even five years ago: the kind of places that make not only returning émigrés but even residents who have never left feel disoriented and out of place—the kind of places that were, during the 1990s, the norm in many parts of China, as well as in other regions of the so-called developing world.[8]

In what follows, I address the intersection of these theoretical concerns through an ethnographic exploration of a range of place-making practices Macau residents engaged in during the transition. How was the legacy of shared sovereignty both expressed and reproduced in ways that Macau residents named and moved through the urban landscape? How did the landscape itself become a central site through which the significance of this legacy was contested? And how did the socioeconomic changes that attended the political transition shape what it meant to call Macau "home"?

Heaven for an Architect

The transition era was by no means the first time that the urban environment of Macau had undergone radical transformation. Macau has been a city since 1586, and, as one historian has argued, its history has been punctuated by brief bursts of rapid change that completely transform the city and its population (Porter 1996). Periods of good fortune, prosperity, and growth, as well as of misfortune, ruin, and decay, have been recorded in and through the changes they have wrought on the physical features of the city as well as in the ways people have talked and written about those changes. The seventeenth-century travelogues of Peter Mundy, the eighteenth-century poems of Wu Li, nineteenth-century paintings of George Chinnery, and twentieth-century short stories by Henrique de Senna Fernandes record delight in the charm of Macau's urban fabric: in the unexpected juxtapositions of European and Chinese architectural elements, in the experience of losing oneself in its tangle of narrow, winding streets or strolling in the stately, shady peace of the Praia Grande. In the early twentieth century, teacher and social critic Manuel da Silva Mendes, who lived most of his adult life in Macau, wrote achingly of the destruction of this urban environment, which he felt had "defined us . . . our being, our life, our history."[9]

The long decade of the transition era brought change of this kind on a staggering scale. Massive land-reclamation projects radically enlarged and altered not only the topography but also the very geography of the city, prompting one Portuguese resident of Macau to joke wryly about the generosity of his government: what other European colonial power had agreed to give back more than double the territory it had occupied hundreds of years earlier?[10] (see Fig. 4). By 1994, reclaimed land already accounted for 56 percent of the total land area of Macau, and two more major reclamation projects had just gotten under way. One of these would enclose the Praia Grande to make two lakes out of the existing sea and plant high-rent office buildings in the middle of what used to be the main anchorage for trading ships. The other would conjoin the two outlying islands, Coloane and Taipa, and build a new city—Cotai—large enough to accommodate 150,000 more residents. On much of this new land, vast blocks of high-rises were built with the labor of over a hundred thousand immigrant workers; in some areas, these were intended for subsidized housing and factories to employ more immigrant workers, and in others, they were dolled up for luxury condominiums to attract middle-class retirees from Hong Kong.

Between 1990 and 1999, major infrastructure projects included a new airport, a new tunnel, a new bridge, a new jetfoil terminal and heliport, a new container port, a new waste treatment facility, a new sports stadium, a new cultural center, and seven new museums. As of the end of 1998, several more such projects were in the pipeline: a marina, a convention center, a theme park, several new green spaces,

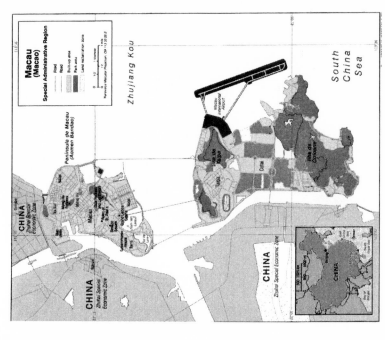

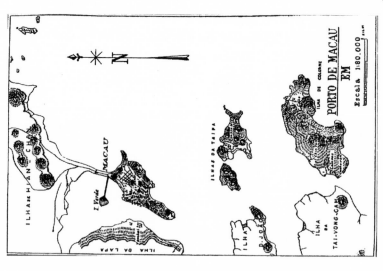

Fig. 4 A 1919 map (*left*) shows Macau consisting of a peninsula and three islands, with a total land area of about 4.5 square miles (11.6 km²). By 2008 (*right*), successive land reclamation projects had decreased the number of islands to one and increased the total land area to over 11 square miles (28.6 km²), with another 2 square miles of reclamation projects in the works (2008 map produced by the Central Intelligence Agency, courtesy of University of Texas Libraries).

the eighth tallest tower on the planet, a bridge linking Macau to Zhuhai and Hong Kong, a Macau extension to the Zhuhai-Canton Railway, and new buildings to house the Legislative Assembly and the courts.[11] At the same time, partly in response to all this new construction, the Macau government undertook a major effort to classify, restore, and preserve some of the architectural structures and ensembles that it considered to be part of Macau's historical and cultural patrimony (see below). Finally, in order to "commemorate the friendship between the Chinese and Portuguese people," in 1992 the governor passed a law authorizing himself to commission large public monuments designed and built by Portuguese artists, to be built at the rate of one per year until the handover.[12] The sheer amount of work that was done on the physical environment meant that civil construction was one of the four leading sectors pushing Macau's economic growth, accounting for approximately 10 percent of the GDP and employing 10 percent of the workforce (R. Tse 1999: 147). In the late 1980s and early 1990s, as one architect told me, "there were over 100 architects working in Macau—that's practically a measurable percentage of the population." This was hardly a surprise, said another Portuguese architect I spoke with in Lisbon who had worked in Macau in the early 1990s, for "Macau was heaven for an architect! In Portugal it takes ten years to build a single building. In Macau in the same amount of time, you could build three buildings on the same spot."

Change on this scale makes itself felt in the everyday of everyone, not just developers and architects. When I lived in Macau in the late 1990s, noise from construction sites—the jatter of jackhammers, the shouts of foremen, the whine and squeal of stonecutters, the deafening clang-thud-clang-thud of pile drivers, the beep-beep-beep of backhoes backing up—was constant during daylight hours. Walk for more than 500 yards in any direction and you would find yourself, at some point, forced off the sidewalk and into the street to move past a bamboo scaffolding or an illegally parked cement truck. One resident of a home for elderly women told me that she had been evicted from dwelling after dwelling in the early 1990s, as one after another her landlords sold their buildings to developers. Others told me, tongue in cheek, that during those years Macau had had not only the highest population density in the world but also the highest density of Mercedes-Benzes per square foot.

This construction frenzy was driven by a transnational economics of speculation and corruption. Much of the building and land reclamation was funded by investors from mainland China, where in the early 1990s, the expansion of the financial system and the weak enforcement of regulations on loans issued by state banks made it easy for state-owned enterprises to use state funds to make unauthorized investments. And many such investors found Macau's low tax rates and comparatively stable economic policies a safer bet than investing in the mainland.[13] Add the facts that in Macau all land was owned by the government and that the process for negotiating the use rights and prices was entirely secret and thus notoriously easy to manipulate for those with money or connections, and the stage was set for massive speculation in construction and real estate. According to one of my interviewees, a Portuguese civil engineer who had worked on one of the major development projects and had watched others unfold, both the investors and the Macau government benefited from this process: borrowing Chinese government funds, one investor would negotiate in secret with a representative of the Macau government for rights to develop existing land or future landfill; then another investor would come in and, again using state funds, buy those rights plus the rights to another, smaller piece of land for a much higher price; then a third would come along, and a fourth, and the process continued with everyone making an enormous profit.[14] Properties would often change hands several times before the ground was even broken—or, in the case of reclamation, before the land even existed. Prices for the housing that was finally built rose so high that locals could no longer afford it, and so the Macau government began offering permanent residence in Macau for an investment of MOP$1 million, hoping to attract buyers from mainland China to fill the empty buildings (R. Tse 1999: 151). But the whole thing came to a screeching halt in mid-1993, when Vice Premier Zhu Rongji, concerned about rising inflation and the growing number of unauthorized and nonperforming state loans, implemented an austerity program that sharply curtailed the availability of credit from mainland banks.

By 1999, all was not well. The speculative spiral had left Macau with a surplus of between 30,000 and 50,000 empty residential and commercial units.[15] These weighed eerily on the city in the form of towering urban villages, thirty stories high, with only one or two windows lit up at night. The abrupt end of the credit free-for-all had left the city sprinkled with the skeletons of abandoned half-built skyscrapers that had sat untouched for years, while work on several new projects, including Cotai New City and the theme park, slowed or stopped.[16] The Portuguese government had classified as heritage sites far more buildings than it could afford to restore; these stood, mildewed and crumbling, and occasionally collapsed. An electrical fire that destroyed a "classified" residence whose façade had been restored by the Cultural Heritage Department raised questions in both the Portuguese and Chinese press as to precisely what was being preserved and why.[17] And grumbling about the money wasted on "ugly" public monuments (this aesthetic judgment being perhaps the only issue on which all of my interlocutors agreed unanimously), when it could have been better spent on social programs or invested for the post-handover government, seemed to grow louder each year.

Whether in the form of intense nostalgia for the sense of sleepy intimacy once afforded by the city, of awe or admiration at the pace of development, of complaints about real estate fortunes made and lost, of chagrin at the lack of centralized planning that led to careless development, or of laments about the lack of interest in the quaint old buildings evinced by the majority of Macau residents, talk about the changes in the built environment of the city was as pervasive as the change itself. In talking about, moving through, and identifying with the changing places around them, Macau residents grappled with the questions of what Macau's past and future sovereign status would mean in their daily lives.

Naming Place

Keith Basso writes, of naming, "whenever the members of a community speak about their landscape—whenever they name it, or classify it, or tell stories about it—they unthinkingly represent it in ways that are compatible with shared understandings of how, in the fullest sense, they know themselves to occupy it" (Basso 1996: 74). Basso's observation is no less true for urban landscapes than for the natural ones he writes of: the way people name places, or do not name them, or name them differently, is an important aspect of how they make sense of the places they inhabit and of the social relations that are entailed. In this regard, the practice of naming, classifying, and speaking about places is perhaps the most immediate expression of, and site of contestation over, sovereign power in everyday life. As we have seen, the different names by which the territory of Macau has been called throughout the centuries tell a contested history of sovereignty. But the ways that Macau residents named the urban structures within the city complicated how this history signified in the present. In inscribing the history of sort-of sovereignty across the contemporary urban environment, these names reproduced the partiality and disunity that that history entailed.

As in countless other places, Macau's pasts echo through its place-names. Names of streets trace histories of forgotten grandeur and despair; they map the ways the city grew and changed with the succession of economic activities that sustained or sapped the lives of its residents. In the oldest parts of the city settled by Portuguese, streets bear the Portuguese names of fortresses that no longer exist (Travessa do Bom Jesus, Estrada de São Francisco), of beaches that have been filled in (Rua da Praia do Bom Parto, Rua da Praia do Manduco); of businesses that no longer operate (Pátio dos Cules, "Coolie Place," marking the center of the human trafficking industry in the nineteenth century;[18] Rua da Felicidade, "Happiness Street," the old red-light district; Rua dos Armazéns, "Warehouse Street"; Beco do Sapato, "Shoe Lane") and of communities that no longer inhabit them (Ramal dos Mouros, "Moors' Extension"; Estrada dos Parses, "Parsee Road").

As in countless other colonial places, an examination of any city map reveals that part of the history that these names record is a colonial one. Scholars have long noted that in colonial cities, "the method of building and naming made present to the visitor the order and the institutions of colonial authority" (T. Mitchell 1988: 161; see also Ross and Telkamp 1985 and Prochaska 1990). The ways that colonial officials named the streets and buildings they built, in other words, were compatible with how they knew themselves to occupy those places, and how they wished others to know it too; it was through the urban environment that the apparently ungrounded ideologies of European colonialism (ideologies of rationality and order, of modernity, of a world that was perfectly knowable and therefore governable) were made sensate (cf. T. Mitchell 1988). To be sure, an enormous number of Macau's streets, buildings, and plazas are named for Portuguese governors, explorers, generals, bishops, businessmen, and other important figures, institutions, and events in the history of Portugal and of its presence in Macau. On one level, then, these names (as well as the design and organization of the objects they identified) made the city a kind of relief map of the "history of colonization and colonialization" (Prochaska 1990: 214), embedding that history into the infrastructure and emplacing it within the city.[19]

On another level, the ways in which these names were made part of the material environment, part of the sensed experience of the city, suggested that the names of places in Macau not only were part of the legacy of Portuguese sovereignty but also encoded a particular interpretation of that legacy. All street signs in Macau are bilingual in Chinese and Portuguese and made of white ceramic tiles with blue trim and lettering, a style reminiscent both of the tradition of *azulejo* (Portuguese ceramic tile) and of the Chinese porcelain (much of which was exported to Europe through Macau) that influenced its development in the seventeenth century. In the mid-1990s, these signs were deemed distinctive enough to merit a display in the Museum of Macau, and miniature replicas of them in the form of refrigerator magnets were sold in souvenir shops around the city. Thus street names, both conceptually and sensually, made the city itself a form of "political expression, didactic in style" (T. Mitchell 1988: 162); the lesson they imparted was that the city of Macau owed its distinctiveness to its history as a "meeting place of two civilizations" and that the material traces of that history were worthy of preserving and enshrining, as well as being a potential source of profit for present-day residents. To paraphrase Mitchell, then, the method of naming and of building names into the urban environment presented to visitors wandering the streets with a half-folded tourist map as their guide, or shopping for knick-knacks near the São Paulo

Ruins, the state's interpretation of the meaning of Portuguese sovereignty and its significance for the future.

But visitors are not residents, and people do not inhabit maps. To examine only maps and street signs and to consider only the presumed intentions of administrators and perceptions of tourists would be to make unwarranted assumptions about how Macau residents knew their city. For the political expression encoded in maps and street signs is by no means unambiguous, and the disjuncture between tourist map and lived experience is one locus for understanding the complexity of how history signifies through place-names. In the old part of town, many streets are small, narrow, and winding, sometimes no more than alleyways; many of them hardly seem big enough to merit a name. But even the smallest alleyways often have names that are long, unwieldy, and confusing. Because most Portuguese names consist of three to four surnames in addition to one or two given names,[20] the effect of peppering the streets with the names of hundreds of Portuguese people can be dizzying, at least for non-native Portuguese speakers. For example, the "Avenida de Almeida Ribeiro" is in a different part of town from the "Avenida do Conselheiro Ferreira de Almeida"; the "Rua de Ferreira do Amaral" is in a different part of town from the "Rua de Coelho do Amaral," although both are named for governors, each of whom has at least two other lanes, alleyways, or plazas named after them. In Chinese, these names are then either transliterated, in which case they become a long and utterly meaningless collection of syllables (the Avenida Almeida Ribeiro is "Nga-meih-da-lei-bei-louh Avenue"/亞美打利庇盧大馬路), or they have entirely different names altogether. So, for example, in Chinese the Avenida do Conselheiro Ferreira de Almeida is Holland Park Avenue (Hoh-laan-yuhn daaih-ma-lou/荷蘭園大馬路), a reference to the fact that it was once a Dutch neighborhood; and despite its long formal Chinese name, everyone—Chinese, Portuguese, and other—refers to the Avenida Almeida Ribeiro simply as San Ma-Louh (新馬路), meaning "new road," for the fact that it was built as recently as the second decade of the twentieth century.[21]

This practice, then, reveals that rather than making sense of the history of Portuguese sovereignty, place-naming often quite literally makes nonsense of it. Perhaps the most telling example is the way the name "Ferreira do Amaral" is inscribed across the city. João de Ferreira do Amaral was the notorious governor whose rule, from 1846 until he was assassinated in 1849, is often considered the first real attempt by the Portuguese state to assert full colonial sovereignty over Macau. There are four public ways in Macau that are named after Ferreira do Amaral in Portuguese, marking his erstwhile status in Portugal as a celebrated hero of imperial expansion. In Chinese, however, whereas the Estrada de Ferreira do Amaral and the Praça de Ferreira do Amaral use the transliteration of "Amaral" (Ya-meih-laat Road/亞美喇馬路 and Ya-meih-laat Plaza/亞美喇前地, respectively),[22] the Rua Ferreira do Amaral, one of the major north–south arteries through the city, is called East Oceanview Street (Dong mong-yeung gaai /東望洋街), and the Istmo do Ferreira do Amaral—the main thoroughfare connecting the most densely populated neighborhoods to the border with China—is most commonly called Border Gate Road (Gwaan jaahp mah-louh /關閘馬路). In this sense, then, the extent to which the history of Portuguese sovereignty in Macau is meaningfully inscribed on the urban fabric depends on which language you speak; yet that history was such that in the 1990s, very few Chinese residents spoke the language that would enable them to recognize the signs of its legacy.

A pocket-size, 180-page booklet published by the Leal Senado provided bilingual, cross-referenced indexes of all street names on the peninsula, descriptions of where they were in the city, and a series of maps on which to locate them (Leal Senado 1992). At first I was delighted to find such a guide, stuck it in my bag and carried it everywhere I went, convinced that it was another essential tool for the good Macau ethnographer. Yet as the weeks and months passed, it stayed in my bag; I rarely consulted it, and never once in the years that I lived in Macau did I see anyone else using it. For, as I came to realize, the disjuncture between Portuguese and Chinese street names mattered only to bilingual strangers: people, like anthropologists, who could and needed to read both Chinese and Portuguese and who had not yet learned to move around the city like natives.

My lesson in how natives moved around the city came one afternoon in early October 1997, about a month after my arrival in

Macau.[23] I had an appointment to interview a Catholic priest who ran a youth center not far from my apartment. Unsure of where exactly the center was, I called in advance to find out; making certain assumptions about the way urbanites orient themselves in the world (and hoping to minimize the possibility of misunderstanding in my then still-tender Cantonese), I simply asked the receptionist for the street address. To my surprise, she didn't know. She asked a colleague, who began rummaging around to find an envelope that might have the address printed on the front. Meanwhile the woman asked me why I wanted the address, and I told her I would be coming to the center that afternoon to speak with the priest. "Oh!" she said, "You want to come here? Then you shouldn't ask for the street address, you should just ask how to get here! Where are you coming from?" This led to a long conversation in which we tried to discover nearby points of reference that I recognized (finally settling on "between the Red Market and Sacred Heart College"), and then a more detailed discussion of the kinds of buildings, alleyways, food stalls, and flower sellers I would pass if I were to start from the Red Market and walk in the right direction. What struck me most immediately was not only that this negotiation was "oriented in terms of the individual making the trip" rather than in universal directions (Blu 1996: 200), but that the markers by which the individual was to orient herself were almost anything but street names.

Within the hour I had a firm understanding of why this was the case. By the time the receptionist had finished giving me directions, her colleague had found the address, and she asked if I still wanted it. Feeling a bit unsteady at the prospect of trying to find a place in the city without actually being able to find it on a map, I said yes; she told me the Center was located at number 30 Luo Yeukhon Sahnfuh Gaai, in which the street name was the Cantonese transliteration of the name and title of a Portuguese priest: "Father Luo Yeukhon Street."[24] But it was precisely my insistence on asking the wrong question—and then relying on the answer to it—that got me into trouble. For, as I followed her directions and arrived at about the halfway mark between the Red Market and the Sacred Heart College, I came across a sign for Rua do Padre António Roliz, in Chinese Luo Sahnfuh Gaai 羅神父街, or "Father Luo Street." Convinced that there could not be two different streets named for Father Luo in the same neighborhood and that perhaps the street sign was using an abbreviated form of the full street name for the sake of convenience, I searched the few short blocks of that street for half an hour, unable to find number 30, asking shop owners and passersby if there wasn't a youth center around here somewhere. Finally, desperate, frustrated, and embarrassed, I found a payphone outside a small grocery store, and called the center again. The same receptionist (who had no idea where I was when I told her the street name) immediately asked me the name of the shop I was calling from and told me to stay right there while she came to get me. She arrived within five minutes, and as she led me back to her office I discovered that the center was located on a tiny alleyway three short blocks beyond Father Luo Street and parallel to it, that was indeed called "Luo Yeukhon Sahnfuh Gaai" 羅若翰神父街, in Portuguese Rua do Padre João Clímaco. The two streets, christened presumably by Portuguese city planners, would never have been mistaken for each other in Portuguese, but were almost indistinguishable in Chinese.

Over the next few months (until I became so accustomed to this mode of orientation, and knew the city well enough, that I never made the mistake of asking for street names) I was told time and again—by everyone from college students to veteran taxi drivers— that aside from a few of the major thoroughfares, no one knew, or used, the names of streets. As I discovered that October afternoon, rather than navigating by streets, Macau natives navigated by landmarks; and in a city as densely populated and densely built as Macau, those landmarks were without exception buildings or monuments: "at the bus stop in front of the Times Building," "by the fountain," "across the street from the phone company," "next to McDonalds," "up from Dom Bosco School," "down from Tap Seac field," "under the cow" (a reference to a well-known shop in Leal Senado Square that specialized in milkshakes and egg puddings, whose signboard boasted a large heifer outlined in white neon). The Rotunda Carlos de Maia, a large plaza that served as one of the main points of access into the biggest and busiest street market in central Macau, had an official Chinese name—"Ga-lou Mai-ye Circle" (嘉路米耶圓 形地)—but it and the whole neighborhood around it were known simply as "Three Lamps" (三盞燈), for the distinctive lamppost that stood at its center. These places were not on any map. Getting directions was, every time, both an extended process of negotiation and an exercise in socialization, for in order to understand how to move from Point A to Point B through urban space, you and your interlocutor would have to inhabit the same social space: which places—out of the close-crowded government buildings, shops, restaurants, markets, parks, alleyways, and apartment complexes that constituted the sociality of urban space—would be recognizable landmarks to both parties?

In this sense, Macau residents' practices of place-naming did reflect the complex signification of sovereignty in Macau. On one hand, the way that Macau residents mapped the city marked the way that social and cultural meanings were inscribed onto urban space: and although these meanings incorporated buildings, monuments, and places that were, in some way, the result of Portuguese colonialism, the way they were named in Chinese rarely acknowledged anything Portuguese about them. Thus, rather than making the city into an expression of colonialization, place-naming was an expression of the irrelevance of Portuguese sovereignty to the lives of the majority of Macau residents. On the other hand, these practices of naming were both legacy and instance of a form of divided sovereignty that encouraged Chinese and Portuguese residents to speak different languages, answer to different authorities, and ultimately, as one Portuguese friend told me, to "inhabit two different cities in the same place."

This, then, is how the history of partial sovereignty and its present-day significance echoes and is made meaningful (or meaningless) through practices of place-naming. But naming is the quintessential sovereign act, and the preceding account, like many other studies of place, leaves unexamined the gaps and holes and unraveled edges, the unspoken or unspeakable, that complicate the sovereign projects of making and naming place. Studies of place-making and -naming that focus on how shared concepts of history, morality, community, or sovereign power are made meaningful through places, be they urban or rural, are indeed crucial to understanding common senses of place. But place, culture, power, and community map neatly onto one another in this approach, and all are cleanly designated by a name: Apache, French, Portuguese, Chinese. They are stories about "living local history in a localized way" (Basso 1996: 6). Indeed, the story I have just finished telling above does the same thing: it demonstrates how the significance of the history of Portuguese sovereignty was proclaimed or made mute through the place-naming practices of different linguistic communities (Chinese vs. Portuguese) in the same location. There is nothing dynamic about this approach; it slices through the tumult and uncertainty of the everyday to examine the physical and linguistic structures that bespeak a shared understanding; it does not examine how those structures (both physical and linguistic) and understandings emerge, what happens when they change, or how the neat concentricity and coterminousness of names, places, and communities might be an illusion, an effect produced precisely through the assertion that place-names mean what they are said to mean, or mean anything at all. The question I address in the rest of this chapter, then, is not simply how different communities (defined by class, ethnicity, language, gender, or anything else) experienced place differently and expressed these experiences through naming practices; the question is how those experiences and expressions were complicated by a social, political, and physical environment that would not stand still. It is an ethnography of urban place-making that examines not only the "localized expressions" through which people name the places around them but what happens when names don't stick and places don't either. It examines how communities express their relationship to the places they occupy and how emplaced communities can come into being almost in spite of themselves.

Naming Non-Places

During the 1990s, Macau was littered with "non-places" in an even more literal sense than Marc Augé (1995) uses the term: although they appeared on the most recent city maps and had transformed the city's skyline, they were places that had no meaningful existence for the city's residents. One area in particular, called NAPE (for "Novos Aterros do Porto Exterior") in Portuguese and San Hau On 新口岸 in Chinese, was a virtual ghost town within the city: a square parcel of reclaimed land jutting out into the bay, on which dozens of squat, cube-shaped buildings had been hastily erected. Few of the buildings, designed as luxury waterfront condominiums and office towers with commercial space on the ground floor, were occupied; no bus lines went there; nor would anyone have occasion even to pass through the area on their way to anywhere else. In the social landscape of the city, it was as if dozens of thirty-story buildings, each the size of an entire city block, did not exist.

In the autumn of 1998, a young Portuguese man residing in Macau quit his civil service job and opened a small bar on the ground floor of one of these enormous uninhabited high-rises closest to the water's edge. Though small, this bar took good advantage of one of the architectural features common to all the high-rises in the area: an arcade running the length of the building where patrons could sit outdoors, protected from sun and rain, and watch the passersby, the activity on the bay, and the lights of Taipa island across the water. By winter, the ground floors of high-rises for three blocks in either direction had been occupied by bars, cafés, noodle shops, and restaurants, turning this area into the evening destination where everyone—tourists, locals, old, and young—went to eat and drink, see and be seen, and enjoy the magical evening breezes that always seemed to spring up at the end of even the hottest summer days.

The problem came in naming this place. How to refer to this area, in order to tell a cab driver where to go or your friends where to meet? The street on which most of these bars were located had a name—the Avenida Doutor Sun Yat-sen—but, although sensible and manageable in both Chinese and Portuguese, it was as meaningless as any other street name in Macau. In Chinese, people often called the area "Macau's Lan Kwai Fong" (澳門蘭桂坊), referring to the two short streets in central Hong Kong, closed to all but pedestrian traffic, that were home to a strip of trendy bars and restaurants where expats, students, white-collar locals, and tourists would gather on weekend nights. In Portuguese, the preferred name was *as docas*, "the docks," a reference to the old dockyards along the River Tejo in Lisbon that had recently been converted into a strip of nightclubs, bars, and restaurants along a pedestrian walkway by the riverbank, that was starting to challenge the old cobblestone hilltop neighborhood of Bairro Alto as the center of gravity for Lisbon's nightlife. Jan, a Hong Kong friend, found the appellation "Lan Kwai Fong" amusing, as Macau's "strip" didn't bear much resemblance to the old buildings, the narrow uphill streets, and the upscale establishments there. Rui, a Portuguese friend, thought the nickname "docas" funny because, although Macau's *docas* is on the water's edge and does have outdoor seating, it is not and never was anything resembling a dock. But there was nothing else to call it; it had no name of its own; it was all but impossible to refer to this place in Macau without referring to another place. Get into a taxi and say "oumun lan gwai fong" ("Macau's Lan Kwai Fong") and you would go straight there; otherwise you'd have to explain that you wanted to go to that street with all the bars on it, right near the Guan Yin Statue (觀音像), which would often prompt the cabdriver to ask for clarification, because there was another street with two or three bars on it near the Guan Yin Temple (觀音堂), in a different part of town. But although the Guan Yin Statue, the latest commissioned work in the governor's public monuments program, had been built quite self-consciously as a landmark, it could scarcely count as such, since it was less than a year old and was one of the most controversial and generally reviled monuments in the city.[25] Ask someone who had been away from Macau for a year or so to meet you at the bars near the Guan Yin Statue, and they would have no idea what you were talking about, since the statue had been erected only a few months previously; try (as I did on a few occasions) to describe the location of both the statue and the bars to Macau natives who had been away a bit longer, and they would look blankly and shrug their shoulders, since only a few years earlier, the entire parcel of land that the statue and the bars and the buildings occupied had been sea.

After almost a year, the problem resolved itself. Several government offices and the headquarters of a major bank relocated into one of the giant office blocks on the reclaimed land, and soon this office complex, Dynasty Plaza (皇朝廣場), gave its name to the entire area. The strip of bars itself still had no name—it appeared on no map—but it became possible to place them in conversation: in Chinese, they were "those bars by Dynasty Plaza" (皇朝廣場嗰啲吧). But those months of limbo, during which the most popular night spot in Macau could not be named except by reference to other night spots in other cities, reveals the extent to which place-making is often far more than "living local history in a localized way." People often make sense of places, or of non-places, through reference to other places.

Making Native Place

For some, however, this tendency of making sense of places through other places was evidence of Macau's most pressing problem: the fact that for the majority of Macau residents, the entire city was a non-place. Time and again Portuguese government officials, city planners, architects, and others complained to me that most residents "have no feeling for the place," they "don't really care about the city," "they don't love the place and don't care what happens to it."[26] They chalked this unfortunate fact up to the largely transient nature of the Chinese population of Macau, and to the fact that well over half the population were "new immigrants" who had arrived in Macau after 1978. Indeed, I was told, prior to the 1990s, even the 40 percent of residents who were born and raised in Macau rarely referred to themselves as "Oumun yahn" or "Macau people"; if you were a Chinese resident of Macau, you would most likely identify yourself as being from Zhongshan or Kaiping or Xinhui or whatever prefecture or province your parents or grandparents had emigrated from. Like Hong Kong, Macau was a "stepping stone society" (A. H. Yee 1989) for everyone but the Macanese: it made sense as a place to which people came from their native place, on their way to someplace else; it was never native in its own right.[27]

During the transition era, this phenomenon became troubling to many people. In the summer of 1996 when I was in Macau doing preliminary fieldwork and language training, my Cantonese tutor asked me to explain to him, as a linguistic exercise, what my study was about. After I stuttered through a description of my interest in all this talk about cultural identity and history in the context of political transition, he gave me an unexpectedly impassioned lesson in why this talk mattered: "Chinese in Macau have historically had a weak sense of belonging to this place," he said, "but without a sense of belonging, we will disappear. If we are not different, we will cease to exist." The belief that the majority of residents had no sense of place was especially disquieting for the Macau Portuguese state, whose project was, after all, that of attempting to displace existing divisions of race, ethnicity, language, and nationality and to replace them with a shared sense of attachment to the place Macau. The urgency of the problem was exacerbated by the ticking of the handover clock: if Macau residents were not made to understand posthaste what made them and their city different, within a few short years after the departure of the Portuguese Macau's uniqueness would disappear, and it would be "just like any other Chinese city." The task of instilling in Macau residents a sense of belonging, and of shaping their everyday experiences of the places they inhabited, became crucial.

Not surprisingly, perhaps, this set of concerns coalesced around another, more palpable process of disappearance: the destruction of the older parts of the city. For, surrounded by and interspersed with the mirrored glass of bank towers, the terraced spirals of high-rise carparks, the soot-stained tile of thirty-story apartment blocks, and the ghost-towns and skyscraper-skeletons that now dominated the skyline, traces of the old Macau still remained. Some of these traces took the form of ruined old buildings of sagging grey brick and gap-toothed, paint-peeled shutters, abandoned by all life except the trees that sprouted from their roofs (see Fig. 5).[28]

Others, including stately private homes and art deco commercial buildings dating from the first decades of the twentieth century, had received more care and use, but nothing was preventing them from being sold to eager real estate developers who would not hesitate to tear them down and put up inexpensive, multistory buildings that could generate more revenue. As the handover approached and the building boom continued apace, some people began to worry that the legendary charm of the "old Macau" was in imminent danger of disappearing into the undifferentiated urban sprawl of south China. These old buildings had to be rescued from the ravages of termites and humidity and human neglect, protected from the greed and carelessness of their owners; otherwise they would be demolished and replaced by "anonymous monstrosities . . . without character of their own" (Porter 1996: 95). Before long, "the mystique that is

Fig. 5   Ruins I: the old Luk Kwok Restaurant on San Ma-Louh in downtown Macau
was just one of dozens of dilapidated old buildings that were on the
government's list of heritage sites (photo by author, 1999).

uniquely Macau's" would be ruined, replaced by "the mundane
sameness of a modern commercial city" (Duncan 1991: 182).

In an effort to forestall this disappearance, during the decade
prior to the handover, the Macau Portuguese state made a concerted
effort to identify, classify, and restore as many "heritage" buildings,
architectural ensembles, and areas as possible and to pass legislation preventing unauthorized alteration or destruction of hundreds
of others.[29] Fortresses, temples, churches, and historical monuments, including the São Paulo Ruins, were renovated, and several
dozen buildings of vernacular architecture—including pawnshops
and pharmacies, brothels and barbershops, hospitals and private
homes—were gutted and girdered with steel instead of rotting wood,
redesigned inside, and repainted outside in pastel yellows, pinks, and
greens (see Fig. 6).[30] Between 1990 and 1997, according to an estimate by the Cultural Heritage Department, approximately HK$69

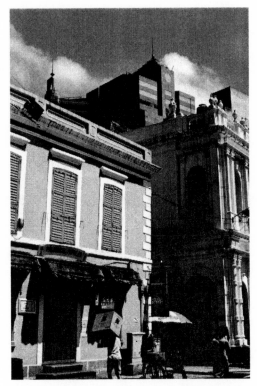

Fig. 6   Restorations I: the Pharmacia Popular and the
Santa Casa de Misericórdia in Leal Senado Square
(photo by author, 1999).

million (US$ 9 million) was spent on restoration work throughout
Macau's peninsula and two islands. Throughout the decade, the
government-run Cultural Institute held photography contests and
exhibitions about Macau's heritage, ran courses on restoration and
preservation techniques, and printed postcards, stamps, and paper
models of heritage buildings; in 1998, it hosted an international
symposium entitled "Culture of Metropolis in Macau," which took
as its theme the need to "establish a past behind the future of
Macau" and, in conjunction, published two special issues of the trilingual *Review of Culture* journal on the subject of "Macau
Património." As the note explaining the journal's cover art explained: "To love and preserve [Macau's] heritage is to move into
the future without [being haunted by] the ghosts of the past."[31]

The opening article in this journal was the translation of a 1970 paper by architect Wong Shiu-kwan, which became widely cited by the dozens of studies of Macau architecture, culture, and identity that were published during the transition era. In the paper, Wong identified in detail all the different ways, and all the different build-ings, in which Chinese and Portuguese architectural styles were blended over the centuries into a hybrid style unique to Macau: southern European verandas and decorative pillars gracing houses with typically Chinese floorplans, Chinese roofs covering typically Portuguese church buildings; even the building materials themselves, Wong demonstrated—the bricks and mortar, wood, stone, and *chu-nambo* (an indestructible mixture of earth, lime, straw, and crushed oyster shells) used to create these effects—were re-engineered and combined in ways that would provide maximum protection against typhoons, heat, and humidity. Wong concluded that "the mutual in-fluences of Chinese and Portuguese architecture produced a special type of architecture that was more suited for the special conditions in Macau. The two styles, Chinese and Portuguese, were combined to form a new identity. The strengths of each were, in Macau, adopted to compensate for the weaknesses of the other" (S. K. Wong 1998: 64). At the Culture of Metropolis symposium, there was talk of applying to UNESCO for status as a World Heritage site, since Macau's patrimony, at least as described by Wong, met the criterion of having "outstanding universal value": it was, wrote the editor of the journal, "a universal lesson, harbinger of a Humanity in which all differences harmonize into a single Unity" (Sá Cunha 1998: 4).[32]

Given its timing—just prior to the handover—and the flowery romanticism of much of its rhetoric, it may seem easy to dismiss this initiative as a classic example of colonial nostalgia.[33] In fact, one of my interviewees, Tiago, a Portuguese architect who had been in-strumental in the heritage and restoration projects in Macau since the mid-1980s, admitted that it was in this spirit of nostalgia—or, as he called it, "anticipated nostalgia"—that he and his colleagues had been able to gain the support of the government. He told me (and other interviewees corroborated) that in the 1980s, there was so much money for the government to make, licitly and illicitly, through land reclamation and real estate speculation that what little heritage legislation or urban planning there was had been ignored or overruled. "I watched the administration destroy plenty of beautiful buildings, plenty of heritage sites in its time," Tiago said. It was only when the Portuguese administrators became aware in 1987 that their days in Macau were numbered that they grew interested in preserving "something of the past, some legacy of the Portuguese presence in Macau that would endure."

But there was more to it than just nostalgia or ideology, Tiago was quick to point out, for the state was not the only champion of the colorful old restored buildings that were now beginning to dot the city like "so many wedding cakes." Playing on the administration's anxieties about its post-handover legacy was a good way to win government funding, but the premise that Macau's old buildings could embody a marketable and potentially lucrative resource due to their quaint and exotic feel was an important rationale for gaining other kinds of support. "When heritage was linked to tourism," explained Tiago, "and it was realized that Macau could be a 'chicken of golden eggs'—that's when people's attitude toward preservation took a turn for the better." Gradually, a greater number of developers, city planners, and investors came to agree that destroying Macau's heritage buildings would ruin the basis of Macau's future prosperity. Some of them began to try to find alternatives that would allow for the maximization of buildable space without further destruction of the picturesque, old-world feel of downtown. The Banco Nacional Ultramarino (BNU) building was a prime example: in 1997, the façade of the old two-story pastel pink bank building was refurbished, but its interior was gutted and replaced with a glass tower some thirty stories tall (see Fig. 7).

In the rhetoric of the heritage initiative, then, all that made Macau the place that it was, historically, culturally, politically, economically—all that made it recognizable as a place at all—became fixed in those physical features of the city that were rapidly disappearing. As the editor of the *Review of Culture* wrote, quite simply, "without its architectural heritage, Macau would not exist" (Sá Cunha 1998: 3). The interesting architectural features of many of Macau's old buildings identified by Wong Shiu-kwan became idolized as symbols of the broader process of cultural exchange and

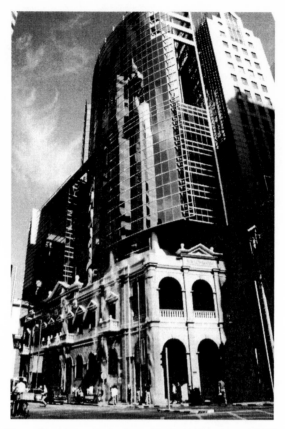

Fig. 7   Restorations II: the Banco Nacional Ultramarino (BNU)
in downtown Macau was a showcase of the adaptive re-use
approach to heritage preservation (photo by author, 1999).

fusion that had characterized the history of Portuguese rule. By producing useful, meaningful places out of the decaying ruins of these
old buildings, the government was emplacing that past in a way that
could serve not only as the basis of the city's future prosperity but as
didactic tools to educate the ignorant: through "architecture, urban
design and landscape," wrote the head of the Department of Cultural Heritage, "residents and visitors can learn about the history of
the place, of the culture inherent to it, and of reasons that are at the
basis of its difference, which it is imperative to maintain" (Departamento de Património Cultural 1997: 9). With such an education,
wrote a prominent Macanese architect, Macau residents would

understand that "the preservation of old buildings, streets, and places cannot simply be discarded as nostalgia . . . [but is] a basic desire of people to identify with their ever-changing living environment by certain reference features. Tangible testimonies of the past provide such reference points by allowing people to identify an environment as home" (Marreiros 1991: 101). In this view, what was necessary in order for Macau residents to call this place home was a proper understanding of the significance of the city's past and of how that past was embodied in the urban structures they encountered every day. Heritage buildings were not simply evidence of a particular past; they were a lasting assurance that that past would not be forgotten. They would continue to foster a sense of place and of home just as surely as the new buildings, "belonging to no particular place or culture," would destroy that sense and make of Macau "an anonymous city, without feeling, pity, or passion" (Porter 1996: 95).

This attempt to get Macau residents to identify with Macau as home was nothing if not controversial. Any attempt to restrict building in an era of rampant real estate speculation is bound to have opponents; Tiago told me that the resistance he met with in Macau was not much different from that he had encountered when working on similar projects in Portugal ten years earlier. His biggest opponents, both there and here, were developers and speculators who had competing interests in the properties protected by heritage legislation. Commercial property owners along San Ma-Louh, the entirety of which was classified as a protected "architectural ensemble," had repeatedly submitted plans to tear down their run-down old buildings and put up taller, newer ones, arguing that Macau's small size meant that as businesses grew they had nowhere to expand but upward, and that anyway it would cost more to restore and retrofit the old buildings in a way that was appropriate for modern commercial purposes than it would to knock them down and start afresh. Each time, their plans had been rejected on the grounds that they violated heritage law. A few of these buildings soon succumbed to fire—torched, it was rumored, by their owners, who thereby made their point in a final and irrevocable manner. But it soon became clear to me that the controversy was not simply due to a clash of economic interests. When people talked about the buildings and the government's attempt to restore them, what emerged were often alternative understandings of the history of Portuguese rule and alternative hopes for its relationship to the future.

As one businessman explained to me, the restrictive legislation and the cost of maintaining heritage buildings was only part of the problem. Mr. Kwok was a businessman and member of the Macau Chinese Chamber of Commerce, arguably the single most powerful civic association in Macau and one that had lobbied against the government's decision to classify certain areas as heritage sites. Of particular concern to Mr. Kwok was the large number of broken-down buildings that remained standing but had not been restored. He admitted that the effort to restore and maintain some of Macau's historic monuments, such as the three major temples and the São Paulo façade, was worthwhile in the interests of tourism, but, he argued, "the Portuguese just go too far! Classifying those old ruined buildings as cultural relics (文物)? What tour guide is going to take their tour to see some ruined old building? What kind of attraction is that?"[34] He had a point. In the São Lázaro district, for example, a swath of two-story buildings dating from the turn of the twentieth century had degenerated into a sway-backed, fire-singed, uninhabitable mess, with no clear timeline for restoration. On San Ma-Louh, the splendid old Luk Kwok restaurant, closed already some dozen years, stood sagging, all moldy timbers, buckled masonry, and partially collapsed roof: this was Macau's heritage? These forlorn structures were indeed, for Mr. Kwok as much as for his adversaries like Tiago, symbols of the history of Portuguese rule—but it was a ruinous history of economic stagnation and decay that called for eradication rather than preservation. Rather than asserting its "difference," Mr. Kwok argued, Macau needed to approximate as closely as possible the history of capitalist modernization behind the success of the other Chinese postcolonial city-states of Hong Kong and Singapore. Skyscrapers, land reclamation, and urbanization were, for him, signs of this success; the classification of ruins as "heritage" was a sign of precisely how irrational, impractical, and out-of-touch Portuguese rule had been—a sign of, in effect, a past without a future. "But let's wait and see," he told me with a sparkle in his eye. "After 1999, I imagine there will be some modifications in the policy about the preservation of heritage sites."

But even among those who believed that preserving as much of the urban fabric as possible was a worthwhile cause, there were objections to the way in which this task had been carried out. One interviewee called it the "kitsch" approach to preservation, which "makes the city look like a movie set rather than a normal city." There were insinuations that despite the rhetoric about creating a past behind the future, the real reason for the state's interest in heritage preservation had more to do with the present: its reluctance to spend the money necessary to modernize the infrastructure (the sewage and water systems, for example) in the older parts of the city, especially since the glut of new buildings meant that no more profit could be made by further development. Other critics pointed out that the state was simply fostering a culture of dependency in which owners of classified buildings would maintain them only for as long as there was government funding to do so. But the complaint I heard most often from long-term Portuguese residents of Macau was that it was a case of too little too late: that by the time the government began listening to the likes of Tiago, it had already allowed—indeed, encouraged—the destruction of the urban fabric that had been the only interesting thing about Macau. One architect I interviewed, who had been living in Macau for nearly twenty years, asked me, "Can you think of any single building in Macau that is worth preserving for its architectural qualities alone? I can't. There are plenty of more interesting buildings in Guangzhou or even in Tianjin." What had been interesting about Macau, he said, was "the way the buildings and streets and everything fit together in a sort of jumble, the general topography of the city—there was a kind of somber mystery about it, it was very interesting and very, very nice. But all this has been lost." According to him, the problem was that the nature of the Portuguese administration here had made long-term planning impossible, or at least implausible. It wasn't that the administration had never had an urban plan; to the contrary, he assured me, there was a long history of urban plans dating back to the nineteenth century. It was simply that every time a new governor arrived, he or his subordinates threw the previous plans out the window, usually in the interests of making a quick profit and retiring to Portugal as soon as possible.

For these residents, what this flurry of interest in Macau's heritage evoked was not colonial nostalgia but a kind of colonial ambivalence: simultaneous pride in what the Portuguese had contributed to the city and chagrin at the thought of what more could have been done. The heritage buildings represented evidence not of a peaceful history of cultural exchange but rather of the legacy of failure and inadequacy of Portuguese rule. "It is as if last year they decided to do in two years everything that they hadn't done in the past 445," fumed Afonso, a Portuguese employee of the Cultural Institute, in late 1998, frustrated at having to work nights and weekends for several months straight in order to keep up with the endless onslaught of urgent cultural projects needing to be completed before the handover. The disproportionate emphasis placed on these disappearing buildings as the primary legacy of the Portuguese presence in Macau had, for him and the architect and a handful of others I spoke with, become an arena for the critical re-evaluation of the history of Portuguese presence in Asia. After all, if the entire legacy of more than four hundred years of Portuguese presence in China could be demolished with a couple of wrecking balls in the space of a few days, what was there to celebrate? If, after all that time, the majority of residents really felt no attachment to the place and no "difference" from the rest of the Chinese people, did that not bespeak the lack of precisely the culture of exchange and hybridity that these buildings were supposed to embody? Did it not simply point up the failure of Macau's Portuguese administrators to construct a solid framework of institutional, linguistic, cultural, and economic affiliations with Portugal and Portugueseness?

A young civil engineer from a prominent Macau Chinese family brought these critiques together in a way that got at the heart of the problem—the distinction between place and non-place. During the Culture of Metropolis conference, Tom Fong distinguished himself by being one of the few participants to draw attention to the problems with the way the government was going about its project. His objection was that in some cases "restoration" consisted of simply tidying up the exteriors of buildings that would collapse under the weight of a single human footstep. "Those restored buildings at the top end of San Ma-Louh—you know, the yellow ones between the bank and the post office—are good for photographs," he said, "but not for people. We went in there for an inspection and we had to tell our engineers not to step out onto the balcony." The government was not making places; in many cases, it was simply whitewashing ruins: pouring money into firetraps in order to prop up a fragile and superficial façade of culture and history. Later, during a lunch break, I overheard Tom explaining to a visiting American architect the problem of overbuilding. He mentioned a large housing project that had been completed nearly a decade earlier but had still not even gone on the market, when he said, "What I think is that any building that is built and not used for ten years is a ruin. They are building ruins!" In a private interview a few weeks later, I confessed to having heard him say this and asked him to elaborate on his analysis. In response, he asked me, "What is a ruin?" and then answered his own question:

A ruin is something wasted, something not properly used. A ruin is a building built for human activity that *has* no human activity or that is not fit for human activity. No one would call your house a ruin, even if it is very old, because you live there and there is activity there. But if you decide to move out and it starts to decay, or if it gets so old and run down that you can no longer live in it and you have to move out, then we can start calling it a ruin. And that is what we have in all those new developments: a bunch of decaying buildings where there is no activity whatsoever.

Thickets of empty skyscrapers and skyscraper skeletons, decrepit old buildings that had been classified but not restored, and some of the showpiece heritage sites whose interiors were unfit for habitation: all these conform to Tom's definition of ruins (see Fig. 8). Whereas Tiago and Mr. Kwok used idioms of "heritage" and "development" to talk about who was ruining what for whom, Tom used the idiom of ruin itself to frame the whole urban environment, and through it the past, present, and future of Macau. Connecting the dots between the incongruities of the built environment, Tom saw the ruins of the colonial past decaying alongside those of a corrupt future. They were evidence neither of the impending capitalist modernity that would finally overcome the irrational constraints of chronic misrule nor of a harmonious past that could serve as the harbinger of an emerging enlightened humanity. Rather, they told an alternative history: the

Fig. 8   Ruins II: in the late 1990s, Macau's landscape was littered
with "ruins" such as these: a high-rise built as an upscale apartment
complex that remained empty for years and its abandoned
half-built twin across the street (photo by author, 1999).

lure of a quick profit made through quasi-legal commerce in a transi-
tory place; the rise and fall of successive modes of livelihood whose
politics make them unsustainable—this was precisely what had
given the city its present (ruinous or fascinating, depending on your
perspective) form.

Yet these critical, even cynical views of how Macau's pasts and
futures were emplaced in the urban environment were not the last
word on the subject, nor did they necessarily imply the lack of a
sense of place. For many people I talked to—especially those in their
twenties and early thirties who had been born in Macau or had
moved there at a young age—had a strong affection for the city,

bemoaned the rapid development that had transformed its skyline, and were glad of the efforts the state was making to decelerate this trend. Some were decidedly nostalgic: I asked one man in his late twenties or early thirties, who was born and raised in Macau but had spent several years studying in North America, how he felt about the changes Macau had undergone in the time he had been away; he responded by interjecting into our Cantonese conversation three English adjectives: "Depressing. Sad. Ashamed." Reverting to Cantonese, he described what a nice place Macau had been to grow up in, how pointless all this overdevelopment had been, and how detrimental to the city's social fabric. Others expressed their attachment to old places in terms of a "feelingful sensuality" (Feld 1996: 91): riding the bus one evening with the friend of a friend, another Macau native who had moved to Hong Kong to attend university and still lived there some ten years later, we passed a small Portuguese-style house on a narrow back street. He pointed it out to me and told me he loved old buildings like those. I asked him why, and he couldn't exactly say. "They're . . . they're just *hóu syùfuhk* (好舒服)," he shrugged, using an untranslatable term that describes pleasant, relaxing, or fulfilling sensations or states of being.

However, the ambiguous political imperatives of one country, two systems meant that many people who expressed a sense of attachment to the cobblestoned plazas, the gray-brick temples, and the pastel row houses still felt the need to position themselves very carefully in relation to the semiotics of these places. The comments of Ah Sun, a young Macau-born Chinese civil servant who had spent time studying both in mainland China and in Portugal, are indicative. Ah Sun responded to my question about what he thought of heritage preservation with a story about two "heritage" monuments that had already disappeared. During the riots that followed the 123 Incident in 1966, he noted, the statue of Vicente Nicolau de Mesquita (a Macanese army officer commemorated in Portuguese sources for his daring and successful attack on a nearby Chinese garrison after the 1849 assassination of Governor Ferreira do Amaral) that stood in Leal Senado Square had been toppled by protesters who found it to be an intolerable symbol of colonial domination. Yet in 1992, when the Macau government dismantled the statue of

Governor Ferreira do Amaral that stood in the plaza in front of the Hotel Lisboa half a mile away, he said, his family and friends had lamented its removal.[35] Ah Sun continued,

I don't want to get into the question of whether it [the removal of the statue] was right or wrong in any sort of political sense. Still—and this is just my personal opinion—I wish they hadn't torn it down. When I was a kid we used to go play in that park. It was a really nice park. A lot of families used to go, kids would play there around the base of the statue, it was a really nice gathering place. And I bet almost no one knew what that statue was or who that guy was. He was just a guy on a horse, right? I bet if you took a poll of all the people who used to play in that park, that almost no one would know or care about its history. So in some ways there was no reason to tear it down. But when they dismantled it, they dismantled part of my childhood with it. They dismantled part of my feeling for Macau (拆咗一部份我對澳門嘅感情).

Aware of the controversial politics inherent in his apparently apolitical remark, Ah Sun carefully distanced himself from any statements about the interpretation of Macau history or Portuguese sovereignty. His fondness for the statue (and, through the statue, for Macau), he insisted, had to do with memories of shared experiences with family and friends, memories that he placed firmly outside the political. Ah Sun contested the state's view that without its efforts, Macau residents would never develop a sense of place; instead, he blamed the state and its overly politicized view of what places mean for chipping away at his deeply felt attachment to his hometown. But he also contended that the state was doing the right thing by preserving as much as it had, for it provided space for the circulation of collective memories that may not be linked to grand narratives of culture, history, nation, empire, or humanity. "You may disagree with the government's interpretation of history," he said, "but at least people get the idea that Macau is worth thinking about. In the past, no one ever thought about Macau, because no one ever believed it was important."

Making Places Native

While the state was attempting to shore up the disappearing uniqueness of Macau and thereby instill Macau residents with a sense of belonging to their city, new urban development projects, those "monstrosities" that some felt threatened Macau's very exis-tence, were transforming the patterns of movement, settlement, and social interaction that are crucial parts of how people define their sense of place. Here, tentatively, ambivalently, even unwittingly, a sense of native place began to emerge, rooted not in the identifica-tion with or against a particular group or in a certain interpretation of history but in the anxious tension between past and future, local and national, "us" and "them."

The parish of Nossa Senhora de Fátima (花地瑪堂區),[36] known broadly as the "northern district" (Zona Norte/北區), was the fastest-growing district in Macau in the 1990s. The area that was in 1996 home to some 40 percent of Macau's population had been, 150 years previously, a narrow isthmus surrounded by the sea. The series of land reclamation projects that created this district began in 1919 with a narrow access road extending to Ilha Verde (青洲); in the early 1990s, the latest, largest landfill and development project, Areia Preta (黑沙環), was completed. By the late 1990s, the rubric "north-ern district" referred to five large neighborhoods (Areia Preta, Ilha Verde, Iao Hon/祐漢, Toi San/台山, and Fai Chi Kei/快子基), which had been expressly designed for industrial complexes and low-income housing projects. These new developments—which had ex-isted on paper in government planning bureaus and real estate devel-opment offices long before they ever took shape in the world—could scarcely have been more different from the older neighborhoods the government was trying to preserve, in both topography and toponymy. The new districts were flat and regular, transected by wide boulevards and uniform housing blocks; most of the streets were numbered (Rua 1 do Bairro de Iao Hon), named after Chinese his-torical figures (Avenida do Comendador Ho Yin 何賢紳士大馬路, Rua de Lei Pou Chon 李寶椿街), or given descriptive or generic names such as "Northwest Road," "Peace Street," or "North Race-course Boulevard."

These neighborhoods had come into existence well within the lifetimes of Macau's long-term residents. Lai San, a Macau Chinese woman in her late twenties, told me of working the dawn hours of her childhood harvesting vegetables on her family's farm in Iao Hon, land that had now sprouted concrete and blacktop, textile factories, auto shops, and the apartment complex where her parents still lived. The father of another acquaintance took great delight in driving me around the northern district, where he and his family lived and worked, and pointing out which of the present-day housing developments, factory dormitories, supermarkets, and parking structures had been mere vegetable fields or open sea when he had arrived in Macau in the 1960s. The construction of these developments, and the exports from the factories they housed, were both catalysts for and results of Macau's economic boom: by 1994, Areia Preta alone was home to over 40 percent of Macau's 1,587 manufacturing and export-processing factories (Wong Chao Son et al. 1997: 54).

An integral part of the boom that gave rise to these neighborhoods was the influx of well over 100,000 "new immigrants" in the space of a decade. The term "new immigrant" (新移民) had a very specific definition, at least in official publications; it referred to "Chinese citizens who have come to Macau, legally or illegally, from mainland China since January 14, 1979" (Wong Hong-keong and Wu 1996: 463).[37] Thanks to China's looser emigration policies after 1978 and to Macau's demand for cheap labor in the 1980s, the number of immigrants skyrocketed. On three occasions between 1982 and 1990, the Macau government granted amnesty to a total of more than 70,000 illegal Chinese immigrants; the city's legally resident population grew by 70 percent in the fifteen years between 1981 and 1996 (Choi and Kou 1998: 37).[38] The number of immigrants from mainland China still living in Macau illegally was estimated, in 1994, to be anywhere between 47,000 and 100,000.

By the 1990s, the majority of these new immigrants, both legal and otherwise, lived in the northern district. The reasons were severalfold: many workers came to Macau through labor-recruiting companies, which provided dormitory housing near the factories in Areia Preta where their charges worked; others, who lived and worked independently, found the housing cheaper in Areia Preta and Toi San than elsewhere in Macau. In addition, it was "closer" to China; as a Iao Hon social worker told me, "Since this part of town is directly connected to the mainland, it's really convenient for people to move in and out between Macau and the mainland." Those immigrants who stayed found that they often became eligible to buy government-subsidized housing in the same area.

Thus, despite the fact that plenty of long-term Macau residents, such as Lai San's parents, lived in the northern district, the new developments came to be associated with new immigrants. And although there was a widespread consensus that Macau's most recent era of prosperity had been built largely with the labor of these immigrants, the neighborhoods where they lived came rather quickly to be considered, in the minds of many long-term Macau residents, alien, confusing, and vaguely threatening. Several long-term Chinese residents of Macau, as well as ex-residents returning to Macau after long absences, told me they always got lost in the northern district. Many claimed that they knew how to get *through* the northern district to the PRC border, because they often went "back to the mainland" (返大陸) for inexpensive dining and shopping, but that the district itself remained, to them, a disorienting maze of buildings that "all look alike" and streets that were laid out in a confusing way. They told me stories of taking the wrong bus and ending up at a deserted terminus with no idea how to get home. In addition, because illegal immigrants sometimes arrived in Macau with the help of organized crime, the large number of illegal immigrants living in the northern district and the relatively high rate of gang-related violence there led to the association of the northern district with criminality. When I was apartment-hunting upon my arrival in Macau, a couple of Macau-born Chinese friends advised me that the neighborhood of Areia Preta, where rents were cheapest, "should be safe for foreigners—but if you were a single Chinese woman, I wouldn't recommend it." The wave of triad violence that caused so much anxiety during the transition era did redraw the map of Macau with regard to crime and violence, since these incidents occurred all over the city—especially in the vicinity of casinos, of which there were none in the northern district. But among many long-term Macau residents, the northern district never lost its taint of alienness and danger.

Another "problem" was that among the immigrants who populated the northern district, a substantial number were natives of

Fujian province, who speak several related dialects unintelligible to Cantonese speakers.[39] Fujianese sailors and merchants have played an important role in Macau since before the arrival of the Portuguese: the well-known origin story of the temple that gave Macau its Portuguese name, the Ma Gok or Ah-Ma Temple (媽閣廟), involves fishermen from Fujian saved from shipwreck by the apparition of the goddess Ah-Ma. In gratitude, they erected the temple that still stands on Macau's southwestern shore. Records indicate that Fujianese sailors in Malacca helped the first Portuguese navigate northward to China. Yet the different linguistic and cultural practices of these Fujianese migrants and their apparent refusal to "integrate" into Macau society gave rise to a certain measure of resentment on the part of some long-term Macau residents:

Fujian people here live like slaves, like slaves! They don't know how to enjoy life. They come here to work, they live up in the northern part of the city, in the ghetto, many of them don't even have their own apartments, and they live all cramped together, and then a bus will go pick them up, like 50 at a time, and take them to work. They work hard and save up their money and send it all back to Fujian. But they do not belong here—they are aliens here, really, they are just like slaves. They do not integrate into Macau society.

"They do not integrate into Macau society" was a complaint commonly made about the new immigrants in general, not only those from Fujian. One University of Macau sociologist who directed a survey among new immigrants echoed this popular sentiment when he concluded, "Most new immigrants have, at best, very tenuous connections with all levels of Macau society; . . . they mostly live entirely within their own social circles. New immigrants lack a sense of belonging to Macau, and some barriers exist between them and Macau people" (Wong Yau Kwan 1990: 168). As one Hong Kong–born Macau Chinese man put it, "Well, racism wouldn't be the right word, 'cause we're all Chinese, but . . . there are certainly snide remarks about people from the mainland squatting and throwing rubbish and this and that, and spitting."

As is often the case in such situations, the comments of the new immigrants themselves depicted a mirror image of the barriers, fears, assumptions, and prejudices that longer-term residents had expressed.

One of my students, a resident of the northern district, found it hard to believe that I and several of my Chinese friends always got lost in her neighborhood. When I said that I did not often go there, she immediately responded, "Oh, all the people you know in Macau must be rich. You should get to know some workers. They'll show you around." She then told me that a friend of hers had lived in Macau for eight years and had never once been to Taipa—one of Macau's two "outlying islands," a short bus ride from downtown, and the location of the only university in Macau, an island whose transformation from agricultural lands into a middle- and upper-middle-class residential district had occurred nearly simultaneously with the development of the northern district. But when I did get to know, through interviews, a group of eighteen immigrant workers from all over China, several of them told me that they didn't necessarily know their neighborhood any better than I did, for they found Macau a lonely, inhospitable, dangerous, and unpleasant place: the crime wave made them fearful of going out except in groups; the streets were too narrow, the air was dirty, it was so noisy, and the density of tall buildings meant you couldn't see the sun for most of the day. Most of them preferred to spend as much of their free time as possible just across the border in Zhuhai, where, it was true, there was more open space, the air was cleaner, the goods cheaper, people could speak Mandarin, and their families could visit them.

And in contrast to the Cantonese perceptions of poor, slavish Fujianese immigrants, an older Fujianese couple, merchants who had maintained an apartment in Macau for nearly twenty years (although they spent much of their time in Fujian) were proud of the contribution they had made to developing the northern district. They invited me to their home for tea one afternoon, picking me up in one of their two Mercedes-Benzes and driving me to their enormous condominium in the heart of Iao Hon. "Twenty years ago," they told me,

Fujian people who came here had to rent apartments from the Cantonese—and the Cantonese didn't like renting to Fujianese because Fujianese would live all crammed together, ten people in a single apartment, four per room, all young single men who had come to Macau to work. But now we Fujianese are the landlords, we're the ones renting apartments to the Cantonese.

That's because we Fujianese are thrifty. We like to save our earnings for the next generation to enjoy. Not the Cantonese, though. If they earn money today, they'll have spent it all by tonight. They don't think about the future. That's why the development of this district over the past twenty years has all been thanks to Fujianese. Twenty years ago this whole area was nothing but vegetable fields and broken-down little shacks. Now it's all high-rises and skyscrapers.

The government built the high-rises, they admitted, but who had moved in first, who had opened the shops and businesses that had made it the bustling neighborhood it now was?

Not all new immigrants, nor indeed all residents of the northern district, could be accused of "not integrating into Macau society." Indeed, it is clear that during the transition era, the term "new immigrant" came to refer not simply to a Chinese person recently arrived in the territory but to a specific social position that involved a particular configuration of class, neighborhood of residence, language, and perceived degree of alienation from Macau society. Thus, for example, when Li Qiulai—a college-educated woman from Shanghai who had learned Cantonese, taught at the University of Macau, and lived on Taipa—referred to herself as a "new immigrant," it always elicited laughter, even though Li came to Macau in 1985, later than many of the new immigrants who lived in the northern district.

In many ways, then, this was a classic example of how fissures along lines of native place arise. As in other places, it involved a sudden influx of people from a different place whose presence simultaneously enabled rapid economic growth and created an enormous strain on the existing social, economic, and urban infrastructure. As elsewhere, perceived differences between the immigrants and "locals" involved a reorganization of urban space, and these distinctions involved markers of class and dialect, and mutual accusations of criminality, alienness, filth, and moral degeneracy (Honig 1992, L. Zhang 2001). The difference was that in Macau, the sense of apprehension and threat was attributed not to immigrants from a particular village or region or province but to a broad spectrum of people from "mainland China." Thus the question of what the history of Macau's sovereign status meant to the present, and what it would mean in the future, did influence many Macau residents' sense of place, although in a way much different from that imagined by the Portuguese administration. I was told several times that the prejudice against mainlanders so prevalent in both Macau and Hong Kong in years past—a prejudice so strong that if you spoke Mandarin Chinese to people in shops or on the street, they would ignore you, scowl, glare, or even spit at you—had all but disappeared now that mainlanders were coming to Macau as investors and tourists with money to spend. Yet as the handover approached, and with it the Chinese state's rhetoric about the long-awaited reunification of the Chinese nation-state, there was an uneasiness afoot as the younger generation of Macau Chinese tried to figure out what to make of that unity. For, although they were clear about what Portuguese rule had *not* meant (namely, most of the things that the Portuguese state was saying it had), they began to realize that it had meant something: they had not experienced the same conditions (i.e., socialism) that had shaped the everyday practices, expectations, and desires of these new immigrants. The same young man who had returned from North America to find himself depressed, sad, and ashamed at the way Macau had changed during his absence told me that he was also bothered by the way people's behavior had changed: "People were never as rude to each other as they are now, they didn't use so much bad language, they were friendlier. . . . Now people are more self-centered." When I asked him why he thought this had occurred, he said, "I think it's from all these mainlanders who have come into Macau, these 'new immigrants' who came in mostly in the early 1990s. They come in, and there are so many of them, and this kind of cultural attitude spreads, like a virus. It's like a virus." The difference in "cultural attitude," he and others told me, was not because mainlanders were uneducated peasants; that perception may have been the basis for the prejudice of his parents' generation, but was clearly no longer the case. The difference was the result of divergent histories and modes of sovereignty. "Because the social system, work habits, and everyday customs in China are so different from those in Macau," wrote the sociologist Wong Yau Kwan, "it is no wonder that new immigrants have a hard time adapting" (Wong 1990: 168). In fact, one Macau Chinese man told me he thought it made sense to refer to "mainland Chinese" as a new social category, Macau's fourth major ethnic group, along with Portuguese, Macanese, and (Macau) Chinese.

It would perhaps be more accurate to say that the new social category that was emerging in these remarks was not "mainlanders" but "Macau Chinese" themselves, and that the sentiment binding this group together was not simply a shared antipathy to mainlanders but an emerging sense of native place. Indeed, in an informal survey I conducted in 1998 of just over 100 students between the ages of 14 to 18 at a Chinese-medium middle school, I asked them to identify their native place (in response to a question, "你是哪里人?" that translates only awkwardly into English, as "You are a person of what place?"); 61 percent responded that they were *oumun yahn*, or Macau people.[40] The political and economic changes of the transition period, which many people feared would sweep away Macau's "difference"—the influx of new immigrants, the boom in new construction, the departure of the Portuguese, the integration into the PRC—were giving rise to a stronger sense of place on the part of a young and growing Macau middle class, which had both the desire and the means to create a past that would be meaningful for themselves in the present. During the transition era, the association between the northern district as an alien and confusing place and the new immigrants as an alien and threatening group, combined with a nostalgic attachment to the *syufuhk* old buildings and sites of their childhood, was one way in which this group expressed a sense of emplacement—or of native-placement, as it were—in Macau. In the following chapter, I examine another venue, the Museum of Macau, in which Macau residents found the subject of their city's sort-of sovereign past represented as a source of pleasure rather than shame and where it became possible to envision Macau, however fleetingly, as a model rather than a ruin.

SIX

The Rubbish Heap of History

On April 18, 1998, a Saturday, the governor of Macau, Brigadier General Vasco Rocha Vieira, and the prime minister of Portugal, António Guterres (who happened to be in Macau to participate in another round of Joint Liaison Group meetings), presided over the inauguration of the brand-new Museum of Macau. The museum had been built from scratch in the space of four years. It occupied the Fortaleza do Monte, the oldest fort in the city, located on a hill right above the São Paulo Ruins. The green space atop the fortress had been transformed into an outdoor theater for the event, complete with red carpets and riser seating. The ceremony opened with a lion dance and speeches by the two dignitaries filled with quotations of nineteenth-century Portuguese poetry and lofty conclusions about the symbolism of the museum's location, which, Mr. Guterres observed, had been transformed from a walled fortress into a "locus of culture with open doors and accessible stairways." The bishop of Macau and the head Buddhist monk blessed the venue, the chants of the monk mingling in the air with the billows of smoke from the bishop's silver censer. Yet it was a relatively small affair, and there were many empty seats. Not only had the governor's office carefully vetted the guest list, but (it was said) they had sent the invitations at the last minute. As a result, several of the invited guests from mainland China, unable to get visas in time, were perforce absent. After the ceremony, the governor and the prime minister led the way for the inaugural museum visit, accompanied by an entourage of high-ranking local government officials and museum staff. They ambled from exhibit to exhibit, nodding as Jorge, one of the museum planning committee members, explained to them the significance of each display; they murmured their appreciation and their questions to Jorge. The rest of us—the twenty or thirty people who had not slipped out after the blessing—trailed quietly and politely behind.

The next day: chaos. It was a Sunday, and the museum opened to the public, free of charge, at 10:00 A.M. By closing time at 5:00 P.M., over 25,000 people had gone through the doors. Around mid-morning, as the crush of visitors inside the museum was beginning to make it impossible for anyone to enjoy the exhibits, the museum staff took to letting in groups of twenty people every fifteen minutes. This kept the crowds outside: the queue at the main entrance wound back and forth through the lobby, down the stilled steps of the upper escalator, across the patio past the museum shop, and three-quarters of the way down the lower escalator. But there were no barriers or velvet ropes to form people into lines in the lobby. Even though staff members had gotten everyone to queue up in remarkably orderly zig-zag fashion, each time the main doors opened to let another group in, the people at the zag end, who were farther back in the line but physically closer to the door than those at the zig end, broke ranks and rushed in first, and the whole line would collapse into a free-for-all. "We were completely unprepared," a staff member later told me.

We had no idea there would be so many people showing up on the first day. There was a fight and practically riots downstairs. This one off-duty policeman showed up with his wife and kids, drunk out of his gourd and complaining because we made him queue up, and when the security guard went over to calm things down, the guy took the nightstick off the guard's belt and clobbered him over the head with it, and then hit one of the women staffing the ticket counter as well—yeah, just walloped her too—and everyone had to go down to the police station to file a report. It was madness.

Inside, the gallery floors were littered with plastic bags and paper cups, museum flyers and candy wrappers; people milled about, discussing the exhibits loudly with others in their group. The atmosphere was downright *yihtnaauh* 熱鬧—literally "hot and noisy," an adjective used to describe events or places that are fun, exciting, and spectacular.

The Museum of Macau was one of ten new museums the government of Macau built in the twelve years prior to the handover.[1] Given what we have seen so far of the cultural politics of Macau in transition and given the takeoff that the leisure economy in China was experiencing at this time, it may hardly seem surprising that the Portuguese government chose to spend millions of dollars on the design and construction of museums that commemorated its legacy while generating income for the city. Nor was this phenomenon unique to Macau; it echoed a similar trend in mainland China, where the number of museums nationwide nearly quadrupled between 1980 and 1999.[2] But because the Museum of Macau was funded entirely by the Macau government, it was the one site in which the departing Portuguese state could give full play to its vision of what the nearly 450 years of its presence in Macau had meant and how that past might shape the way Macau residents thought about themselves as Chinese—or as different from all other Chinese. The museum would help dispel the image of Macau as a colonial backwater sustained by illicit activities and of the Portuguese administration as having generated, presided over, and benefited from this constellation of iniquities. It would help fashion a unified sense of identity and belonging among the various communities that called Macau home. The Macau once known as the "City of Sin" would now be refashioned as "Macau: City of Culture"—a slogan engraved in stone in the museum's exit hall.

Unlike the state's efforts in other realms, the Museum of Macau met with remarkable success: Macau residents' response to the museum was far more enthusiastic than anyone, including the residents themselves, had expected. By the second day, the staff was better prepared, and the number of visitors smaller; but even eighteen months later, in July 1999 when I did six weeks of fieldwork in the museum, the dynamic had not changed. The number of visitors had shrunk to an average of 8,000 per month, but on those occasions when the museum was full—especially with large groups from schools or old-age homes, or tours from the mainland or Taiwan— the docents had to shout to make themselves heard over the din, and the Filipino security guards apologetically but constantly shushed visitors' sometimes exuberant reactions to the exhibits. Indeed, the vast majority of visitors I talked to—mainlanders or Macau locals, Chinese or not, grownups or children, old folks, Australians, Portuguese, Hong Kongers—told me they enjoyed the museum. The interviews I conducted on the museum floor were not likely to elicit much criticism (due in no small part to my demeanor, standing in the exit lobby with a tape recorder, notebook, and pen, and a museum staff I.D. tag around my neck), although I always asked in as many ways as I could if there were things about the museum that could be changed or improved. But even in unsolicited comments I overheard in the museum and in numerous informal conversations I had elsewhere with people who had visited the museum, I heard far fewer criticisms than I had expected. A Macanese man from California who was in town visiting relatives said he had always hated museums but in this one found himself thoroughly fascinated. Friends from Hong Kong and the United States whom I expected would cynically see the museum as a colonial artifact told me they found it beautiful, world-class, first-rate. Students who had been dragged to the museum on a class trip didn't want to leave. Macau residents who had been skeptical about the huge expense of building the museum told me that it was worth every penny.

In this chapter I examine the dynamics of this success and ask how the museum succeeded in presenting a view of Macau's pasts that residents found compelling. But I also want to pay attention to the difficult terrain on which this success was built, for this terrain shaped the kind of success that was possible. At every step of the way, the process of creating the museum had provided the ground for charged moral debates about the meaning of Portuguese sovereignty, both as a historical condition and as the present-day power to represent the value of the past. Whereas the museum planners felt their project was both necessitated and hindered by residents' lack of any sense of the value of their past, some residents reviled the museum's misunderstanding, misuse, and misrepresentation of that past. Although the popularity of the museum suggests that its representational strategies managed to overcome these divisive politics remarkably well, the behavior of all those enthusiastic visitors on opening day—shouting and littering and brawling in the lobby—

raised questions as to what exactly it had succeeded at. The museum remade Macau in a standardized, systematized form that replaced the city's jumble of differences and unsavory associations with a narrative about the civilizing influence of international commerce and shared sovereignty. But the very attempt to represent this narrative in a way that would enable the broadest possible spectrum of Macau residents to identify with it both opened up new spaces in which residents could evaluate Macau's past and its relationship to their future and undercut the unifying, "systematizing" project of the museum itself.

Valuing the Past

The Museum of Macau was the most expensive, most publicized, and most visited museum built during the 1990s museum boom. Quotes on the final cost of the museum vary, but it was in the vicinity of US$16–17 million. Carlos Bonina Moreno, the Portuguese architect in charge of creating the museum (to whom all the staff referred to, respectfully and affectionately, by his almost transcendental title, "the Architect"), had lived in Macau since 1982, and had earned a name for himself by designing the Maritime Museum in the late 1980s. According to him, this new project had arisen from a dinner-table conversation with Governor Vasco Rocha Vieira. "The governor said to me, 'I want to create a museum that will tell the story of Macau, will you build it for me?' That was it," Moreno told me in our first interview, a few weeks after the museum opened to the public.[3] "No instructions, no deadlines, no collection, no venue, no budget, no staff"—just a personal request and an implicit target date: the museum needed to be completed well before the handover.[4] Moreno convened a committee of museum planners, who got to work choosing a location, hiring staff, plotting a "storyline," and assembling a collection. The process of creating the museum, he claimed in a newspaper interview just prior to the inauguration, was like making a movie: "We chose the location, we wrote the script and we looked for the artists. We looked for objects that contributed to the story of Macau. . . . The most important thing for us [was] not to have objects of great value but exhibits that tell the story—the story of Macau and all that represents its soul" (*Macau Travel Talk*, n.d.: 7). He emphasized that from the beginning, he and the other members of the museum planning committee had wanted to move away from the "traditional" museum form, which he found to be pedantic, "sterile," and "temple-like." They wanted instead to create a museum that was "as much for the senses as for the mind" (Edwards 1998)—or, as the Architect put it in an interview with me, "a museum for normal people, not intellectuals."

In many ways, the Museum of Macau was a classic heritage project. Although it was not intended to be a history museum in the strict sense (because, as one of the planning committee members told me, Macau history was far too complex to be represented in a single museum), Macau's past was its principal subject. The attempt to engage "normal" people through a fusion of education and entertainment; the labeling, restoration, and nostalgic contemplation of historical sites and objects; and the idea that the unique past residing in those sites and objects could both define the people of Macau as an autonomous group and be marketed profitably to a growing transnational audience of cultural tourists echoed similar projects in countless other places.[5] Richard Handler has written convincingly of the "objectifying logic" exemplified by heritage projects—a logic that "allows any aspect of human life to be imagined as an object" that can be possessed, preserved, consumed, or commodified by the collective individual of the nation (Handler 1988: 141–42). But a study of how heritage projects represent the value of the past must push this metaphor a step further, asking what *kind* of object the past is imagined as. Artifact, commodity, talisman, text: each of the myriad ways of imagining any given object entails a different understanding of that object's purpose and its relationship to individuals, communities, and other objects. Each way of classifying an object is a different way of conceptualizing its value, and each conceptualization of value structures differently the way the objectified past may be represented and the kinds of present-day social relations this representation may engender.

On one hand, in 1990s Macau, the past was often spoken of as a resource or raw material (or a set of resources and raw materials) that could be worked into a marketable, profit-generating commodity that would allow the city to tap into a growing transnational leisure market. As the Macau government explored avenues for economic development that would help the city diversify away from its dependence on gambling, a variety of bureaucrats, real estate developers, and tourism industry leaders began to agree that, properly worked up, Macau's past could be packaged and sold in ways that would translate Macau's "difference" into tourist dollars. A Portuguese friend who worked in the Macau Government Tourism Office (MGTO) told me this was the reason for the museum boom: "It all boils down to an attempt to diversify the product we can offer to tourists." As of the summer of 1999, there were as many museums in Macau as there were casinos.

At the same time, however, the museum staff viewed the importance of their actions precisely in terms of fending off the ravages of transnational capitalism. They imagined the raw materials of Macau's past as having a value that was unique, untranslatable, and imperceptible to those who sought the value of the past solely in its economic exploitability. This was the past as fetish object, with the power to transform each decaying pile of bricks, each moldy document, each historical fact unearthed from the mass grave of unremarked events that constitute the past, into one more testament to and component of Macau's uniqueness in the modern world. Imagined thus, the past had the power to transform Macau residents from rootless, self-absorbed immigrants into citizens who understood themselves as inheritors and protectors of that uniqueness. In his speech at the inauguration of the museum, the governor who had commissioned it praised it as "an institution that will valorize the city in an extraordinary way by bringing into focus its image as a place whose distinguishing characteristics include ethno-cultural harmony, tolerance, and the affirmation of citizenship" (Vieira 1998). The Architect, too, told me that he felt this was the museum's true purpose. For him, the museum's target audience was not the busloads of tourists on their way home from the casinos but the population of Macau. Noting that more than half of this population had moved to Macau during the economic boom of the past two decades, he said:

A society needs to have some common culture or traditions, like a cement bonding it together. Otherwise, it is just like living in one of those high-rise buildings you see being built all over Macau now, where you can live right next door to your neighbors for so many years, and still never know them, never even say "hello" to them. The museum can help create a common identity, a common language and culture. This is the role of the museum in the city.

Both literally and metaphorically, then, the Architect saw the museum as creating an alternative system that would counter the divisive social effects of capitalist development.

Far from being unique to Macau, this bifurcated understanding of the value of the past is central to the heritage concept. Recent studies of museums, historical theme parks, and World Heritage sites in China demonstrate how heritage discourse thrives on the fusion of these two conceptions of value. They argue that such sites are spaces in which circuits of political, economic, and moral value (at the local, national, and transnational levels) intersect and make cultural nationalism, local identity, consumerism, and state legitimacy indistinguishable from one another and naturalize them as timeless characteristics of Chinese culture. In China as elsewhere, "heritage" thus signals a condition in which the interests and ideologies of state and market have coincided so completely that the past is opened up as both justification for and new frontier of capitalist accumulation and subject-making.[6] In this analysis, heritage discourse effects interpretive closure on the past, obscuring the relations of domination that structured that history (and continue to structure our appreciation of that history) and providing a unified, universalized, and "self-congratulatory" narrative through which viewers should understand the past's relationship to the present and the role that past has played in the creation of present-day communal identities.[7]

Yet virtually all these studies note that the meanings visitors take from heritage sites exceed the ideological intentions of the designers. This "excess" is often seen as a gap in an otherwise seamless ideological text, an unintended consequence that marks the limit-point of ideology.[8] But closer examination of how these texts are produced and how viewers interact with them reveals the oversimplifications in this analysis. In the Museum of Macau, the fusion of divergent

ways of valuing the past was far more fractious than heritage discourse let on. The creation of gaps was hardly unintended; it
was crucial to effecting the convergence of contradictory ways of
valuing the past—contradictions that became apparent, if they
hadn't been already, in the very articulation of the heritage project.
These were fundamental contradictions not only about the interpretation of Macau's colonial past and what parts of that past were
worth preserving but also about how and by whom the past could
best be transmitted to the future and for what purpose. In short, the
museum planners had to contend with all the contrary views about
the nature of colonialism and sovereignty, Chineseness and non-
Chineseness, and the contours of community and belonging that the
process of political transition had raised. Later in the chapter I explore the effects of this gap-making strategy; first, however, I examine these contradictions and their consequences for the museum.

What Is a Museum?

As we have seen, questions about the value of displaying Macau's
past dogged the museum project from its very inception. It also
shaped the kinds of work that its staff felt able or compelled to do.
The dozen or so museum staffers I interviewed, like the Architect,
understood the importance of their own labor in terms of its moral
significance. When I asked one senior administrator, a Macau Chinese woman, why she thought the Portuguese had wanted to build
such a museum in the first place, she admitted that she thought all
the government's "beautiful words" about fostering a sense of identity and belonging were just so much PR; the real reason, she maintained, was that the Portuguese state wanted to make itself look
good on its way out. One of the Portuguese staff members concurred,
saying that the city government had wanted to improve residents'
image of the Portuguese and to change the widespread impression
that the government never did anything for the public. But this
cynicism about the state's motives for building the museum did not
diminish these staff members' own enthusiastic commitment to
the project of presenting, as the same senior administrator put it,
an "honest assessment of Macau's past," one that would actively

involve the community in reflecting on the "true spirit" of Macau
and transmitting that spirit to future generations.

The staff's sense that the museum's main value was ethical rather
than economic in nature was reinforced by the fact that once it was
up and running, it was not administered by MGTO, which ran several of the other new museums in town, but by the Cultural Institute,
which administered, among other things, the Cultural Heritage Department, the city archives, the Central Library, a semi-scholarly
journal on Macau culture and history, and several research scholar-
ships. The museum staff saw the decision to place the museum under
the control of the Cultural Institute as a sign that the government
considered the museum an educational institution whose primary aim
was to foster ongoing research and teaching about Macau's past,
rather than a "tourist attraction" on a par with food festivals and the
Macau Grand Prix, whose primary goal was the generation of income.[9] Everyone I asked was pleased with this decision but feared that
the fact that it had taken the government several months to reach it
betrayed lingering doubts about the true value of the museum.

In fact, as time went on, many staffpeople felt that the value of
their labor was misunderstood. One day in the summer of 1999, the
same administrator who had earlier dismissed the state's "beautiful
words" called me into her office at lunchtime because, she told me,
she wanted to explain why the museum did not work "the way we,
the staff, want it to." This was, she said, primarily because no one
outside the museum, not even in the government that commissioned it, believed that there was any substantial work to be done
once the museum was up and running. Several of her colleagues
echoed this sentiment on other occasions. "They think it is a permanent exhibition, a static thing, not a living museum," said Cristina, a young Portuguese woman in charge of educational programs
and community outreach. "They think of it like a monument," said
another. The director (a Macau Chinese woman who had worked
for the museum for several years before being appointed to the direc-
torship in December 1998) told me she had been surprised and dismayed to learn the extent to which people in Macau—even her own
superiors in the government—saw the museum as nothing more
than a "tourist attraction." No one seemed to understand that

Macau's past could have a value outside its commodifiable potential. But who, she asked, would argue that the Louvre is primarily a "tourist attraction," even though it is the first place tourists go in Paris? Although she and the rest of the staff of just over thirty people (including the support crew of computer programmers, drivers, groundskeepers, and security guards) were chronically overworked, she had a hard time justifying to other government departments and to the public why she needed so many employees: once the museum was "finished," they asked, couldn't it operate with just a ticket-taker and one or two guides? The museum staff felt they had to educate the people of Macau, including their own superiors, not only about the value of their past but also about the value of a museum. The first temporary exhibition to be designed, organized, and mounted after the museum's inauguration was entitled "What Is a Museum?" and explained to visitors what kinds of work went into running a museum, what made a museum different from other attractions on the tourist itinerary, and why it was an important institution for a city like Macau to have.

The Heart of Macau

One of the first decisions the planners made about the museum—where to put it—was one of their most divisive and revealed early on the kinds of problems that differing conceptions of the value of old places and objects would engender. The Architect and his colleagues decided that the Fortaleza São Paulo do Monte (usually known as the Fortaleza do Monte, 大炮台, or the Monte Fort) would be the ideal location for a museum dedicated to celebrating the history and culture of Macau. Built between 1617 and 1626, the Monte Fort forms part of a complex of buildings, including the São Paulo Church, that has been called the "acropolis" of Macau: the political, military, religious, symbolic, and erstwhile geographic center of the city. The Jesuits had built the complex and were its first owners and residents; but in 1623, with the arrival from Portugal of Macau's first resident governor, the Jesuits were kicked out and the fort was transformed into the governor's residence and the center of Portuguese state and military power. As the city grew, the state used the fort for a variety of purposes: it served at various times as a residence of the military commander, a prison, a barracks, and (beginning in 1965) a meteorological observatory and public park that ranked high on the list of tourist sites. The fort had long dominated civilian life as well as the military: salvos had been fired from its cannon during state visits or at the death of dignitaries; signals had been hoisted from its flagpoles to warn of fire or approaching typhoons; and criminals punished atop its ramparts to serve as lessons to the populace. More recently, during the 1992 International Music Festival, it had served as the venue for a more positive (if not more edifying) spectacle, as its grounds were transformed into an open-air theater for a performance of *The Barber of Seville* (Teixeira and Silva 1998: 88–91). The changing uses of the fort through the centuries spoke to the changing nature of the Portuguese presence and the changing forms of urban life in Macau.

The Monte Fort was also the setting for one of the city's founding legends. On June 24, 1622, at the height of Macau's prosperity and on a day when most of the able-bodied Portuguese men were away at the Canton trade fair, the Dutch navy attacked Macau with more than 600 men. The Dutch were expecting a quick victory over the few priests, administrators, and slaves who remained in the virtually defenseless city. But a single cannon shot, fired by a Jesuit priest from atop the half-built fort, fortuitously hit the Dutch powder kegs, destroying their ammunition, killing several commanding officers, and causing such disorder among the troops that the handful of defenders easily drove them back to the sea. The legend goes that during the citywide celebration after this victory, the slaves who had fought most valiantly were granted freedom in recognition of their courage in defending the city, and Chinese officials in Guangzhou sent gifts of rice in gratitude and celebration.[10] A few months later, upon request from Beijing, the Portuguese in Macau sent cannon and troops to aid in the Ming armies' struggle against the Manchus in the north; in the ensuing year, Chinese officials recognized the wisdom of allowing the Portuguese to fortify the city—a step they had long resisted (Boxer 1937). Thus (during the transition era, at least) the story of this miraculous victory was told as the story not of the triumph of Portuguese empire, but of Macau as a site where the interests of Portugal and China converged. Until 1999, the anniversary of the battle (which was also the feast day of St. John the Baptist, who became the patron saint of Macau) was celebrated every year as Dia da Cidade, or "City Day."

In short, as my friend from MGTO laconically put it, the Monte Fort was "a prime piece of real estate"—valuable by virtue of its location, its history, and its symbolic potency. Although the planning committee had considered several sites for the museum, the Architect told me it was almost immediately clear that the fort was the best choice, not only for its proximity to tourist circuits and parking but, more important, because, as he put it, "It is the heart of Macau; Macau was born there." Moreover, he felt that transforming a fortress into a center of culture and learning would symbolize the museum's message about the ultimately peaceful and enlightened course of Portuguese rule in Macau.

Yet for critics of the Portuguese, housing a museum dedicated to representing the "soul" of Macau in a site so powerfully associated with the Portuguese state and military was symptomatic of the whole problem with the Macau heritage project: it suggested the degree to which the Portuguese obsession with heritage was nothing more than the attempt to continue their colonial presence by other means. In the months before the museum opened, one Macau Chinese friend (who had never hidden from me his dislike of the Portuguese) wondered aloud whether, given its location, the Museum of Macau would be "one of those museums that has a room with portraits of all the colonial governors." I told him that I'd seen the plans for the museum and they did not include such a room. Even so, he said, he didn't envision himself having any interest in visiting a museum built by the Portuguese, nor for that matter any museum that celebrated Macau's past, which he saw as characterized by prejudice, greed, corruption, and national humiliation. The fort was an "ideal" location for the museum only for those who already accepted the narrative that the museum was designed to tell.

In this sense, although the symbolic value of the museum's location appeared self-evident to the planners, much work had to be done to ensure that this value was evident to all. The publicity surrounding the construction and inauguration of the museum afforded many opportunities to tell and retell the origin story of the fort. This story was also included as the subject of an exhibit inside the museum: a small interactive video screen played a simple computer-animated version of the battle and eulogized the valiant defenders of the city, without mentioning their ethnic composition.[11] Indeed, during a tour I tagged along on in the summer of 1999, one of the docents explained to a group of middle-school students that this exhibition told the story of the day that "we Macau residents (我哋澳門居民) defended Macau against the Dutch." By directing public attention to this origin story—rather than to any of the other events that had taken place in the fort in the 400 years of its existence—the museum designers framed the fort as a symbol of the common interests of Portugal and China and the defense of those interests as the very foundation upon which Macau had been built. Within this narrative, then, even a Portuguese fortress could be evidence not of imperialism and aggression against China but of the shared sovereignty that formed the basis for the distinctiveness of Macau's "system."

But according to the Architect, there were two practical problems with locating a museum on this site. First, the Monte Fort was well named for its position atop a hill with a commanding view of the city, and, like any good fort, it took some effort to get to. You had to climb the hill, reaching the main entrance either from the west, following a footpath that meandered southward from the São Paulo Ruins, along a stretch of green below the rough *chunambo* walls of the fort and up a steep, uneven stone staircase; or from the east, tracing a series of ever-narrower, ever-steeper streets that wound upward between aging four-story apartment buildings whose iron-grated balconies were strung with plants and laundry and whose ground-floor shops spilled their buoyant clutter of merchandise out onto the street. The planners feared that, as the Architect put it, "If people have to get all hot and exhausted trying to get here, they won't come." Second, the planners estimated that the museum would need at least 1,500 m^2 of exhibition space, but the only existing building on the fortress grounds (an early twentieth-century structure that had been used as the city's meteorological observatory) was far too small. The question was how to create such a space in a way that would not destroy the historic structures and ambience of the fort and yet be easily accessible from the São Paulo Ruins and the street below.

Building the museum underground—into the hill itself—solved both problems. But it also provoked further questions as to what the value of this location, and of the tangible traces of Macau's past, really was. For as they dug, the team encountered abundant evidence of the very past they were seeking to preserve: the foundations of the building where the first Portuguese governors of Macau had resided; the remains of structures from the São Paulo Seminary; an old rubbish heap that contained ceramic pieces from the late Ming dynasty; and a 33-meter-long portion of stone wall, six meters tall and two meters thick, that predated the construction of the fort itself by at least a decade.[12] In order to make space for the museum, the planners and Portuguese archaeologists brought in especially for the excavation decided to document, photograph, and remove the foundations of the governors' house, to pull the ceramics out of the rubbish heap, and to demolish most of the wall. In conversations with me and in interviews with the press, they downplayed the significance of this decision, noting only that some archaeological remains discovered during the process of excavation had been carefully restored and included in museum displays and that a portion of the old wall had been left standing and unobtrusively incorporated into the foyer of the museum. But the handling of these discoveries was lambasted in a series of articles published in the *Macao Daily* shortly after the museum opened, in which writer Chan Dou (1998a, b, c, d) accused the museum designers of amateurism, ignorance, and stupidity. Chan agreed with the museum designers that the Monte Fort was the perfect location for a museum dedicated to the history of Macau, because it was "the site of the greatest historical value in Macau" (澳門最具歷史價值的焦點). But the remains of the governors' residence inside, Chan argued, also "had enormous historical value. After all, how many architectural structures dating from the Ming dynasty still exist in Macau?" (Chan 1998b). In an article the next day, he continued: "These sites don't belong to any one person, any one ethnic group, or any one institution; they are the heritage (文物財產) of this place. What sense does it make to demolish them and shovel away the remains? Who came up with such an idiotic idea?" (Chan 1998c). The implicit answer to this last question—it was the Portuguese government's idiotic idea—indicated that far from improving the image of the Portuguese state in the eyes of the public, the museum project thus far had, for at least part of that public, affirmed the alienness and illegitimacy of a government that treated the evidence of its own past so cavalierly and had such a wrongheaded vision of how the past mattered to the present day.

In the summer of 1999, I asked the museum director what she thought of these accusations. She understood the concerns behind them, she said, but in the end

> they had to decide which would better serve the public—having a big open pit there on top of the fort, which was one of the only green spaces in that whole part of the city, or having a museum there. Besides, the plans were all completed and the work was already under way. To abandon the site at that point, to find another site for the museum and start all over again, just in order to leave the fort as an archaeological site, didn't make sense.[13]

All projects of heritage preservation beg the fundamental question of what should be preserved and why, and require their planners to make difficult decisions about the relative value (aesthetic, didactic, historical, and financial) of the objects and sites under their control. Such decisions reveal their assumptions about how the past matters. In this case, it became clear that the designers considered the Monte Fort a valuable location for the museum primarily because of the narrative significance it would take on as a museum dedicated to a particular interpretation of the past, rather than to the unmediated material evidence of that past it already contained. This tension between the value of historical authenticity on one hand and of narrative and aesthetic mediation on the other was even more pronounced when it came to conceptualizing the value of the objects in the museum's collection.

The Rubbish Heap of History

As of the summer of 1999, the museum's permanent collection consisted of around 3,000 objects. Everyone who had worked with the museum since its inception was quite proud of the fact that, four years earlier, they had begun with zero objects and created the collection as they built the museum. As the Architect noted at the outset, the designers had not built the museum to house a collection of objects already deemed valuable; they found, or created, the objects necessary to tell a story about the value of the past. But again, divergent ways of imagining this value often entailed incongruous ways of representing it.

On one hand, a large number of objects in the museum were replicas of other objects: plaster "terracotta" soldiers, Styrofoam steles, fiberglass cannons, plastic molds of shrimp dumplings and carrot cakes, newly tailored "traditional" costumes, reproduced photographs, aluminum swords.[14] These objects were often displayed alongside, or as part of, dioramas and models—modes of representation that, as Kirk Denton (2005: 576) has pointed out, "eschew 'authentic' artifacts and embrace the patented inauthenticity of recreated scenes." Although the display captions and tour docents were usually careful to indicate which objects were replicas, the museum staff also emphasized that the authenticity of the objects did not matter. In this sense, as a Portuguese friend of mine (a teacher who had lived in Macau for several years and who himself had loaned some objects to the museum) noted, "It is a principle similar to the 'antique' furniture shops you see in the vicinity of the museum. It doesn't matter so much if the things inside are fake-old or really old." What was being packaged and sold, in both the faux-antique shops and the museum, was customers' sensory experience of antiqueness and authenticity. In the Museum of Macau, as in other similar museums, objects were valued not for their unique aura or their ability to provide "historical testimony" (Benjamin 1968: 221) but for their capacity to evoke "pastness" in carefully managed ways. In a logic by which the past was a raw material primed for commodification, it made sense to represent it through simulacra, endlessly reproducible and exchangeable, making of the past an infinitely renewable resource. In this sense, the museum staff again seemed to be working with an anti-fetishistic concept of the value of objects: the transformative power of the past lay not in the objects themselves but in the story those objects could be made to tell.

On the other hand, the fact that the museum included "real" artifacts clearly did matter. Small placards made note of objects donated by local individuals or institutions, and docents always emphasized that certain objects—the bells that once tolled in the tower of the

São Paulo Church, the bellhop's uniform from the old Bela Vista hotel, the wedding dress worn by a Macanese bride in the 1920s, the Neolithic potsherds excavated from the beaches of Coloane, or the shards of seventeenth-century porcelain unearthed from the old Santo Agostinho monastery—were "real." For the designers were equally adamant that the museum should be not only *for* the people of Macau but also (as Cristina put it) "a product of Macau, made by the people of Macau." They wanted the museum's representation of Macau's past not only to appear authentic but to *be* an authentic self-representation by Macau residents.[15] And for this purpose, simulacra, with their qualities of anonymity and reproducibility, would not serve. Macau's heritage was not something that could be reproduced just anywhere, by anyone; it was rooted, reflected, and sustained in the material culture and daily lives of the people of Macau. This reflected precisely the kind of fetishistic understanding of the value of objects that the use of replicas seemed to disavow: the idea that the transformative power of the past actually resides in old things and that, should those things disappear, the past and its power would disappear with them.

This idea of the past as a nonrenewable resource that was vanishing before their very eyes animated the actions of many staff members I spoke with. When I asked Cristina about the provenance of the "real" objects in the museum, she replied:

About half the stuff in the museum comes from the rubbish heap. Literally! [We] walked around the city for hours looking in rubbish dumps. They dismantled one of the old pawnshops—closed it down and dismantled the building, and no one claimed the stuff inside, so they threw it in the trash. [We] got *so much* stuff from that dump. I used to walk around town with [one of the planning committee members], and she would just pick up some old piece of junk that looked worthless, and it would turn out to be something really interesting. Really. We looked in every rubbish heap in the city.[16]

Jorge, a history teacher from Portugal and a member of the museum planning committee, told me of going into swaybacked, abandoned old buildings, risking life and limb to salvage pieces of furniture, kitchen shrines, window shutters, or the sliding doors with thick wooden bars that let air in and kept strangers out and were almost as ubiquitous in nineteenth-century Cantonese houses as steel window grates are in Cantonese apartments today. He had spotted, in a house that was condemned and falling to pieces, the carved wooden votive tablet dedicated to the Earth God that now adorned the wall above the stairs to the mezzanine. The story of his efforts to retrieve the tablet was often included in docents' comments on tours.

I was never sure if Cristina and Jorge were attuned to the irony of this image of a handful of Portuguese civil servants rooting through the rubbish of a largely Chinese city, pulling from the refuse objects that they felt represented the "soul" of its people. But the sense of salvaging the city from its own rubbish heaps clearly heightened the staff's sense of the urgency of their project. For it confirmed the idea that the people of Macau were complicit in the disappearance of their heritage—not because of ideological resistance, but because of their ignorance of the multiple kinds of value that old things could have. This impression was only substantiated when, in the attempt to create a museum of and by the people, the planners solicited donations of objects from the community. "We accepted everything," said the Architect, "no matter if it was valuable or not. We just wanted people to feel that this would be their museum." But as it turned out, he said, these donations did not add up to much. And this, the staff lamented, was because Macau residents just did not understand the historical value of antique objects. As Grace, the young Macau Chinese woman in charge of the Conservation Department, put it,

This museum is a good place to preserve the old things of Macau. If we didn't have this museum . . . maybe people would destroy them or damage them. But now that we have this museum, people will think, OK, *if I want to throw this thing away*—before they throw things away, they will think, *oh, why not take it to the museum and put it in the museum?*

I was startled by the idea that even potential donors would conceive of the museum as being full of objects that would otherwise belong in the rubbish. Working from my own assumptions about the value of museum pieces, I asked Grace why, if someone had an object they believed museum-worthy, they wouldn't try to sell it instead. She replied,

We have had the experience, some donors, they say, *oh, if the museum doesn't want it, we'll just throw it away* [. . .] Because for them, most objects don't have market value, they have [only] historical value. Like a piece of paper, maybe it has [some scribblings] by a famous writer, but maybe the local people would think, *oh, for me it's just a piece of paper.* But maybe for the historian it's a valuable manuscript. It's a different perspective, a different point of view.[17]

As Grace points out, the problem was not Macau residents' ignorance of the potential exchange value of genuine historical artifacts. There really was no market for the old suitcases Cristina and her colleagues had pulled from the pawnshop dumpster or the worm-eaten window shutters Jorge had rescued from the bulldozers. But according to Cristina, it was this single-minded approach to value that both hampered the attempt to build a museum "of the people" and gave the museum its *raison d'être.* The ideas that objects in general, not just in the museum, could be conduits for historical consciousness and that historical consciousness itself should be of value to everyone in the community because it was the constitutive cement of that community would have to be part of the museum's educational mission.[18]

Yet as the museum grew, it developed its own financial, spatial, and narrative economy, and the value of historical objects began to be measured in new and conflicting ways. By 1999, storage space was dwindling, the red tape necessary to register donated objects (or to get rid of registered objects) was proliferating, and the museum became more selective in accepting donations. Although the official collections policy was still being drafted in the summer of 1999, Grace told me that "for the museum to acquire an object these days, it must be related to Macau culture, and also related to our themes." For example, she continued:

In our permanent collection, we have a theme on tea. So, if somebody donates a very beautiful teapot, maybe we would accept it. But of course it must be a valuable one. Unique. If you can find it in the market, it's not valuable. I mean, unique. Or . . . you have seen that we have some documents from a wedding? Yeah. But we only have one set. So, it would be nice if somebody wanted to donate another set of wedding documents, like a wedding certificate or something . . . But if it's just a piece of paper, or something that has nothing to do with our themes, we would not accept it. Even if it's old.

After the museum opened, although the museum staff was still concerned with educating people about the value of "old things," they were forced to start making different distinctions of value, becoming more discriminating in decisions about what counted as the raw materials of Macau identity. Like the Monte Fort, the value of potential museum objects was measured not by their price, beauty, age, or uniqueness but by their ability to fit the story the museum was designed to tell. I next describe that story and the techniques used to tell it and then examine in more detail the responses Macau residents had to seeing their city's past represented in this way.

The Story of Macau

Pushing open the heavy tinted-glass doors to enter the museum from the lobby, you find yourself in a dark, cool room, with walls and floor of stone. A placard on the facing wall informs you in Chinese, Portuguese, and English that you are about to travel along "a 'time corridor' towards the first encounter," that will allow you to better compare some "significant developments of the [Chinese and European] civilizations up to the sixteenth century"—that is, up to the moment that the first Portuguese set foot on Chinese soil. A wide corridor extends to your left; two long spotlit vitrines, each one guarded by a statue approximately six feet tall, line the walls on either side. The statues are fiberglass replicas of a granite "Iberian Peninsula Warrior (first century B.C.)" and a terracotta "Xi'an warrior (Qin Dynasty, 221–207 B.C.)," and the two glass cases correspond, respectively, to "European" and "Chinese" civilizations. Each case holds six displays describing (as one of the museum planners put it) "how the major problems of civilization were solved." Six topics— Writing, Philosophy, Empire, Religion, Technology, and [East-West] Contacts—are each represented by a small group of objects and a descriptive paragraph in three languages. The six displays are spaced directly across the corridor from one another, allowing the visitor to move either back and forth between civilizations, or sequentially down through the ages, beginning, on the European side, with

Fig. 9   The Museum of Macau's "Time Corridor" displays the accomplishments of
"European" and "Chinese" civilizations throughout the ages, culminating (on the
far wall) in the establishment of Macau (photo by author, 1999).

Egyptian hieroglyphs, and running through Socrates, aqueducts, and
Catholicism, and culminating in the sixteenth-century Portuguese
voyages of "discovery"; or, on the Chinese side, with the origins of
Chinese writing, and then on to Confucius, Qin Shihuang, gunpow-
der, and bridges, and culminating in the fifteenth-century voyages of
Admiral Zheng He. Along the way, the corridor narrows perceptibly,
bringing these two civilizations closer together in space, through
time. They do not physically meet but are brought together in the
viewer's gaze by a black video box centered on the far wall, with red
holographic writing that reads "MACAU / 澳門" (see Fig. 9).

This entrance hall, physically and conceptually bracketed off
from the rest of the museum as a kind of preface, sets up the representative strategies for the whole first floor. It establishes symmetry
and equivalence between two cosmopolitan civilizations, two privileged bearers of culture, China and "the West"—even the two warriors at the entrance are exactly the same height, although the Iberian soldier is cut off at the knees. And it establishes Macau as the
product of the inexorable encounter between these civilizations:
the culmination of four thousand years of world history.

This corridor empties into a cul-de-sac, the Archaeology Room, which features displays of Neolithic potsherds discovered in Macau and cross-dated maps of similar archaeological finds in the Pearl River Delta region. Miniature dioramas invite you to imagine what life was like for the Neolithic settlers of Macau, and what might have happened during the "first encounter" between Portuguese mariners and Chinese mandarins at Macau. Add to this a few maps and ceramics from the fifteenth and sixteenth centuries, and the scene has been set: Macau has been established as an ancient, peaceful, continuously but sparsely populated Chinese territory, where Portuguese traders, representatives of a civilization as advanced as the Chinese, came to sell their wares to their formidable yet welcoming Chinese hosts. Macau is about to be transformed by foreign trade.[19]

In the main hall of the first floor, these themes of symmetry, equivalence, and the civilizing influence of foreign trade are developed. The Commerce area describes how China and the world, via Macau, transformed each other. Large interactive wall maps show the trade routes that spanned the world from Lisbon to Manila to Acapulco, converging on Macau. A three-dimensional cross-section of a typical Portuguese ship's hold is stocked with bales of silk, bars of silver, clay jars of ginger and pepper and cinnamon, crates of tea leaves, and porcelain dishes tied in bundles. A series of interactive wall-mounted exhibits explains the importance of Chinese silk, tea, and porcelain to Europe's economy and culture. This section establishes a cosmopolitan Macau, central to the processes of world trade and rightful bearer of the epithet "bridge between east and west."

The Administration and Defense area—where one might expect to find those portraits of Portuguese governors or other representations of Portuguese sovereignty over Macau—develops the theme of harmonious and mutually beneficial coexistence. A miniature diorama depicts Macau's first foundry and emphasizes that the cannon cast there not only were used in Macau but were exported to Europe and, in the seventeenth century, sent to Beijing for use in the Ming dynasty's losing struggle against the Manchu invaders. It is here that the video of the 1622 Dutch attack reminds visitors of the joint interests of the Portuguese and Chinese in Macau. And mounted side-by-side on the wall are two fiberglass reproductions of stone steles, one carved with a crown and a coat of arms, the other with rearing dragons and the characters "imperial decree" (聖旨); beneath them is a long glass cabinet displaying, on one half, a series of official documents in Portuguese, and on the other half, a long scroll in Chinese and Manchu, bearing the seal of the Daoguang emperor. Although not explicitly stated, it is clear that these are symbols of joint sovereignty, of the symmetry and symbiosis between Chinese and Portuguese governance over Macau.[20]

The themes of civilizational symmetry and enlightened exchange are further developed in the area called Meeting of Cultures, which portrays two major religious traditions associated with China and Portugal. Along one wall, a series of display nooks hold, one after the other, a miniature model of the Lin Fung Temple 蓮峰廟,[21] examples of Chinese religious art, "Luso-Chinese interactions in religious art," examples of Christian religious art, and a miniature model of the São Lourenço Church.[22] A multimedia exegesis of the symbolism of the São Paulo façade emphasizes its bicultural imagery and the fact that it was a cooperative effort between Italian Jesuit designers and Japanese craftsmen. A glass case with drawings, paintings, and texts about "The Jesuits in the Imperial Court" traces the arrival of the Jesuits in Macau, the career of Matteo Ricci, the friendship between the Kangxi emperor and the Jesuits in Beijing, and the "remarkable cooperation in scientific endeavors between Europe and China" that ensued. An engraving of Matteo Ricci and the well-known Chinese Catholic Paul Xu Guangqi 徐光啟 standing side by side, both dressed in the robes of Chinese literati, echoes the symmetry between the Iberian and Chinese warriors at the museum's entrance and implies that this was an era in which Westerners recognized China as a civilization equal to their own.

Thus the first floor sets up Macau as a central hub of exchange in the early modern world, a world prior to the system of nation-states, in which commercial, political, and cultural traffic occurred between civilizations and religions rather than nations and colonies. Merchants, missionaries, artists, architects, and even soldiers are the enlightened protagonists of a story about the establishment of Macau as a "city of culture" and a point of convergence between civilizations. The question of Portuguese sovereignty is not even posed, let alone answered; rather, the idea that Macau prospered under a kind of shared sovereignty is implied, aestheticized, and, as James Hevia has put it in reference to a different museum, "safely ensconced under the seemingly apolitical and sanitized sign of heritage" (Hevia 2001: 222).

To get to the second floor, you pass along the mezzanine, a long loft overlooking the first floor lined on one side by near-life-size replicas of the façades of Portuguese- and Chinese-style buildings painted in the pink, blue, yellow, and green pastels that are the distinctive hues of the heritage buildings outside. As you mount the stairs, you can peer in the door of a "typical" Chinese house to see the dark interior with its rough table and chairs; on a screen at the back runs a video loop showing four elderly Chinese people playing mahjong. A little further along you reach the entrance to the fort's cistern room, where the ambience of the Porto Interior (or "Inner Harbor," off Macau's western shore) is recreated with the use of nearly life-size model boats, buildings, and mannequins, while on a large screen overhead, a documentary film plays about the marriage customs and folk songs of the *seuiseuhng yahn* 水上人, or "waterborne people," who lived on their boats anchored in the harbor.[23] The mezzanine is a liminal section, bringing you down from the dizzying heights of civilizations and history to the interiors of the city, its harbors and homes, and out of the distant past into a familiar but timeless zone.

The second floor of the museum, Popular Arts and Traditions, was the favorite of most visitors and staffpeople I spoke with. Its aim, according to the Architect, is to portray "the old Macau, a Macau that no longer exists except in the memories of its oldest residents." In practice, this appears to mean Macau between the 1920s and the 1960s, and the focus is on the sights, sounds, smells, and surfaces of daily life—work, play, domestic life, rites of passage—that had all but disappeared from 1990s Macau.

The Commercial Activities area, for example, is illustrated by life-size replicas of the interiors of four "typically" Chinese shops—a joss-shop, a Chinese bakery, an herbal pharmacy, and a pawnshop; by miniature models of a firecracker factory that existed in Taipa in the mid-twentieth century, of the interiors of factories making

incense and matches, and of the distinctive architecture of the traditional pawnshop tower (a five-story gray-brick building with narrow
slits for windows, which had been a distinctive feature of Macau's
skyline in the nineteenth and early twentieth centuries), along with
posters and objects demonstrating the products of these enterprises.
But the most popular exhibit on the whole floor was "Hawkers'-cries
of Macau" (Pregões de Macau/街頭叫賣聲), which featured a life-
size diorama of an "old Macau" street with five life-size plaster mannequins dressed and posed in the manner of the itinerant broom
sellers, junk collectors, knife sharpeners, sticky-rice dumpling ven-
dors, and herbal tea peddlers who used to roam the streets drumming
up business with their distinctive cries (see Fig. 10). The display
window is fronted by a series of five viewing nooks, each nook fitted
with speakers that, when you press a button, plays a recording of one
of the hawker's calls. These calls unfailingly elicited laughter and
mimicry and exclamations of recognition among people who had
lived in Macau, and, on occasion, stories about how they or their
mothers would conduct business with the street peddlers from the
comfort of home by lowering out of the window a basket on a string.

By focusing on the publicly sensual aspects of these economic activities—the sound of the hawkers' cries, the look and feel of a shop,
the "park-like atmosphere" of the firecracker factories[24]—these exhibits intersperse "real" objects with replicas and miniatures to perform a kind of culturizing work on the daily practices of "old
Macau." Forms of (Chinese) labor are represented as part of Macau's
unique heritage, while the social conditions surrounding this labor
disappear. Typified, anonymous, and aestheticized, they are stripped
of the signs of exclusion (along lines of ethnicity, language, class,
gender) that would have structured the social relations that produced them; instead, they stand as evocative icons of an imagined
collective past.

The strategy of typification continues as you turn the corner from
the Hawkers' exhibit and arrive in the Domestic Life area. Immediately you find yourself in front of another popular exhibit: a table
laden with (plastic models of) the cakes and savories of a "typical"
chá gordo, or Macanese high tea. Although marked explicitly as a
Macanese practice, in this instance, the hosts are anonymous, the

Fig. 10   The itinerant broom seller and herbal tea peddler were part of the
"Hawkers'-cries of Macau" display, one of the most popular exhibits
in the Museum of Macau (photo by author, 1999).

occasion unnamed, and everyone is invited to the table. Similarly, the "Macanese Room" and the "Chinese Room," the two other major exhibits in the Domestic Life area, are re-creations of "typical" living spaces in an earlier era: they are not actual re-creations of anyone's living room, nor are they overtly labeled as being upper-middle class, though they clearly are. A wall display on "domestic life"—one of the few exhibits patently gendered female—shows images of activities and objects that might have been found in these rooms: black-and-white photographs of women sewing and vacuuming; a book of cross-stitch patterns published in Shanghai; a vintage sewing machine and a wooden embroidery box. In the Leisure Activities area, an exhibit called Traditional Games of Macau features a cabinet full of colorful kites, carved sticks, and paper dolls and a video that demonstrates how "the children of Macau" used these objects in play. An exhibition on marriage, another favorite of many

visitors, recreates a private space that has come to function as one of
the most public symbols of a homogeneous "Chinese tradition"—a
Chinese wedding chamber, complete with an ornately carved rose-
wood wedding bed, carved wooden chests, tables, utensils, and picture frames, and an equally ornate sedan chair in the space opposite.

Interspersed with these typified representations of "Macau culture" are dioramas that recreate specific places in Macau, identified
by name: most often, public spaces that have changed beyond recognition, such as the São Francisco Garden, the Pagoda Square Ba-
zaar, and the Hong Gung Temple Market.[25] These exhibits take
places familiar to anyone who has spent time in Macau and defamil-
iarize them by depicting what they might have looked like in the
late nineteenth or early twentieth century: low, tidy, colorful buildings; spacious, tranquil, and well-manicured public gardens; bustling
shops and wharves, and little traffic. These landscapes, which successive waves of construction have made unrecognizable to today's
Macau residents, make the city itself a focus of nostalgic desire by
creating a kind of shock or cognitive gap ("*That's* what it used to
look like?!"), explicitly inviting visitors to use their historical imagination to close that gap.[26] This strategy of representation, rather
than bringing interpretive closure to the meaning of museum objects
as signs of a particular narrative about the past, widens that interpretive gap, inviting visitors to make what they will of the juxtaposition
of past and present.

On the second floor, then, the Macanese appear for the first time,
and any direct reference to Portuguese governance disappears, as do
almost all representations of Portuguese people. Yet the most striking thing is the extent to which the "unique culture" of Macau is
predominantly, though not exclusively, Chinese. The implication is
that the Portuguese presence allowed Chinese culture to flourish
while providing the possibility for cultural hybridity in the form of
the Macanese, and that the "unique culture" which resulted is to be
found in the everyday practices, the homes, workplaces, and bed-
rooms of Macau residents, who are invited to value these intimate
aspects of their personal and familial pasts as part of Macau's communal heritage—part of its "system." It presents a vision of Chineseness that is not overdetermined by concerns of state sovereignty or

the grand designs of empire and civilization but finds its most evocative expression in the ingenuity and aesthetic beauty of the minutest details of daily life.

Unlike the second floor, Cristina admitted to me, "you can basically just whiz through the third floor." Charged with the theme of representing "contemporary Macau," the exhibits on this floor make little sense, thematically speaking, and many of them are not really about the present at all: they trace the careers of noted Macau writers since the sixteenth century and of Macau's urban development since the 1920s; they demonstrate the role Macau played as a haven for refugees in World War II, and as a base for the revolutionary activities of Dr. Sun Yat-sen; they display "old things" donated by various local institutions (the Dom Bosco School, the Bela Vista Hotel); and they situate Macau in a global context with a display on the Macanese diaspora and a small world map showing the location of two other cities called Macau (one in Brazil and one in France).[27] A glass case displays various elements of "Macanese" architecture (an explanatory placard makes it clear that this refers to the architectural style that developed in Macau, not to architecture designed by Macanese people), which resulted from the "hybridity, coexistence [and] . . . exchange of influences" between Chinese and European architectural forms. A video gallery plays three short films on the changes Macau has undergone in recent decades. But the most popular part of this floor were the three computer terminals near the exit that challenge visitors, game-show-like, to take a quiz on the myriad facts they learned in the museum. In the narrative logic of the museum and of heritage thinking more broadly, however, the thematic incoherence of the third floor makes sense: all that is interesting about contemporary Macau are the few remaining traces of its vanishing past, whose disappearance is the most salient characteristic of the present. The only gesture toward the future is the exhibit closest to the exit, which explains the Macau Basic Law and the design of the new SAR flag; although intended to express confidence in the future of a city with such a cultured past, viewed from another angle it simply suggests that the handover will be the end of all that made Macau unique.[28]

Conspicuously absent from the museum's story of Macau are any references to violent, controversial, or unsavory events. There is nothing about the opium or the coolie trade, nothing about the one-armed Governor Ferreira do Amaral; no mention of the disputed 1887 treaty or the general strike of 1922, of the border skirmishes of the 1950s or the 123 Incident of 1966–67. Nothing about the poverty of and discrimination against the *seuiseuhng yahn*, or about their forced relocation in the 1980s; no indication that dozens of firecracker factory employees were killed in explosions or that hundreds of refugees died of starvation on those quaint city streets during World War II. The only clue to the enormous role played by gambling in Macau's economy is the small exhibit along the corridor leading toward the exit, which displays an early twentieth-century roulette wheel and slot machine against a painted backdrop representing the interior of a "typical" Macau gambling hall (known as a "fantan club") of the early twentieth century, which bears little resemblance to modern-day casinos.[29]

The museum staff was clearly accustomed to questions about why these elements had been left out. Most of the time in interviews I didn't even have to ask about it; staff members would volunteer the fact that they were often asked this question and offer their explanations gladly. As the Architect put it in a newspaper interview, "Some isolated situations of conflict . . . are not that important when considering Macau's long history as a peaceful meeting place between the Occident and the Orient" (Bruning 1998). Jorge told me that during the planning committee meetings, they encountered no problems with their interpretation because they had carefully expunged any themes they thought Beijing might find sensitive; when in doubt, they asked the advice of an ethnic Chinese member of the committee, a historian of Hong Kong who was "very attuned to the Chinese sensibility."[30] The planning committee, Jorge said, had intentionally tried to "choose the things of unity instead of the things of, you know, of . . . division." After all, the main audience for the museum was the Chinese and the Macanese: the designers did not want to antagonize the very people for whom the museum was supposed to be a unifying, community-building cement. A third member of the planning committee told me, even before I started my research, that they had never intended to present an objective accounting of the past; the museum had been "a political project" right from the start.

But this is precisely the point, if we understand politics as a struggle over the representation of value. The Architect's comment that moments of conflict are just "not that important" in the history of Macau indicates that the parts of the past that he valued were those that could give shape to the state's vision of a cultural solidarity cross-cutting the lines of ethnicity, language, class, and nationality that had long divided Macau residents. Cristina summed up why she thought their approach—evoking the past as a series of surfaces, smells, sights, and sounds, rather than the critical examination of abstract historical and social processes—was the root of the museum's success.[31] "A lot of museums are sort of sterile," she said.

Not this one. We want people to *smell* Macau. That's why you'll notice, in the cistern area with the exhibit about Porto Interior, there's a bit of rotten old salt fish hanging up on the post there. Of course it's covered with wax to preserve it, but you can still smell it—you walk into that exhibit and it smells exactly like Porto Interior. That's what I feel about this museum, is that it is just an extension of the streets of Macau, with air-conditioning. The air-con is the only difference.[32]

According to Cristina, it was the sensual evocation of the past that made the museum both lively and lifelike, both entertaining and authentic. But it was the difference—the air-conditioning—that made it attractive. Not literally the air-con, of course (although on a steaming subtropical summer day, the attraction of spending a couple of hours in a fiercely air-conditioned environment is not to be underestimated), but the knowing gap between the museum's selective realism and the real "old Macau" outside. The museum's representation of the past derived its appeal from the creation of such cognitive gaps, rather than from the accretion of cognitive knowledge.[33] Rather than effecting narrative closure on the past, it widened the interpretive gap, blurring distinctions between authentic and inauthentic, official and popular, public and private, resistance and cooptation, the actual and the possible. In the next two sections, I argue that although this strategy was the basis of the museum's success in legitimizing multiple pasts as part of the city's heritage, it created problems of its own: how to assess whether the museum was succeeding at its task of getting Macau residents to value this standardized vision of their heritage as the basis for a shared subjectivity rather than simply as a source of revenue and how to ensure that the legitimacy of this vision would be evident to all museum visitors, not just Macau residents.

"It's Like a Street Market in Here"

One afternoon around half past three, a visit from a group of forty twelve-year-olds from a Catholic middle school overlapped with two groups from homes for elderly women. Within minutes the museum went from the serenity of a quiet day—the silence broken only by the echoing footsteps of the security guards and the muted melodies of classical music piped in over the public address system—to pandemonium. Children ran through the exhibition halls, jumping off benches and sliding across the smooth stone floors, stopping suddenly in front of a display that caught their eye, mimicking the sounds of interactive exhibits and reading the captions aloud at the top of their lungs to their friends ("Macau!! International Trading Port!!," they yelled while standing in front of the large wall map that traced the sixteenth-century trade routes from Macau to Europe, Mexico, and Japan). They imitated the recorded cries of the street-hawkers, and made up cries of their own. They picked up and handled whatever could be picked up and handled; it was not until several of them accidentally broke the plastic case of a television monitor playing a video loop on the history of Chinese coins that a security guard and the harried teacher joined forces to get the children to line up and stand still (if not quietly) behind the replica of Macau's first printing press. Meanwhile the two large groups of elderly visitors had broken up into smaller knots; some wandered from exhibit to exhibit based on whatever caught their eye while others who had visited before made straight for their favorite exhibits. "Let's go upstairs and see that broom-seller," one elderly woman called to her friends. "Yeah, that's a good one! Let's go!" Others discussed the accuracy of the exhibits on the recent past, measuring the objects on display against the yardstick of their own memories. The noise was deafening. At four, the governor was due to arrive with a delegation. Lillian, one of the staff members who had come out onto the museum floor to help translate between the teacher and the Filipino security guard, caught my eye as she hurried through the main hall of the first floor, and with a grin called to me, "So crowded, it's like a street market (街市) in here!"

Lillian was clearly amused by the scene—she added that at least the governor would be happy to see that the museum was so popular. Later, however, when I paraphrased her remark to other staff who asked me how things were going up there on the museum floor, their reactions were mixed. Everyone found the comment amusing, and knew exactly what she meant: just as Macau's street markets (whose fresh produce, fish, and meats most Macau residents preferred to the air-conditioned but overpriced shrinkwrapped provisions of the supermarket) were crowded and noisy and *yihtnaauh* and full of people moving around between displays of objects, so was the museum at times of heavy traffic. And certainly, it was evidence of the museum's popularity. But the comment also provoked discomfort. Cristina thought this raucous behavior, like that of the crowds on opening day, reflected visitors' disappointingly single-minded conception of the value of the museum. She lamented that, especially during the first two weeks when admission was free of charge, people "weren't being careful in the museum, they didn't care much about the exhibits. It's like if you have to buy a ticket, somehow you respect it more. Also, when we had activities for kids, with games and corporate sponsors giving prizes, it wasn't like the kids were interested and having fun—they just wanted to get the prizes and get out of there. They and their parents would rush around collecting all the free promotional stuff they could, and then leave." Grace also thought that teaching people how to behave in a museum would have to be a significant part of their work:

In my opinion, the local people, especially students, they don't really know what's the point of visiting a museum. I remember the first week, when museum admission was free, most of the people who came in, they didn't really enjoy seeing—well, I cannot say they did not enjoy, but they did not appreciate—seeing what they did. They just came in and talked loudly, they didn't really appreciate the objects. . . . They even sat down inside to eat and drink. Personally, I think they don't know how to visit a museum. They [treated it] like an amusement park. The children were running around, jumping over the benches, and the parents didn't even say "no no no," they just let them do it. So I think a museum is a place for them to learn how to appreciate valuable things.

The idea that museums are engaged in a civilizing, modernizing mission is not new, nor is it unique to Macau (see Bennett 1995, Duncan 1995, and for China, R. Watson 2004). But the contradictory ways of conceptualizing the value of the past in the Museum of Macau engendered contradictions in deciphering the boisterousness of local visitors. On the one hand, Cristina and Grace viewed the visitors' behavior as a sign of disrespect, and further evidence that Macau residents could think about the value of the past only in commodity terms. In this view, it was a sign of the museum's failure to create Macau subjects who embodied the appreciation of history and knew how to behave in its presence.

In a separate interview, however, Jorge reminded me that the museum planners had deliberately set out *not* to create "a traditional museum, like the Louvre," which he thought of as a kind of "holy space" in which "you may not speak, may not touch, and it is almost forbidden to look." Cristina spoke approvingly of a different kind of *yihtnaauh*—that which was created by small groups of elderly women who would come to the museum after doing the morning shopping and spend hours inside: "They really get enthusiastic about it, saying 'Oh yes yes, this is exactly the way it was, do you remember, this is exactly how it was!', or 'No no, this isn't how it was, it was more like that . . . ' Chinese and Macanese alike, they really seem to get into it, to interact with it. And this is exactly what we wanted to do with this museum." In this sense, she viewed the visitors' behavior and the comparisons to a street market as a sign of the museum's success at creating an environment—very everyday, very Macau—in which local residents felt at home while engaging in an embodied and participatory manner with a range of representations of how and why their pasts mattered to the future: a museum whose only difference from the streets outside was the air-conditioning.

The Reality Effect

Other visitors I interviewed spoke of their appreciation of the museum in ways that were precisely what the museum planners had hoped for. Whenever I asked people what they liked about the museum, almost without exception they expressed their greatest enthusiasm about the second floor, saying they found it "really real"

(好真). Several people mentioned that they had especially enjoyed the street hawkers' exhibit because it "really is like the real thing!" (好似真㗎). A Hong Kong tourist was impressed by how well the second floor had "recreated the ethos of a bygone era" (召回往日風貌). On occasion, I witnessed elderly women stopping to bow three times in front of the replicas of small door shrines or votive tablets that had been built into the walls of exhibits meant to demonstrate what "old Macau" had looked like, just as they would have done if they had passed a real street shrine outside. From time to time I saw people nearly overcome with emotion and disbelief when they encountered an object that had been an identifiable part of their own lives: in one case, a man found the image of his school-aged self in an enlarged photograph of a boys' choir from the 1970s; in another case, one of my students wrote of the surge of nostalgia she felt when she saw on display an old Chinese-style door that was either an exact replica of or perhaps indeed was the very door to a building (now demolished) that she used to pass by every day on her way to school as a child. Every single day I heard visitors saying to each other excitedly, "This is just how it used to be!," "Look, son, these are the games I used to play as a kid! No one plays these anymore!," or discussing the degree of verisimilitude of particular exhibits ("Oh, I remember the peddler in San Ma-Louh who used to make painted flourpaste figurines like these, but they were never *this* nice . . . "). One small group of visitors from Macau—two middle-aged women and an older couple—all agreed that the museum was "good" because it was "so real, it's like Macau was before, it's all very familiar to older people, they see the exhibits and can explain everything to the younger generation." These reactions suggested, despite the misgivings of Cristina and Grace, that the museum had achieved a degree of legitimacy as a representation that was of and for, if not by, the people of Macau. As Cristina told me, "We hoped people would come and have fond memories of what Macau used to be like, and bring their grandchildren to visit as well, so that when the grandchildren grow up they will have fond memories of the museum as a place they used to go with their granny who would tell them all about the old Macau." In such interactions, the museum both legitimized Macau residents' experiences and stories about the past by including them as part of Macau's heritage and drew legitimacy from them by implying that the museum's narrative corresponded to, even emerged from, the everyday memories of Macau residents.

But the assertion that certain exhibits (or the museum as a whole) were "really real" did not mark visitors' passive acceptance of the state's vision of the role Macau's past had played in producing a unique cultural identity among its residents. The "reality effect"— the extent to which heavily mediated representations of people, places, or communities are read by those very people as realistic depictions of certain aspects their lives—is hardly as transparent as it may seem. As Sarah Friedman (2006: 605) has pointed out in a different context, film viewers may very well identify with "a film that they also reject as an inaccurate portrayal of both their past and present lives," finding certain images or tropes or narrative twists evocative of their own life experiences while at the same time rejecting the film's objectification of their lives as stereotyped and inauthentic. Similarly, Macau residents' reactions to the museum's representations of Macau's recent past could be labeled neither cooptation nor resistance, for, by evoking the past in a space and in a way that was sanctioned by the state, the museum allowed visitors' own memories to draw power both from official ideologies and from their ability to elude those ideologies.

In trying to explain the feeling evoked by the Chinese door, for example, my student likened it to her reaction whenever she heard the Portuguese national anthem. She assured me that she had no love of Portugal, but the anthem reminded her of childhood nights, lying in bed while her grandparents listened to the radio in the next room; every night at the end of the broadcast the local radio station would sign off by playing the Portuguese national anthem. Hearing this anthem today, she said, always made her feel safe and happy. Similarly, her reaction upon seeing the door was not to admire its Sino-Portuguese design or to reach abstract conclusions about the importance of maintaining the icons of Macau's unique history; it was an empathic, sensory memory of this very door and the immediate social context in which she had first encountered it as a child. The shock and amusement of seeing valued by their inclusion in a museum objects that would otherwise have been forgotten or discarded or that conjured memories which would otherwise have been considered too personal or trivial to be publicly commemorated seemed to be an important part of the enjoyment that people from Macau derived from visiting the museum.[34] Part of the pleasure was the thrill of transvaluation, of seeing the private become public, the useless become priceless. The very idea of dignifying Macau's recent past with a museum partook of this kind of pleasure. Many old Macau residents, fed up with representations in the international media of their city as characterized by corruption, backwardness, and criminality, were pleased to see a public institution that highlighted instead the contributions it had made to the modern world; this did not mean they accepted the Portuguese state's claims to legitimacy. Those reeling from the physical transformation of their sleepy city were gratified by the thought that the places and lifeways they remembered but had seen destroyed in the rush to economic development should be immortalized in a museum; this did not mean they felt there was reason to preserve those places or lifeways outside the museum.

One afternoon I interviewed two elderly Chinese women and their younger companion (a woman I guessed to be in her late thirties) who were sitting in the exit lobby resting their feet and waiting for the rest of their group to catch up. When I asked if they had enjoyed the museum, all three responded enthusiastically. One of the older women told me that she had enjoyed looking back on how life was when she was young and that the museum was good because it was "very real," because "these are all things we used to see and use." The younger woman, also from Macau, had also enjoyed her visit, but not for the same reason; she had found the same exhibits to be *dak-yih* (得意)—a term that in Cantonese means, depending on the context, something like "quaint," "cute," or "interesting"—but clearly outside her own experience of "reality."

As I asked them about which exhibits they had liked and why, the older women began to explain what kind of memories the exhibits had conjured up for them. "People used to be so patient, so hardworking; and they used to be really *lek* 叻 ["clever," "talented"]! Everything used to take more effort than it does now. Things we used to make by hand they can now make by machine; we used to have to walk everywhere, and now everyone has motorbikes."[35] I sat with them for perhaps fifteen minutes, as the two older women recounted for each other, myself, and their younger companion the things they had seen and done and used when they were young, how difficult it had been, how much work it had been just living. So was it worthwhile recalling all these hardships? I asked. They all agreed that it was valuable, "because everything has changed so much, and it's important for the young people to understand this." This sentiment—that "young people can learn about what Macau used to be like, and see how much it has changed"—was a refrain I heard again and again from older Macau residents who visited the museum, as well as from the younger people who accompanied them. The museum was valuable not because it publicly commemorated an idealized past but because it provided a space in which visitors could mark, recall, and collectively travel the almost unimaginable distance between the past and the present. This reason for wanting to recall the past was not unique to Macau residents. Similar refrains could be heard all over China in the 1990s as people tried to come to grips with the breathtaking pace of change they had witnessed in the space of two decades and were encouraged by the state to frame this change in a progressive narrative of economic development and increasing national prosperity. In this sense, these women seemed to articulate this progressivist narrative and with it a kind of resistance to the museum's idealization of "the old Macau." They did not consider the old Macau to have been either *dak-yih* or unique, nor were they at all eager to preserve its traces in their lives. But they did not feel alienated by or angered at the museum's aestheticized representation of the hardships of the past.[36] Rather, they delighted in the opportunity it presented to recount other pasts and other reasons for wanting to remember those pasts. The pleasure they derived from telling their tales of hardship and from their repeated visits to the museum (this was their second visit) was at least twofold: that of appreciating their present situation, and that of seeing their past ways of life, their labor, their own talent and cleverness, appreciated publicly by the state and by younger generations.

In this sense, the museum's success lay not in its creation of a unified ideological story of Macau's past that residents found meaningful but in its ability to create a series of evocative gaps that allowed a

wide range of individual meanings to be interpellated and legitimized as part of the heritage of Macau. But the strengths of this
mode of representing the value of the past were also what ensured
that it would be of limited appeal. Indeed, the temporal and ideological limits of this strategy of representation were all too evident,
at least to some. One of the few detailed critiques of the museum I
heard during the course of a visitor interview came from a middle-
aged man (I never even asked his name; let us call him Wu) who
had been born in Macau but had moved to the mainland as a child.
After ascertaining that I was not Portuguese, he praised the museum
for its ability to "capture the best of Macau. They really captured
every aspect of the way life used to be in the sixties. It all felt so familiar! For the Portuguese to build this museum just before they
leave, it's really—I think it's really valuable (好有價值)." But when
I asked if he thought anything about it should be changed, Wu replied, hesitantly at first but then with increasing conviction:

There *is* one thing. In the future, with more mainland tourists visiting
[Macau]—you know, people from the interior have a very strong sense of
ethnic pride (民族感很深), so especially in one exhibit—I don't know if
you saw it or not, the street hawkers' exhibit? With the guy peddling herbal
tea? This exhibit, we—we locals, we Cantonese—we can feel this is local
history. But people from the interior, they have a different feeling. They
think, why did they portray Portuguese culture as so good (葡國文化搞得
那麼好), and then portray Macau people as so . . . so ignorant? Really ignorant. The museum should be more careful in this respect. They are, after
all, Chinese; they should emphasize the cultured aspects (有修養那部份)
of Macau, not just these street-hawkers and such. Of course when *we* see it
we feel a sense of familiarity (有親切感), but in the future—it's a question
of being evaluated by history (是一個歷史評價的問題).[37]

Wu insisted on the distinction between "we locals," whose memories
allow them to understand the museum's evocative representation of
everyday pasts as real and familiar, and mainlanders who, informed
by a nationalist pride grounded in the collective memory of "national humiliation" by Western imperialists (a narrative still taught
in schools and promoted in films, television programs, and museums
around the PRC), would read this representation as a veiled insult to
the Chinese people. Wu feared that mainlanders would object to the

museum's valorization of precisely those elements that Macau people enjoyed for their "realness" and would read the whole second floor of the museum as an unfortunate, perhaps deliberate lapse in the narrative of perfect civilizational symmetry established on the first floor. According to him, measured against the CCP's view that history is an omniscient force that will in the future sit in judgment of the present, that the autonomous subject of that history is the Chinese people, and that the value of heritage lies in its ability to foster patriotism, this kind of real did not belong in a museum. The rubbish heap was where it should have stayed. This past could not provide the foundation for Macau's future; rather, it was precisely what would have to be overcome for Macau to prosper as a part of the Chinese nation-state. For them, he feared, the museum's valorization of rubbish would not signify harmony, equality, and tolerance, nor would it function as a celebration of Macau's "system," of local cultures and communities; it would simply reinscribe the city's image as a colonial backwater and a cultural desert.

I must say that I did not talk to any mainlanders who expressed this view. Most of the mainland visitors I spoke with were more impressed by the museum's aesthetics and the interactive technology than they were critical about the content of the exhibits.[38] More than an accurate representation of mainlanders' views, then, the apprehension expressed by this one man, Macau-born and mainland-raised, gives poignant expression to the anxiety about what Macau's past would actually come to signify in the post-handover future. On one hand, he articulated precisely the sense of difference that the Portuguese state was hoping to inculcate in Macau residents: the sense of a "we" that includes everyone from Macau, and that involves a way of thinking about the past and its ramifications in the present that is decisively unlike the "they" on the other side of the border. On the other hand, he seemed to be saying, the handover will mean that Macau people will have to admit that the CCP's interpretation, though less familiar, is more correct. His remark that the museum administrators should know better because they "are, after all, Chinese," implies that this defamiliarizing interpretation of Macau history is not just ideologically different from that of the museum; it is—or will soon be—the only truly Chinese interpretation possible.

Conclusion

The Museum of Macau certainly succeeded in the task of getting many Macau residents to value a variety of pasts for a variety of reasons. What was less clear was whether it succeeded in getting them to value the state's standardized vision of Macau's sort-of sovereign past as the basis for a system and a sort-of Chinese subjectivity that would be worth preserving and protecting after the handover. Although the museum, like other heritage projects, did its utmost to popularize a unified, universalized, and self-congratulatory narrative of Macau as a bridge between civilizations, the tactics the designers chose to adopt in order to downplay the potentially divisive and alienating politics of representing Macau's past—emphasizing the evocative and sensual character of the exhibits, removing objects from their social contexts and displaying them as icons of pastness rather than explanations of the past—provided a space for the mobilization of a wide range of memories that had little to do with the ideological uses to which the past was put. As a result, the image of Macau that emerged in the comments of visitors looked less like a bridge and more like a petri dish—a common ground for disparate memories, sown for contradictory reasons, growing toward divergent futures.

Yet the mere fact of having a public space dedicated to the telling of those disparate memories may have done more than anything to ensure that Macau residents would be able to bring those pasts into their futures, for whatever reasons they deemed suitable. In this sense, the rowdy throngs on opening day attested not to Macau residents' inability to appreciate the value of the past but rather to their desire to see their multiple pasts valued in ways that they found meaningful, and their hope that in the museum they would find what they were looking for. In the next chapter, I examine the stories of other Macau residents whose ambivalence toward their hometown was misread by the state as a sign of apathy rather than passion, but whose narratives contain incisive critiques of the significance of Portuguese sovereignty, the meaning of Chineseness, and what they both might someday come to mean.

SEVEN

Outlawed Tales

On the cleared space of the nightclub's dance floor, now serving as a makeshift stage, a spotlight comes up. It illuminates a woman with reddish-brown hair sitting on a chair in the corner, gently rocking back and forth. Tremulously, she begins to sing in the slow minor key of a *fado*:[1]

Macau, terra minha	Macau, my land
Trazes a lembrança de uma quinta	You evoke pastoral memories
És coberta de folhas e flores	Swathed in foliage and flowers
São alegres as tuas cores	Festive are your colors
Macau, terra de lendas	Macau, land of legends
Os contos são tuas fazendas	Your treasures are your stories
Os monumentos históricos que tens	Your historic monuments
E o ambiente português que manténs	And your Portuguese ambience
Macau, viveste sempre longe da tua mãe	Macau, you've always lived so far from your mother
Macau, és a menor da tua família	Macau, you're the smallest in your family
És tranquila e bonita	So tranquil and pretty
Símbolo de paz	A symbol of peace
E da beleza	And of beauty
Macau, terra minha . . .	Macau, my land . . .

She trails off, voice choked and eyes shining. Sitting in the audience of several dozen people cramped onto the mismatched benches, bar-stools, and rattan chairs that have been drawn up into orderly rows for the event, I wonder how many people in the audience understand or recognize the lyrics she is singing. And I wonder what in the world could have led the Macau government to prohibit this play, entitled *Macau One Two Three*, from being performed in a state-owned theater. Is this folk song, written by a Macanese *tuna* (string band), not an expression of the very themes of nostalgia, emplacement, tolerance, and historical consciousness that the state has been at such pains to articulate in its textbooks, its museums, and its heritage projects? Shouldn't the Portuguese government be thrilled to witness this song sung by a Eurasian actress in a production written and performed by a politically progressive underground theater troupe run by ethnic Chinese based in Hong Kong? Would that not validate the state's truth claims about the unique history and identity of Macau and its people and silence the critics who see these claims as mere colonial artifice?

But we were crammed into this tiny, privately owned nightclub because two nights previously, the government had suddenly canceled the group's original booking at the main hall of the Macau Conservatory. The play and the government's response to it became the center of a furious public debate, late in the summer of 1998, about censorship and the politics of culture. What the controversy made clear was not just the simplistically ideological nature of the state's culture project but also the fact that the state did not have a monopoly on the way that themes of nostalgia, belonging, identity, Chineseness, and sovereignty circulated in transition-era Macau.

In tracing the state's efforts to make Macau residents aware of their unique cultural identity, I had been told time and again that the problem was that the majority of Macau's residents simply had no sense of belonging to the city, no sense that Macau was different from any other Chinese place, no sense that this difference might be something valuable. There was little recognition that those Macau residents who identified as ethnic Chinese might have an awareness of the relationship between their experiences of Portuguese sovereignty in Macau and their sense of Chineseness that differed from the state's—an awareness that might not even be articulated in terms of identity. In this chapter, I examine three alternative commentaries about the nature of Macau's "difference" that demonstrate how Macau residents expressed a sense of belonging to their city in ways that were lost, disregarded, or actively suppressed by both the Portuguese and the Chinese states during the years before the handover. These commentaries express a degree of ambivalence that made them not just politically incorrect but altogether irreconcilable with the notion of "identity" as it was used by the Portuguese in the transition era. They give voice to the problems inherent to this and other concepts, such as nationality and citizenship, that attempt to express complex and often ambivalent senses of community and belonging in objectifiable or emblematic terms. And they present a challenge to contemporary anthropological theories of the increasing flexibility of citizenship and identity in the face of the reconfiguration of state sovereignty in a transnationalizing world.

Identity and Chineseness

One reason that so few proponents of "Macau's unique identity" even recognized the existence of these alternative expressions of belonging was the translingual nature of the state's culture project. The term the Portuguese used to promote this sense of belonging among residents of Macau—*identidade*—was one that did not translate well into Chinese. Portuguese-language versions of the governor's speeches, educational initiatives, the texts of museum programs, and cultural events all began with references to Macau's *identidade cultural* or the *identidade própria de Macau* (identity unique to Macau). But the term "identity" has no exact equivalent in Chinese. In some instances, such as in the phrase "identity card," it is translated as *shenfen* 身份; but this means something closer to "social status" and implies, in a restricted sense, one's juridical identity and, in a broader sense, one's position or standing within a larger social structure. In this broader sense, *shenfen* is a thing that some people can have more of than others.[2] In social science dictionaries, "identity" is often translated *rentong* 認同, which implies a sense of "acceptance of," "agreement with," even "assimilation to"; and placed in conjunction with the word for "cultural"—*wenhua rentong* 文化 認同—it is an academic neologism that most people in 1990s Macau found unfamiliar and puzzling.[3] Rather than taking this opportunity to familiarize Macau residents with new terminologies that would reflect their new forms of consciousness, however, the translators of the official speeches and the Chinese proponents of Macau culture and history chose to render the concept "identidade cultural" as *wenhua te-se* 文化特色: cultural characteristics. Thus, as Richard Handler (1994: 31) has pointed out, although the modern concept of identity "presupposes the oneness, continuity, and boundedness of the person, agent, or group," *te-se* implied a collection of traits, qualities, or objects that did not necessarily cohere into any kind of unity; in Macau, *te-se* was often used to refer to objects such as heritage buildings and Macanese food, rather than to forms of consciousness or social relations. Despite the linguistic and semiotic gulf between *identidade* and *te-se*, however, it seemed that what Portuguese officials did share with their Chinese translators was a reified sense of identity as something that existed objectively in the world, as tangibly as a cathedral or a Macanese dumpling, whether or not anyone realized it was there. They spoke of their project not as one of creating a sense of identity but as one of making Macau residents *aware* that this identity existed and that it had been theirs all along.

It was this discrepancy that made it possible for Macau Chinese to say things like "Macau identity is just an invention of the Tourism Office," while still insisting that the way Macau residents thought about themselves and their relationship to the people around them was fundamentally different from that of people from the mainland or Hong Kong. But it also meant that, on one hand, translingual discussions of Macau identity often went nowhere, not only because they entailed divergent views about the locus and nature of Macau's difference and of the role of the Portuguese state in producing it, but also because they involved divergent understandings of what difference those differences made: for how could a mere collection of interesting buildings and food items constitute a challenge to the meaning of being Chinese? On the other hand, in order to hear alternative views on what, if anything, made Macau people different from other Chinese people, and how, if at all, that difference should be protected, one had to listen for language that sounded very little like the state's official discourse on identity. The three commentaries that follow provide examples of how individual and collective experiences of sovereignty in Macau—be it Chinese or Portuguese—

shaped Macau residents' views of themselves and their city in ways that complicated, undermined, or transfigured the value of this difference.

Macau One Two Three

Written and performed by the Hong Kong–based Asian People's Theatre Festival Society (亞洲民眾戲劇節協會) and co-produced by Stone Commune (石頭公社), a Macau-based artists' collective, the play *Macau One Two Three* consisted of three one-act solo performances—A Portuguese Story, A Macanese Story, and A Chinese Story—that together told "the story of Macau of the past four hundred years." After touring Kenya, Portugal, England, and Hong Kong during July and August 1998, the production came to Macau, where it was scheduled to run for two nights (August 21 and 22), in English and Chinese, in the main hall of the state-run Macau Conservatory. Two nights before it was to open—a month after Stone Commune had completed the application procedures and paid the MOP$700 (US$90) rental fee to use the venue—the producers received a phone call from the director of the conservatory, Carol Chiu, who informed them that the Cultural Institute of Macau (ICM) was revoking its permission to use the venue. A spokesperson for Stone Commune said the reason ICM had given her was that the play had "political content" and that this was "not an opportune moment for it to be performed publicly" (含政治成分,不適合現時公演). Stone Commune went to the press, and the papers in Macau and Hong Kong picked up the story, accusing the Macau government of censorship.[4] Meanwhile, the play's producers found a new venue: Tribo, a small African-themed bar owned by a Portuguese man, located on the ground floor of a low-income housing block in Areia Preta.

But this was just the beginning of the controversy. The members of Stone Commune published an open letter to the governor, demanding an explanation for the many unanswered questions raised by the case: Why had they not been notified in writing of the ICM's decision? Why had they heard from Chiu, who was a personal friend of several of the Stone Commune members, rather than directly from the ICM? Why had these concerns not been aired earlier, when they first applied for the permit? If the problem was the "political content" of the play, why had it not been a problem when they performed it in Portugal? Was the government prepared to compensate them for their losses, and if so how? Would the ICM take responsibility for the damage this incident had done to Macau's international image and to the confidence of the Macau people in the right to freedom of artistic expression?

There was no immediate official response, but various government sources suggested that the problem had been not one of censorship but a breach of bureaucratic procedure: Chiu had approved Stone Commune's application when this decision was not hers to make. The president of the ICM, Heidi Ho, "should have been consulted about this performance, and she was not" (*O Futuro*, August 25, 1998). In fact, Ho had found out about the performance only when she saw promotional posters for it on the street, at which point she had contacted the director of the Conservatory, instructing her to cancel the performance and ask the producers to submit another application for evaluation by the proper authorities.

On August 31, the governor of Macau, Brigadier General Vasco Rocha Vieira, gave a press conference in which he assured Macau residents that they lived in a "space of freedom":

There has never been censorship nor has the government of Macau ever given the slightest indication that such a thing could happen. What happened in the case of the ICM's performance venue was a problem at the level of administration. I consider it an administrative error. . . . The government of Macau has given more than enough proof that it works tenaciously to ensure that rights, guarantees, and liberties can be a palpable, concrete and deep-rooted reality in the territory.   (*JTM*, September 1, 1998)

Unfortunately for the governor, the very journalists he was speaking to were among those who best remembered the incidents of censorship that had occurred in the territory just in the previous three or four years. In 1996, on the thirtieth anniversary of the 123 Incident, two journalists (one Chinese and one Portuguese) at the local television station had produced a documentary on the events, but the station had "indefinitely postponed" its airing. In the early 1990s, the Macau government had commissioned a well-known Portuguese sociologist, Boaventura de Sousa Santos, to write a book about Macau. But when it was completed and found to present a critical take on the Macau government's positions on democratization, localization, corruption, and social welfare, the government shelved it with no explanation. Finally in 1998, Santos took it to Portugal and had it published independently.[5]

For these reasons, the government's explanation held little water with anyone. Stone Commune considered the governor's words "an attempt to evade the politics of the situation," and asked the High Commission Against Administrative Corruption and Illegality to investigate. Cultural organizations around the territory signed a petition protesting the threat to artistic freedom. Portuguese- and Chinese-language papers in Macau and Hong Kong ran editorials attacking the government not only for jeopardizing Macau residents' constitutional rights to freedom of expression but also for hypocrisy. When, in September, the undersecretary for culture (who was responsible for the ICM) suggested that the director of the Conservatory was a new employee who did not understand the rules for renting out the venue, a Chinese journalist countered that this simply demonstrated that censorship was the rule (*Va Kio Daily*, September 21, 1998). In November, Stone Commune again applied for permission to use the Conservatory for a repeat performance of *Macau One Two Three*, but the Conservatory and the ICM pushed responsibility for the decision back and forth and never responded to the request.

One of the many questions raised by this controversy was what exactly may have been so politically sensitive about the play. Since no one in the government would admit to having said it was too political—and since no one outside the government believed the official explanation—observers were left to infer what the problematic content was. The consensus was that the government had objected to the name *Macau One Two Three*, understanding it as a reference to the 123 Incident in 1966–67. As we have seen, this incident was left out of most of the government-sponsored historical narratives about Macau, since it contradicted the image of harmonious East-West relations and the benign, beneficent nature of the Portuguese presence in Macau. Yet most people who saw the play, including the cultural attaché to the Portuguese consulate in Hong Kong, argued that there was in fact nothing remotely political about it and that the title referred not to a historical event but to the structure of the play itself: three perspectives on three separate experiences of Macau.

The first act, the "A Portuguese Story," was the fictionalized biography of an acquaintance of the troupe members. Played by Hong Kong Chinese actor Choy Kam Ho 蔡錦濠, the character was a man named António, who appeared with long hair and dressed in a cape. He proceeded to tell his life story, a story of constant disillusionment: born and raised in Mozambique of Portuguese parents, as a child he was puzzled by the violence, racism, and cruelty that surrounded him and bored by the school where adults seemed to squeeze all the adventure and poetry out of the language and history that had produced such epics as *The Lusiads*.[6] He went to university in Lisbon, where he joined the radicals who supported the liberation of African colonies; he was jailed and drafted and sent to Africa to fight for the colonizers. The revolution eventually succeeds; everyone dances with joy at the prospect of a free, socialist Mozambique. But the dream dies; corruption and injustice are rampant, disillusionment complete. He hears of a teaching job in Macau—so close to China, the socialist paradise—and accepts it immediately; he goes to Macau, studies Chinese, wears a Mao cap, and learns to drink rice wine. But once again he is disillusioned: by China (how could the vanguard of the revolution be revealed as a counterrevolutionary gang?), by the Portuguese in Macau (how could the heirs of the socialist revolution be interested only in cars, clothes, women, and money?), and by his Chinese students, who are studying Portuguese only to pass the civil service exam and show no interest in adventure or poetry. He quits teaching and opens a small bar with some friends. He plans to stay after the handover. He hopes that by hosting performances by artists from around the world, he might, in a small way, help make Macau a better place.

The second act, "A Macanese Story," starts with the song that opens this chapter. The actress, Veronica Needa, a Eurasian woman born in Hong Kong who lives in England, plays a Macanese character named Julia, whose task it is to explain the Macanese to the audience. As she explains who her ancestors were, she dons items of clothing to represent the nationalities of the women that Portuguese men settled down with in Macau. She teaches the audience a few words of *patuá*, explaining how the Portuguese vocabulary and Chinese grammar melded into a new and particularly expressive tongue. Likewise, she explains, the Macanese are an intermediary class between the Portuguese and the Chinese, despised by both the Portuguese above them (she stands on a chair and looks imperiously down her nose) and the Chinese below them (she squats, glances up, and spits). Her grandfather had five children but would have his picture taken only with the fifth one: the first-born was too dark, the second too straight-haired, the third too slanty-eyed, and the fourth too flat-nosed. She tells the story of the Macanese boy and the Chinese girl who fall in love and marry, against the wishes of their parents, and who live together happily for a while, until they begin to encounter "cultural differences" that appear insurmountable until a child is born who learns the languages and cultures of both his parents and reunites the whole family.[7] This, she tells us, is one story; but there are stories with different endings. There's the story of the fair-skinned Macanese boy, the son of a judge, whose privilege allows him to get away with all kinds of mischief; he joins a gang, deals drugs, and ends up shot to death in his Mercedes-Benz. There's another story of the Macanese boy who looked, spoke, ate, and acted Chinese, and whose only connection to his Portuguese heritage was his surname, which he lost when he married into a wealthy Hong Kong Chinese family, taking their name and becoming indistinguishable from the Chinese.[8] Many of us, she says, fear the same thing is happening to us. We are speaking more Cantonese, celebrating more Chinese festivals, without even realizing it. More and more of us are leaving Macau. Tuna Macaense, the band that wrote that song, used to have sixteen members, then ten, now only six. But those six are still singing, she says, and she ends with another rendition of the song with which she began.

The third act, "A Chinese Story," was performed by Evelyn Choi 蔡愉穎, a native of Macau who had moved to Hong Kong for university. It was the story of her memories of Macau. She remembers her parents hiring a *triciclo* (a three-wheeled pedal-rickshaw) to take them around town: "this is Meia Laranga"—as she asks her mom for money to buy a handful of shrimp chips; "this is Praia Grande"—as she plays tag with her siblings; "this is Statue Square"—as she sits still for photo after photo before finally telling her dad she'd rather play hide-and-seek than have her picture taken. She remembers asking questions: passing by "Coolie Street," she asked what a "coolie" was and was bewildered to learn that Macau had once been a center for the sale of human beings; in school, learning that Vasco da Gama had sailed to India in 1498 and Zheng He sailed to India in 1405 and Africa in 1420, she asked, "So, wasn't Zheng He cleverer than da Gama?" (那, 鄭和唔係叻過達加馬麼?). When she heard about the riots that had shaken Macau in 1966, she remembers asking, "So Dad, were you involved in the riots?" "So Dad, were the policemen who beat up the people Portuguese, Chinese, or Macanese?" "So Dad, were you happy when the Portuguese governor gave in to the demands of the Chinese?" She remembers that all her questions had been met with silence, but this didn't stop her from asking them. When she moved to Hong Kong, she found everything there very different. She came back to Macau for visits and looked up her old school friends, only to find that everything in Macau had changed too. She goes on another *triciclo* tour, this time lamenting the disappearance of the old shops and buildings. One of her classmates brags of her attractiveness to Hong Kong boys, who like her Portuguese passport; another tells her how little the government cares about providing social services for the people in the northern district, how crowded and filthy it is, with garbage piled up on the streets, and how the other day she had seen a cop standing on the corner when someone dropped a dirty diaper out of a high-rise window that practically hit him on the head, but he just ignored it. "Just like the government." She remembers the "true story" of the Restaurant of the Eight Immortals, which was closed after it was discovered that the owner had been serving dumplings made with the flesh of people he had murdered.[9] She remembers feeling, and still feels, conflicted toward her "homeland" (家園): love and hate, hate and love, in equal measure.

An article in the newspaper *Son Pou* 訊報, published prior to the Hong Kong or Macau performances, recounted how the play had gotten its controversial name. The director, Gus Mok, asked Evelyn

Choi what she knew about the Portuguese in Macau. She said she knew very little but remembered learning the words *um, dois, três* in school. They tentatively titled the play *Macau One Two Three*, and when the troupe later learned that this was the name of an incident in the 1960s, they thought it more, rather than less, appropriate: "It was a key moment in the history of Macau and the coexistence of its people, and so it seemed even more logical that *Macau One Two Three*, should be the title of this educational play."

This explanation is even more revealing of the shortcomings of the government's take on Macau identity than if the play had been an exposé of police brutality some thirty years past. The fact that the only thing a Chinese woman born, raised, and educated in Portuguese Macau knew about the Portuguese was how to count to three suggests a rather different conception of what the Portuguese presence had meant to the majority of people living in Macau: absolutely nothing. The structure of the play and the content of the stories reinforce this sense that these three people are inhabiting three different Macaus that have little to do with one another. Little hybridity happens in these vignettes. We see no cultural or even commercial exchange between civilizations. The strong identification each character has with the territory derives from the very distinct experiences each one has of it. The story does not open the question of what Chineseness is or could be or suggest that the history of Portuguese sovereignty created anything in Macau but a sociopolitical backdrop against which each character, each ethnic group, encountered its own joys and disappointments. The Portuguese character comes to Macau to escape the disillusionment of his youth and is only further disillusioned by the lack of any true cultural exchange he finds in his classroom or among his Portuguese friends. The Macanese character calls herself "one of the true sons and daughters of Macau" and experiences the "pure" Portuguese and Chinese as intolerant, racist, and threatening. The Chinese character is enraptured by nostalgia for her childhood and encounters Portuguese people only in the silence of her father's response to her questions about the 123 Incident and in the frustration that others express about "the government." Although all three individuals are portrayed sympathetically, they tell histories critical of the forces that they feel have structured Macau society: self-interest, prejudice, corruption, fear.

After the November performance I attended, the troupe turned up the house lights and took questions. This performance had been in English (the Cantonese performance had been earlier in the day, and I had not been able to attend; the actors did not feel comfortable performing in Portuguese); although the proportion of Portuguese, Macanese, and foreigners in the audience was certainly higher than it would have been at the Chinese performance, there were also plenty of local Chinese in attendance. The only member of the audience who was critical of the play was a Portuguese man (an economist working for the government who was in Macau on a two-year contract) who wondered aloud what such a critical play could offer that might be positive or inspiring. The troupe members answered that they had been careful to end each act with a positive vision—the Portuguese man who had decided to stay, the Macanese woman who had kept on singing, the Chinese woman whose hatred of Macau's problems could not negate her love for the city and her deep sense of belonging. And the mere fact that these three stories had been collected and performed in the same place at the same time, they felt, was itself a positive thing, a step toward crossing the enormous gap that exists, and has always existed, between these communities.

In this sense, the perspective of *Macau One Two Three* resonated with that of a number of people I spoke with, both Chinese and Portuguese, who found the government's insistence on hybridity, cultural exchange, and mutual understanding to be exaggerations at best, and preposterous at worst. The play did echo the state rhetoric of cultural identity in several ways: it made the same claims about the trifold ethnic composition of Macau's population; it recognized that despite the differing historical and structural conditions of their presence in Macau, the members of all three communities (but no others) had equally legitimate attachments to the city; and it suggested that Macau's uniqueness was, for better or worse, a product of the coexistence of these three groups on the same soil. But it took quite a different line on what that uniqueness entailed: ambivalence, disappointment, and hatred as much as pride, nostalgia, and love. In this sense, it is significant that no one but a few high-ranking officials in the Macau Portuguese government (who may or may not have seen the script) seemed to consider this play "political," and only one Portuguese man, himself a recent arrival to Macau, found it "critical." The rest of the comments that evening, and in the press after both performances, praised the play's producers for their remarkably accurate portrayal of the ambivalence that Macau's "uniqueness" inspired in its natives.

Monica

Other Chinese residents of Macau were more positive about what made Macau people different, but their analyses of how the history of Portuguese sovereignty had shaped that difference, and how that difference should best be articulated, could hardly have been more at odds with that of the state. Monica was an ethnic Chinese woman, born and raised in Macau, who worked as an administrator at the Museum of Macau. Given where she worked, I thought she would have an interesting take on all this talk about identity and asked her during our interview if she had any comment. To my surprise, after thinking for a moment, she confessed that she found the whole question rather alien. Identity, she told me, was something people needed only when they lived in situations of instability or insecurity, cut off somehow from their roots and their culture—like the Portuguese in Macau, living so far away from home. "The Portuguese have been here so long, they want to keep emphasizing how long they have been here. So they need to take up the question of identity. But we don't need an identity. We are Chinese. Chinese living in Macau. We just live the way we live, we have our families and our little traditions or ways of doing things, and we just keep doing them that way, as we were taught."[10] I asked what she meant by these "ways of doing things," mentioning that when I first arrived in Macau I had been surprised at how different it was from my experiences of the mainland or any other Chinese places I had lived. She replied: "Of course it's different from the mainland, because in the past thirty or fifty years, the Communists really made an effort to destroy things of the past. They made a conscious effort to destroy their past. But here in Macau," she said, "we live more naturally, we do things as we used to do them and don't try to force an unnatural break with our past. Hong Kong Chinese are very materialistic; mainlanders are very politicized, they live constantly in a highly political environment. But in Macau people just live naturally, the way we know and like." She mentioned the strong sense of nationalism that prevailed among many mainlanders, and said this too was not something Macau people needed. "So," she said, "we don't talk about identity much, because it's really not necessary. Identity is not something we feel the need of."

This is a remarkable statement in many ways, not least because it came from an administrator of a museum whose primary goal was to valorize Macau identity. On one hand, she denied the need for identity, because Chinese (in Macau) are "just Chinese." This echoes the words of the European researcher quoted in the Introduction, who lamented that Macau was peopled with coffee-drinking Chinese. But it also echoes the comments of Dr. Jacques, the principal of the Portuguese Liceu, who equated the construction of a "Macau identity" with an unnatural colonial project and deemed natural only a local "consciousness" that is lived rather than learned. In this sense, Monica and the principal share an understanding of identity—as opposed to "Chineseness" or "consciousness"—as a concept that is ideological, colonial, and alien to Chinese people.

On the other hand, where Dr. Jacques implied that teaching students about Macau history would be one way to denature their identity, Monica went on to equate nature with history: mainlanders are unnatural because they have broken with their past, and Hong Kong people because they have sold their past out from under themselves. But Macau people live "naturally" because they do things in line with their history, their traditions, their customs; they have no need of the artifice of identity. Although the Macau Portuguese state had been stressing the need for Macau people to learn about and capitalize on their historical and cultural identity because they had nothing else (economically, politically, linguistically, ethnically) to distinguish them from their neighbors, she suggested that it was precisely Macau people's lack of a need for identity, itself due to the "natural" relationship they enjoyed with their own past, that distinguished them from their neighbors. Mainland Chinese nationalism, the Portuguese obsession with Macau's identity, and the clamor about Hong Kong identity just prior to the 1997 handover she read as signs that these people had become, by design or by oversight, cut loose from the ground of their history.

The role of the state (and, by extension, of the Portuguese) here is a more complicated one, simultaneously irrelevant to and enabling of the day-to-day workings of culture. This same woman told me that despite having been born and raised in Macau, she had had no substantial social interaction with a Portuguese person until she was twenty-six years old. But at the same time, implicitly, it was the presence of the Portuguese state—with all its inefficiency, corruption, and lame-duck, *laissez-faire* policies—that enabled Macau to avoid the destruction of its past. One of the elected officials of a clan association told me that Macau had the highest per capita number of civic associations of any city in China, precisely because the Portuguese state had "ignored" Chinese society in Macau—but this meant that Chinese residents had been able (or obliged) to maintain the "old-fashioned" social institutions that could now be claimed as markers of the organic purity of Macau Chineseness.

This echoed many statements I heard from Macau Chinese about the extent to which Cantonese culture in general, especially in Macau, had preserved a greater number of, and more "traditional," Chinese practices than anywhere else.[11] In contrast to the stereotypes held by northern Chinese of Hong Kong and Macau as "cultural deserts," crassly commercialized societies whose essential Chineseness has been diluted by uncontrolled exposure to the West, a variety of Macau Chinese told me of "traditional" Chinese cultural practices—religious rituals, linguistic structures, styles of martial arts—that could no longer be found in the mainland or Hong Kong but were still common in Macau. Perhaps the best-known example was the Drunken Dragon Festival (醉龍節), celebrated on the eighth day of the fourth lunar month by the Macau Fishmongers' Union. Originating among the itinerant performance troupes of Guangdong province, the Drunken Dragon Festival (which commemorates a complex story involving a plague-ridden village, a Buddhist monk with a magical jade sword, a drunken fisherman, and a snake reincarnated as a dragon whose spirit imbues a cassia tree with curative powers) was still practiced as an annual event in Macau, even as it had died out (or more accurately, had been eradicated) in the rest of Guangdong province half a century before. More than these easily identifiable public rituals, however, many Macau people—even those who dismissed the state's talk about identity as nothing but "an invention of the Tourism Office"—often spoke of a difference in "mindset" (心理) or "lifestyle" (生活方式), some quality of social existence that made Macau a better place to live than Hong Kong or mainland China. "We are more conservative (保守), more old-fashioned than Hong Kong people," a student at the Macau Polytechnic Institute told me. "We are more relaxed and take life more slowly. If you want to have a big career, you should go to Hong Kong. But if you just want to have a decent job, raise your family, live a comfortable life (小康生活)—then I much prefer Macau."

Macau natives were not the only ones to see Macau in this light. Li Qiulai, the college professor who had moved to Macau from Shanghai in 1985, told me that she felt that one of the defining traits of the Chinese people and culture was a strong sense of *renqing* (人情味): a term translated variously as "human feelings," "human obligations," "reciprocity," and "empathy." The diversity of these translations indicates the complex set of meanings denoted by *renqing*. Anthropologist Yan Yunxiang has suggested that "*renqing* entails a basic emotional empathy and understanding of others and, related to this, a set of moral obligations and social norms" (Yan 1996: 3). As such, it has deep roots in Confucian moral codes and is often acknowledged as central to all Chinese social relationships, forming the basis of civility, even of civilization.[12] Echoing the sentiments of the museum administrator almost exactly, Li Qiulai told me that on the mainland because of the Cultural Revolution and in Hong Kong because of the fast pace of economic development, "people's hearts have changed (人的心都變了). The Cultural Revolution made people more calculating and less trusting; development in Hong Kong has created a more cutthroat competitive atmosphere, so [in both places] the sense of *renqing* has all but disappeared." But in Macau, she continued, these elements of Chineseness that have been lost elsewhere still remain. Indeed, this was one aspect of

Macau that visitors from Hong Kong remarked on repeatedly, ascribing to it everything from the warmer attitudes of the waitstaff in restaurants to the more forgiving attitudes of motorists on Macau's narrow streets to Macau's political culture in which shouting campaign slogans through megaphones—an accepted practice in Hong Kong political campaigns—was a sure way to alienate any potential constituency. One Hong Kong couple shook their heads in amazement as they told me that when they had been trying to hail a taxicab on a busy Macau street, another person who arrived after them but managed to get a cab before they did actually let them take his cab because they had been there first. "We've never seen *that* happen in Hong Kong."

To articulate Macau's difference in terms of greater *renqing*, then, was to propose that Macau residents' uniqueness lay not in their hybridity or their "Latinized" ways but in the unusual strength of their claim on the moral core of Chineseness. It was also to acknowledge, if only in a backhanded way, that the history of Portuguese sovereignty had created the conditions under which this and other forms of "authentic" Chinese culture could be maintained. Although hardly a deliberate policy, it had been a kind of unintended silver lining behind the Portuguese state's particular brand of ambiguous sovereignty. By declaring itself sovereign over Macau, the Portuguese state had sheltered the city from the drastic political and economic policies that had transformed, for better or worse, the regions around it; at the same time, in refusing to govern the Chinese in Macau in line with the norms of modern sovereignty, it allowed "traditional" Chinese civic institutions, which tended to reinforce personalistic ties and a sense of moral obligation, the autonomy they needed to flourish and remain not just relevant but indispensable to the functioning of Chinese society in Macau.

Louis

The third narrative, a family history, is not a story that Louis Cheung, its narrator and protagonist, unfolded for me neatly and chronologically in formal interviews.[13] Rather, it is one that he built—for me, for himself, for his children—in bits and pieces over a year and a half: verbally, as he told me anecdotes and answered my questions; visually, as he leafed with me through photo albums and family business records and drew branches of family trees on paper napkins; ritually, as he took me on visits to local graveyards where some of his ancestors were buried and to his native place in Guangdong province where others still lived. Although I call this a family history, to a large extent it is a story primarily by and about Louis himself. It is by him because, although I got to know his wife and children and met many members of his extended family, few of them were interested in or able to discuss family history with us. It is about him because it reveals perhaps less about his ancestry than about his sense of what ancestry means—how ancestry and its entailments place him in the world. Louis invited me to help him document the history of his family and his own life—happy, I believe, to have someone as interested as he in thinking about the intricacies and ironies involved in the creation of ties by blood and marriage and about the relationship of a variety of pasts to the present. Because the story presented here was one that I witnessed him build, I present it largely in his own words. In what follows, the italicized text is taken from a brief written document, "The Cheungs' Family Tree," that Louis compiled (in English) after his first trip to his native place in 1985; the set-off quotations are the speaking voice of Louis himself, who told me stories of ancestors and descendants on various occasions, as we sat, in the kitchen of his house on Taipa island, at his office in the northern district, or in the noisy noodle shop downstairs, drinking tea laced with lemon, speaking English laced with Cantonese.

But in another way, the chronicle presented here is mine more than his, for one of the things that drew me to Louis as an interlocutor was the depth and candor with which he thought and spoke about many of the issues that I had come to Macau to understand or that I had encountered along the way. Although I only occasionally sought out his thoughts in any formal way on the research questions I was pursuing in other venues (the museum, the schools, the heritage sites), I found that the stories he told often touched in unexpected ways on the questions that had led me to these sites. Louis had little use for the Portuguese administration or for any of the identity-speak it embraced in its final years; yet I think his story expresses, perhaps better than any so far, the contradictions and ambivalences inherent in the attempt to claim the history of the Portuguese presence as the defining characteristic of Macau and its people. My story of Louis and his family—which may or may not be his story—is one that confounds both the state's vision of the relationship between sovereignty, identity, and belonging, on one hand, and anthropological theories of citizenship in the age of transnationalism on the other.

I first met Louis Cheung 張智樂 in November 1997, when, looking for leads in understanding the role played by civic associations in Macau Chinese social life, I went to interview members of the Macau Cheung Clan Association (澳門張祖聯誼會), of which Louis was past president and an active member. Louis is an ethnic Chinese businessman, born and raised in Macau. In many ways, he appears to be an incarnation of the state's construction of the emplaced, hybrid, historically conscious subject who could have been produced only in Macau: he has a strong interest in the history of his family, which has been in Macau for six generations, and he is a devoted Catholic whose father pulled himself and his family out of rural poverty on Taipa by attending Catholic school and learning Portuguese. In 1935 Louis's father opened a store that eventually became a family business and a well-known Macau institution—trading in both Chinese and Portuguese merchandise, provisioning the Portuguese government and military as well as Chinese charitable organizations—for more than fifty years. In the sense that Louis and his family occupied an economic niche as a "bridge," facilitating "commercial and cultural exchange between East and West," they appeared to be both products and symbols of Macau's uniqueness as the state constructed it during the transition era.

From a different perspective, however, Louis also appeared to be the quintessential "flexible citizen," a phrase coined by Aihwa Ong to describe a kind of subjectivity, prevalent among the business elite of Hong Kong, that partakes of the "cultural logic of flexible capital." A sign of the global age, and both post- and anti-national, the flexible subject is mobile and "ungrounded," employing strategies to "evade, deflect or take advantage of political and economic conditions in different parts of the world" (Ong 1999: 2). The "ungrounded identities" of the subjects of Ong's study are produced by an eschewal of old notions of place, history, and the "moral meaning of citizenship" and by the embrace of an amoral, entrepreneurial view of citizenship in which any lingering ambivalence is replaced by an unflinching instrumentalism. The possession of multiple passports, the pursuit of philanthropic endeavors and of certain Chinese cultural practices such as *fengshui*, and even the selective but careful adherence to the principles of filial piety, Ong argues, are meaningful among these elite not as expressions of patriotism, cosmopolitanism, or refinement but as strategies for accumulating various forms of capital—social, cultural, political, and economic.

As we shall see in greater detail below, Louis also seemed to partake of the "ungrounded personal identities of traveling men" that Ong (1999: 20) argues have become the norm among the transnational Chinese merchant class. Having first studied in Taiwan and then studied and worked in the United States for ten years, Louis carries a US passport. In the late 1990s, his mother, five of his six brothers and sisters, and his grown son and daughter from his first marriage lived in the United States or Canada; the sixth sibling was established in southeast Asia. Louis himself returned to Macau from North America to run the family business in 1974, but between 1976 and 1983 he went back to the United States to pursue his education in business management. In 1983, he returned again to Macau to expand the business, but was forced to close it a few years later. In 1991, he and his wife of nineteen years divorced after having two children and several years of a trans-Pacific "commuter" marriage. By the late 1990s, he was remarried to a woman from Macau, with whom he had a young daughter; Louis, an elderly cousin, and a niece were the only members of his patriline who still lived in Macau. Although his work for a small Hong Kong–based transnational firm rarely required him to travel farther than Hong Kong, his family commitments still took him to North America as often as finances and vacation time would allow; his clan association activities kept him connected to his native place in Guangdong province, and his involvement in Catholic organizations kept him in touch with people, issues, and events in Hong Kong, Taiwan, Manila, and Rome.

Both of these thumbnail sketches of Louis and his family are as accurate as they are incomplete; it is the tension between them, the way that Louis lives them both, that is revealing. For, on one hand, Louis articulated little of the sense of belonging to Macau that (according to the state anyway) his particular family history should have engendered; yet neither did he fit Ong's bill of the flexible citizen as consummate rational actor, "outwardly mobile, aligned more toward world market conditions than toward the moral meaning of citizenship in a particular nation" (Ong 1999: 119).[14] What Louis's stories reveal are the unwarranted assumptions that both these theories of subjectivity—that promoted by the Macau Portuguese state during the transition and that argued by Ong—make about how nation-state sovereignty or its absence shapes subjectivities, collective or individual. Both share the idea that new kinds of subjectivity should or can or are displacing the more conventional concepts of political identity expressed through citizenship: the Macau-Portuguese state was attempting to demonstrate how the ties between blood, territory, nation, and state expressed in the concept of citizenship could and should be cross-cut by cultural affiliations based on shared experiences of locality and history; Ong suggests that the emergence of global capitalism has transformed (for the elite diasporics who are the subject of her study) older sensibilities about the moral resonances of nation, territory, history, and state. Neither the Macau Portuguese state nor Ong takes into account the way that accumulated experiences of particular forms of sovereignty may shape the very conditions of possibility, or impossibility, of these new subjectivities.

The Cheung family history, as constructed by Louis, begins with the Jin invasion of the city of Kaifeng (in today's Henan province), capital of the Song dynasty, in the early twelfth century. The Song court fled south, and loyal official Cheung Yung Fung moved with them, taking a position as a magistrate in Huizhou, Guangdong province. *Ancestor Yung Fung moved south with the Songs in 1127, 860 years ago. Ancestor Fu Man settled in Heishi village more than 600 years ago. Twenty-seven generations have been living in this village.* Louis does not know in what year—or what decade—the first Cheung of his family arrived in Macau. He knows that twenty-first-generation ancestor

Tong Kan 東勤 and his son Siu Wing 少榮 boarded a boat in Heishi village and ended up in Taipa and estimates that that must have been in the early nineteenth century. "But why they settled on Taipa, not Macau or Hong Kong or somewhere, I'll never know," laughed Louis. "They must have been heading for somewhere else and got lost."

Louis's stories began to flow with increasing certainty once the Cheungs reached Taipa:

My grandfather's father [Kai Chong] was an opium smoker. He sold every-thing they owned. One time his wife (who came down to Taipa from Hei-shi village after him) went up to the hill and cut some grass for fuel, you know, and she sold them and got—you know those coins with the holes in the center, they used to tie together with string? A string of cash. She came home and put it on the table and went to get a drink or wash her hands or whatever, and that string of cash disappeared. My grandfather [Wing Fai] was still a small boy. He comforted his mother, saying, "Don't worry, I'll borrow some money and I'll work hard, as hard as I can, and we'll repay our debts double." So I think he started a business. A grocery. But a very old-fashioned grocery—you know what a *jaahp fo póuh* 雜貨鋪 is? Yeah, not ex-actly a grocery store, but a store selling things like pickles, tofu, things like that. And then another shop—I don't know who ran that, it was still going when my mother married [my father]—it was a place selling clothes for the dead, we call them *sau-yi* 壽衣 [literally "longevity clothes"].

My grandfather married my grandmother, who gave birth to eight daughters and one son. Only two survived. One was the eldest aunt, and the second was the eighth aunt, who was ten years older than my father. Until the ninth [child was born]. My grandmother told my grandfather that he had to marry a concubine, because she had already given birth to nine children and only two daughters had survived. So my grandfather married again, which was very common in those days, but he told my grandmother, "I won't be happy if you don't have a son before the second wife does." And then the concubine gave birth to number 10, a daughter. And then my grandmother and the second wife gave birth to two children more or less one year apart, or maybe it was even the same year. And they were both boys. My father was from my grandmother, not the concubine, and he was the elder, a year or a few months older. After that the second wife had [children number] 12, 13, 14, 15, all daughters....

My father was eleven years old when his father died, and I think my grandmother didn't know how to read. When he was maybe 14 or 15, my father could see that he wouldn't have any career by staying in such an

environment. His elder sister, ten years older than him, who was very conservative, she said, "Don't leave, just stay home, sell some merchandise,
make some money, and just be conservative." And my father broke with all
that advice by going to Macau to attend Portuguese school. The school he
went to was a seminary, very famous, called Sang-Yeuhk-Sat 聖若瑟修院
[Seminário de São José]. At the age of 15 or 14. In those days, before the
bridge was built, there was no means of transportation [between Macau and
Taipa]. We had to take ferries, and the trip took about one hour or so, and
the schedule was not frequent at all. So my father had to stay at the house
of his good friend in Macau. And my father told me that he grew up in such
a difficult environment. He had to read by—well, maybe not by candlelight,
but there was just one lightbulb, and people were lying not very far away
from him smoking opium. Yeah. In such an environment. And he was
studying Portuguese. There was no Portuguese-Chinese dictionary then.
None. And he didn't know English. He had to check a Portuguese-English
dictionary and then an English-Chinese dictionary in order to find a word.
But he spoke fluent, perfectly fluent, perfect Portuguese. If you heard him
on the phone you would not realize he was Chinese, you would have
thought that he was Portuguese. [As an adult] he had a lot of Portuguese
friends, and very good relations with the government. Many heads of [gov-
ernment] departments were his schoolmates.[15]

In 1935, Louis's father, Man On, and another man named
Cheung established a dry goods store on San Ma-Louh, near the
Leal Senado. Nine years later, Man On's partner sold him his shares
of the business, and the shop became a family enterprise. Thanks to
Man On's ties to the Portuguese community, after World War II, the
shop began to get government contracts. They also supplied the
Tung Sin Tong 同善堂, a Chinese-run charity, with goods to dis-
tribute to the poor. Man On helped found the Cheung Clan Association, was involved in the Chinese Chamber of Commerce, and
chaired several other community associations. Aside from his connections with government, he was friendly with the most powerful
members of the Chinese community, including Ho Yin 何賢.[16] Not
wishing his children to receive a "communist" education, in the
early 1950s, as many Chinese-medium schools in town began raising
the new flag of the People's Republic of China, Man On sent his
sons to study at Yuet Wah College 粵華中學, a Catholic boys'
school. While he was there, Louis became a Catholic.

My father wouldn't allow me to be baptized. He said there are only three reasons for a Chinese to be baptized. The first would be to get *gaujaiban* 救濟品 [relief supplies]. Either they would give them only to Catholics, or they would recruit you to be a Catholic in order to get the stuff. The second reason was to get a better salary. In the old days, if your name was Wingsit Cheung, or Cheung Chi Lok, like my name, your salary would be 80 dollars per month. But if your name was Louis Cheung, you'd get 100 dollars, even for the same position. It was discrimination. Absolutely, racial discrimination. Now if your name was Louis Clayton, you'd get 120. If my name were Cheung Chi Lok, there's no way I could just change it to Louis Clayton, right? No way I'd change it. So might as well just accept the fact that I'm getting paid 80 dollars per month. But once I got baptized, I'd be given a Christian name, "Louis." So, "Louis Cheung," oh, that's not bad, 100 dollars, I'd get 20 dollars more. Well, if I'm called Louis Cheung, I might just as well be called Louis Clayton, and get 20 dollars more. But this would be very disgraceful. To give up your history like this would be very disgraceful. My father hated that. And the third reason would be to meet girls. Because a lot of girls would get baptized. They would go to Catholic school. All the most famous girls' schools in Macau were Catholic schools: Santa Rosa, Sacred Heart, and the others. But, [my father] said, whoever gets baptized after the age of 30 has real faith, they really believe it. So I waited until I was after 30 to be baptized. And until now, I'm still a Catholic. And I never changed my last name. No.[17]

Louis began his family history from a moment of displacement brought about by political transition and loyalty to a sovereign (the Song bureaucrat fleeing south with the court). The history tells, on one hand, of the success that can come from hard work, filiality, perseverance, and adherence to tradition; at the same time, it acknowledges that conditions of opium addiction, debt, poverty, and illiteracy could be overcome only by breaking with family and tradition and immersing oneself in an alien language, culture, and institution. The story that Louis told me about his father is at once the story of a colonial system of privilege and discrimination that put Chinese residents of Macau at a disadvantage, and the story of how his father managed to work that system to his advantage without abandoning his sense of Chineseness or his political loyalties. Man On had been a supporter of the KMT, and all the shop's records were dated by the Nationalist calendar, in which 1912, the first year of the Republic of China, was Year 1.

One of the things that struck me about Louis's family stories was the extent to which they were almost always tangibly emplaced:

The 23rd generation, Kai Chong (啓祥), 24th generation Wing Fai (永輝), [and] 25th generation Man On (民安) were all born on Taipa Island and lived there. Twenty-sixth generation Iok Ling, Chi San, and Terry were all born in Taipa; Paul, Chi Lok and Josephina were born at 8 Pátio das Paredes; Rosanna was born at 10 Avenida Costa Ferreira. Twenty-seventh generation Valerie through Raymond were born in Macau; Andrew, Brendan and Alton were all born in the United States of America; Artie through Ava were born in Canada; William was born in the U.S.; Susana and Arlo were born in Indonesia; Richard and Robert were born in Canada. In other words, of the 27th generation clansmen, no one was born in Taipa. Only Valerie and Catherine [and Louis] are still in Hong Kong and Macau.

This liturgy of the birthplaces of five generations of Cheungs maps the family through time and across space, invoking both their intimate familiarity with specific places in Macau and their progressive dispersion across nations and continents. In fact, Louis often "spoke with place" (Basso 1996) and seemed to pride himself on his ability to speak in detail of the histories of particular places. He could tell me the name of the street on which his mother was born ("it was on Hahwaan Gaai 下灣街, I don't remember the number") and could rattle off the addresses of the four buildings the family business had used as warehouses in the late 1960s. Louis's immediate family—his father and mother and their seven children (of whom Louis was fifth, born in 1944)—lived upstairs from their shop, and on summer evenings, he told me, they would often pass the time sitting by the bronze statue in the main square opposite the house. Since I knew that the building he had grown up in was now classified as part of Macau's architectural heritage, I asked him if he knew much about its history. He told me that his aunt had told him that when she was a child, an elderly neighbor had told her that she remembered watching the building being built; he guessed it must have dated from the late nineteenth century. His family had rented the building in 1935 and had purchased it in 1953, when he was nine years old. He showed me photographs of himself as a teenager, posing for the camera on the ledge of the building's flat roof; he told me of being woken from an afternoon nap one Saturday in December 1966 by the noise of crowds on the square below, and watching from his bedroom window as crowds ransacked the Leal Senado and pulled down that bronze statue, which was a likeness of Nicolau de Mesquita, a Macanese army officer who had led an attack on the Chinese garrison at Passaleão (北山嶺) in retaliation for the 1849 assassination of Governor Ferreira do Amaral.

When I got to know him in the late 1990s, Louis lived in the very location (although not the same building) where his father had been born and his grandmother had died. He made a point of telling his daughter, when she came for a visit from California, the long story of the evolution of that plot of land: how, in 1950, his father had gained exclusive rights to the five rundown old buildings that occupied the lot by agreeing to pay the 300 patacas it would cost to build a wall around them, in compliance with a government directive to clean up Taipa village; how he'd rented it for $80 a year, first to a Portuguese sergeant working at the army base just up the hill and then to a relative who needed extra storage space for the hardware store he ran across the street; how Louis himself had spent a few thousand patacas in the late 1960s to knock out some walls and join the buildings together, put in a patio and fix it up well enough so the family could take the boat over from Macau for weekend barbecue parties; how, after the Macau-Taipa bridge was built in the early 1970s, they'd converted the building into a warehouse and then, in 1991, remodeled it as their primary residence.

Yet according to Louis, all this knowledge, all these accumulated experiences of and stories about places in Macau, did not translate into a sense of belonging or nostalgia. When I asked, he told me that he had no particular "feeling" (感情) for the places of his youth. As for the house he grew up in, on two occasions (once in the 1970s and again in the early 1980s), he had tried to get permission to tear it down and build a new thirteen-story building on the site; he'd gotten estimates and a contractor, but his plans were frustrated when, *in media res*, the government classified the building as part of Macau's cultural heritage and informed him that it was against the law to make alterations to its exterior. In 1985, due to growing competition from chain stores and the recession caused by the signing of the Sino-British Joint Declaration on Hong Kong, Louis closed the family business, which had grown into an enterprise employing over seventy people. It was then that he sold the San Ma-Louh building and moved back to the place of his father's birth on Taipa.

Neither did he articulate any regret at the development that was transfiguring his city and displacing, literally, his family. In the fall of 1997, Louis told me that the old Taipa graveyard in which his ancestors were buried was going to be razed and converted into a public park. As the fields of ginger flowers and vegetables that once covered the island's low-lying flats were quickly being replaced by towering apartment buildings, the Taipa Municipal Council had felt the need to create more green space to attract families to fill the empty buildings and had announced its plan to dig up the graves of Taipa's oldest burial ground and move them to one of the newer cemeteries on the island. At Qingming (the grave-sweeping festival celebrated fifteen days after the spring equinox) the following spring, Louis invited me to join him and his elderly cousin as they went for the last time to the old graveyard to sweep the graves of his ancestors.[18] We tramped through the overgrown grass, searching for quite a while to find the graves of his grandfather and great-grandfather, that of his grandmother (who had been buried separately), and of his cousin's mother. We eventually found them and performed the requisite ritual: burning three sticks of incense, bowing three times, clearing away the dead leaves from the low, horseshoe-shaped grave. Louis had told me earlier that he hoped his son would visit from California before the graves were dug up, so he could show him the place where his ancestors had lain for generations. But on this day I seemed more upset than he was by the thought that real estate speculation and overdevelopment were displacing even the dead. I had read dozens of historical accounts of Chinese villagers taking up arms against those who dared disturb their ancestral burial grounds (indeed, it was said that this was the last straw that had triggered the assassination of Governor Ferreira do Amaral in 1849); even I, I thought, would have been dismayed if the Boston-area cemetery where my own grandparents' remains were buried had been dug up due to shortsighted city planning. But after we somewhat hastily finished at the old graveyard, Louis gladly took me to visit the graves of the previous two generations—Tong Kan and Siu Wing, the two who had come to Taipa from Heishi, together with their wives—which had already been moved to the new resting place Louis had chosen for them: the small Catholic cemetery across the street.

Indeed, Louis told me, he felt no real attachment to Macau; he would leave in the wink of an eye, he said, and never look back, if he could find a job that would pay as well in real terms as the one he had there. I admit that I was puzzled by Louis's apparent indifference to the places he had been born and raised, an indifference that I saw as a disjuncture between the fact of emplacement and its meaning. My surprise at his indifference, of course, had more to do with my own assumptions about the relationship between place, memory, and nostalgia than with his, and my attempts to engage him in conversation about it met with little success. But then, unexpectedly and in a different context, Louis himself provided a clue.

After the cemetery visit, we took his cousin home and went back to Louis's house in Taipa village for a cup of tea. He suggested with a smile that instead of tea, we should try making Portuguese coffee again. Last time I had been there, he had told me he knew a way of making "Portuguese-style coffee" by hand, a method involving coffee powder, hot water, and a lot of stirring. He had tried to make it for me then (over the protests of his wife, who suggested that American coffee was easier and better-tasting, and besides all that stirring might scratch the china), but it hadn't turned out. This time, his wife was busy with their toddler, so he heated water and we talked while he stirred; occasionally I took over the stirring as he picked up my pen to illustrate a point.

As we chatted, I told him I was in the midst of researching the attempt to introduce a Macau history curriculum into the middle schools, because I was interested in how the government was going about its project of making people feel proud of being from Macau.

He paused stirring and looked at me. "Make people feel *proud* of being from *Macau?*"

"Yes," I responded.

He laughed, briefly and quietly, with what I read as a combination of derision and incomprehension, looking down at the cup of Portuguese coffee he was laboring over.

The phone rang, and we were interrupted.

When he returned, he suddenly asked me if, in my interviews, I had met other people with views like his. Or was he peculiar?

I asked what he meant.

"I mean that I still believe the Portuguese are invaders. I still consider them to be invaders. Whether by force, militarily, or economically, politically, religiously, whatever—they are invaders. This is not their place, but they have stayed here for four hundred years." He explained that he found it very difficult to understand Chinese residents of Macau who so willingly cooperated with, even celebrated, the Portuguese authorities in Macau. "I can't understand," he said. "I can't understand.

I mean, if you live peacefully in your home, and all of a sudden, or maybe gradually, someone comes in, some others—I don't care what race, or even E.T.'s [space aliens]—some others come in, they bribe your family or your partner, or they use force or whatever, and occupy your place, and settle down, as if nothing ever happened. And they ask you to move into a small room, they say, "Oh Cathryn, you may move into this room, you have complete freedom, you can do whatever you want, I'll feed you and I'll . . ." And then they entertain their friends, and decorate the house and—and they still allow you a lot of freedom, you can go out, you can invite people to come in, except you have to observe their regulations, or they say, "You have to turn the lights off at 8 PM," or "You can't make any noise"—it's quite true, I mean, at night when people sleep you shouldn't scream or make a lot of noise, but [*gentle tone now*] this is my place, it's not your place. How come you can come over to my place and then say to do this and this—even if it's good for me? Actually the entire house is mine, I mean, we live here, and we're not fighting or anything. Maybe I'm poor, maybe I'm weak. Or maybe I'm sick and you cure me, maybe you give me medicine to cure me. . . . But what should I do? What should you do? If you can't fight, you are not strong enough, and perhaps you might need their aid. . . . But what should your attitude be? Be very grateful? Be very hateful? Or just stay where I should, you ask me to move here and I move here? You invite me to join your celebration, [and I say] "Oh sorry, I'm busy, I'm not feeling well, I can't make it." Why do you have to honor someone who occupies your place? [pause] Can you understand that? [pause] They never think about these things, they never think. . . . It may be understandable after the signing of the Joint Declaration. For the last few years, well, even if I praise you, well, everybody in the world knows that you're going to get out a few years from now. I can understand that. But before the signing of the Joint Declaration. . . . Why? [pause] Well, they don't have to protest, they don't have to fight against them, they don't have to, but on the other hand, or on the same hand, they don't have to be . . . too *positive*. I feel ashamed, I really feel ashamed. Very ashamed."[19]

Here Louis answered his own heartfelt question, the question of the colonial subject: "What should your attitude be?" His ambivalent response—neither "grateful" nor "hateful"—acknowledges that the policies of an alien government may be reasonable, even beneficial to the governed, while still denying their legitimacy. It translates into the impossibility of feeling pride in his family's long history in Macau or belonging to the places in which that history happened.

But Louis was equally uncomprehending of the politics of Macau's impending postcoloniality. For, despite his US passport, he considered himself a Chinese patriot. He was, like his father, a loyal supporter of the KMT, and he could not understand how the one country, two systems policy could be understood as "patriotic." Louis was one of the few people I met who questioned (out loud, in my presence) the meaning of the term "patriotism" as it was used in Macau:

This one country, two systems policy, how can it be patriotic? Being patriotic means agreeing with the government, and if you have one country with two systems, you are saying that what the government does is OK for some people in your country, but not for you. It's making a division out of what should be unity, and unity means only one. So it is a big contradiction. They all say they love China so much, but do they really? How can they? It's like if a child is adopted, and his biological parents are poor peasants but he loves them very much, and then his adopted parents are wealthy people who live in the city and play tennis and are well educated and are bankers or whatever. And if the child really loves his parents, he should either go and share his wealth with them, give them the money and education and help them improve their lives, or, if that is impossible for some reason, if he really loves them he should give up his rich lifestyle and go back and live with them in their poor village. That's love. It is conditionless love, the kind of love a husband and wife or parents and children should have. And if we are talking about *ngoi-gwok* 愛國 [patriotism, literally "love-country"], that would be the true patriot.[20]

The complexity and density of Louis's stories reveal a profoundly ambivalent subjectivity: at once firmly placed but denying any sense of place; fascinated with the past but uninterested in preserving its material traces; proud of and filial toward his father, but uncomprehending of anyone who (like his father) would actively collaborate with the Portuguese administration; a Chinese patriot with a foreign passport. This ambivalence, it seems to me, cannot be fully explained either by the Portuguese state's assertions about Chinese residents' single-minded concept of value that made them unable to appreciate their unique history or by Aihwa Ong's assertions about flexible citizens' notion of citizenship, shaped by a world in which the logic of transnational capital is total and every aspect of life is structured by the drive for accumulation of capital in its myriad forms.

That Louis's sense of "ungroundedness" had little in common with the Hong Kong elites described by Ong became clear to me when I asked him about his US passport. One day, when the fires of the Macanese nationality controversy were burning at their hottest, I had asked Louis when he had gotten American citizenship, why he chose to get it, and what kind of passport he had before. He laughed and told me he had a good story about that, and that next time I came to his house he would tell it to me.

So on this hot summer Sunday afternoon, we sat in his home office, which was crammed with files and papers and folders, water stains covering the ceiling, an old typewriter taking up space on the desk, covered and unused, since the desktop computer had its own hutch at right-angles to the desk. The wall-mounted air-conditioning unit hummed reassuringly. Where there were no bookshelves, the walls were bare, except for a large framed black-and-white photo portrait of Louis's father: a thick-set, well-groomed, bespectacled man of middle age, radiating confidence and dignity. Louis rummaged through the drawers of his filing cabinet for a few moments and almost immediately found what he was looking for. Onto the desk he plunked two piles of booklets fastened together with rubber bands. These were the forms of identification, some valid and some expired, that had at some point been possessed by himself, his ex-wife, and his son. He undid the rubber bands and spread them out on the desk.

"Now," he started the little show-and-tell session with his own IDs,

these days I have a U.S. passport and a Portuguese passport. I have a Hong Kong ID card and a Macau ID card. I have a Salvo-Conduto, which is an identification card allowing Portuguese passport-holders to enter Hong

Kong and stay for seven days without a visa. I have a *yihng biht jing* 認別證 or *bilhete de identidade de cidadão nacional*, a national ID card for Portuguese citizens, a U.S. Social Security card, a re-entry permit for Hong Kong, a re-entry permit for the U.S., a "home-returning" permit (回鄉證) for the mainland, four valid drivers' licenses (Macau, Hong Kong, U.S., and Canada) and one expired one (Taiwan).

He took great glee in this proliferation of paper identities, which, as he noted, was not strictly legal: by law he was allowed to have either a Hong Kong or a Macau ID card, not both.

    With a prologue like that, I expected that the "good story" would be one about the joys of flexibility. But the story he told was rather one about the hassles, expense, and logistical maneuvering necessary to living and traveling with multiple identifications. When he and his first wife, Angela, who was from Hong Kong, were living together in Macau with their young son Douglas, they faced the problem of maintaining their residency rights in Hong Kong while living permanently in Macau. They tried to solve the problem by staying in Macau as "Hong Kong residents visiting Macau"; whenever they entered Macau from Hong Kong, they would do so on their Hong Kong identity cards and needed to make a trip back to Hong Kong every few months. This trick worked quite well until they wanted to travel overseas.

    Because there was no international airport in Macau, if they wanted to go anywhere, they had to travel through Hong Kong. At that time, Louis had a Portuguese passport, and Angela got one shortly after marrying him; but Douglas, who had been born in Hong Kong, had only a Hong Kong British passport. (As the son of a Portuguese national, Douglas would also have been eligible for a Portuguese passport, but according to Louis this would have required a lengthy—and, for non-Portuguese speakers who had to hire a Macanese notary to fill out the forms on their behalf, expensive—application process.) As Louis explained it, the problem was that "in order to depart from Hong Kong on a Portuguese passport, we needed to have our date of arrival in Hong Kong stamped in the passport as well; Immigration won't give you an exit stamp if they don't see an entry stamp. But because Douglas had a British passport, his point of origin was assumed to be Hong Kong, so his passport should not have had a Hong Kong entry stamp." Louis and his wife could simply travel on their Portuguese passports from Macau to Hong Kong and then abroad. But if Douglas were to travel on his British passport from Macau to Hong Kong, it would get stamped with an entry date showing that Hong Kong was not in fact his point of origin. Then the authorities would see that he had not been living in Hong Kong, and he might lose his status as a permanent resident. In brief, while Angela and Louis needed Hong Kong entry stamps in their Portuguese passports, their son, who was too young to travel alone, had to avoid getting one in his British passport.

So Louis and his wife devised a plan. Because Douglas was a child, he was listed together with Angela on her Hong Kong re-entry permit. When the family traveled back and forth between Macau and Hong Kong, on business or to visit family, Angela and Douglas would travel on her Hong Kong re-entry permit. If they traveled together, the permit would be stamped "entry [or exit] plus one." The permit assumed the point of origin to be Hong Kong, so any exit-plus-one stamp would have to be cleared by an entry-plus-one—in other words, there had to be one round trip each time. "Otherwise," Louis chuckled, "if Angela had an exit-plus-one on her way from Hong Kong to Macau, and then just an individual entry on her way from Macau to Hong Kong, Immigration might think she had taken Douglas to Macau and sold him or who knows what!"

This, then, solved the problem of getting Douglas to Hong Kong without stamps in his passport, but now Angela would be in Hong Kong without an entry stamp in her Portuguese passport. So she would have to leave Hong Kong and enter again, this time on her Portuguese passport. With the exit-plus-one stamp on her re-entry permit cleared, she could travel as an individual; so she would leave Douglas with relatives in Hong Kong, return to Macau on her re-entry permit, meet up with Louis, and travel back to Hong Kong on her Portuguese passport. Their Portuguese passports would be stamped "entry"; Douglas's British passport would have no stamp, and they would then be ready to go anywhere they liked— "although," Louis laughed, "I don't know what the immigration officers in America or Canada or wherever must have thought, seeing two Portuguese parents and a British son who were all Chinese!"

Upon their return to Hong Kong, the whole thing happened in reverse: at the airport immigration checkpoint, Angela and Louis would get the date of entry into Hong Kong stamped on their Portuguese passports, and would need to get an exit stamp within thirty days. They would leave Douglas with relatives in Hong Kong and return to Macau together. There Angela would turn around and travel back to Hong Kong on her re-entry permit bearing the individual exit stamp; as she entered Hong Kong, she would receive an individual entry stamp, which would clear the individual exit stamp. She could then pick up Douglas and return to Macau, acquiring an exit-plus-one stamp and starting the whole sequence all over again.

Louis told this story with amusement, not annoyance. I think his amusement came from his ability to outwit the authorities who viewed the system of passports and identification cards as a means to pin people down, rather than freeing them to live and move across borders. The delight Louis took in his accumulation of legal identities and in his maneuvering around multiple levels of bureaucratic localization seemed to demonstrate—in contrast, for example, to the Macanese discussed in Chapter 3—how little the state's categorizations really mattered, and how Chineseness is constituted more importantly of things like kinship ties and cultural practices. It seemed to be one more story about a flexible citizen, about the (southern) Chinese propensity for understanding passport identity as a strategic identity, as opposed to the Western view (which Louis imputed to North American immigration officials) in which national identity is as indelible as "race."

But this view is complicated by the fact that Louis was not being asked to choose one of these legal identities over another. This much became clear in something Louis admitted to me much later when, at the close of a rambling discussion about Macau's complicated relationship with Taiwan, the role of the Catholic church in Asia, and the meaning of socialism, he came back to the question of why and how he got his US passport. He said,

If I didn't have an American passport, the Macau government would consider me Portuguese. And as you know, that's not something I would like. Now, I can tell you that I consider myself Chinese, but there is no way in my life that I would ever be willing to consider myself a subject of the People's Republic of China. The problem is, if I tell people that I am Chinese, after 1999 I will be given a Macau SAR passport, and that would mean I would have to acknowledge that I am a citizen of the PRC. And I can't do that. I won't do that. So I can tell *you* that I am Chinese, but to other Chinese I say that I am an American. What else can I do? *Huigui* [the handover] is inevitable. It is going to happen. But I do not want to make a choice about whether or not to accept an SAR passport.

Stunned by the passion of this denial, the likes of which I had never heard anyone utter in a year and a half of asking people in Macau about sovereignty and Chineseness, I asked him whether, if he were somehow in a position to make such decisions, he would prefer the Portuguese to remain in charge of Macau. "Fortunately," he replied with a smile,

I'm not in that position. All I know is that if you forced me to choose between calling myself American, Portuguese, or Chinese, I would say that I am American. And if you really forced me, if you held a gun to my head and forced me to choose between being Portuguese and being a citizen of the PRC, I would have to call myself Portuguese. Even though I don't have the slightest relationship with Portugal or anyone or anything Portuguese— I don't speak the language, I don't like the people or the Portuguese character. But if you forced me to choose between being Portuguese and being a citizen of the PRC, I would choose Portuguese. You know the saying *ren ru fu zhong* 忍辱負重?[21] It means choosing the lesser of two evils—there's not much of a choice.[22]

He broke off here and grinned, as surprised as I was at the oddly confessional quality of his statement. "Wow," he said, "for all these years I've never been able to tell anyone this, and now I can tell you my *samsing* 心聲 [innermost thoughts]. You're the only one I can tell."

What becomes clear here is that Louis's sense of "ungroundedness" stemmed not from an amoral view of citizenship as a means to maximizing advantage but precisely from his very passionate political beliefs about the illegitimacy of the rule of either the Portuguese or the CCP. Although Louis's stories reveal yet again the myriad practical reasons for claiming multiple citizenships, they also demonstrate the extent to which flexibility and ungroundedness do not necessarily supplant older notions of history, place, kinship, and a passionate nationalist sensibility. For him, holding citizenship (at least, Chinese citizenship) necessarily means being patriotic, and patriotism, as he said, means "unity"—accepting not just the same living conditions but also the same political beliefs as his compatriots. The advantage a US passport can provide, then, is not just economic security; it allows him to avoid having to answer the question of the moral meaning of citizenship in a situation in which he finds no acceptable answer. To be sure, Louis takes full strategic advantage of his multiple passports: he uses his US passport to travel overseas to visit family, his home-returning-permit to visit his native place or to go across the border to Zhuhai for inexpensive seafood, and his Macau ID to reside comfortably in a place where he can achieve a standard of living that would be out of his reach anywhere else. But this does not mean that his notions of citizenship and nationality are transparently instrumentalist, infinitely flexible, or inherently separable from his conceptions of history, culture, and place. To the contrary, they are shaped by his very sense of history and belonging, as well as his profound, if profoundly ambivalent, relationship with place. And in this sense, his story reflects the ambivalence that lies at the heart of all citizenship—not just flexible citizenship—as a category of collective subjectivity in the modern world: it is (as Derrida has remarked about the law) simultaneously too general to capture the unique experience that each individual brings to the definition of being Chinese (or Portuguese or American) and too narrow to do justice to the complexity and wide-ranging significance of the term "Chinese." Louis's story suggests that the flexibility of citizenship in the era of transnationalism is not so much the undoing of earlier configurations of citizenship as it is an expression of the ambivalence that has inhered in the concept of citizenship from the beginning. It points to the limitations of any attempt to express or to study collective subjectivity through categories such as citizenship and identity that are structured by the precepts of modern sovereignty.

Conclusion

Stories like the three presented above were not out of the ordinary in transition-era Macau. To be sure, the *Macau One Two Three* performance and the controversy it sparked were not everyday occurrences, but the sensibility they expressed—of frustration mixed with nostalgia and a kind of ambivalent, world-weary optimism—resonated with the remarks of many people I spoke with in other contexts during the transition era. Although I did not come across many people with Monica's ability to articulate their ideas about identity, history, and culture, her thoughts about the meaning and locus of Macau's difference were echoed by a wide range of Macau residents, as well as among many visitors from Hong Kong and the PRC whose experience of Macau's difference was all the more keen precisely because it was unexpected. And although I met few people as willing as Louis to think and talk about their family histories, their life stories, and their *samsing*, his views were indeed not "peculiar." His dubious identification with Macau was articulated by others who shared his antipathy toward the Portuguese and the history of imperialism they represented, while still recognizing that they would not be where and who they were had things happened differently.

But the fact remains that, in important ways, these were still "outlawed" tales. The *Macau One Two Three* production was literally outlawed, banned from being shown in state-run venues. Monica's comments about the uselessness of "identity" and her thoughts on where Macau's true uniqueness lay were widespread structures of feeling that were rarely, if ever, expressed in the public sphere. And Louis felt the impossible choice demanded by the disjuncture between his political beliefs and "Macau reality" to be so troubling that he could not voice them to anyone but a sympathetic foreigner who had promised him anonymity. The air of confidentiality, even transgression, that attended the telling of these stories stood as a reminder that, ironically, despite the ostensibly "united front" on Macau history and Beijing's qualified support for the Portuguese state's efforts to assert the cultural uniqueness of Macau, public discourse about the history of Portuguese sovereignty and the significance of the impending handover was still dominated by totalizing, either-or rhetorics that left little room for the articulation of ambivalence or complexity of feeling.

Conclusion

A weed from Catholic Europe, it took root
Between the yellow mountains and the sea,
And bore these gay stone houses like a fruit,
And grew on China imperceptibly.

Rococo images of Saint and Saviour
Promise her gamblers fortunes when they die;
Churches beside the brothels testify
That faith can pardon natural behaviour.

This city of indulgence need not fear
The major sins by which the heart is killed,
And governments and men are torn to pieces:

Religious clocks will strike; the childish vices
Will safeguard the low virtues of the child
And nothing serious can happen here.

—W. H. Auden, "Macao" (1939)

The ideal of sovereignty continues to be a source of both hope and despair in the world today. Movements taking as their goal the achievement of political sovereignty have continued to proliferate, as have modifiers of the term—such as food sovereignty, energy sovereignty, cultural sovereignty, environmental sovereignty—denoting the realms of human activity in which the exercise of sovereign power is thought necessary or desirable. The hopeful see sovereignty as a means to fulfilling the promises of freedom, self-determination, social justice, dignity, and ethnic solidarity. The despairing see it as a basis for perpetuating bloodshed, thuggery, totalitarianism, and the politics of exclusion. These reactions are as extreme as the idea of absolute authority that underpins the principle of sovereign power.

But although their polemicism reflects the urgent meaning that sovereignty holds for many groups around the world, it often precludes more nuanced discussions of what exactly sovereignty entails and what the alternatives might be.

During Macau's transition to Chinese rule, conditions were such that one alternative to this polarizing vision of sovereignty came into view, if only hazily and fleetingly. To be sure, the entire premise of the handover was structured by the logic and demands of nation-state sovereignty: the Chinese state wished to regain supreme authority over people and territory that had historically been defined as Chinese. From this perspective, in Macau as in Hong Kong, the one country, two systems policy that guided the transition to Chinese rule was simply a "framework for managing an alternative type of economy—the market economy—which stood in such sharp contrast to the Chinese planned economy" (Ghai 2000: 94). But in practice, as this book has shown, the process of Macau's political transition raised far-reaching questions about the meaning of sovereignty, in the past and in the future, and about how particular configurations of sovereignty could or should or had affected Macau residents' sense of their own Chineseness. To an extent impossible in neighboring Hong Kong, it opened up the possibility of interpreting the old agonistic stories that underpin received histories of the modern world—stories of colonialist exploitation vs. nationalist response, the West vs. China, traditional vs. modern—in new and multiple shades of gray. And it provided a way to think about this little Portuguese backwater as being in the vanguard of a cosmopolitan Chinese subjectivity.

Perhaps it has become obvious by now that in the process of studying the various ways this alternative view was articulated in the everyday of Macau's public sphere, I came to find it both intellectually and ethically enchanting. But I confess to this enchantment as if it were a dirty secret, for I have also never been able to shake the conviction that it is a sign of my own hidden complicity with the colonial project, or at least of my naïveté and willingness to be distracted from harsh reality by strings of pretty words. The reality, I keep telling myself, is there in the testimonies of many informants. The Portuguese were invaders. They were racists. They were hopelessly inept administrators. Macau under Portuguese rule was ruinous. It was a laughingstock. It was a venal place. It was useful as a stepping-stone and not much else. The portrayal of all that was good about Macau was nothing more than colonial nostalgia for a world that never was; lusotropicalism was nothing more than a colonialist smokescreen, just as the Portuguese state's denial of its own imperialism was its greatest and most cynical imperialist gesture. So ingrained in me are the classic critiques of colonialism that whenever I feel myself beginning to listen instead to the testimonies of other informants—who spoke of their love for Macau, their ambivalence toward Portuguese rule, their pride in what made them simultaneously thoroughly Chinese and thoroughly different from other Chinese people, their affirmation of the more relaxed and compassionate attitudes that they felt characterized life in Macau, and their nostalgia for the old city that had been demolished before their very eyes and replaced not so much with serviceable new buildings as with towering icons of capitalist development—I reprimand myself and repeat to myself that the more closely Macau adhered to the precepts of national sovereignty and economic development, the better off its residents would be. The ambivalence of my reaction is precisely why I want to end by following the instincts of my own enchantment and endorsing, if only tentatively, the utopian sentiments I found in this alternative view. I suggest that in Macau's unsystematic system we may find something that did provide a model for a better world, as well as a better model for thinking about the world.

To see Macau as a model for the world rather than a failure to live up to the global norms of modern state sovereignty, one need only contrast it to the ideologies of unity and uniformity that are entailed in those norms. Narratives of modern sovereignty tell of a form of power that functions uniformly and absolutely across space and through time within a given territory (and uniformly does not function outside the borders of that territory). From this perspective, the Portuguese state in Macau looked like nothing so much as a failure, and the one country, two systems policy a new and dangerous experiment whose contradictions could, if not carefully policed, threaten the foundations of the Chinese nation-state. Similarly, the concepts of collective subjectivity that are, in current usage, structured by the principle of modern sovereignty—including that of identity—entail "a sameness across time or persons . . . [that] is expected to manifest itself in solidarity, in shared dispositions or consciousness, or in collective action" (Brubaker and Cooper 2000: 18). It was this ideal of sameness that led Louis to despair of ever being able to call himself Chinese and that caused Macau's lack of systematicity to appear as a problem rather than a delight.

These ideologies of unity and uniformity present analytical as well as political problems. They are utopian dreams that have all too often been mistaken for descriptions of reality or prescriptions for reality as it should be. They are analytically misleading, because they mask the heterogeneity that pervades all aspects of human life, and politically unsustainable, since successive waves of violence (both physical and psychic) are often justified with reference to the mirage of a perfect oneness just up ahead.

But, as this book has shown, in transition-era Macau alternative narratives of sovereignty and subjectivity challenged all attempts to impose uniformity. On one hand, these narratives framed both the history and the future of sovereignty in terms of compromise, collaboration, accommodation, and differentiation. They asserted that the Portuguese presence in Macau had been not sovereign colonial rule but a kind of partial sovereignty, alternately shared and contested between China and Portugal: a form of power whose limits were continuously shifting and open to question. This meant that no state, indeed no single institution, could assert authority over all aspects of public (or, for that matter, private) life. Viewed from this perspective, Macau was not, as the Macau Portuguese state would have it, a multicultural city, insofar as multiculturalism is a unitary ideology that advocates the understanding and appreciation of cultural difference. Rather, it was a city of niches—economic niches, political niches, linguistic and educational niches—that formed outside the range of what was possible according to the standards of nation-states.[1] The very history of Macau as a "meeting point between East and West," for example, was the history of its role as a niche for illegal or quasi-legal forms of commerce—a role that has continued up to the present day. Similarly, the absence of state control of the education system within Macau allowed the development of a far greater diversity of educational institutions than was possible in either China or Portugal. Although many lamented the poor standards that this diversity had produced, most agreed that it had mitigated the Portuguese state's ability to shape young (Chinese) minds and had helped foster a robust (Chinese) civil society open to a range of perspectives on the meaning of Chineseness from the PRC, Taiwan, Hong Kong, and elsewhere. To rephrase the metaphor that one interviewee used to describe Macau, these niches were like pools that form alongside a rushing stream: not sad, isolated puddles cut off from the world at large, but fertile, productive spaces, necessary to the sustenance of life—the good life—on earth.

These narratives also suggested that people and activities within a given territory could be subject to multiple sovereign powers whose authority ebbed and strengthened, expanded and contracted, over time, and still remain part of a single coherent locality, defined in geographical, cultural, economic, social, and even political terms. Macau residents often articulated a sense of connectedness or commonality that did not entail uniformity: this is, after all, what the metaphors of the Paris metro and the petri dish, as well as the idea that Macau's different communities inhabited different cities in the same space, expressed. Viewed from this perspective, Monica's statement that "we don't need identity, we are Chinese" is not an oxymoron but a critique of the insistence that the only valid forms of community, belonging, or social cohesion are those that can be articulated in the unitary terms of identity. It is a proud assertion of a sense of Chineseness that does not live or die with the state but emerges from and is reproduced in the intimacies of daily life. To say this is not to suggest that, in the end, Chineseness really is a cultural formation unaffected by state practices and imaginaries of power; to the contrary, the explicit contrast that Monica draws between Macau and its neighbors (they need identity; we don't) is a confirmation of how Chinese subjectivities are powerfully shaped by different imaginaries and practices of sovereign power. Without a sovereign that embraced modern nation-state standards, Monica and others argued, communities in Macau had never developed the sharp edges of purportedly uniform identities (ethnic, class, racial, or national), and as a result Macau had managed to escape the catastrophic conflicts that devastated other regions during the twentieth century.

In this sense, although some commentators have interpreted W. H. Auden's poem about Macau (quoted in the epigraph) as a sardonic dismissal of a petty, indulgent place that will never amount to anything, I can't help but see in Auden's vision of Macau a prescription for a utopia indeed. There is something to be said, after all, for mere peaceful coexistence—be it of saints and gamblers, churches and brothels, or of a series of diverse linguistic, ethnic, religious, and political communities—rather than an artificial and enforced unity. There is certainly much good to be said of living in a place where nothing serious happens because men and governments find no reason to tear each other to pieces.

But even as I became enchanted with the potential this alternative view of sovereignty held for envisioning a better world, I also became convinced that just because it becomes possible to imagine sovereignty differently does not mean that we must necessarily do so. The circular career of lusotropicalism—a post-colonial nationalist discourse about hybridity that was turned seamlessly to the service of Portuguese imperialism in Africa—is enough to remind us that simply replacing binaries with multiplicities or seeing complexity and interconnectedness where we once saw simple, hard-and-fast distinctions is not in itself a cause for celebration. Despite the sparks of utopian potential evident in Macau's un-system, Macau was certainly no utopia. And the specific conditions that held in Macau are not necessarily transposable to other places and times. For these reasons, what I propose in this book is not a new universal theory of sovereignty that will free the world from antagonisms and imbroglios; it is, rather, an approach that refuses to be drawn in by assertions of uniformity (at the level of the locality, the nation, or the globe) and insists instead on the validity of systems of living together that are unrecognized as such—and that therefore are able to emerge and survive under the radar, in the belly of the modern world.

Admittedly, most Macau residents were not attuned to the utopian potential in their way of life. Even among those who did feel that Macau could serve as a model for a more peaceful and tolerant world, no one I knew rejected the idea that China should and one day would be unified under a single sovereign power. Indeed, many Macau residents looked forward to the handover not simply because it would rid them of the corrupt, inefficient Portuguese state, but because it really was a momentous historical occasion. The widespread narrative of China's modern history as a still-incomplete journey from subjugated, humiliated, and divided nation to a fully sovereign, self-determining nation-state was still a powerful one, and it was also the reason China's resumption of sovereignty over Hong Kong and Macau was celebrated not only by Macau residents but by "Chinese populations all over the world, regardless of their political loyalties" (R. Chow 1998: 5). The handover represented not so much a victory for the CCP as one more step toward ending China's century of national humiliation and fulfilling its destiny as a strong, united, respected sovereign nation. The question that still lingered in the minds of many Macau residents, however, was: What kind of difference would the handover make?

Huigui la!

I left Macau in September 1999, three months before the handover and just over two years after I had arrived. In the months before my departure, arrangements for the transfer of administrative sovereignty were moving apace. As predicted, Edmund Ho 何厚鏵, a prominent banker and the son of Ho Yin (leader of the Macau Chinese community in the 1960s), had been chosen as chief executive. He had appointed his administrative staff, whose members were ready to take office. "Localization" was nearly complete, since all but the highest-ranking Portuguese civil servants and the staff needed to plan and run the handover ceremonies had been sent back to the government jobs awaiting them in Portugal. Aside from a quarrel about the handover venue itself (the Macau government had been planning to hold it in the brand-new multi-million-dollar Cultural Center, but Beijing insisted that its auditorium was too small), and the problem of Broken Tooth Koi, who still sat in his Coloane prison cell awaiting trial, by September it was clear that the Portuguese and Chinese governments had for the most part succeeded in their goal of ensuring a "smooth transition."

On December 12, 1999, I returned to Macau for a ten-day visit. Some Macau Chinese friends thought it odd that I would fly all the way from California just for the handover. Many of them were planning to leave Macau that week, to avoid the crowds and to take advantage of the four-day holiday for a trip to Hong Kong, the mainland, or the beaches of southern Thailand. But for reasons both professional and personal, I wanted to witness the event that had overshadowed every aspect of public life in Macau for as long as I had known it.

The city was decked out. That it was almost Christmas and almost the turn of the new millennium made the decorations more elaborate. Leal Senado Square and the plaza in front of the Hotel Lisboa were awash in neon. The handover mascot, a chubby little cartoon bird flying upward, adorned the "Macau 99" banners that plastered the walls of restaurants and shops; it was outlined in neon and affixed to the outsides of skyscrapers along with slogans such as "Macau Returns" or "Welcome Macau's Return to the Motherland" or even "Macau Comes Home!" Public thoroughfares and parks were aflutter with alternating Chinese and Portuguese flags of exactly the same size and height. Paper lanterns shaped like fruits and flowers graced the green spaces created by traffic roundabouts or divided roads. Twisted old banyan trees were draped with colored lights that spiraled around their trunks and ran crazily up and down their branches. The fences around construction sites and abandoned buildings—pragmatic chain-link fences designed to keep out bodies, not gazes—had been covered with plywood, whitewashed and stenciled with the bridge emblem that adorned the SAR flag. Everyone remarked on how beautiful the city looked. "It hasn't been this pretty in twenty years!" said the cabbie who brought me from the jetfoil terminal back to my old apartment on the night I arrived. He then quickly changed his mind: "It hasn't been this pretty in 450 years!" With the amount of neon decorating the streets and buildings, I replied, for once Macau must have been visible from the moon.

I spent the afternoon and evening of December 19 wandering the streets, accompanied by an acquaintance, a photographer who had come from Hong Kong to try to capture the event on film. I did not wish to tag along with journalist friends who would be in the press box at the official ceremony. No one I knew was having a handover party. Most of my Portuguese friends and acquaintances had already gone back to Portugal, and those who remained were working backstage at the handover ceremonies. Several Chinese friends were involved in the ceremonies as well, working as ushers, helping with press coverage, or participating in the "cultural events" that preceded the banquet. Others who had not headed out of town told me they planned to stay home, watch the events on television, and catch up on some household chores. It was not quite the non-event that Ah Man had predicted when he joked that everyone would wake up one morning and realize that the handover had happened last week, but after so many years of preparation and expectation, of living teleologically toward this moment, many Macau residents could not help but find the event anticlimactic.

It was unusually cold, wet, and windy that evening, a fact that provoked ominous jokes about heavenly portents. Just after dark, my companion and I walked down to Macau's Lan Kwai Fong to watch the massive fireworks display that was supposed to kick off the festivities, only to find that the event coordinators had canceled it for fear that the strong winds would blow some festive sparks onto the flammable tent where the VIPs of the evening—Chinese President Jiang Zemin and Prime Minister Zhu Rongji, Portuguese President Jorge Sampaio and Prime Minister António Guterres, Macau Governor Vasco Rocha Vieira, and 3,000 invited guests—were dining. We then wandered up to Three Lamps, where Stone Commune was sponsoring a sparsely attended Alternative Handover Celebration featuring a series of short films and performance pieces by local artists. Toward midnight, we made our way over to Leal Senado Square, which was packed with spectators. An enormous stage had been erected along San Ma-Louh, facing the square, but by now the live performances had ended and a huge television screen positioned stage left was broadcasting live footage from inside the handover building. We found a spot with a relatively unobstructed view and stood our ground.

And then it was happening. Suddenly everyone's attention was on the screen, watching a select corps of soldiers, Portuguese from one side and Chinese from the other, marching silently and slowly in from the wings. The next day, a Portuguese acquaintance who had worked on the Committee for the Handover Celebration Activities told me that this was the single most difficult aspect of the whole event to choreograph: the Chinese and Portuguese soldiers have such different marching styles, he said, that it was almost impossible to get them to synchronize closely enough to reach center stage at the exact same moment. The only sound being broadcast from inside the tent was the measured footsteps of the soldiers, but the square was far noisier. When the camera zoomed in for the first time on the soldiers of the People's Liberation Army, a great cheer went up from the crowd. The first close-up of Jiang Zemin watching the soldiers elicited another long, loud cheer.

I looked around me at the cheering crowd and the three teenage boys next to me, who were leaning on one another, grinning and horsing around as much as the cramped space allowed, clearly thrilled by the whole event, and realized that I was not understanding this event from their perspective. Had my whole project been a failure? Had I been so captivated by the romanticism and implicit promise of the alternative vision of Macau history and so drawn to the people who espoused it that I had missed something fundamental about what the handover meant for the vast majority of Chinese people, in Macau or elsewhere? Perhaps it all really was just as simple as the newspapers had made it seem: Chinese people who had endured four hundred years of foreign domination were overjoyed at the prospect of unification with their own people. "Of course we're happy," I remembered hearing people say during the Hong Kong handover, which I had witnessed at the beginning of my fieldwork in 1997, "we are all Chinese." I had wondered then, as I wondered now, what this meant. I thought of the variety of Macau Chinese informants who had said to me, over the past two years, in one way or another, "If we are not different, we will cease to exist." Was Macau's difference, I had wondered, really so fragile, so dependent on the historical presence of a weak foreign government? Tonight I could not help thinking that maybe it was. It seemed that with the departure of a few hundred civil servants, it could be swept away by the roar of the crowd.

But in the next minute, I could not help laughing. As Jiang got up to give his speech, a voice over the public address system in the tent gave the command, in Mandarin, "Qi li!" 起立 (All rise!). Immediately the boys next to me started mimicking the voice, "Qi li!," trying out the foreign sounds of Mandarin on their tongues and laughing at the results. It was difficult to hear Jiang's short speech above the crowd.[2] But as he finished speaking and sat down, a female voice came over the sound system at the square and summarized, in rapid Cantonese, the speech Jiang had just made in Mandarin. The message welcoming the people of Macau into the warm embrace of the motherland, the message through which their leader hailed them as fully and finally Chinese, had to be translated into a language they could understand.

Later that night down at "the docks," the party continued. In every bar, small knots of people gathered around televisions showing live coverage of the post-handover programs and the swearing-in ceremonies of the new government, while the patrons seated at tables and bars glanced over from time to time and remarked on how stuffy and boring the ceremonies looked. When the television showed the newly ex-governor Rocha Vieira leaving Macau for the last time, I was sitting in Casablanca, a bar run by Carlos, a Portuguese freelance writer who had been in Macau for a dozen or so years. He and several other Portuguese who were planning to stay in Macau waved a drunken, happy goodbye, shouting obscenities at the image of the departing governor and his wife. I asked Carlos if he weren't sad to see the Portuguese administration go. "I am a Portuguese, and I am proud of my country and my culture," he proclaimed tipsily. "But I am not proud of those militarist bastards who were running this place! I am glad they are gone! They give us a bad name, I want nothing to do with them! They do not represent me!" Later, other Portuguese people I knew who were planning to stay echoed Carlos's sentiment, hoping that the transfer of sovereignty would make it easier for local people to appreciate Portuguese people and culture, as well as the Portuguese aspects of their own history, since they would no longer be associated with the illegitimacy of the Portuguese state.

Toward dawn on December 20, 1999, as hundreds of well-wishers lined the streets near the Portas do Cerco to greet the People's

Liberation Army as it marched into Macau, I found myself with friends at Moonwalker, a bar frequented by a mix of Chinese, Macanese, Portuguese, Filipinos, Thais, Australians, Americans, and others, laughing and line-dancing and singing along to the Filipino band's cover of "My Achy Breaky Heart." By morning, all the Portuguese flags in town had been replaced by Macau SAR flags, smaller and shorter than the Chinese flags, lest anyone forget the proper relationship between locality and nation. In the days and months after the handover, nothing much about daily life in Macau changed. For a while, whenever someone proposed or performed the slightest variation from routine, others would say jokingly, "We're in China now!" The joke was, of course, that despite the declarative nature of this simple statement of fact, what it meant, and what it implied about where Macau had been before, was entirely unclear.

In the years after the handover, a great deal about Macau did change. From 2001 to 2005, I taught anthropology and Chinese studies at the University of Macau, and during those years as well as on frequent visits since then I have been able to witness some of these changes firsthand. The handover anniversary has become an annual public holiday, celebrated with gala concerts and fireworks displays, but the era of Portuguese administration is a distant memory. Macau history is seldom talked about except by way of a tourist attraction. In 2001, the SAR government refused to renew STDM's monopoly on casinos in Macau and opened the gaming industry up to limited competition. The urban landscape was once again transformed as the Las Vegas Sands Corporation, Wynn Resorts, and Stanley Ho's new organization, Sociedade de Jogos de Macau, broke ground on several new casino-hotel complexes, each more gigantic and grandiose than the next. Some say the arrival of the Vegas corporations transformed Macau far more thoroughly than the mere transfer of sovereignty ever could have, and in some respects they are right. Where the civil service was once the highest paying and most coveted job in town, today the casinos pay far higher wages than any other employer in the city, and a high school dropout can earn more as a dealer than a trilingual college graduate working for the government. The casino companies brought a minor flood of Americans and American influence to this city that once styled itself an alternative to Anglo-American hegemony. At the same time, closer economic integration with the Pearl River Delta, the enormous new demand for labor in the casinos, and the PRC's loosening of travel restrictions to Macau led to a new influx of mainland workers and tourists and influence. The slot machines in the casinos do not accept patacas, only Hong Kong dollars or renminbi; all the signs in the interior of the Sands Casino are in the simplified Chinese script that was once exclusively used in the mainland; and when ordering dim sum at the Cantonese restaurant in the old Hotel Lisboa, one must speak in Mandarin because the local waitresses have all found better-paying jobs in the American casinos and have been replaced by young women from northern provinces. By 2007 Macau had 26 casinos, and they were generating more revenue than all the casinos in Las Vegas combined. The prices of residential and commercial real estate skyrocketed; the stationery shops, record stores, and small restaurants that once made Leal Senado Square a destination for locals as well as tourists closed down, evicted in favor of transnational chains like Starbucks and discount cosmetics shops like SaSa that cater to mainland tourists and that can pay double or triple the rent. In the spring of 2005, I found my students who had graduated two years previously bewildered and concerned. Despite the promises of no change for fifty years, Macau had once again been transformed, and so quickly. Was there really no future for them outside the casino industry? Would they have to delay marrying and having children indefinitely because they were now unable to afford an apartment in one of the buildings that had been standing empty for nearly a decade? Would Mandarin and English replace Cantonese and Portuguese as the linguas francas of the city because that was where the money was? Had Macau simply traded the familiar incompetence of the Portuguese for a new, more commercialized form of imperialism? One of my students told me that for the first time in her life, she was thinking of leaving Macau and trying her luck in the job markets or graduate schools of Hong Kong, Shanghai, Taipei, or almost anywhere else.

But on the streets in back of the glittering new "strip," something of Macau's quirky old system remains, for better and for worse. In

2006, the secretary for transport and public works, Ao Man Long 歐文龍, was arrested on 76 separate charges of corruption (through which he had amassed personal assets of over US$100 million during the six years of his tenure) and eventually sentenced to 27 years in prison, thus spectacularly giving the lie to the idea that corruption had been a peculiarly Portuguese problem and severely undermining the trust that many Macau residents had placed in their post-handover government. Some of the questions raised by the Portuguese state during the final years of its existence still echo in the public sphere. The Chinese government applied for, and in 2005 received, UNESCO World Heritage status for several complexes of old buildings in Macau that "provide a unique testimony to . . . one of the earliest and longest-lasting encounters between China and the West based on the vibrancy of international trade." It celebrates "the special relationship established between the Chinese and Portuguese" that "favoured an important interchange of human values in the various fields of culture, sciences, technology, art and architecture over several centuries."[3] One student of mine wrote a paper arguing that Macau should require Portuguese to be taught in its middle schools, so as to cement the city's competitive advantage in China's burgeoning trade with Brazil. The city's Portuguese legacy is mentioned in an unfailingly positive light whenever Macau, like Foshan or Chengdu or any other city in China, is called on to promote its local culture or its attractiveness to foreign investment. Some would argue that this diminishes Macau's difference, since it suggests that Macau is only as unique as every other city in China. But to say this is to take as fact that which in the transition era was a hotly contested claim: that Macau's history of Portuguese rule really did make it fundamentally unlike any other Chinese city, as dissimilar as the wonton and the apabico.

In the years since the Macau handover, too, a great deal about the world has changed. In the first decade of the twenty-first century, public attention in the United States has become far more focused on the threats to national sovereignty posed by "global terror," "global warming," and the "global financial crisis" than by transnational corporations or the WTO. Questions about the need, the legitimacy, and the limits of sovereign power in Iraq, Palestine, North

Korea, and the United States have overshadowed fears about the "China threat." Yet today more than ever we may take lessons from Macau's transition. If we would understand the specificity and the peculiar force of sovereignty as both a dream of justice and a source of brutality, we must pay attention to culturally bound conceptions of legitimacy as well as the ways these conceptions are ignored and manipulated by those in power. If we would see our way past the nightmarish narrative of a neoliberal empire relentlessly remaking the world in its own singular image, we must remind ourselves of the tentative nature and partial reach of all sovereign claims and keep attuned so that we may recognize other systems of living together that elude their grasp. And if we would envision, in order to see how it might succeed, a better world, we would do well to consider the possibilities as well as the perils of imagining sovereignty differently.

Reference Matter

Notes

Complete bibliographic information on the items cited here in the author-date format can be found in the Works Cited, pp. 363–97.

Introduction

1. For analyses of the symbolism of these carvings, see Hugo-Brunt 1954 and Cheng 1999.

2. Macau's currency, the *pataca* (MOP), is pegged to the US dollar at a rate of 7.8 to 1.

3. Wong Hon-keong and Wu 1996: 525. The phrases "stability and prosperity" (安定繁榮) and "a smooth transition" (平穩過渡) became slogans of Macau's transition.

4. Camilleri and Falk 1992: 16–17. I shall not rehearse the rich history of this field of political philosophy. In this section I have drawn on Biersteker and Weber 1996, Camilleri and Falk 1992, T. Hansen and Stepputat 2001, Hinsley 1966, and Latham 2000.

5. See, e.g., Appadurai 1996, Boyarin and Boyarin 1993, Hall 1991, Hardt and Negri 2000, Huntington 1993, Ong 1999, Ong and Nonini 1997, Radhakrishnan 1995, and Tölölyan 1991.

6. As Foucault (1980: 102) puts it, "We should direct our researches on the nature of power not towards the juridical edifice of sovereignty, the State apparatuses and the ideologies which accompany them, but towards domination and the material operators of power, towards forms of subjection and the inflections and utilisations of their localised systems, and towards strategic apparatuses."

7. See, e.g., Mamdani 1996, Ong 2003 and 2006, Povinelli 1998, and Stoler 2002.

8. T. Hansen and Stepputat (2006: 297) argue explicitly for this approach, suggesting that leaving aside the question of "formal ideologies of rule and legality" in favor of examining *de facto* sovereignties allows for a more complex understanding of the multiple forms that sovereign claims may take, as a "tentative and always emergent form of authority grounded in violence that is performed and designed to generate loyalty, fear, and legitimacy from the neighborhood to the summit of the state." Although I find this approach stimulating, I fear that it collapses, under the rubric of sovereignty, too broad a variety of modes of exercising power, many of which would not be recognized as "sovereign" by the people they implicate.

9. Here I am influenced by Foucault (1980: 90, 98), who argues that the exercise of power should be viewed not in terms of repression but in terms of a struggle; and that individuals are never only the "inert or consenting target of power" but are "always also the elements of its articulation."

10. See, e.g., Taussig 1987. Foucault (1997: 74) writes that modern liberal states work through a "rationalization that obeys . . . the internal rule of maximum economy."

11. In saying this I do not mean to suggest that "experience" should be taken as a foundational category (cf. Joan Scott 1991); these experiences and what they signified were certainly structured by social and political relations, which I discuss in greater detail throughout the book. The point here is that through the men and women who made up the state in Macau, the very different social and political relations that had structured notions of national sovereignty in Europe, Africa, the PRC, and Macau were brought to bear on the policies and politics of transition-era Macau.

12. One exception is the book *Is Taiwan Chinese?*, in which Melissa Brown (2004) sets out to address this question head on. However, I find her main premise, that "actual identities" can and should be separated out from the "ideological" claims made about them, problematic.

13. Ang 2001, R. Chow 1998, Chun 1996b. As they point out, we now have the ability to conceptualize difference within Chineseness but only among those individuals or populations considered *a priori* Chinese in some (usually racialized) way.

14. Cecilia Jorge (2004: 40) traces the name *apabico* to the Indian word *apa*, or small pancake, and the Portuguese *bico*, or tip, for the small point of dough that sticks out after the dumpling is pinched closed.

15. Special economic zones (SEZs), of which the cities of Zhuhai, Shenzhen, Shantou, and Xiamen were the first, were a product of the economic reform policies of the 1980s. Writes George Crane (1996: 161–62), "Modelled originally on the export processing zones in other developing

countries, the SEZs were originally envisioned as areas where foreign investment would be both permitted and controlled in an effort to gain national economic advantage from world markets." By the mid-1990s, however, there was no longer anything particularly special about these special zones, as "the exceptionalist rhetoric central to their identity has crystallized into a model for China."

16. In 1995, the Macau International Airport opened, allowing air travel to and from a handful of destinations in the PRC, Taiwan, Japan, and southeast Asia. In 1999, a bridge linking the newly reclaimed land between Macau's two outlying islands with Zhuhai's Hengqin Island was inaugurated, opening a second route into mainland China.

17. These estimates are based on figures from 1996, when official sources put Hong Kong's total land area at 415 square miles (1,076 km^2) and total population at 6,305,413, and Macau's total land area at 9 square miles (23.5 km^2) and total population at 440,000. By 2005, however, massive land reclamation projects in Macau had increased its land area to 10.8 square miles (28.2 km^2); and even in 1996, unofficial figures put Macau's population closer to 500,000, taking into consideration the illegal immigrants not counted in the census.

18. The possibility (be it a hope or a fear) that Hong Kong would exert an economic, political, and cultural influence on the rest of China was summed up in a phrase that circulated in China in the 1980s: "Shenzhen is Hongkongized, Guangdong is Shenzhenized, and the whole country is Guangdongized" (quoted in Ming K. Chan 1994: 177).

19. The term "Macau Portuguese government" is a translation of the Chinese term 澳葡政府. Although this is a somewhat awkward locution in English, it is the easiest way of distinguishing between the governments of Lisbon and Macau, and between the pre- and post-handover administrations.

20. Message from the governor in "Macau na expo," *Jornal tribuna de Macau*, June 19, 1998.

Chapter 1

1. For a discussion of history as a moral force, see Ng and Wang 2005; for examples of the language of taboo, heresy, and heterodoxy in Chinese history, see Spence 2001 and Unger 1993; for an example of popular representations of these taboos, see Cha 1997.

2. The phrase "the Chineseness of China" is Wang Gungwu's (1991); he also suggests that a sense of a shared history is constitutive of Chineseness.

As Jun Jing puts it, "a worthy Chinese is supposed not only to remember a vast amount of information related to the past, but to draw on this past as the basis of moral reasoning" (Jing 1996: 17). See also Ryckmans 1986 and Schwarcz 1994.

3. See Jin 1988: 133.

4. See, e.g., S. Chu 1996, who argues that it is the Chinese people's consciousness of "their history of several millennia" that makes them so unwilling to view Taiwan as an independent nation.

5. On May Fourth iconoclasm, see T. Chow 1960 and E. Wang 2001; on the KMT's stance as the protector of Chinese tradition, see Chun 1996a; on speaking bitterness, see Anagnost 1997 and Rofel 1999; on culture fever, see J. Wang 1996; on the commodification of tradition, see Oakes 2000.

6. Robert Young (1990) and Prasenjit Duara (1995), for example, both argue that the Hegelian concept of history as a process of evolution toward the self-awareness of universal Reason girded the West's claim to mastery over the non-Western Other.

7. Andrew Ross explains the *padroado* as follows: "the two crowns [of Spain and Portugal] were given the right to rule over lands 'discovered' by them. In turn they had to undertake the costs of christianising them. In this way the Spanish and Portuguese crowns extended, into the new colonies, the rights they had in Europe of choosing who should be appointed to all senior ecclesiastical posts" (A. Ross 1994: xii). A series of papal bulls and treaties between 1454 and 1508 set out the contours of this agreement and eventually set the line of demarcation between Spanish and Portuguese spheres of influence at 370 leagues (about 1,100 miles) west of the Cape Verde Islands.

8. In the brief history of Portuguese Asia that follows, I draw on Alden 1996, Boxer 1968 and 1969, T. Coates 2001, Pearson 1987, Subrahmanyam 1993, and Souza 1986.

9. How many Portuguese (including *reinois* and *mestiços*) were in Asia at the height of Portugal's influence is almost impossible to determine, in part because contemporary records could not monitor Portuguese fertility or mortality rates in Asia, and in part because officials could not easily track the movements of private traders, missionaries, and deserters across the vast expanse of the Estado da Índia, especially when these subjects did not wish to be kept track of. In addition, for the purposes of imperial head-counts, the term "Portuguese" was used less often than categories such as *casado* (married settler), *ministro* (government official), *soldado* (soldier), *lançado* (rebel or deserter) and *solteiro* (individual merchant with no fixed abode)—categories that sometimes overlapped, that could refer to anyone considered to have

Portuguese "blood," and that sometimes included Asian converts to Christianity. However, best guesses suggest that the number of European-born Portuguese residing in the Estado da Índia (from Mozambique to Macau) never exceeded 10,000 at any one time (Subrahmanyam 1993).

10. Historian Holden Furber dubbed the era between 1500 and 1750 the "Age of Partnership" as a way of highlighting the "friendly and cooperative" nature of relations between Westerners and Asians during that period, and of distinguishing it from the age of "European conquest and domination" that followed (Furber 1969: 716, 719; see also Kling and Pearson 1979). I find "partnership" a rather innocuous term to describe the volatile, often violent, usually asymmetrical relations that obtained between the various groups, but I take Furber's point that the different world-historical conditions that held sway in the nineteenth and twentieth centuries produced new models and ideologies for the exercise of power that displaced those existing in the sixteenth and seventeenth centuries.

11. See especially Boxer 1969 and Pearson 1987.

12. Portuguese embassies were sent to Guangzhou in 1517 and to the Ming court in Beijing in 1520, but (according to contemporary Portuguese accounts) the unruly behavior of one man, Simão de Andrade, ruined the initial good impression made upon the Chinese by the efforts of the first ambassador, Simão's brother Fernão Peres de Andrade. This story is told in many Chinese histories as well, but according to the *History of the Ming*, there may have been a more compelling reason for Ming opposition to the Portuguese. In 1520, the court learned that the Portuguese had, in 1511, sacked and captured Malacca, a faithful vassal state. The ousted king of Malacca fled to nearby Pahang and sent a series of delegations to Beijing seeking the Ming's help in regaining his throne (see Chang 1934, Chen 1996, and Wade 1997). The Ming court's rejection of the Portuguese embassy in 1521 was certainly informed by this news. The presence of the Portuguese in the South China Sea and later in Macau gave rise to longstanding disagreements within both the Ming and the Qing administrations as to the potential advantages and risks of allowing Chinese subjects to engage in sustained trade with the Portuguese. For details, see Boxer 1968.

13. Of these islands, most notable and readily identifiable were Lampacau (浪白澳) and São João (上川島), both near Macau (see A. Gomes 1957 and Chang 1934).

14. Chang 1934: 70–71.

15. There is considerable controversy over the Portuguese settlement at "Liampo"—whether it existed as a permanent settlement, whether "Liampo" is really "Ningbo," and whether it was really destroyed by Chinese

forces in 1542. The most famous story of the sacking of Liampo is re-counted in Fernão Mendes Pinto's epic 1614 *Peregrinação* (Pinto 1996). Al-though long accepted as an eyewitness account of the destruction of Liam-po, it has recently been recognized as at best an embellishment of the truth. As for "Chincheu," Pinto also describes a prosperous Portuguese enclave there that was demolished by Chinese troops in 1549; this is almost cer-tainly fiction, although there is evidence that there were small temporary Portuguese settlements at Quanzhou and frequent skirmishes with Chinese troops around the busy port city of Zhangzhou. See Chang 1934.

16. See, e.g., Tam 1994.

17. Ah-Ma is a nickname for the goddess Mazu 媽祖, also known as Tianhou 天后, or "Empress of Heaven," who is worshipped all along the southeastern seaboard of China and Taiwan as the protector of seafarers.

18. Rendered variously in sixteenth- and seventeenth-century Portuguese sources as "Amaqua," "Amagao," "Amaquam," "Amacao," "Maquao," and "Macoa," the name was eventually standardized to "Macau" in Portuguese and "Macao" in English. For a summary of the derivation of the name Macau and the confusion that attends it, see Porter 1996: 36–41. For a more in-depth discussion, see L. G. Gomes 1997: 65–78.

19. Many of these "Japanese pirates," known in Chinese as *wokou* (倭寇), were, in fact, Chinese subjects driven to illicit activities (from illegal trading to the sacking and looting of towns and cities) by the social and economic dislocations of the Ming-Qing transition. For more on the *wokou*, see K. So 1975 and Wills 1979.

20. See L. G. Gomes 1997: 16.

21. In early Qing texts this name was often rendered 嶴門. Huang Qichen (1999: 6) notes that the first recorded reference to "Aomen" was in a document written in 1564, but in official documents this name continued to be used interchangeably with Haojing and Haojing'ao throughout the seventeenth century.

22. How this name was rendered in Chinese characters also varied: probably it originated as Oyster Mirror Bay (蠔鏡澳 Haojing'ao), for the shallow, calm, oyster-rich waters of the delta flats; but it was usually written homonymously as Moat Mirror Bay (濠鏡澳). A literature professor at the University of Macau told me that the substitution was probably made be-cause the character for oyster, which features a "worm" radical, was consid-ered inelegant as a place name. Incidentally, Huang Qichen (1999) notes that in the *Suma oriental* by Tomé Pires (a narrative of Pires's time in Asia in 1512–15), there is at least one reference to Macau as "Oquem," which is

a reasonably close Portuguese rendering of the Cantonese pronunciation of Haojing (Hou-gehng).

23. As Boxer (1968: 3) notes, "the Chinese names for Macau are legion." In addition to the variants of Haojing mentioned above, Huang Qichen (1999: 6) lists Jinghai 鏡海 (Mirror sea), Jinghu 鏡湖 (Mirror lake), Haohai 濠海 (Moat sea), Haijing 海鏡 (Sea mirror), Haojiang 濠江 (Moat river), Lianyang 蓮洋 (Lotus sea), Xiangshan'ao 香山澳 (Fragrant hills bay), Longya men 龍崖門 (Dragon cliff gate), and Ma Jiao 馬交 (Mating Horse). This plethora of names is multiplied by the fact that the land area now known as Macau was often better known by the names of the waters that surrounded it. For example, Shizimen 十字門 (Cross gate) referred to the cross-shaped channels separating the islands just off the coast of the Macau peninsula.

24. From a poem entitled "Xiangshan'ao" written in 1684 by Du Zhen, a trusted official of the Qing Kangxi emperor. Kangxi sent Du on an inspection tour of the coastal areas of Guangdong and Fujian in 1683, to report back on the possibility of opening up several coastal cities to international trade. On the day of his departure from Macau, Du presented this poem to his Portuguese hosts in Macau in gratitude for their hospitality. See Tang Kaijian 1996.

25. See Tam 1994: 68 for a summary of how the interpretation of the payment of ground rent as a bribe has been taken up by both the political left and right in twentieth-century Chinese historiography.

26. 金劄 denotes a communication from a high-ranking official to an inferior, thus reinforcing the sense that the emperor viewed the Portuguese as subject to his power.

27. According to Huang Qichen (1999), in 1614, responding to a series of memorials from southern officials suggesting that the unruly and well-armed Portuguese be expelled in the interests of national security, the Ming court ordered that, in the interests of trade, the Portuguese be allowed to settle in Macau.

28. Both Chinese and Portuguese sources suggest that everyone involved understood that the Portuguese remained in Macau at the sufferance of the emperor. A memorial from Governor-General Zhang Minggang of Guangdong and Guangxi to the Wanli emperor in 1615 explains: "From reports we know that Macau is in Xiangshan, that our soldiers have the place surrounded on sea and land, and that the foreigners there depend on us for all their food and daily necessities. If we suspect them of harboring ill intentions, we can first cut off these supplies and leave their throats parched, and

then eliminate them easily with one slash of the knife" (Chen 1996: 6). And in 1635, António Bocarro reported that "the peace that we have with the King of China is as he likes it, for since it is so far from India, and since he has such vastly greater numbers of men than the utmost that the Portuguese could possibly assemble there, never did we think of breaking with him whatever grievances we may have had, because they have only to stop our food-supplies to ruin our City" (quoted in Boxer 1984: 27). For a discussion of the legal status of foreigners and Chinese subjects in Macau in the late Ming and early Qing, see Tang Kaijian 1997.

29. This comparison is the subject of some controversy among Chinese historians, and indeed the parallel is not total, especially since the Han dynasty policy involved more of a divide and conquer approach in which one foreign group was chosen to keep the others in line, often sparking interethnic conflict. But the parallel seems more appropriate in the seventeenth century when the British and Dutch appeared in the South China Sea: at that point, the Chinese state quite openly agreed to allow the Portuguese certain privileges in return for their promise to keep these other "red-haired" foreigners at bay.

30. Historians Jorge dos Santos Alves and Wu Zhiliang suggest two other periodizations. Alves (1996: 206) argues that the era of Portuguese sovereignty over Macau began in 1784 when for the first time a Portuguese ambassador was sent to Beijng in the attempt to "prove and defend Portugal's right to sovereignty over Macau, which it had obtained by conquest." Wu argues that the colonial period began in 1844 when Portugal declared that Macau, Timor, and Solor were to be administered as a single province and ended in 1976 when the promulgation of the Organic Statute of Macau provided Macau much greater political autonomy from Portugal (quoted in H. S. Yee 2001: 22).

31. Great Britain's role in pushing for and winning this diplomatic victory was crucial. A confluence of political and economic factors (primarily British attempts to monopolize the import of opium to China, and France's aggressive intentions on China's southwestern borders) were the proximate reasons that Britain and Portugal had for forcing the issue. See A. Coates 1978, Gunn 1996, F. G. Pereira 1991, Saldanha 1996a, and Tam 1994.

32. By 1930, Portugal's empire included Macau and Timor; the cities of Goa, Damão, and Diu in India; and Angola, Mozambique, Portuguese Guinea, and the islands of Cabo Verde and São Tomé and Principe along the Atlantic coast of Africa.

33. Note that the Portuguese word *condomínio* expresses quite literally the sense of joint dominion or shared sovereignty.

34. Article 73 of the United Nations Charter requires member-states that have "administrative responsibilities for territories whose peoples have not yet attained a full measure of self-government . . . to develop self-government, to take due account of the political aspirations of the peoples, and to assist them in the progressive development of their free political institutions."

35. Little has been written about the policies toward Macau pursued by the KMT government from which the Communists wrested power in 1949. Huang Qichen mentions that the KMT made moves to regain sovereignty over Hong Kong and Macau in the fall of 1945, hoping that the end of the Japanese occupation of China would be an opportune moment to address this question (as it indeed was in other European colonies in Asia). Demonstrations, vitriolic articles in the Chinese press, and minor border clashes created a tense and uncertain atmosphere; in the late 1940s, a survey conducted by the Guangdong People's Association for the Promotion of the People's Movement to Take Back Macau (廣東民眾收回澳門活動促進會) reportedly found that over 70 percent of its 127,000 respondents supported the use of force to take Macau. But because the KMT felt that "the current international climate makes this problem a difficult one to solve in the short run," this movement came to naught (see Huang 1999: 493–95; also Magalhães 1992: 21–30).

36. See Shipp 1997: 96 for the English version of this text and Tam 1994: 263 for the Chinese.

37. Most observers attribute this refusal to the PRC's reluctance to disturb the Hong Kong economy, which was its main source of foreign currency at the time. But Tam (1994: 259–60) notes that after 1974, the Portuguese socialist government's increasingly friendly relations with the Soviet Union may also have caused China to be wary of forging closer ties with Portugal.

38. In the preface to the first Portuguese edition of *Casa grande e senzala*, Freyre calls Boas "the one teacher who left the most lasting impression on me" ("a figura de mestre de que me ficou até hoje maior impressão"). He continues, "It was while studying anthropology under Professor Boas that . . . I learned to understand as fundamental the difference between *race* and *culture*; to discriminate between the effects of purely genetic relationships and those resulting from social influences, cultural heritage and the environment. This entire work hinges on this basic differentiation between race and culture" (Freyre 1966: xxxi–xxxii).

39. This summary of Freyre's argument is provided by Gerald Bender (1978: 5).

40. Freyre expounds these ideas with increasing conviction and universality in *O mundo que o Português criou* (The world the Portuguese created), published in 1940; *Um Brasileiro em terras portuguesas* (A Brazilian in Portuguese lands), published in 1953; and *O Luso e o tropico* (The Portuguese and the tropics), published by the Salazar government in 1961. In contradistinction to the Salazar government, Freyre argued that the process of "hybridization" was bidirectional: not only had the Portuguese "Europeanized" tropical cultures, but many habits, fashions, and ideas now considered thoroughly European had been brought to Europe by Portuguese returning from the tropics.

41. In 1926, a military coup ended the First Republic (a period of short-term dictatorships, factionalism, and political violence) that followed the republican revolution of 1910. Salazar became prime minister in 1932 and remained in power until he was incapacitated by a stroke in 1968. His successor, Marcelo Caetano, ruled until a 1974 military coup toppled the regime. Shortly thereafter, the Socialist Party was elected to power. See Macqueen 1997.

42. Bender notes that although Salazar espoused some of the main tenets of lusotropicalism—the ideas that racism did not exist in Portugal and that Portuguese colonialism was superior to other forms of colonialism—he rejected others, such as Freyre's rejection of racial explanations of "backwardness" and his emphasis on the equality of Portuguese and African civilizations, in favor of the blunt assertion that Africans were "intrinsically inferior" (Bender 1978: 7). Freyre's own attitude toward Portuguese colonialism in 1960s Africa seems to have been ambivalent: in *The Portuguese and the Tropics*, he overtly supported the Salazar regime (see Freyre 1961), but elsewhere he insisted that lusotropicalism was a sociological concept, not a political one, and expressed sympathy for Africans' desire for independence from Portuguese rule (Castelo 1998: 26–27).

43. Perry Anderson (1962) calls lusotropicalism a "systematic falsification of reality." Basil Davidson surmises that "even the soberest of researchers, when confronted with language like [Nogueira's], may be inclined to clutch wildly at his hair and wonder if words in Portugal can possibly be thought to mean what they mean elsewhere" (Davidson, Preface, in Ferreira 1974: 13).

44. In Macau, but not only there. João de Pina-Cabral (1989: 6) has argued that "the myth of racial tolerance" is "one of the most enduring ideological traits relating to Portuguese identity." Gerald Bender noted that "even today . . . many of the Portuguese who consider themselves 'anti-colonial' continue to believe in a number of the tenets of lusotropicalism"

(Bender 1978: 3). And Miguel Vale de Almeida (2004: 61–62) traces the influence of lusotropicalist thinking into the work of leading contemporary sociologist Boaventura de Sousa Santos, who has argued that Portuguese culture is a "border/frontier culture" and that Portugal was "too close to its colonies to be wholly European and too far from Europe to be a true colonizer."

45. Cláudia Castelo (1998: 14) notes that Soares—who, as an outspoken leader of the opposition to Salazar in the late 1960s and as head of the Portuguese Socialist Party in the 1970s, had been imprisoned and exiled by the Salazar government—has on other occasions expressed his admiration for the same theory that Salazar used to justify colonialism. Soares gave a speech in Recife, Brazil, in 1987, in which he said that although lusotropicalism "was misused by the old regime," it was also "admired" by those committed to "the free, democratic, modern Portugal that I represent."

46. In fact, during more than two years of fieldwork in Macau I never once heard the term "lusotropicalism" mentioned in *any* context. I often heard Portuguese people in Macau argue that Portuguese colonialism was less racist and less totalizing than the British, French, or Dutch versions. But it was not until a colleague who works in Angola listened to my description of the state orthodoxy on "cultural identity" in Macau and identified it as late-model lusotropicalism that I became aware of the extent to which this theory had been used to justify Portuguese rule in Africa. I am indebted to Ricardo Ovalle-Bahamón for this insight.

Chapter 2

1. This argument has been made eloquently by Tsing 1993 and Stewart 1996. For a similar argument about China's ethnic minorities and the production of Han "normalcy," see Gladney 1994, Litzinger 2000, and Schein 2000.

2. See B. Silva 1994 and Meagher 2008.

3. Luís Vaz de Camões (ca. 1524–80) is Portugal's national poet, author of the epic poem *The Lusiads*, which details Vasco da Gama's journey to India; Camões himself is reputed to have spent time in Macau shortly after its establishment in 1557. Sun Yat-sen had a medical practice in Macau in the late nineteenth century and published articles advocating revolution in a local newspaper there; the home he had built in Macau in 1912 for his first wife still stands.

4. Barend ter Haar (1998: 16) writes that the English term "triad" derives from "several alternative autonyms of the Heaven and Earth Gathering" (天地會), a loosely connected series of male brotherhoods operating in

southern China and Southeast Asia since the late eighteenth century. Brotherhoods within the Heaven and Earth Gathering take names such as Three Dots (三點會), Three Rivers (三河會), or Three Unions (三合會) (16). Contrary to the assumptions of much of the Western literature on triads, Haar argues, the number three does not refer to the philosophical trinity of "heaven, earth, and man," but rather to "the three dots of the water radical on the left of the character Hong (洪), which is the common family name of all Triad members."

5. In 1995, Hong Kong residents accounted for 77 percent of visitors to Macau (Cao 2000: 188).

6. See, e.g., "Macau: Gangsterland," *Economist* (US edition), May 9, 1998, p. 41; Gee and Azevedo, "Good Cops, Bad Cops," *Asiaweek*, October 30, 1998; Todd Crowell and Law Siu-lan, "Troubled Transition," *Asiaweek*, April 24, 1998; "War on Triads," *Asiaweek*, December 10, 1999; Cathy Hilborn, "Making a Killing," *Far Eastern Economic Review*, March 12, 1998, pp. 26–29; Bertil Lintner, "End of an Empire," *Far Eastern Economic Review*, December 24, 1998; and John Colmey, "Tales from the Dragonhead," *Time*, April 20, 1998.

7. See "Japan Puts Macao on Danger List over Gang Violence," *Japan Economic Newswire*, May 19, 1998; U.S. and Foreign Commercial Services, "Consular Information Sheet—Macau," August 29, 1997.

8. In January 1999, the chief of police issued a press release claiming that 60 percent of the murder cases in 1998 had been solved; by then, this came across as too little, too late (*South China Morning Post*, January 28, 1999).

9. Interview with K. Mok, November 19, 1997, in Cantonese.

10. The editors of the Macau paper made light of Camões's statement by "reporting" that, upon hearing this news, the *Washington Post* closed its Chicago bureau and Michael Jordan of the Chicago Bulls boarded an airplane bound for Macau.

11. Not long after my arrival in Macau, I met one family in which this saying was literally true: one of the older brothers in a family of eight children was a police officer, and one of the younger brothers had dropped out of school and was, a middle brother told me rather vaguely, employed by the triads. This was also the premise of one of the most famous Hong Kong gangster films of all time, John Woo's *A Better Tomorrow* (英雄本色). But for most Macau residents, the metaphorical truth of this expression was more disturbing than its literal meaning.

12. I heard countless stories about police officers who were also alleged triad members. A Portuguese friend told me, in hushed and anxious tones,

of coming home from work early one afternoon to discover that his domestic helper had been using his hall closet as a clearing-house for cocaine and heroin shipments. He immediately called the police and gave all the details of the case, as well as his personal information, to the detective who came to his house; six months later, my friend saw the detective's name on the list of men who had been arrested and charged with being the "brains" behind the 14K triad. Another friend told me she had witnessed an off-duty police officer assault a Filipino security guard; the guard refused to press charges, and only after she kept insisting that it was his right to seek compensation did he tell her that he had heard the policeman was also a triad.

13. Interview November 12, 1997, in English and Portuguese.

14. Interview with Chan Keng Wuhn 陳景垣, September 13, 1997, in Cantonese and Mandarin.

15. Interview with Ng Kuok Cheong, October 8, 1997, in Cantonese and English.

16. For the British response to Maoist-inspired violence in Hong Kong in 1967, see I. Scott 1989. For British attempts to curb triad influence in Hong Kong, see Jones and Vagg 2007.

17. Liu summarizes: "In 1993, Mr. Tao Si-ju (陶駟駒) [then China's Minister of Public Security] made a statement which caused a stir in Hong Kong. At a press conference given on 8 April 1993 . . . Mr. Tao stated categorically that triad members were good people and patriots." Liu concedes that Tao may have felt authorized to make such a statement because Premier Deng Xiaoping had reportedly said the same thing, on the record, in the 1980s (T. M. Liu 2001: 114). Deng himself may have been, intentionally or not, paraphrasing Sun Yat-sen's praise of the "nationalist, anti-Manchu origins" of triads and other secret societies (cf. Ownby 1996: 6); he was certainly fitting into a long line of twentieth-century Chinese political leaders, from Sun Yat-sen to Chiang Kai-shek, who found allying with triads and other secret societies to be far more rewarding than attempting to suppress them.

18. In fact, I was stunned at the frequency with which I heard Macau people express the (mistaken) belief that, thanks to the stern hand of the Communist Party, triads did not exist in mainland China.

19. Even then, Macau was treated as a special case: its residents were subject to neither the evacuation orders nor the general prohibition on maritime trade that the Qing imposed on its subjects between 1655 and 1680. See Huang 1999: 167–72.

20. Cf. Chesneaux 1971 and 1972, Fei-ling Davis 1977, Tao 1981, Wakeman 1972, and Yuan Dingzhong 1961. Murray (1994) provides an

excellent discussion of both the Chinese and the Western historiography of the triads.

21. Haar (1998: 265) argues that the slogan typically attributed to the triads of the eighteenth and nineteenth centuries—"Overthrow the Qing, Restore the Ming" (反清復明)—is misleading in that it divorces apparent political aims from the millenarian ideologies that underpinned it. Instead, he argues, the triads combined messianic religious imagery with the specific expectation that a young prince Zhu, descendant of the ruling house of the Ming, would return to the throne and usher in a "perfect age."

22. To be clear: I do not mean to imply here either that Chineseness connotes criminality or that the triads are "the epitome of a 'typically Chinese' form of exclusionist, corporate group" (Haar 1998:3).

23. See Bolton et al. 1996. Bolton and his co-authors also assert that there is a difference between triads and organized crime, implying that something about triad organizations—their structure, their "jargon," or perhaps simply their professed historical ties to the nineteenth-century triad groups—sets them apart.

24. This was the English translation provided in the subtitles of the film for the Chinese phrase 人在江湖, which translates more literally as "a person in the *jianghu*." That the translators used "hero in a troubled world" to render this in English demonstrates the extent to which *jianghu* mythology entails a sense of valor defined against a social world in decline.

25. It was, however, allowed to play in Hong Kong. As is normally the case with films released in Hong Kong, while the movie was still in cinemas, illegal VCD copies of it were already available on the street for less than the price of a single movie ticket. Although bootleg film and CD sales are a known source of triad income, it was reported that Broken Tooth took a dim view of this practice when it threatened to interfere with his own box-office returns. Consequently, over the course of a couple of evenings in mid-May, while Broken Tooth sat in jail, 14K members smashed up shops where pirated copies of his film were on sale. Illegal sales of *Casino* ceased, though only temporarily (see T. M. Liu 2001: 160).

26. The other defendants included Broken Tooth's younger brother Wan Kuok-hung 尹國雄 and retired Macau police detective Artur Chiang Calderon. All were convicted.

27. The key points that Broken Tooth's lawyer, Pedro Redinha, objected to were the prejudicial statements by the head judge; that same judge's ruling that defense lawyers should have no contact with their clients until after all testimonies had been heard; and the breaches of procedure in appointing a judge to replace Mendes and a lawyer to replace Redinha. A

story in *Asiaweek* suggested that there never had been a bomb in the police chief's car and that the police had fabricated the whole story as a pretext to arrest Broken Tooth. See United Nations Human Rights Commission, Communication no. 925/2000 (December 15, 1999), CCPR/C/73/D/925/2000; and Gee and Azevedo 1998.

28. This paper, *Ponto final,* was known for its critical stance toward the Rocha Vieira administration. In contrast to *Ponto final's* coverage of the trial, the Macau Chinese papers tended to present a much more staid, facts-only kind of reporting, and the Hong Kong Chinese papers barely covered the proceedings at all.

29. See Guedes 1991.

Chapter 3

1. The "Resolution on Nationality" was how Nuno referred to this document. Its full name in English was "A Clarification by the Permanent Committee of the National People's Congress on Some Questions Regarding the Application of the Nationality Law of the People's Republic of China in the Macau Special Administrative Region." In Chinese and Portuguese, this was "關於對＜中華人民共和國國籍法＞在澳門特別行政區實施作出解釋的建議" and "Esclarecimento do Comité Permanente da Assembleia Nacional Popular sobre várias questões quanto à aplicação da Lei de Nacionalidade da República Popular da China na Região Administrativa Especial de Macau." For brevity's sake, I am using Nuno's term.

2. The phrase "bright lines and clear taxonomies" is Patricia Williams's. See Williams 1991: 8.

3. In this approach I draw on important work in the anthropology of law, which examines how law becomes the language of both sovereign power and those who would oppose, manipulate, or negotiate with it; how it constitutes the very subjects in whose interests it is invoked; and how extra-legal concepts and categories inform both the practice of law and the public understanding of it. See, e.g., Biolsi 1995, Brenneis 1996, Comaroff 2001, Collier and Suárez-Navaz 1997 and the papers in the issue of *Identities* it introduces, Coombe 1996, Coutin 2000, Coutin and Chock 1997, Lazarus-Black 2001, Lazarus-Black and Hirsch 1994, Maurer 1996, Merry 1993 and 2000, and Riles 2000.

4. For more on Portuguese language and Macanese identity, see Simões 1993a.

5. Although Stanley Ho, the richest man in Macau by far and owner of the gambling franchise from 1962 to 2002, is Eurasian (being the grand-

nephew of Sir Robert Ho Tung), speaks Portuguese, and was married to Clementina Leitão, a Macanese woman, he is not considered Macanese. He does not deny his Eurasian ancestry, but in public he identifies as Chinese, and I have never heard anyone challenge his claim to Chineseness.

6. Pina-Cabral gives the Cantonese as *touh saang jai* 土生仔, loosely translatable as "local-born folks," which does not specify an ethnicity or nationality but emphasizes the localness of the Macanese. Although it is true that this is a colloquial way of referring to the Macanese, it is an abbreviation of the longer "local-born Portuguese" and does not include all locals. When Macau Chinese people want to emphasize their status as locals, they say they are *oumun wahyahn* (澳門華人, Macau Chinese) or more emphatically, *touh saang touh jeuhng* 土生土長, "locally born and raised." In my experience, this latter phrase was never confused with *touh saang jai*.

7. For other discussions of Macaneseness, see A. Amaro 1988, Batalha 1977, V. Cunha 1998, Forjaz 1996, Morbey 1994, Pina-Cabral 2002, F. Silva 1979, and H. S. Yee 1997.

8. I believe Nuno was paraphrasing Wittgenstein's (1997: 31) observation that "the words 'This is a king' . . . are a definition only if the learner already 'knows what a piece in a game is.' That is, if he has already played other games, or has watched other people playing and 'understood.'" From taped interview, in English, January 20, 1999.

9. Liao Zixin's (1995: 161–62) description is worth quoting at length, as it expresses many of the negative stereotypes of the Macanese: "They [the Macanese] have low social status in the eyes of the continental Portuguese, while in Macau they enjoy privileged social status as the offspring of the ruling colonialists and live a carefree life immune to censure, often gaining access to elevated positions and high salaries in the Government despite ignorance and incompetence. They are prone to act outrageously, [are] impervious to public opinion, and tend to wield their power heavy-handedly but with absolute impunity. Contradictory tendencies to be self-deprecating but arrogant compete within them, which [means] that this group of Macau Portuguese approaches life with a philosophy not entirely compatible with that of the Portuguese from Portugal. What emerges in the Macanese is a culture without roots. Influenced by the way of life in Macao, and fully integrated into local society, they have undoubtedly assimilated to some degree into Chinese culture. Yet they are largely excluded from the wider Chinese world."

10. In this sense, the Macanese were not unlike the Hong Kong Eurasians described by Vicky Lee (2004: 4), who fit both into Western ideologies of "degeneration, transgression, adulteration, impurity, regression and

moral laxity," and Chinese ideologies of the betrayal of race, nation, and lineage, as well as into the belief that "Eurasians were the ideal hybrid race . . . bringing together the best of both worlds, amalgamating two great civilizations."

11. Article 42 of the Basic Law states that "the interests of the residents of Portuguese descent in Macao shall be protected by the Macao Special Administrative Region in accordance with the law, and their customs and cultural traditions shall be respected."

12. As Michael Dowdle (1999: 287) has asserted, "Everyone agrees that there is no real rule of law in China." Chinese Deputy Permanent Representative to the UN Shen Guofang has argued explicitly that the implementation of international law should never be allowed to violate the sovereignty of the nation-state (quoted in *China Daily Online*, Wednesday, November 10, 1999). See also Alford 1999, Hintzen 1999, and Peerenboom 1999.

13. For example, after the NATO bombing of the Chinese embassy in Belgrade in 1999, the Chinese media expressed outrage that the United States and its allies justified their "extremely cruel acts of aggression" through the "fallacy that human rights are above state sovereignty" (quoted in J. Wang 2001). See L. Liu 1999a for a discussion of the extent to which international law appeared, to the Chinese officials who first encountered it in the mid-nineteenth century, to be little more than an extension of British imperialism. Cf. also Comaroff (2001: 306), who remarks that the Tswana of South Africa referred to law as "the English mode of warfare."

14. In 1997, President Jiang Zemin, in his political report to the Fifteenth Communist Party Congress, stated that "the task of our Party is to establish the rule of law and construct a socialist country with the rule of law."

15. Already in the late 1960s Anthony Dicks (1984: 127) noted that "deciding which inhabitants of Macao are Chinese [is] a question that is of potentially some importance" to the central government, given that the Portuguese government had, in 1967, effectively "recognized without qualification China's right to protect the interests of the Chinese inhabitants of Macao." For a comparison of the complex interactions among the legal concepts of nationality, residence, and sovereignty in Hong Kong, see Ghai 1999.

16. In the Ming (1364–1644) and early Qing dynasties (the mid-seventeenth through early nineteenth centuries), for example, the state treated Chinese who had emigrated to other sovereign lands not as potential subjects but as traitors who had abandoned their homeland and their families in the pursuit of profit (Yen 1985: 19; Duara 1997: 43). By the late nineteenth century, the Qing court's recognition of the need to protect

thousands of Chinese indentured laborers in the Americas, and Euro-American insistence that China behave like the other members of the "family of nations," led the Chinese state to begin offering protection to Chinese residing outside China and to seek their support in return (Yen 1985). This approach intensified into the early twentieth century: the Republican revolution of 1911 that brought the KMT to power was funded partly by Chinese who were citizens of other nation-states; well into the 1970s, the KMT government viewed "jurisdiction over [ethnic] Chinese abroad as a right and responsibility of the Chinese government" (S. Fitzgerald 1972: 76). In the early years of the PRC, the Communist Party called upon ethnic Chinese abroad to advance the cause of anti-imperialist liberation in the lands where they had settled and invited them "home" to participate in building the new China (Y. Lu 1956: 15); but by 1957, increased persecution of ethnic Chinese in southeast Asia and China's inability to protect them caused the CCP to relinquish these claims (T. Hsia and Haun 1976). As ultra-leftism waxed in the Maoist era, Chinese who had resided overseas were once again viewed with suspicion and hostility, as potential spies and counterrevolutionaries. In the 1980s and 1990s, with the stunning rates of economic growth and interregional investment between Chinese populations of Asia, North America, and Australia, the Chinese government began promoting "myths of common origin" of all Chinese in ways that emphasized "discourses connecting race, nation and territory" (Louie 2000: 645).

17. Ien Ang (2001: 50) writes of experiencing the same thing in reverse: a Chinese cab driver in Sydney, upon learning that Ang did not speak Chinese, told her it would be easy for her to learn because she had Chinese blood.

18. In my use of this term I draw on Giorgio Agamben's (1998) discussion of potentiality and sovereignty.

19. Almost without doubt, the term the author had used in her original Chinese essay was *oumun yahn* 澳門人, rather than *touh saang pou yahn* 土生葡人. *Oumun yahn* is a term that translates only awkwardly into either Portuguese or English, as "Macau person" or "Macau people." This expression is a common way, *mutatis mutandis*, of specifying a person's "native place," be it Shanghai, Chongqing, or New York. Unlike *touh saang pou yahn*, it carries no explicit ethnic or national marker. See Chapter 5 for a discussion of the importance of native-place identification in China.

20. In Chinese, "cultura macaense" was rendered as 澳門文化, or "Macau culture." See Macau Sempre Statutes, Chapter III, Article 6, Paragraph i.

21. Interview in English, February 24, 1999, from notes written up afterward.

22. Indeed, Macau Sempre's attempt to redefine the word "Macanese" evidently failed to convince many. During the 1996 elections, Macau Sempre sponsored a slate of candidates (both Macanese and ethnic Chinese) to run for Legislative Assembly, based on this platform of multiethnic commitment to Macau; but, as Mario put it, "we didn't even get enough votes to elect a left arm, let alone a whole person." I never heard an ethnic Chinese person from Macau refer to herself as Macanese; not even all Macanese people wanted to be called "Macanese." I first heard objections to this term in April 1999, shortly after the third Encontro das Comunidades Macaenses. It was voiced in rather vague terms in Portuguese by a Macanese man from Australia, who said that many of the overseas participants in the Encontro had felt confused and uncomfortable at the use of the term Macaense, which they felt was "a form of political propaganda." He and most of the Macanese he knew preferred to call themselves, in *patuá, filho-Macau.*

23. Under Portuguese rule, both the Macanese and the Chinese were subject to a glass ceiling in terms of political participation—no one but a Portuguese national was ever appointed governor of Macau, and in the 1990s, when Jorge Rangel (an ethnic Macanese with Portuguese citizenship) became Undersecretary for Administration, Education, and Youth, he was the first and only non-ethnic Portuguese to fill such a high-ranking position. However, the Organic Statute that had governed Macau since 1976 included no explicit citizenship requirement for any government post.

24. Quoted in *Ponto final,* 30 October 1998, p. 18.

25. Great Britain granted some three million Hong Kong residents (just under half of Hong Kong's 1996 population of 6.3 million) the right to carry "British National Overseas" passports, which made international travel easier than a Chinese passport but did not permit them to live or work in Great Britain. Skeptics of Portuguese "generosity" countered that the difference was a matter of scale, and that of those 130,000 Macau residents, the overwhelming majority would very likely never emigrate to Portugal; they were a safe bet.

26. This paragraph and paragraph 2 below are my translations from the Chinese text of the Resolution published in AMRB, December 30, 1998, p. A-2.

27. See, e.g., the *Va Kio Daily* 華僑日報 of January 21, 1999, which describes the Resolution as "generous" and characterizes Portuguese objections as "nitpicking" (挑剔). The *Macao Daily* (澳門日報)—which was

both the most widely read newspaper in Macau and the only one owned by the Chinese Communist Party—ran articles about the nationality law with the word "generous" in the headline in at least three separate editions in the two months following the publication of the Resolution (January 9 and February 2 and 16, 1999).

28. Compare to Virginia Domínguez's (1994: 1) story of Susie Phipps, the woman who had herself declared "white" in a Louisiana court. Press reports wrote that "Raised White, a Louisiana Belle Challenges Race Records that Call Her Colored."

29. Plenty of studies have demonstrated that notions of nationality and citizenship are profoundly racial ones, in China as well as Portugal. See Dikötter 1992, for China; see Ovalle-Bahamón 2003, for Portugal; and more generally, see Balibar and Wallerstein 1991, Gilroy 1991, Manzo 1996, and B. Williams 1995.

30. The longer explanation Nuno gave me went like this: from the perspective of Portuguese law, nothing short of formally renouncing Portuguese nationality (via the bureaucratic channels set up for this purpose in Portugal) would change a Macanese person's status as a Portuguese national; acquiring Chinese nationality would change nothing. Only if a Macanese actively renounced Chinese nationality would she become eligible for diplomatic protection by Portugal when living or traveling in Chinese territory (in other words, she would lose her *de facto* dual citizenship status and be viewed exclusively as a Portuguese citizen). The same thing held true from the perspective of Chinese law: the only way Macanese people born in Macau could change their nationality status was if they actively renounced Chinese nationality. If they "opted for" Chinese nationality, they would not be changing their status since, under Chinese law, they were already considered Chinese nationals by virtue of their Chinese descent and/or their birth in a Chinese territory. In this sense, Nuno pointed out, the "choice" was only a choice (in the sense of refusing one of two possibilities) for those Macanese who wished to be considered Portuguese nationals while they were in Macau and the rest of China.

The situation of Chinese in the Netherlands East Indies at the turn of the twentieth century provides an interesting parallel. According to Wang Gungwu (1981), China's first nationality law, promulgated in 1909, "conceded that the Chinese in the Netherlands East Indies could become Dutch subjects, [but] it insisted that even such Dutch subjects would still be Chinese whenever they returned to China." In 1999, the Macanese were in very much the same position, except that the Resolution highlighted the fact that China's nationality law provided a way to renounce even this partial claim to Chineseness.

31. This was also the case, for example, in Mexico prior to 1997, when dual nationality was recognized in light of the increasing numbers of Mexican emigrants to the United States who did not adopt US nationality in order to avoid losing Mexican nationality (Ramírez 2000: 313).

32. One of Macau's Chinese-language newspapers also ran an article about a "Portuguese person" who had opted for Chinese nationality (*Si Man Pou*, November 26, 1999).

33. The term *zhongguoren* means "Chinese person" but connotes belonging to the Chinese polity. It may also be used to refer to citizens of China who are not ethnically Han. It stands in contrast to *huaren*, which is more commonly used in Macau and other places outside China to denote a person who identifies as ethnically and culturally Han Chinese but may not be a citizen of the PRC. I use the admittedly awkward phrase "nationalized Chinese personhood" to reflect this distinction. At no point in the debate did anyone suggest that the Macanese should be considered *huaren* or Han Chinese. In fact, I heard intimations (from researchers and bureaucrats with connections to Beijing) that those Macanese who did choose to adopt Chinese citizenship might and should, at some point in the future, be identified as China's fifty-sixth ethnic minority (*shaoshuminzu*).

34. This was a committee of 100 members, 60 of whom were from Macau (the remaining 40 being from the PRC), that was in charge of laying the groundwork for the post-handover government.

35. To clarify the difference between filiation and descent, Nuno gave the example of an ethnic Chinese person born in Mozambique, who is a Mozambican citizen by birth, and who marries a Mozambican citizen. "So they are not Chinese nationals, ok? So imagine they come to live in Macau. And they have a child here. In accordance with the Chinese nationality law, [that child] is not automatically a Chinese national, because even though he was born in Chinese territory, neither of his parents is a Chinese national. But according to the first part of this Resolution, this child *is* a Chinese national. Because he is of Chinese *descent*, and he was born in Chinese territory."

Chapter 4

1. See, e.g., Bourdieu 1991, M. Brown 1985, Chai 1977, Cooper 1984, Kalia 1980, Reed-Danahay 1996, Segal 2000, 2005, Vickers 2003, and Willis 1981.

2. See, e.g., Unger 1993 and E. Wang 2001.

3. This included, in the 1997–98 academic year, eighteen middle schools, eighteen schools offering both primary and secondary education, and eight schools offering pre-primary, primary, and secondary education (Wu Zhiliang and Ieong 1999: 333).

4. Here I take as analytically distinct two concepts often used interchangeably: that of the local or locality, and that of place. "Locality" I take to be a question of scale: of determining, in spatial terms, the contours of a social group, a set of practices or commitments; "place" I understand to be the set of meanings, attachments, and histories that a particular group, entity, or individual imputes to a given locality. See Chapter 6 for a discussion of place-making in Macau.

5. Sociologist Albert Yee (1989) coined the phrase "stepping stone society" in reference to Hong Kong, but I often heard it applied to Macau as well. See also Ngai 1999.

6. Interview July 23, 1996, tape-recorded, in English.

7. For examples of the many analyses of the problems of localization in these three arenas, see Santos and Gomes 1998, Ramos et al. 1997, and H. S. Yee 1993.

8. Ignatius Ts'ao (1999) describes the cumbersome process of translating Macau's legal code. Chinese equivalents had to be found not only for the elaborate legalese of thousands of pages of documents but also for the concepts that formed the basis of the Portuguese legal system, which differed considerably from the British system on which Hong Kong law was based (and thus made a simple transposition of Hong Kong's legal code impossible). The process was further complicated by an almost complete dearth of Chinese lawyers trained in the Portuguese system, and of Portuguese lawyers who could speak or write Chinese (ibid.: 72).

9. This tension was sharpened in January 1999, when the Hong Kong government asked Beijing for a "reinterpretation" of a ruling given by the Hong Kong Court of Final Appeal (CFA). The ruling involved a group of mainlanders who sued to be given the right of abode in Hong Kong on the grounds that they were relatives of Hong Kong residents. The CFA found in favor of the plaintiffs, arguing that the Basic Law of the Hong Kong SAR granted the right of abode to persons whose parents did not have the right of abode at the time of their birth as well as to those born out of wedlock to a father who was a Hong Kong permanent resident. Arguing that this ruling would allow nearly 700,000 mainlanders to have the right of abode in Hong Kong (and an estimated million more, when those first 700,000 themselves became permanent residents) and that such a large and sudden influx of immigrants would overwhelm the city's infrastructures, the

Hong Kong government appealed to the Standing Committee of the National People's Congress, which determined that in order for a person to seek right of abode, one or both parents had to have been a resident at the time of the applicant's birth. This intervention sparked a crisis of confidence in the rule of law in Hong Kong, as constitutional scholars viewed it as a sign of "the unlimited and unchallengeable power of the NPC to impose any meaning on the Basic Law." See Ghai 2001.

10. Prasenjit Duara (1995: 3) points out that "the nation seeks its ultimate moorings in history." Tsing (2004) argues that the advocates of global capitalism (and their critics), too, seek to make their vision of globality seem real to the rest of us in part by depicting its evolutionary continuity with earlier forms of market interactions and ideologies, while claiming a variety of futures: a long-term future in which economic downturns are mere turbulence in the flight path toward ever-increasing returns on investment, a millennial future in which time and space disintegrate into a spectacular simultaneity.

11. See, e.g., Fitzgerald 1995 and Tsin 1999.

12. Although in some respects it is true that the Chinese Communist Party "closed" China to flows of capital, people, and information originating in Europe, Japan, and the United States, it is astonishing how quickly and completely the transnational commitments of Maoist China have been forgotten. Publications on China's foreign relations in the 1960s and 1970s are filled with descriptions of the flows of capital, labor, and diplomats between China and countries in Africa, India, and southeast Asia, along with dire predictions about the globalist pretensions of Maoism. But by the mid-1990s, in China and elsewhere the Maoist era was regarded as one of isolationism and closure rather than commitment to a competing globalist project. The rhetoric by which the CCP itself refers to the economic policies of the post-Mao period as "reform and opening up" (改革開放) reinforces the sense that Maoism was a condition of closure. But this should be seen for the transnationalist claim that it is, rather than as a transparent description of reality.

13. This awkward translation is an attempt to convey the sense that a demonstrated commitment to one's (or one's family's) place of origin in China is in and of itself patriotic.

14. For a discussion of the *aiguo aixiang* rhetoric among Chinese Americans returning to China, see Louie 2004. Edmund Ho, who became Macau's chief executive on December 20, 1999, was praised in precisely these terms in a biographical article entitled "Edmund Ho: Proud to Be *aiguo aixiang*" (何厚鏵: 愛國愛鄉無愧我心), published to mark the fifth

anniversary of the handover and the end of his first term in office (see Zhang Ying 2004).

15. See Ong 1999: 215. Other such spatial breakings-up of sovereign power exist in the PRC. Five autonomous regions at the province level (the Tibetan, Inner Mongolian, Xinjiang-Uyghur, Ningxia-Hui, and Guangxi-Zhuang autonomous regions) and thousands of autonomous prefectures, counties, and townships allow groups that have been formally defined as "minority nationalities" some autonomy in deciding how to implement national policies (see Ghai 2000 and Heberer 1989). In the 1980s, SEZs (initially only Shenzhen, Zhuhai, Xiamen, and Shantou but later expanded to include several other coastal cities and the entire province of Hainan Island) were created in which foreign investment, stock markets, and other elements of capitalism would be "both permitted and controlled" (G. Crane 1996: 77). Both the autonomous regions and the SEZs thus constitute exceptions to centralized socialist governance. But neither allows a different type of economy, a separate tax system, or an entirely different legal code than that of the PRC; nor do they grant the residents of these regions and zones the autonomy over virtually all domestic matters that Hong Kong and Macau have.

16. The CCP's 1994 definition of patriotism included "accept[ing] the principles of peaceful reunification and 'one country, two systems.'" By this definition, it would have been unpatriotic to suggest that Macau and Hong Kong should have the same "system" as the mainland (*Beijing Review*, quoted in He and Guo 2000: 36).

17. Scholarly works and documentary collections on the history of Macau education published during the transition era include Aresta and Barata 1996; Aresta et al. 1997; Claro and Alves 1997; J. Costa 1999; Deng n.d.; Feng 1999; Huang n.d.; Liu Xianbing 1994a, 1994b, and 1995; Lu Deqi 1995; Mendes 1996; Simões 1993b; and Zhang Wenqin 1995 and 1999.

18. See, e.g., Cremer 1992, Fei Chengkang 1988, Lamas 1998, Pires 1988, Huang 1999, Liu Xianbing 1994a, Porter 1996, Wu Zhiliang 1996, and Zhang Wenqin 1995 and 1999.

19. Consider, for example, Samuel Huntington's (1993) controversial but often-cited essay on the "clash of civilizations," which divides humanity into a series of distinct religio-cultural civilizations that could easily be mapped onto any world atlas. For analyses of the changing concept of "civilization" in China, see Anagnost 1997 and Duara 2001, 2003.

20. See Duara 2001 for a discussion of how civilizational discourse became articulated to nationalism.

21. By 1592, the school had 200 students (Teixeira 1982: 183). See also Aresta and Barata 1996 and Liu Xianbing 1994b.

22. Wu Li was converted to Christianity and wrote a series of poems about Macau while studying theology at the college. His "Thirty Miscellaneous Poems on Macau" are collected in Chaves 1993.

23. According to Liu Xianbing 1994b, the Portuguese crown contributed 1,000 cruzados to the school every year from the taxes collected at Malacca; according to Alden (1996: 531), in the 1630s, the college "owned two junks and held shares in several other craft."

24. Chen Tan 陳坦, *Kangxi yu Luoma shijie guanxi wenshu* 康熙與羅馬使節關係文書 (Documents on diplomatic relations between Kangxi and Rome), quoted in Liu Xianbing 1994a: 19.

25. The Rites Controversy was a theological and political debate in which Ricci and other Jesuits (notably Alessandro Valignano), realizing that the imperative for Chinese Christians to become Europeanized was a major obstacle to their conversion, argued that Chinese who converted to Christianity should be allowed to continue performing certain Confucian rites (such as "ancestor worship") because these rites were essentially secular cultural rituals rather than religious and therefore pagan. They also argued that existing Chinese terms originating in Confucian classics could be used in translating Christian concepts, such as *tian* (天) for "heaven" and *shangdi* (上帝) for "God," because these Chinese terms were philosophical (rather than religious) and did not refer to a transcendental entity other than the Christian God. These policies certainly eased the Jesuits' acceptance by Chinese elites, for whom the performance of Confucian rites was socially and politically indispensable, but earned them enmity and accusations of heresy from other Catholic orders, who for the better part of a century attempted to convince Rome to declare this policy heterodox and to censure the Jesuits. In 1715, they finally succeeded at this task when Pope Clement XI issued a decree forbidding Chinese converts from practicing Confucian rites or using *tian* or *shangdi* to refer to the Catholic Heaven or God. See Alden 1996, Ross 1994, and Mungello 1989.

26. Kangxi wrote a decree of his own in response to Pope Clement XI's declaration that the practice of Confucian rites was incompatible with Christianity: "Reading this proclamation, I have concluded that the Westerners are petty indeed. It is impossible to reason with them because they do not understand larger issues as we understand them in China. There is not a single Westerner versed in Chinese works, and their remarks are often incredible and ridiculous. To judge from this proclamation, their religion is no different from other small, bigoted sects of Buddhism or

Taoism. I have never seen a document which contains so much nonsense. From now on, Westerners should not be allowed to preach in China, to avoid further trouble" (see "Decree of Kangxi," in D. J. Li 1969: 22). The Jesuit scientists, however, were allowed to continue their work at the observatory in Beijing, which they did until the pope disbanded the Jesuit order in 1773.

27. For Portugal, see Wheeler 1978 and Freitas 1999; for China, see Bailey 1990.

28. In China, the idea of mass education as the responsibility of the state was a relatively new one; as Paul Bailey (1990: 2) notes, "the state had traditionally left whatever formal elementary education that did exist to local communities, gentry and lineages." In Portugal, this idea had been around at least since the mid-nineteenth century, but had never been very well implemented. At the time of the 1910 revolution, 79 percent of Portugal's population was illiterate (Wheeler 1978).

29. The Escola Comercial, established in 1878 by the Associação Promotora da Instrução dos Macaenses, was designed to provide young Macanese with an "education for diaspora," teaching them the skills they would need to find white-collar work in other cities of Asia (see Simões 1993b). Macau was also home to two of China's pre-eminent education reformers: Zheng Guanying 鄭觀應, who in the 1880s drafted the first plan for a national education system in China, was educated in Macau and later retired there; and Chen Zibao 陳子襃, an advocate of vernacular education and education for women, established in 1899 in Macau one of the first schools in China to use vernacular materials (Feng 1999; see also Bailey 1990: 73–74). In addition, Protestant mission schools in Macau in the late nineteenth century were among the first to educate Chinese women and the disabled; several of the graduates of these schools went on to open or inspire others to open similar institutions on the mainland (see Guo 2005).

30. Alexandre Rosa, executive coordinator of the Commission for Education Reform in the early 1990s, discerned four distinct "systems" of education in Macau, based on language of instruction: "Chinese, accounting for 76 percent of schools and 86 percent of students; Portuguese, with 11 percent of schools and 5 percent of students; Luso-Chinese, with 7 percent of schools and 3 percent of students; and Anglo-Chinese, with 5 percent of schools and 6 percent of students" (Rosa 1991: 32). These different "systems" were also run on different administrative models; for example, students in PRC-affiliated schools attended six years of elementary plus six years of secondary school, divided into "lower" and "upper" secondary (represented in shorthand as 6+6 or 6+3+3); the Hong Kong model, following

the British, involved five years of secondary school plus a twelfth year of college prep (6+5+1); the Taiwan model, 6+3+3; and the Portuguese model followed a 4+2+3+2+1 pattern (primary, preparatory, junior secondary, senior secondary, and pre-university). There were also combinations and recombinations of these. See Bray 1992: 329–30.

31. Bray and Tang (1994) criticized the lack of "local" textbooks even in subjects such as mathematics, not to mention social studies, history, or geography. They found regrettable the prevalence, in mathematics textbooks used in Macau's schools, of examples, drawings, and units of measurement taken from Hong Kong, the PRC, England, or Portugal, arguing that when "the lack of local textbooks fails to make the subject relevant to the local context . . . an opportunity may have been missed to make schooling more relevant to daily life" (37).

32. The process of educational reform in the 1990s led to dozens of publications detailing the causes and remedies for the sorry state of education in Macau. See, e.g., Bray 1992, Bray and Koo 1999 and all the essays in it, Bray and Tang 1994, Bray and Hui 1991, Hu 1994, Rangel 1991, Rosa 1991, So Chiu Fai 1994, J. Tan 1993, K. C. Tang 1998, F. H. Tang and Morrison 1998, and A. H. Yee 1990.

33. Rosa 1991 notes that as of 1991, 50 percent of teachers in Macau's schools had completed secondary-level education, but only 37 percent had any post-secondary teacher training. Adamson and Li (1999: 44–45) note that in 1996–97, the average starting salary for teachers in private schools was between MOP$7,000 and 10,000 (approx. US$900–1,280) per month, whereas their counterparts in government-run schools started at a monthly salary of MOP$17,500 to 21,500 (approx. US$2,250–2,750).

34. See J. Tan 1993: 55 for an overview of the history textbooks used in seven secondary schools in Macau. Many of the schools used Hong Kong textbooks to teach world history, but they often switched to mainland or Taiwan textbooks for Chinese history.

35. This was the case until 1991, when the privately run University of East Asia—which had been, since its establishment in 1981 by Hong Kong investors, the only institution of tertiary education in Macau—became the public University of Macau.

36. See, e.g., Bray 1992, Hui and Poon 1999, and A. H. Yee 1990.

37. Alexandre Rosa (1991: 33) echoes Rangel's dissatisfaction: "Historically, education in Macau developed . . . with the almost total lack of intervention by the administration in terms of delineating the educational policy of the territory."

38. This phrase echoes Deng Xiaoping's national program of pursuing "socialism with Chinese characteristics" (具有中國特色的社會主義), made famous in the 1980s.

39. This assertion, which I heard informally from a small number of educators and slightly more often from Macau residents not involved in education, is argued forcefully by Hui and Poon 1999. They assert that "colonial governments commonly try to maintain their influence in colonies in post-colonial periods, and . . . education is one of the major social institutions for actualising such influence" (99). The authors take the expansion of public education initiated by both the Hong Kong and the Macau governments as evidence of their "imperial initiatives in cultural and economic expansion in China" (116).

40. On local history instruction in Taiwan, see M. Liu and Hung 2002; for Hong Kong, see Vickers 2002 and 2003.

41. Founded in Guangzhou in 1889 by the Baptist Convention of Guangzhou and Guangxi provinces, Pui Ching was one of the first modern schools in China to be established by Chinese Protestants. In January 1938, to escape the Japanese occupation, the Guangzhou branch of the school relocated to Macau (which was safer than Hong Kong because of Portugal's neutrality in World War II). After the war, the Macau branch continued operation. In the mid-1990s, K–12 enrollments were around 3,000. Although nominally a Protestant school, religious instruction was limited to one hour per week, and the school accepted students regardless of creed.

42. The school was named for a prominent Macanese educator, Luís Gonzaga Gomes, who died in 1974.

43. Although the widespread perception was that the student body consisted primarily of Portuguese from Portugal, according to the principal, in 1998 more than half of the Liceu's nearly 1,000 students spoke Chinese or another language at home. The Liceu also ran night classes for adults without a high school degree, and the Liceu complex housed an affiliated primary school that also followed the Portuguese primary curriculum.

44. The Escola Portuguesa was run by the Fundação Escola Portuguesa de Macau, whose funds came from two sources: the Portuguese Ministry of Education (51 percent) and the Orient Foundation (49 percent). The latter is a nonprofit organization established in 1988 with funds from STDM (which was, from 1962 to 2001, the sole holder of the license to run casinos in Macau) as part of its agreement to contribute to the city's cultural and economic development.

45. In a separate interview, a vice-principal of the Escola Portuguesa told me that in 1998–99, there were 1,500 students in Portuguese-medium

schools in Macau, all of whom would (if they stayed in Macau) converge on the Escola Portuguesa, which was already having difficulty accommodating its target enrollment of 600.

46. Interview June 5, 1998, in English, from notes written up after the interview.

47. Interview February 5, 1999. I have masked the identity of this person to protect confidentiality, due primarily to the extreme reluctance Z showed in talking to me about this subject.

Chapter 5

1. Goodman notes that also "in traditional China . . . geographic origin was generally the first matter of inquiry among strangers" (Goodman 1995a: 5; see also Tuan 1996).

2. Stereotypes abound about the traits of people from particular places in China and are often subscribed to by the groups they describe: people from Guangdong are supposedly good at business, whereas those from "the north" care more about politics; men from the Northeast are more prone to fistfights, but southerners talk problems out; people from Chaozhou are wily and suspicious of outsiders, and women from Hangzhou are said to be the most beautiful in all of China. Attributions such as these operate on all levels, from region to province to county to village.

3. As Myron Cohen (1994: 96–97) writes, "At all levels of society, and among those serving or representing the state, it was considered that one dimension of being Chinese was to have a place of origin somewhere in China. . . . Acceptable localisms were incorporated by the state and the elite into Chinese cosmopolitanism." For the culturalist framework of native-place belonging among transnational Chinese, see Ong and Nonini 1997 and Tu 1994b.

4. Lucien Pye (1993: 115) notes that the sense of humiliation at China's loss of control over portions of its territory, which the CCP built into a platform for revolution, meant that treaty ports were seen and experienced as "sordid, immoral cities—squalid places that needed, as the conquering Communists certainly believed, to be totally cleaned out." More specifically, certain places within those cities became known as icons of the arrogance of foreigners and the humiliation of the Chinese: consider the recurrent myth of the public park in 1930s Shanghai whose gate boasted a sign reading "Chinese and Dogs Not Allowed." See Bickers and Wasserstrom 1995 for a discussion of the persistence and periodic re-emergence of this myth.

5. See, e.g., Waldron 1993 and Anagnost 1997; on heritage sites, see Hevia 2001, Flath 2002, and the works cited in my discussion of heritage in China in Chapter 6.

6. One recent exception is L. Zhang 2006.

7. See, e.g., Massey 1994, Dirlik 1999, and Moore 1998, 2005.

8. Author and literary critic Dai Jinhua (2000: 208) writes of the "giddy and aggressively rapid urbanization of the 1990s" that, although exciting, leaves "even a 'homegrown' Chinese suddenly stripped of hometown, homeland, and home country, and abandoned to the beautiful new world." Li Zhang (2006: 466) notes the same phenomenon in Kunming, where, after a massive effort to "modernize" the city in advance of the 1999 International Horticultural Expo, many long-term residents "could no longer find their way around."

9. See Mundy 1907, Chaves 1993, Instituto Cultural de Macau and Chinnery 1997, H. Fernandes 1993, and Mendes 1996.

10. For an analysis of the geographical growth of Macau, see Wong Hon-keong and Wu 1996: 5–6. Major land reclamation projects continued apace throughout the late twentieth and early twenty-first centuries, which made accurate figures for the land area of Macau difficult to obtain. In 1994, reclaimed land accounted for 56 percent of the total land area of Macau, and about two-thirds of the land area of the peninsula (see Wong Chao Son et al. 1997: 72). For details on individual reclamation projects, see Taylor 1994 and Prescott 1993.

11. The Macau-Zhuhai bridge was completed just in time for the handover. See Lopes 1998. For details on the Cotai project and future expansion, see Chui et al. 1999. As of 2010, the railway had yet to be completed (or even begun).

12. For details through 1997, see "Os novos monumentos," *Revista Macau*, 2d ser., no. 61 (May): 42–48.

13. Although Macau and Hong Kong ranked high as sources of foreign direct investment in mainland China, this investment was bidirectional. At the end of 1993 it was estimated that the total investment in Macau from China was more than MOP$60 billion (Maruya 1999: 143n11).

14. Interview, in English, October 29, 1998.

15. Raymond Tse (1999: 151) puts the number at 34,000 vacant units of a total of 149,000 residential units, for a vacancy rate of 20–25 percent. He does not give a figure for vacancy rates of commercial units.

16. The phenomenon of half-built buildings abandoned in mid-construction was so common throughout Guangdong province in the 1990s that they acquired a name of their own: *lanwei lou* 爛尾樓, literally "rotten-

tail buildings," since they had had a solid beginning or "head" but foundered before the ending or "tail" could be completed.

17. See, e.g., "Fachada ICM" in *Macau hoje*, December 9, 1997, p. 5.

18. See B. Silva 1994: 45, 52. According to the 1992 publication *Arruamentos da cidade de Macau*, there is a *rua* (street), a *travessa* (lane) and a *pátio* (place) that all bear the name *dos Cules* in Portuguese. In Chinese, the street is called Tintong Gaai 天通街, the lane is called Giufu Hong 轎夫巷 (Sedan-chair-bearer Lane), and the place is known as either 苦力 圍 (Coolie Circle) or 聚龍里 (Assembly of Dragons Place).

19. One Portuguese author describes the Praia Grande in the nineteenth century as "a waterfront promenade where the colonial government and some foreign commercial companies built their headquarters. . . . [These structures] were a reproduction . . . of the ideals and concepts of imperial, and thus colonial, luxury and opulence as they were practiced by Portuguese, European, and especially British architects, which imprinted on the colonial city much of its segregationist character—a segregation that was as much racial as spatial" (Burnay 1998: 98).

20. João de Pina-Cabral (1994: 123) notes that this is a result of Portuguese naming conventions, whereby "a person must receive . . . her mother's father's surname followed by her father's father's surname," but that often people will choose to maintain additional "[sur]names to which they have a right," especially if these names are prestigious.

21. Manuel Alves (1990: 62) notes that this phenomenon of calling streets by different names occurs even in Portuguese; for example, he notes, "one of the first street names that Portuguese who have recently arrived in Macau learn is 'Rua das Mariazinhas,' whose real identification is split between 'Rua de S. Domingos' and 'Rua de Pedro Nolasco da Silva'—which very few people know by these names."

22. This is according to the official government map issued in 1992 (Leal Senado 1992). In the *Macau Atlas*, compiled by three Chinese historians and geographers and published by the Macau Foundation in 1997, the Praça Ferreira do Amaral—named for the eponymous statue that once occupied its center and was dismantled in 1992—is depicted on the map, but is given no name at all (Wong Chao Son et al. 1997).

23. Karen Blu (1996: 200) describes a similar experience she had soon after arriving in rural North Carolina to do fieldwork among Lumbee Indians. She noticed that the way Lumbees gave directions differed from that of the rural Midwesterners among whom she grew up: for the Lumbees, directions "were usually couched in terms of places I already knew how to get to ('You know the Union Chapel road, well, you go to the second crossroads

and turn left . . . ') [and] were always oriented in terms of the individual making the trip" rather than in terms of the universal directions of north, south, east, and west. For Blu, this difference between the ways that residents of two rural farming areas expressed the individual's relations to the surrounding space led her to an understanding of the complex historical and social factors that impact the way that Lumbees think about, and thus express, concepts of place and community.

24. Bear in mind that since in Chinese surnames come before given names, "Luo" is a transliteration of the priest's surname.

25. This 20-meter-high statue, described as a Portuguese interpretation of Guan Yin, the Buddhist goddess of mercy, was designed by Portuguese architect Cristina Leiria (who was rumored to have gotten the contract because she was a "friend" of the governor). Most Macau residents I spoke with disliked it: some found it simply unattractive; others saw it as a symbol of the Portuguese *mis*understanding of Chinese culture; and the most vehement found it downright insulting.

26. I heard this even from Tiago, an architect and advocate of heritage preservation who (as we shall see) held the state responsible for the destruction of Macau's urban fabric and insisted that the debate about heritage was not a "Portuguese vs. Chinese" matter—it was not that the Portuguese wanted to preserve and the Chinese wanted to tear down everything to put up skyscrapers. But other interviewees said or implied that they believed it to be precisely a Portuguese vs. Chinese question: that after the handover, the Chinese would tear down every last remnant of Portuguese colonialism and try (as every other southern Chinese city was trying) to become like Hong Kong.

27. See Siu 1996 for a description of a similar phenomenon in Hong Kong.

28. Many of these buildings had been left to crumble because their ownership was disputed due to Macau's archaic property registration system or was divided among a dozen or more descendants of the original owner, who could not agree on a future course of action. These problems were complicated by the fact that the owners of many buildings had long since moved permanently overseas and were virtually impossible to trace.

29. In 1976, the Macau government passed the first law governing the preservation of historic buildings and created the Commission for the Preservation of Macau's Heritage. In 1984, this heritage law was strengthened and the list of classified sites expanded to include over 130 buildings, monuments, and neighborhoods. In most classified areas, property owners were forbidden to destroy or make alterations to the exterior of the buildings, and

any plans for new buildings would be subject to approval by the commission. It was not until the late 1980s, however, that the heritage preservation initiative came into full swing, as the commission was upgraded into a government department with an annual budget in the millions, allocated for the restoration of dilapidated but classified sites. See Marreiros 1991, Departamento do Património Cultural 1997, and Prescott 1993.

30. According to a report given at the Culture of Metropolis Symposium by a representative of the Departamento de Património Cultural, as of 1998 they had done major restoration work on 60 private buildings, thirteen Chinese temples, two libraries, and one church; 25 more buildings were slated for restoration "in the next years" (Durão 1998). Minor or external work had been done on a number of other buildings, including two forts, three churches, and three Chinese temples. The budget for restoration had jumped from HK$700,000 in 1991 to $25 million by 1996. See also Departamento do Património Cultural 1997.

31. "Preservar e amar o Património é lançar-se ao futuro sem fantasmas do passado" (Instituto Cultural de Macau 1998: 2).

32. "Uma lição universal, símbolo antecipado de uma Humanidade onde todas as diferenças se harmonizam na mesma Unidade." In fact, Tiago and others had been trying to get the Macau government to apply for World Heritage status for several years already, but it was apparently not until 1998 that Governor Vasco Rocha Vieira began to seriously entertain the idea. A UNESCO representative was invited to attend the Culture of Metropolis conference and returned again in the winter of 1998 to discuss the issue further. As it turned out, this was already too late. The application had to be submitted and followed through on by the sovereign state of the applicant nation; but the application process would take at least eighteen months, while only fourteen months remained to the Portuguese in Macau. After 1999, the Macau SAR government renewed this initiative: in 2002, the central government in Beijing began the application process on behalf of Macau, and UNESCO World Heritage site status was granted in 2005. While this application process was attended by as much or perhaps even more fanfare as the abortive application of the late 1990s, the exhibitions, photo competitions, and celebrations that attended it were largely about placing Macau in the context of the vast number of places in the PRC that are already on the list—the Great Wall, the Forbidden City, Qin Shihuang's tomb, and so on—thus framing Macau's "universal value" as a distinctly Chinese accomplishment.

33. Renato Rosaldo (1989) popularized this term in a different context: he uses it to describe the fascination colonizers come to feel for the native

culture they have destroyed in the process of colonization. I am using it to describe the desire of colonizers to relive the "good old days" of colonial wealth, power, and privilege—days that always seem to be bygone.

34. Many European and American tourists found these ruins precisely the most attractive part of Macau; they lent an air of archaic mystery and melancholy to the city that was rare in the bustling modernity of south China.

35. The statue was removed on October 28, 1992, reportedly at the behest of Lu Ping, then vice director of the State Council's Office for Hong Kong and Macao Affairs.

36. For administrative purposes, the Macau peninsula is divided into parishes—a fact that reveals the deep and lasting influence of the Catholic church in the social administration of the city. In addition to Nossa Senhora de Fátima, there are four other parishes on the peninsula: São Lourenço (風順堂區), Sé (大堂區), Santo António (聖安多尼堂區), and São Lázaro (望德堂區). For details, see Wong Hon-keong and Wu 1996: 8–9.

37. This definition is often qualified even in government practice. The head of the Instituto de Acção Social de Macau (IASM or 社會工作司) told me that different government departments have different ways of categorizing new immigrants: her office defined a new immigrant as anyone who arrived from the mainland after 1979, but for the purposes of housing subsidies or welfare payments, some government departments considered anyone who had resided in Macau for seven years or more to be a resident, and those who had been in Macau less than seven years new immigrants.

38. Macau's population statistics, especially those from the 1981 census, are notoriously unreliable (see Matos 1990). Census data reports also vary widely depending on how individual authors interpret such terms as "floating population" and "resident population," and whether and how they include estimates of "illegal immigrants." Figures provided by the Macau Census and Statistics Department indicate that from 1981 to 1996, the resident population grew from 240,000 to 410,000, an increase of 70 percent (Choi and Kou 1998: 37)—much of which was accounted for by amnesties granted to over 130,000 illegal immigrants. As of 1996, the population was officially 415,850, although unofficial estimates put the total at well over 500,000. Some sources estimate that the population had already hit this number in 1988 (see H. Tse 1990: 79).

39. Again, accurate numbers are hard to come by. One 1994 estimate put the number of Fujianese males employed in Macau's construction sector alone at 70,000, or a seventh of Macau's total population (Zheng et

al. 1994: 17). In 1999, another source estimated the total number of Macau residents who identified as Fujianese at 110,000 (Zheng 1999).

40. A total of 108 questionnaires were completed. Because I was not allowed access to the classroom, I prevailed on a history teacher to administer the survey in her classes. Of the 42 who did not respond *oumun yahn*, 35 said they were *Zhongguoren* (Chinese); four indicated a specific place: Xinhui (a county near Macau) 2, Zhongshan 1, and Fujian 1; two left the space blank; and one said he was an earthling (地球人). Of the 66 people who identified themselves as *oumun yahn*, 60 listed their place of birth as Macau; five said they were born in China (Zhongguo), and one in Hong Kong. When asked for their *jiguan* or place of origin, however, not a single person answered "Macau": seven replied "China" (Zhongguo); 14 wrote "Guangdong province," 4 "Hainan province," 3 "Fujian province," 1 "Changsha" (a city in Hunan province); and 30 listed districts in Guangdong province (Zhongshan 13; Xinhui 7; Kaiping 2; and one each from Dianbai, Heyuan, Jiangmen, Doumen, Zhuhai, Taishan, Panyu, and Heshan).

Chapter 6

1. The other nine were the Maritime Museum (opened in 1987); Taipa House Museum (1992); Macau Grand Prix Museum (1993); Wine Museum of Macau (1995); Post, Telephone, and Telegraph Museum; Museum of Sacred Art in the São Paulo Ruins (1997); Sacred Art Treasury in São Domingos Church (1998); Macau Art Museum (1999); and Nature and Agriculture Museum on Coloane.

2. According to Kirk Denton (2005: 566n4), the number of museums in China rose from 365 in 1980 to 1,357 in 1999, with construction continuing or even accelerating into the twenty-first century.

3. Interview on May 30, 1998, in English, from notes written up after the interview. Below, all unattributed quotations from the Architect are taken from this interview.

4. The Architect told me that even the deadline had been negotiable: although it needed to be done before the handover, he himself had decided on the target date of April 1998.

5. See, e.g., S. Crane 2000, Handler 1988, Hevia 2001, Hewison 1991, Kirshenblatt-Gimblett 1998, and Lowenthal 1998.

6. Anagnost 1997, Corner and Harvey 1991, Denton 2005, Flath 2002, Hewison 1991, Hevia 2001, Oakes 2000.

7. David Lowenthal (1994: 41) describes late twentieth-century heritage and identity discourse as "swim[ming] in a self-congratulatory swamp of collective memory."

8. See, e.g., Hevia 2001 and Ma 2001.

9. Indeed, the museum proved to be a cause for government expenditure rather than a source of income. According to the museum's head accountant, based on the income from the first eight months of the museum's existence (April–December 1998), its projected income for all of 1999 would not even be enough to cover the electricity bill for the year (interview July 23, 1999).

10. For a complete account of this incident, see Boxer 1938.

11. The animated representation of the battle was rather diminutive—even cute, if such a word can apply. A group of cartoon ships sails up to shore and a line of dots representing Dutch soldiers disembarks and moves toward the center of the peninsula; a larger dot, representing a cannonball, is lobbed toward them and explodes, sending the soldier-dots helter-skelter back to their ships, which turn tail and sail quickly away. The absence of any mention of who the "residents" were who so valiantly defended their city is particularly ironic in light of Boxer's contention that the Dutch may have chosen to attack Macau when they did precisely because they believed there would be no resistance from ethnic Chinese residents. In 1621, English merchant Richard Cocks (1883: 326–27) wrote, "It is very certen that with little danger our flleet of defence may take and sack Amacon in China, which is inhabeted by Portingales . . . and ¾ partes of the inhabetantes are Chinas. And we are credably informed that, these last two yeares, when they did see but 2 or 3 of our shipp within sight of the place, they weare all ready to run out of the towne." According to Boxer (1938: 21), two days prior to the attack, the Dutch navy sent three officers and a translator to the Chinese settlement in Macau to ascertain whose side the Chinese population would take, or if they would remain neutral; but they encountered "not a single person, and returned without having obtained any information."

12. Clementino Amaro (1998: 132), one of the archaeologists from Portugal who oversaw the excavation of the fort, estimates that the wall was built at the same time as the College of St. Paul's, which was completed in 1606.

13. Interview with Teresa Fu, July 22, 1999 (paraphrased from notes written up after the interview).

14. Denton 2005 notes a similar principle in museums all over China during the same period.

15. In my interviews with museum staff, I often heard assertions as to the thoroughly "local" character of the museum. Cristina quite proudly called it a "homemade museum," and in his speech at the museum's inaugu-

ration, the governor emphasized the fact that "practically the whole museum was conceptualized and realized with recourse to local resources, both human and material, which lends [it] a very specific and genuine character" (Vieira 1998). The idea that the staff was entirely local was something of an overstatement; most of the planning committee members were Portuguese from Portugal, although many of them had lived in Macau far longer than would be necessary to be legal residents. And it was certainly a skewed idea of who "the people of Macau" were: as another staff member (a Chinese woman) pointed out, "in the beginning, there were no Chinese people involved," and when she joined the staff in 1996, none of the documentation was in Chinese, nor was the collections registry set up to be able to handle entries in Chinese. By 1999, this had changed drastically; of the 30-odd full-time staff members (not counting the Filipino security guards), only one was Portuguese, and most of the rest had either been born in Macau or had spent most of their lives there.

16. Interview, in English, June 3, 1998 (from notes written up after the interview).

17. Tape-recorded interview, June 23, 1999, in English.

18. See Ryckmans 1986, who suggests that this lack of appreciation of objects was not a sign of ignorance, but of a peculiarly Chinese attitude toward the past. In explaining the relative dearth of ancient monuments or buildings in China, he argues that "the past which continues to animate Chinese life . . . seems to inhabit the people rather than bricks and stones." See also Mote 1973, who writes that "Chinese civilization did not lodge its history in buildings. . . . The past was a past of words, not of stones." In contrast, Li Zhang (2006) suggests that residents of Kunming do see the built environment—the bricks and stones of their city—as important "containers" for collective memory. She suggests that the tendency to bulldoze old buildings and discard old objects has more to do with ideologies of progress and the linear approach to history entailed in nationalist thinking (in China and elsewhere) than with any essentially "Chinese" way of being in the world.

19. Note the resonance with many mainland museums, which, in the era of "economic reforms," present commerce and the entrepreneurial spirit as two of the "fundamental truths" of the Chinese nation (Denton 2005).

20. Critic Chan Dou (1998d) noted that there was actually no correspondence between the stele, which reads "Imperial Decree," and the Chinese- and Manchu-language document displayed in the cabinet beneath it, which was a mandate conferring a title upon a county official from Guangdong province dating from the Qing dynasty.

21. Lotus Peak Temple, one of the oldest temples in Macau (built in 1592), which served as the accommodations for high-ranking Qing officials visiting Macau—including Lin Zexu 林則徐, who tossed more than two million pounds of opium into the sea just north of Macau.

22. One of the oldest Catholic churches in Macau, whose parish has traditionally been Macanese.

23. The *seuiseuhng yahn*, known more commonly by the pejorative term "tanka" 蛋家, have been described by one anthropologist as "a floating population" in the literal sense: living on their boats, the Cantonese *seuiseuhng yahn* specialized in fishing and water transport, developed distinctive variations of Cantonese folk music, dress, and religious practice, and were regarded as a separate (and despised) social group by the land-based Cantonese (Peixoto 1987; see also E. Anderson 1972). Despite the fact that communities of *seuiseuhng yahn* were scattered all along China's southern coastlines and rivers, several people told me that these *seuiseuhng yahn* were the "real" Macau. When I explained to a full-time docent at the Museum of Macau that I was interested in how museums represented Macau's "unique culture," she told me I was in the wrong place; at the Maritime Museum they had a much more thorough explanation of the *seuiseuhng yahn*, and they were really what made Macau unique. In English- and Portuguese-language books about Macau in the late nineteenth and early twentieth centuries, the women of this community figure especially prominently, since they were known to Europeans as prostitutes and servants. One of the best-known short stories by the best-known Macanese author, Henrique de Senna Fernandes, is a love story between A-Chan, a young *seuiseuhng yahn* sold into prostitution by her destitute parents, and a Portuguese sailor stationed briefly in Macau during World War II (H. Fernandes 1997).

24. The captions point out that because of the constant danger of chain explosions, these factories consisted of a number of small buildings set far apart from one another around a central pond; the door and windows of each building were blocked by walls two or three feet in front of them, so that explosions would be contained. The pond, the spacious surroundings, and plenty of acacia trees for shade, the captions say, created a "park-like" atmosphere.

25. In the museum display, this is romanized as "Hong Kong" Temple Market. I have changed the spelling to avoid confusion, for the name of the temple refers not to the city of Hong Kong, but to the Cantonese nickname of the god Kang Zhen Jun 康眞君, Hong Jan Gwan, dubbed "Venerable Hong" or Hong Gung 康公.

26. Some captions address visitors directly, inviting "you" to remember or imagine or feel. The diorama of the São Francisco Public Garden (加思欄花園) exhibit is one example. By the 1990s, the pagoda that used to be the center of this garden had been rebuilt as a distinctive octagonal structure housing a small library—a well-known but not particularly significant landmark, surrounded by a few bushes and trees. The garden itself had been bisected by a street and paved over for a parking lot. The diorama, however, recreates the public garden as it looked in the 1930s, and the English caption begins: "We hope that this model of the St. Francisco Garden brings back wonderful memories to you." Because Chinese grammar allows the subject of the sentence to be assumed, the Chinese caption does not use the same deictic markers as the English but still conveys the idea that the diorama is intended to allow the viewer to "recall the look and feel of the São Francisco Garden of yesteryear."

27. In the trilingual captions accompanying the exhibit on the diaspora, the term is "Macanese" in English, "Macaense" in Portuguese, and, in Chinese, "澳門人"—that is, the generic term for "Macau people," rather than the specific term *touh saang pou yahn* or "local-born Portuguese," that refers to Portuguese Eurasians in Macau. The paragraph starts by referring to the ethnically unmarked phenomenon of emigration from Macau ("in the middle of the XVII century, the population of Macao, experiencing difficult economic times, was forced to emigrate"), and imperceptibly shifts to discussing diasporic "Macanese" in the narrow sense (rendered in Chinese as 土生葡裔), who maintain ties with their hometown and actively "preserve their cultural identity" through "Casas de Macau." The exhibit shows flags from the twelve Casas de Macau around the world, as well as photographs of reunions and activities they sponsor.

28. It is significant in this regard that when I returned to the Museum of Macau in the summer of 2009 after not having visited for four or five years, all the exhibits on the third floor had been scrapped and the entire floor converted into a space for temporary exhibits.

29. Fantan 番攤 is the name of a game popular in Chinese communities in the nineteenth and early twentieth centuries. It involved placing a large number of buttons, coins, beans, or other objects in a pile while players bet on how many would be left over after the croupier removed as many as he could in groups of four. Crosbie Garstin (1927: 103), a British novelist and travel writer who visited Macau in the mid-1920s, describes Macau's fantan houses, a few dozen of which were licensed by the Macau government: "The table is on the ground floor and a certain number of gamblers can be accommodated about it, but others ascend to the first and second stories

and get a bird's eye view of the table down a well cut through the two floors, so that looking upward you see two circles of faces peering down upon you. Bets are taken up above by attendants who convey the money to and from the table in little baskets swinging on the ends of strings." In the painted backdrop of the museum display, even the fantan clubs appear "cultured" and multiethnic, as European gamblers (in tuxedos and evening gowns) and Chinese gamblers (in "traditional" Chinese gowns) alike sit daintily on the balcony, watching the action below.

30. Interview July 15, 1999. In fact, the language of "peaceful cultural exchange among Europeans and Chinese" that predominated in the Museum of Macau recalls the state-run museum in Chengde, dedicated to demonstrating "the interchanges and harmonies of culture between the Han and Tibetan people" (Hevia 2001: 232).

31. This approach was hardly unusual in late twentieth-century museums. See Walsh 1992 and Kirshenblatt-Gimblett 1998.

32. The stink of salt fish permeating the Porto Interior exhibit calls to mind the horse droppings that are allowed to litter the streets of Colonial Williamsburg, as signs of the authenticity of this representation of the past (Handler and Gable 1997).

33. The museum's most outspoken critic, Chan Dou (1998d), criticized this strategy not because it whitewashed the past, but because its evocative, gap-filled narrative was not pedagogical enough: "After seeing this whole museum," he writes, "visitors would still not have the slightest idea about the more systematic historical changes Macau has undergone over the past 400+ years. . . . My impression is that the designers just divided up a bunch of different objects into categories and piled them up, without a shred of comprehensive consideration about how to display the history of Macau."

34. Gyan Prakash (1992: 171) describes a similar dynamic of recognition at work among "native" visitors to the Madras Museum of the late nineteenth century. This strategy of including "worthless" objects in the museum generally worked, as intended, to produce this kind of shock of familiarity, although on occasion I heard people saying, somewhat derisively, things like "if they want old suitcases, I can give them old suitcases!"

35. From tape-recorded interview, July 8, 1999, in Cantonese.

36. This is a criticism often levied at heritage museums. See, for example, Bob West's (1988) analysis of the Ironbridge Gorge sawmill museum in England: "What angered me about [it] was that the 'reality' it produced actively disorganised and thus rendered illegitimate, any alternative account of what this experience of work amounts to."

37. From tape-recorded interview, June 22, 1999, in Mandarin.

38. The closest I heard to a criticism was in another interview with a group of mainland journalists and educators, who told me they had thoroughly enjoyed the museum but had found the content a bit lacking. One of them attributed this to the fact that because Macau was "only" 400 years old, there wasn't much history to represent.

Chapter 7

1. *Fado* is a genre of Portuguese folk music that is often said to reflect the "soul of the Portuguese nation." The name derives from the Latin *fatum*, or fate, and fado songs are almost always about love, loss, separation, death, and *saudade* (longing).

2. Thus, the phrase 他很有身份 (literally, "he has a lot of *shenfen*") is a comment on the high standing that an individual has achieved in a given field. Occasionally, *shenfen* is also used to translate "identity" in the broader sense. In 1997, Stone Commune published a 24-page booklet entitled "身份/Identity" to accompany an art exhibit of the same name; in this case, it clearly was intended to reference identity in the social scientific sense.

3. Increasingly, in social science work on identity in Chinese or in translations of works from English, the two terms are combined, as *shenfen rentong*. But this is an even more academic phraseology, not a term that anyone in Macau would use to talk about themselves.

4. Newspapers that ran stories about the case included *Macao Daily* 澳門日報, *Va Kio Daily* 華僑報, *Son Pou* 訊報, *Macau Pulse* 澳門脈搏, *Ponto final*, *Macau hoje*, *Jornal tribuna de Macau*, and *O Futuro* in Macau; the *Hong Kong Standard*, *South China Morning Post*, *Ming Pao* 明報, the *Hong Kong Economic Journal* 信報, and *Sing Tao Daily* 星島日報 in Hong Kong, and *United Daily News* 聯合報 in Taiwan, as well as newsletters for theater professionals in Macau and Singapore.

5. I had a small taste of censorship myself when preparing a public talk on my research. In the abstract of the talk, which was circulated to newspapers along with the press release publicizing the event and distributed to the audience at the talk, I described my research as exploring how state and civic actors were trying to "ensure that Macau maintains its unique culture and, as such, its autonomy after 1999." A few days prior to the talk, I received a phone call from the sponsoring organization—a government-run institute—asking my permission to remove the final clause for fear that it would be too political: "We don't like to mention 'culture' and 'autonomy' in the same sentence."

6. Luís de Camões's epic poem, *Os Lusíadas*, completed in 1572, describing the travels of Vasco da Gama's first voyage to India. As Richard Helgerson (1992: 28) notes, the poem "has no single hero . . . it celebrates the deeds of a nation," and does so by representing the motives for Gama's voyage as being the search for glory and honor rather than the search for "Christians and spices" (a quote that is usually attributed to da Gama himself). It has thus become Portugal's national poem—"a representation of who [the Portuguese] have been, who they are, and who they would be"—and Camões has become Portugal's national poet (Helgerson 1992: 36).

7. In fact it is a synopsis of *A Trança feiticeira* by Macanese novelist Henrique de Senna Fernandes (H. Fernandes 1993).

8. This echoes the story of Wallace Nolasco, the protagonist in novelist Timothy Mo's 1978 book *The Monkey King*.

9. This was not the first time I had heard Macau Chinese people tell this story of human-flesh dumplings (人肉餃子)—an urban legend common to virtually every Chinese city I've been in—as a "true story," one that somehow reflected something uniquely terrible about Macau. One informant pointed out to me the very location where the restaurant used to be, indicating that the reason it was now a boarded-up ruin was that no one would rent a building so prone to be haunted by vengeful souls.

10. Interview July 22, 1999, in English, from notes written up after the interview.

11. The ongoing dispute over where the center of Chineseness lay was evident in the way people talked about dialects. On meeting a foreigner who could speak both Mandarin and Cantonese, native Mandarin speakers would often express their appreciation by remarking, "Wah, she can speak both Chinese (中文) *and* Cantonese (粵語)!"; whereas native Cantonese speakers would reverse the terms: "Wah, she can speak both Chinese (中文) *and* Mandarin (國語)!"

12. For other discussions of *renqing* and social relationships in China, see Ambrose King 1989 and Mayfair Yang 1994.

13. All identifying features of this man and his family, including personal names, place-names, and business ventures, have been changed in order to protect their privacy.

14. Ackbar Abbas (1997: 5) makes a more extreme statement about the political orientation (or lack thereof) of flexible citizens: for them, he argues, "the only form of political idealism that has a chance is that which can go together with economic self-interest, when 'freedom,' for example, could be made synonymous with 'free market.'"

15. Tape-recorded interview, November 25, 1997.

16. Ho Yin was one of the most influential residents of Macau in the 1960s and 1970s. A wealthy businessman who made his fortune from gold trading, Ho was head of the Chinese Chamber of Commerce, had a seat on the Macau Legislative Council, and was a delegate to the PRC's National People's Congress. "Thus," writes Steve Shipp (1997: 92), "Ho was a key figure in virtually every major decision affecting Macau, whether instigated by Portugal or China or by Macau itself." Ho's son Edmund was chosen by the PRC to become the first chief executive of the Macau SAR after the handover.

17. Tape-recorded interview, November 25, 1997, in English and Cantonese.

18. As it turned out, this was not the last time Louis was able to visit these graves. The plans for the public park, like so many other plans in this era of constant change, were never realized.

19. Interview March 21, 1998, from notes written up immediately afterward.

20. Interview May 26, 1998, from notes written up immediately afterward.

21. The phrase *renru fuzhong* means, literally, "bearing humiliation, shouldering a heavy load" and is used to describe someone whose circumstances force them to make an unpopular decision.

22. Interview May 26, 1998, from notes written up immediately afterward.

Conclusion

1. I thank Anna Tsing for this insight and for the image of the niche.

2. I later read the full text of the brief speech, in which Jiang (2000) extolled the "friendship between the peoples of China and Portugal and the friendly cooperation between the two countries."

3. From http://whc.unesco.org/en/list/1110 (last accessed March 26, 2007).

Glossary of Cantonese Characters

Character	Pronun-ciation	Mandarin equivalent	Meaning
乜, 乜野	māt, mātyeh	甚麼	what
冇	móuh	沒有	none, have not
叻	lek	聰明, 利害	clever, strong, capable
好似	hou chíh	很像	resembles
佢	kéuih	他/她	he, she
佢哋	kéuihdeih	他/她們	they, them
咁	gám	這樣	so, like this
呢喥	nīdouh	這里	here
呢啲	nīdī	這些	these
畀	béi	給	to give
係	hàih	是	yes, to be
唔	m	不	not, no
得意	dākyi	可愛, 有趣	cute, unique, interesting
㗎	gaa	—	*final particle to make a strong assertion*
嘅	ge	的	*possessive particle*
嘅嗻	ge-ze	—	*final particle to express diminution*

361

Character	Pronun- ciation	Mandarin equivalent	Meaning
咗	jó	了	*indicates completed action*
啲	dī	一點, 一些	some, a few
嗰嗲	gódouh	那里	there
嗰啲	gódī	那些	those

Works Cited

Abbas, M. Ackbar. 1997. *Hong Kong: Culture and the Politics of Disappearance*. Public Worlds, vol. 2. Minneapolis: University of Minnesota Press.

Adamson, Bob, and Siu Pang Li. 1999. "Primary and Secondary Schooling." In *Education and Society in Hong Kong and Macau: Comparative Perspectives on Continuity and Change*, ed. Mark Bray and Ramsey Koo, 35–58. Hong Kong: Comparative Education Research Centre, University of Hong Kong.

Agamben, Giorgio. 1998. *Homo Sacer: Sovereign Power and Bare Life*. Stanford: Stanford University Press.

Alden, Dauril. 1996. *The Making of an Enterprise: The Society of Jesus in Portugal, Its Empire, and Beyond, 1540–1750*. Stanford: Stanford University Press.

Alford, William. 1999. "A Second Great Wall? China's Post-Cultural Revolution Project of Legal Construction." *Cultural Dynamics* 11, no. 2: 193–214.

Almeida, Miguel Vale de. 2004. *An Earth-Colored Sea: "Race," Culture, and the Politics of Identity in the Postcolonial Portuguese-Speaking World*. New Directions in Anthropology, vol. 22. New York: Berghahn Books.

Alves, Jorge Manuel dos Santos. 1996. "Natureza do primeiro ciclo de diplomacia luso-chinesa (séculos XVI–XVIII)." In *Estudos de história do relacionamento luso-chinês*, ed. Antonio Vasconcelos de Saldanha and Jorge Manuel dos Santos Alves, 179–215. Macau: Instituto português do Oriente.

Alves, Manuel Luís. 1990. "O espaço territorial de Macau: identificação, evolução e ocupação." In *Population and City Growth in Macau*, ed. D. Y. Yuan, Wong Hon Keong, and Libânio Martins, 59–77. Macau: Centre of Macau Studies, University of East Asia in association with Macau Census and Statistics Department.

Amaro, Ana Maria. 1988. *Filhos da Terra*. Macau: Instituto Cultural de Macau.

———. 1998. *Das cabanas de palha ás torres de betão: assim cresceu Macau*. Estudos e Documentos. Lisbon: Universidade técnica de Lisboa, Insituto superior de ciências sociais e políticas, and Livros do Oriente.

Amaro, Clementino. 1998. "O Colégio de S. Paulo e a Fortaleza do Monte: intervenção e leitura arqueológicas." In *Um museu em espaço histórico*, ed. Museu de Macau, 114–56. Macau: Museu de Macau.

Anagnost, Ann. 1997. *National Past-Times: Narrative, Representation, and Power in Modern China*. Body, Commodity, Text. Durham: Duke University Press.

———. 2004. "The Corporeal Politics of Quality (*Suzhi*)." *Public Culture* 16, no. 2: 189–208.

Anderson, Benedict R. O'G. 1991. *Imagined Communities: Reflections on the Origin and Spread of Nationalism*. Rev. ed. London: Verso.

———. 1994. "Exodus." *Critical Inquiry* 20, no. 2: 314–27.

Anderson, Eugene. 1972. *Essays on South China's Boat People*. Asian Folklore and Social Life Monographs. Taipei: Orient Cultural Service.

Anderson, Perry. 1962. "Portugal and the End of Ultra-Colonialism" 3 pts. *New Left Review*, nos. 16–18: 84–102.

Ang, Ien. 2000. "Can One Say No to Chineseness? Pushing the Limits of the Diasporic Paradigm." In *Modern Chinese Literary and Cultural Studies in the Age of Theory*, ed. Rey Chow, 281–300. Durham: Duke University Press.

———. 2001. *On Not Speaking Chinese: Living Between Asia and the West*. London: Routledge.

Appadurai, Arjun. 1996. "Sovereignty Without Territoriality: Notes for a Postnational Geography." In *The Geography of Identity*, ed. Patricia Yaeger, 40–58. Ann Arbor: University of Michigan Press.

Appadurai, Arjun, and Carol Breckenridge. 1988. "Why Public Culture?" *Public Culture Bulletin* 1, no. 1: 5–9.

Aresta, António, and Aureliano Barata, eds. 1996. *Liceu nacional de Macau: genealogia de uma escola*. Macau: Direcção dos serviços de educação e juventude.

Aresta, António, Aureliano Barata, and Albina dos Santos Silva, eds. 1997. *Documentos para a história da educação em Macau*. 2 vols. Macau: Direcção dos serviços de educação e juventude.

Asad, Talal. 2004. "Where Are the Margins of the State?" In *Anthropology in the Margins of the State*, ed. Veena Das and Deborah Poole, 279–88. Santa Fe, NM: School of American Research Press.

Auden, W. H. 1939. *Journey to a War*. New York: Random House.

Augé, Marc. 1995. *Non-Places: Introduction to an Anthropology of Supermodernity*. London: Verso.

Bailey, Paul J. 1990. *Reform the People: Changing Attitudes Towards Popular Education in Early Twentieth-Century China*. Edinburgh: Edinburgh University Press.

Balibar, Etienne, and Immanuel Maurice Wallerstein. 1991. *Race, Nation, Class: Ambiguous Identities*. London: Verso.

Barmé, Geremie, and John Minford, eds. 1988. *Seeds of Fire: Chinese Voices of Conscience*. New York: Hill and Wang.

Barthes, Roland. 1957. *Mythologies*. Paris: Éditions du Seuil.

———. 1977. *Image, Music, Text*. New York: Hill and Wang.

Basch, Linda, Nina Glick Schiller, and Cristina Szanton Blanc. 1994. *Nations Unbound: Transnational Projects, Postcolonial Predicaments, and Deterritorialized Nation-States*. Langhorne, PA: Gordon and Breach Publishers.

Basso, Keith. 1996. *Wisdom Sits in Places: Landscape and Language Among the Apache*. Albuquerque: University of New Mexico Press.

Basso, Keith, and Steven Feld, eds. 1996. *Senses of Place*. Santa Fe, NM: School of American Research Press.

Batalha, Graciete. 1977. *Glossário do dialecto macaense*. Coimbra: Imprensa da universidade.

Bender, Gerald. 1978. *Angola Under the Portuguese: The Myth and the Reality*. Berkeley: University of California Press.

Benjamin, Walter. 1968. *Illuminations*. Ed. and with an Introduction by Hannah Arendt. New York: Schocken Books.

Bennett, Tony. 1995. *The Birth of the Museum: History, Theory, Politics*. London: Routledge.

Berlie, Jean, ed. 1999. *Macau 2000*. Hong Kong: Oxford University Press.

Bickers, Robert A., and Jeffrey Wasserstrom. 1995. "Shanghai's 'Dogs and Chinese Not Admitted' Sign: Legend, History and Contemporary Symbol." *China Quarterly*, no. 142: 444–66.

Biersteker, Thomas, and Cynthia Weber, eds. 1996. *State Sovereignty as a Social Construct*. Cambridge Studies in International Relations. Cambridge: Cambridge University Press.

Biolsi, Thomas. 1995. "Bringing the Law Back In: Legal Rights and the Regulation of Indian-White Relations on Rosebud Reservation." *Cultural Anthropology* 36, no. 4: 543–71.

Blu, Karen I. 1996. "'Where Do You Stay At?': Homeplace and Community Among the Lumbee." In *Senses of Place*, ed. Keith Basso and Steven Feld, 197–227. Santa Fe, NM: School of American Research Press.

Bolton, Kingsley, Peter Pau-fuk Ip, and Christopher Hutton. 1996. "The Speech-Act Offense: Claiming and Professing Membership of Triad Society in Hong Kong." *Language & Communication* 16, no. 3: 263–90.

Bourdieu, Pierre. 1987. "The Force of Law: Toward a Sociology of the Juridical Field." *Hastings Law Journal* 38: 814–53.

———. 1991. *Language and Symbolic Power: The Economy of Linguistic Exchanges*. Cambridge, UK: Polity, in association with Basil Blackwell.

Boxer, C. R. (Charles Ralph). 1937[?]. *Expedições militares portuguêsas em auxílio dos Mings contra os Manchus, 1621–1647*. Macau: Escola tipográfica salesiana.

———. 1938. *A derrota dos Holandeses em Macau no ano de 1622*. Macau: Escola Tipográfica de Orfanato da Imaculada Conceição.

———. 1963. *Race Relations in the Portuguese Colonial Empire, 1415–1825*. Oxford, UK: Clarendon Press.

———. 1968. *Fidalgos in the Far East, 1550–1770*. Hong Kong: Oxford University Press.

———. 1969. *The Portuguese Seaborne Empire, 1415–1825*. 1st ed. New York: A. A. Knopf.

———. 1984. *Seventeenth-Century Macau in Contemporary Documents and Illustrations*. Hong Kong: Heinemann (Asia).

Boyajian, James. 1993. *Portuguese Trade in Asia Under the Habsburgs, 1580–1640*. Baltimore: Johns Hopkins University Press.

Boyarin, Jonathan, and Boyarin, Daniel. 1993. "Diaspora: Generation and the Ground of Jewish Identity." *Critical Inquiry* 19, no. 4: 693–725.

Bray, Mark. 1992. "Colonialism, Scale, and Politics: Divergence and Convergence of Educational Development in Hong Kong and Macau." *Comparative Education Review* 36, no. 3: 322–42.

Bray, Mark, and Philip Hui. 1991. "Curriculum Development in Macau." In *Curriculum Development in East Asia*, ed. Colin Marsh and Paul Morris, 181–201. London: Falmer.

Bray, Mark, and Ramsey Koo, eds. 1999. *Education and Society in Hong Kong and Macau: Comparative Perspectives on Continuity and Change*. CERC Studies in Comparative Education, vol. 7. Hong Kong: Comparative Education Research Centre, University of Hong Kong.

Bray, Mark, and Kwok-chun Tang. 1994. "Imported Textbooks, Non-Interventionist Policies and School Curricula in Macau." *Curriculum and Teaching* 9, no. 2: 29–42.

Brenneis, Donald. 1996. "Speaking Law, Making Difference." *Political and Legal Anthropology Review* 19, no. 1: 117–24.

Brown, M. 1985. "Implicit Values in the Social Science Curriculum: Male and Female Role Models." In *Education and Social Stratification in Papua New Guinea*, ed. M. Bray and P. Smith, 176–81: Melbourne: Longman Cheshire.

Brown, Melissa. 2004. *Is Taiwan Chinese? The Impact of Culture, Power and Migration on Changing Identities.* Berkeley: University of California Press.

Brubaker, Rogers. 1992. *Citizenship and Nationhood in France and Germany.* Cambridge: Harvard University Press.

Brubaker, Rogers, and Frederick Cooper. 2000. "Beyond 'Identity.'" *Theory and Society* 29, no. 1: 1–47.

Bruning, Harald. 1998. "Spirit and Soul of Macau Captured at Mountain Fort." *Hong Kong Standard*, February 14.

Burnay, Diogo. 1998. "Mutações e arquitecturas: arquitectura e colonialismo em Macau." *Revista de cultura*, 2d ser., 35/36: 95–106.

Butler, Judith. 1993. *Bodies That Matter: On the Discursive Limits of "Sex."* New York: Routledge.

Camilleri, Joseph, and Jim Falk. 1992. *The End of Sovereignty? The Politics of a Shrinking and Fragmenting World.* Aldershot, Eng.: Edward Elgar.

Cao Yunhua. 2000. "Relations Between Macao and South-East Asia." In *Macao 2000*, ed. Jean Berlie. Hong Kong: Oxford University Press.

Castanheira, José Pedro. 1999. *Os 58 dias que abalaram Macau.* Lisbon: Publicações Dom Quixote and Livros do Oriente.

Castelo, Cláudia. 1998. *O modo português de estar no mundo: o luso-tropicalismo e a ideologia colonial portuguesa (1933–1961).* Biblioteca das ciências do homem. Porto: Edições afrontamento.

Cha, Louis (Jin Yong). 1997. *The Deer and the Cauldron: A Martial Arts Novel.* New York: Oxford University Press.

Chai, Hon-chan. 1977. *Education and Nation-Building in Plural Societies: The West Malaysian Experience.* Canberra: Development Studies Centre, Australian National University.

Chan Dou 陳渡. 1998a. "Jin yu qi wai" 金玉其外 (Skin-deep). *Macao Daily* 澳門日報, July 7.

———. 1998b. "Zainan" 災難 (Disaster). *Macao Daily* 澳門日報, July 8.

———. 1998c. "Yuchun xingjing" 愚蠢行徑 (Idiocy). *Macao Daily* 澳門日報, July 9.

————. 1998d. "Wuming wushi" 無名無實 (Nothingness). *Macao Daily* 澳門日報, July 10.

Chan, Ming K. 1994. "Decolonization Without Democracy: The Birth of Pluralistic Politics in Hong Kong." In *The Politics of Democratization: Generalizing East Asian Experiences*, ed. Edward Friedman, 161–85. Boulder, CO: Westview Press.

Chang, T'ien-tse. 1934. *Sino-Portuguese Trade from 1514–1644: A Synthesis of Portuguese and Chinese Sources*. Leyden: E. J. Brill.

Chau, L. C. 1999. "An Analysis of Postwar Economic Growth in Macau: Lessons on Development Strategy and Prospects." *Portuguese Studies Review* 7, no. 2: 54–67.

Chaves, Jonathan. 1993. *Singing the Source: Nature and God in the Poetry of Chinese Painter Wu Li*. Honolulu: University of Hawai'i Press.

Chen Wenyuan 陳文源. 1996. "*Ming shi lu* Pu Ao shiliao jizai" 〈明實錄〉葡澳史料記載 (Historical materials on Portugal and Macau in the *Veritable Records of the Ming*). *Revista de cultura* 26 [Chinese ed.]: 155–64.

Cheng, Christina Miu Bing. 1999. *Macau: A Cultural Janus*. Hong Kong: Hong Kong University Press.

Chesluk, Benjamin. 2004. "Visible Signs of a City out of Control: Community Policing in New York City." *Cultural Anthropology* 19, no. 2: 250–75.

Chesneaux, Jean. 1971. *Secret Societies in China in the Nineteenth and Twentieth Centuries*. Ann Arbor: University of Michigan Press.

Chesneaux, Jean, ed. 1972. *Popular Movements and Secret Societies in China, 1840–1950*. Stanford: Stanford University Press.

Chio, In Fong 趙燕芳. 1999. "Issue of Nationality of Macao-Born Portuguese"/"Aomen tusheng Puren de guoji wenti" 澳門土生葡人的國籍問題. *China Law/Zhongguo falü* 中國法律, Supplement for Macao's Return/Aomen huigui tekan 澳門回歸特刊: 28–30/ 93–96.

Choi, Fátima, and Kou Chin Pang. 1998. "Intercensal Population Changes in Macau, 1981, 1991 and 1996." In *Macau and Its Neighbors Toward the 21st Century*, ed. Rufino Ramos and D. Y. Yuan, 37–43. Macau: University of Macau and Macau Foundation.

Chow, Rey. 1993. *Writing Diaspora: Tactics of Intervention in Contemporary Cultural Studies*. Arts and Politics of the Everyday. Bloomington: Indiana University Press.

————. 1998. "Between Colonizers: Hong Kong's Postcolonial Self-Writing in the 1990s." In *Ethics After Idealism*, 149–67. Bloomington: Indiana University Press.

————. 2000. "Introduction: On Chineseness as a Theoretical Problem." In *Modern Chinese Literary and Cultural Studies in the Age of Theory,* ed. Rey Chow, 1–25. Durham: Duke University Press.

Chow, Rey, ed. 2000. *Modern Chinese Literary and Cultural Studies in the Age of Theory: Reimagining a Field.* Asia-Pacific: Culture, Politics, and Society. Durham: Duke University Press.

Chow, Tse-tung. 1960. *The May Fourth Movement: Intellectual Revolution in Modern China.* Cambridge: Harvard University Press.

Chu, Shulong. 1996. "National Unity, Sovereignty, and Territorial Integration." *China Journal* 36: 98–102.

Chu, Yiu-kong. 1996. "International Triad Movements: The Threat of Chinese Organized Crime." *Conflict Studies* 291: 1–25.

Chui Sai Peng 崔世平 et al., eds. 1999. *21 shiji Aomen chengshi guihua gangyao yanjiu* 21世紀澳門城市規劃綱要研究 (Twenty-first-century Macau city planning guideline study). Macau: Fundação para a cooperação e desenvolvimento de Macau.

Chun, Allen. 1996a. "From Nationalism to Nationalizing: Cultural Imagination and State Formation in Post-War Taiwan." In *Chinese Nationalism,* ed. Jonathan Unger, 126–47. Armonk, NY: M. E. Sharpe.

————. 1996b. "Fuck Chineseness: On the Ambiguities of Ethnicity as Culture as Identity." *boundary 2* 23, no. 2: 111–38.

Claro, Rogério, and Maria Irene Alves. 1997. *A administração escolar em Macau, 1979–1982.* Macau: Direcção dos serviços de educação e juventude.

Coates, Austin. 1978. *A Macao Narrative.* Hong Kong: Oxford University Press.

Coates, Timothy J. 2001. *Convicts and Orphans: Forced and State-Sponsored Colonizers in the Portuguese Empire, 1550–1755.* Stanford: Stanford University Press.

Cocks, Richard. 1883. *Diary of Richard Cocks, Cape-Merchant in the English Factory in Japan, 1615–1622.* Works issued by the Hakluyt Society, vol. 66. London: Hakluyt Society.

Cohen, Myron. 1994. "Being Chinese: The Peripheralization of Traditional Identity." In *The Living Tree: The Changing Meaning of Being Chinese Today,* ed. Tu Wei-ming, 88–108. Stanford: Stanford University Press.

Collier, Jane, and Liliana Suárez-Navaz. 1997. "Sanctioned Identities: Legal Constructions of Modern Personhood." *Identities* 2, no. 1–2: 1–27.

Comaroff, John. 2001. "Colonialism, Culture, and the Law: A Foreword." In *Law and Social Inquiry* 26, no. 2: 305–14.

Coombe, Rosemary. 1996. "Marking Difference in American Commerce: Trademarks and Alterity at Century's End." *Political and Legal Anthropology Review* 19, no. 1: 105–15.

Cooper, Barry. 1984. "On Explaining Change in School Subjects." In *Defining the Curriculum: Histories and Ethnographies*, ed. Ivor F. Goodson and Stephen J. Ball. London: Falmer Press.

Corner, John, and Sylvia Harvey. 1991. "Mediating Tradition and Modernity: The Heritage/Enterprise Couplet." In *Enterprise and Heritage: Cross-Currents of National Culture*, ed. Corner and Harvey, 45–75. London: Routledge.

Corner, John, and Sylvia Harvey, eds. 1991. *Enterprise and Heritage: Cross-Currents of National Culture*. London: Routledge.

Costa, João Paulo Oliveira e, ed. 1999. *Cartas anuas do Colégio de Macau (1594–1627)*. Macau: Fundação Macau and Comissão territorial de Macau para as comemorações dos descobrimentos portugueses.

Costa, Maria de Lourdes Rodrigues. 1997. *História da arquitectura em Macau*. Colecção documentos & ensaios. Macau: Instituto Cultural de Macau.

Coutin, Susan Bibler. 2000. *Legalizing Moves: Salvadoran Immigrants' Struggle for US Residency*. Ann Arbor: University of Michigan Press.

Coutin, Susan Bibler, and Phyllis Pease Chock. 1997. "'Your Friend, the Illegal': Definition and Paradox in Newspaper Accounts of U.S. Immigration Reform." *Identities* 2, no. 1–2: 123–48.

Crane, George. 1996. "'Special Things in Special Ways': National Identity and China's Special Economic Zones." In *Chinese Nationalism*, ed. Jonathan Unger, 148–68. Australian National University Contemporary China Papers, no. 23. Armonk, NY: M. E. Sharpe.

Crane, Susan A. 2000. *Museums and Memory*. Cultural Sitings. Stanford: Stanford University Press.

Cremer, R. D., ed. 1992. *Macau: City of Commerce and Culture. Continuity and Change*. 2d ed. Hong Kong: API Press.

Cui Zhitao 崔志濤. 1998. "Tusheng guoji wenti sanzhong keneng" 土生國籍問題三種可能 (Three possibilities for the Macanese nationality problem). *Macao Daily* 澳門日報, October 19.

Cunha, Esperança. 1999. "Nacionalidade: porque optar?" *Ponto final*, January 22.

Cunha, Luís Sá. 1998. Editorial. *Revista de Cultura*, 2d ser., 34: 3–4.

Cunha, Vanessa. 1998. *Sobre a identidade e a morte: histórias macaenses*. Colecção cadernos de investigação. Macau: Instituto Cultural de Macau.

Dai Jinhua. 2000. "Imagined Nostalgia." In *Postmodernism & China*, ed. Arif Dirlik and Zhang Xudong, 205–21. Durham: Duke University Press.

Dai Yixuan 戴裔煊. 1987. *Guanyu Aomen lishi shang suowei ganzou haidao wenti* 關于澳門歷史上所謂趕走海盜問題 (Macau history and the so-called expulsion of pirates). Macau: San Kwong Press.

Dannen, Fredric. 1997. "Partners in Crime: China Bonds with Hong Kong's Underworld." *New Republic* 217, no. 2–3 (July 1997): 18–24.

Das, Veena. 2004. "The Signature of the State: The Paradox of Illegibility." In *Anthropology in the Margins of the State*, ed. Veena Das and Deborah Poole, 225–52. Santa Fe, NM: School of American Research Press.

Das, Veena, and Deborah Poole, eds. 2004. *Anthropology in the Margins of the State*. School of American Research Advanced Seminar Series. Santa Fe, NM: School of American Research Press.

Davidson, Basil. 1969. *The Liberation of Guiné: Aspects of an African Revolution*. Foreword by Amílcar Cabral. Middlesex, Eng.: Penguin Books.

Davis, Fei-ling. 1977. *Primitive Revolutionaries of China: A Study of Secret Societies in the Late Nineteenth Century*. Honolulu: University Press of Hawai'i.

Davis, Mike. 1992. *City of Quartz: Excavating the Future in Los Angeles*. New York: Vintage Books.

de Leeuw, Hendrik. 1933. *Cities of Sin*. New York: Willey Book Company.

Deng Kaisong 鄧開頌. 1995. "16–18 shiji Aomen dong-xifang keji wenhua jiaoliu zhi biaoxian ji zuoyong" 16–18世紀澳門東西方科技文化交流之表現及作用 (Technology and cultural exchange between East and West, 16th–18th centuries). In *Aomen jiaoyu, lishi, yu wenhua lunwen ji* 澳門教育,歷史與文化論文集 (Essays on Macau education, history, and culture), ed. Lu Deqi 盧德祺, 172–84. Guangzhou: Xueshu yanjiu zazhi she.

Denton, Kirk. 2005. "Museums, Memorial Sites and Exhibitionary Culture in the People's Republic of China." *China Quarterly* 183: 565–86.

Dicks, Anthony. 1984. "Macao: Legal Fiction and Gunboat Diplomacy." In *Leadership on the China Coast*, ed. Göran Aijmer, 90–128. Studies on Asian Topics, no. 8. London: Curzon Press.

Dikötter, Frank. 1992. *The Discourse of Race in Modern China*. Stanford: Stanford University Press.

Dirks, Nicholas. 1990. "History as a Sign of the Modern." *Public Culture* 2, no. 2: 25–32.

Dirlik, Arif. 1999. "Place-Based Imagination: Globalism and the Politics of Place." *Review: Fernand Braudel Center* 22, no. 2: 151–87.

Dirlik, Arif, and Xudong Zhang, eds. 2000. *Postmodernism & China*. Durham: Duke University Press.

Djao, Wei. 2003. *Being Chinese: Voices from the Diaspora*. Tucson: University of Arizona Press.

Domínguez, Virginia. 1994. *White by Definition: Social Classification in Creole Louisiana*. 2d ed. New Brunswick, NJ: Rutgers University Press.

Douglas, Mary. 1966. *Purity and Danger: An Analysis of Concepts of Pollution and Taboo*. London: Routledge & Kegan Paul.

Dowdle, Michael. 1999. "Heretical Laments: China and the Fallacy of 'Rule of Law.'" *Cultural Dynamics* 11, no. 3: 287–314.

Dreyfus, Hubert Lederer, Paul Rabinow, and Michel Foucault. 1983. *Michel Foucault, Beyond Structuralism and Hermeneutics*. 2d ed. Chicago: University of Chicago Press.

Duara, Prasenjit. 1993. "De-constructing the Chinese Nation." *Australian Journal of Chinese Affairs* 30: 1–26.

———. 1995. *Rescuing History from the Nation: Questioning Narratives of Modern China*. Chicago: University of Chicago Press.

———. 1997. "Nationalists Among Transnationals: Overseas Chinese and the Idea of China, 1900–1911." In *Ungrounded Empires: The Cultural Politics of Modern Chinese Transnationalism*, ed. Aihwa Ong & Donald Nonini, 39–60. London: Routledge.

———. 2001. "The Discourse of Civilization and Pan-Asianism." *Journal of World History* 12, no. 1: 99–130.

———. 2003. *Sovereignty and Authenticity: Manchukuo and the East Asian Modern*. State and Society in East Asia Series. Boulder, CO: Rowman & Littlefield.

Duncan, Carol. 1991. "Art Museums and the Ritual of Citizenship." In *Exhibiting Cultures: The Poetics and Politics of Museum Display*, ed. Karp and Lavine, 88–103. Washington, DC: Smithsonian Institution Press.

———. 1995. *Civilizing Rituals: Inside Public Art Museums*. Re Visions. London: Routledge.

Durão, Luís. 1997. *Na afirmação de uma identidade*. Macau: Instituto Cultural de Macau.

———. 1998. "Cultural Heritage Policy in Macau." Paper presented at the International Symposium on the Culture of Metropolis in Macau, September 14–18, 1998, Macau.

Edkins, Jenny, Nalani Persram, and Véronique Pin-Fat, eds. 1999. *Sovereignty and Subjectivity*. Critical Perspectives on World Politics. Boulder: Lynne Rienner.

Edwards, Anastasia. 1998. "Macau's Rich Past Given a Future." *South China Morning Post*, April 17.

Escobar, Arturo. 2001. "Culture Sits in Places: Reflections on Globalism and Subaltern Strategies of Localization." *Political Geography* 20: 139–74.

Fang, Yi-tao. 1998. "An Opinion on the Choice of the Leading Sector in Macau's Current Economic Development." In *Macau and Its Neighbors Toward the 21st Century*, ed. R. Ramos, R. Wilson, J. R. Dinis, and D. Y. Yuan. Macau: University of Macau and the Macau Foundation.

Farquhar, Judith, and Zhang Qicheng. 2005. "Biopolitical Beijing: Pleasure, Sovereignty, and Self-Cultivation in China's Capital." *Cultural Anthropology* 20, no. 3: 303–27.

Fei Chengkang 費成康. 1988. *Aomen sibai nian* 澳門四百年 (Macao 400 years). Shanghai: Shanghai renmin chubanshe.

Fei Xiaotong 費孝通. 1991. *Xiangtu Zhongguo* 鄉土中國 (Earthbound China). Hong Kong: Sanlian.

Feld, Steven. 1996. "Waterfalls of Song: An Acoustemology of Place Resounding in Bosavi, Papua New Guinea." In *Senses of Place*, ed. Steven Feld and Keith Basso, 91–136. Santa Fe, NM: School of American Research Press.

Feng Zengjun 馮增俊. 1999. *Aomen jiaoyu gailun* 澳門教育概論 (An introduction to education in Macau). Guangzhou: Guangdong jiaoyu chubanshe.

Fernandes, Henrique de Senna. 1993. *A trança feiticeira*. Macau: Fundação Oriente.

———. 1997. "A-Chan, a tancareira." In *Nam van: contos de Macau*, 9–20. Macau: Instituto Cultural de Macau.

Fernandes, Moisés Silva. 2006. *Macau na política externa chinesa, 1949–1979*. Lisbon: Imprensa de ciências sociais.

Ferreira, Eduardo de Sousa. 1974. *Portuguese Colonialism in Africa: The End of an Era*. Paris: UNESCO Press.

Fitzgerald, John. 1995. "The Nationless State: The Search for a Nation in Modern Chinese Nationalism." *Australian Journal of Chinese Affairs* 33: 75–104.

Fitzgerald, Stephen. 1972. *China and the Overseas Chinese: A Study of Peking's Changing Policy, 1949–1970*. Cambridge: Cambridge University Press.

Flath, James. 2002. "Managing Historical Capital in Shandong." *Public Historian* 24, no. 2: 41–59.

Fok, Kai-cheong. N.d. (1996?) *Estudos sobre a instalação dos Portugueses em Macau*. Lisbon: Gradiva; Macau: Museu marítimo de Macau.

———. 1991. "O debate Ming acerca da acomodação dos Portugueses e o aparecimento da 'Fórmula de Macau.'" *Revista de cultura* 16: 13–30.

———. 1996. "The 'Macau Formula' at Work: An 18th Century Qing Expert's View on Macau." In *Estudos de história do relacionamento luso-chinês,* ed. António Saldanha Alves and Jorge dos Santos, 219–34. Macau: Instituto português do Oriente.

Forjaz, Jorge. 1996. *Famílias macaenses*. Macau: Fundação Oriente and Instituto Cultural.

Foucault, Michel. 1978. *History of Sexuality*. New York: Pantheon Books.

———. 1980. *Power/Knowledge: Selected Interviews and Other Writings, 1972–1977*. Ed. Colin Gordon. Brighton, Eng.: Harvester Press.

———. 1997. *Ethics: Subjectivity and Truth*. Ed. Paul Rabinow. Essential Works of Michel Foucault, 1954–1984, vol. 1. New York: New Press.

Foucault, Michel, and Paul Rabinow. 1984. *The Foucault Reader*. Middlesex, Eng.: Penguin Books.

Freitas, Maria Luísa A. V. de. 1999. "Civic Education, Social and Personal Development and Citizenship Education: Changes in Portugal through the 20th Century." In *Young Citizens in Europe*, ed. Alistair Ross. London: CiCe.

Freyre, Gilberto. 1951. *O mundo que o Português criou*. Lisbon: Edições livros do Brasil.

———. 1953. *Um Brasileiro em terras portuguesas: introdução a uma possível luso-tropicologia, acompanhada de conferências e discursos proferidos em Portugal e em terras lusitanas e exlusitanas da Ásia, da África e do Atlántico*. Rio de Janeiro: J. Olympio.

———. 1961. *The Portuguese and the Tropics: Suggestions Inspired by the Portuguese Methods of Integrating Autochthonous Peoples and Cultures Differing from the European in a New, or Luso-Tropical Complex of Civilisation*. Lisbon: Executive Committee for the Commemoration of the Vth Centenary of the Death of Prince Henry the Navigator.

———. 1966. *Casa-grande e senzala: formação da família brasileira sob o regime de economia patriarcal*. 13th ed. Rio de Janeiro: José Olympio.

Friedman, Sarah. 2006. "Watching *Twin Bracelets* in China: The Role of Spectatorship and Identification in an Ethnographic Analysis of Film Reception." *Cultural Anthropology* 21, no. 4: 603–32.

Fung, Anthony. 2001. "What Makes the Local? A Brief Consideration of the Rejuvenation of Hong Kong Identity." *Cultural Studies* 15, no. 3/4: 591–601.

Furber, Holden. 1969. "Asia and the West as Partners Before 'Empire' and After." *Journal of Asian Studies* 28, no. 4: 711–21.

Garstin, Crosbie. 1927. *The Dragon and the Lotus*. New York: Frederick A. Stokes.

Gee, Alison Dakota, and Paulo Azevedo. 1998. "Good Cops, Bad Cops." *Asiaweek*, October 30.

Geertz, Clifford. 1973. "Deep Play: Notes on the Balinese Cockfight." In *The Interpretation of Cultures*, ed. Clifford Geertz, 412–53. New York: Basic Books.

———. 1996. Afterword. In *Senses of Place*, ed. Steven Feld and Keith Basso, 259–62. Santa Fe, NM: School of American Research Press.

Ghai, Yash. 1999. *Hong Kong's New Constitutional Order: The Resumption of Chinese Sovereignty and the Basic Law*. 2d ed. Hong Kong: Hong Kong University Press.

———. 2000. "Autonomy Regimes in China: Coping with Ethnic and Economic Diversity." In *Autonomy and Ethnicity: Negotiating Competing Claims in Multi-Ethnic States*, ed. Yash Ghai, 77–98. Cambridge: Cambridge University Press.

———. 2001. "Citizenship and Politics in the HKSAR: The Constitutional Framework." *Citizenship Studies* 5, no. 2: 143–64.

Gilroy, Paul. 1991. *'There Ain't No Black in the Union Jack': The Cultural Politics of Race and Nation*. Black Literature and Culture. Chicago: University of Chicago Press.

Gladney, Dru. 1994. "Representing Nationality in China: Refiguring Majority/Minority Identities." *Journal of Asian Studies* 53, no. 1: 92–123.

Gomes, Arthur Levy. 1957. *Esboço da história de Macau, 1511–1849*. Macau: Repartição provincial dos serviços de economia e estatística geral (Secção de propaganda e turismo).

Gomes, Luís Gonzaga. 1997. *Macau: um município com história*. Macau: Leal Senado de Macau.

Goodman, Bryna. 1995a. *Native Place, City, and Nation: Regional Networks and Identities in Shanghai, 1853–1937*. Berkeley: University of California Press.

———. 1995b. "The Locality as Microcosm of the Nation? Native Place Networks and Early Urban Nationalism in China." *Modern China* 21, no. 4: 387–419.

Guedes, João. 1991. *As seitas: histórias do crime e da política em Macau*. Macau: Livros do Oriente.

Gunn, Geoffrey. 1996. *Encountering Macau: A Portuguese City-State on the Periphery of China, 1557–1999*. Boulder, CO: Westview Press.

Guo Weidong 郭衛東. 2005. "Jidu jiao yu Zhongguo jindai nüzi mangren jiaoyu" 基督教與中國近代女子盲人教育 (Protestant missions and education for blind women in modern China). *Revista de Cultura* (Chinese ed.) 57: 77–86.

Gupta, Akhil. 1995. "Blurred Boundaries: The Discourse of Corruption, the Culture of Politics, and the Imagined State." *American Ethnologist* 22, no. 2: 375–402.

Haar, Barend ter. 1998. *Ritual and Mythology of the Chinese Triads: Creating an Identity.* Sinica Leidensia. Leiden: Brill.

Hall, Stuart. 1991. "The Local and the Global." In *Culture, Globalization, and the World-System: Contemporary Conditions for the Representation of Identity,* ed. Anthony King, 19–39. Binghamton: SUNY Binghamton, Department of Art and Art History.

Handler, Richard. 1988. *Nationalism and the Politics of Culture in Quebec.* New Directions in Anthropological Writing. Madison: University of Wisconsin Press.

———. 1994. "Is 'Identity' a Useful Cross-Cultural Concept?" In *Commemorations: The Politics of National Identity,* ed. John Gillis, 27–40. Princeton: Princeton University Press.

Handler, Richard, and Eric Gable. 1997. *The New History in an Old Museum: Creating the Past at Colonial Williamsburg.* Durham: Duke University Press.

Hansen, Mette Halskov. 1999. *Lessons in Being Chinese: Minority Education and Ethnic Identity in Southwest China.* Studies on Ethnic Groups in China. Seattle: University of Washington Press.

Hansen, Thomas Blom, and Finn Stepputat. 2001. *States of Imagination: Ethnographic Explorations of the Postcolonial State.* Politics, History, and Culture. Durham: Duke University Press.

———. 2006. "Sovereignty Revisited." *Annual Review of Anthropology* 35: 295–315.

Hardt, Michael, and Antonio Negri. 2000. *Empire.* Cambridge: Harvard University Press.

He, Baogang, and Y. J. Guo. 2000. *Nationalism, National Identity and Democratization in China.* Sydney: Ashgate.

Heberer, Thomas. 1989. *China and Its National Minorities: Autonomy or Assimilation.* Armonk, NY: M. E. Sharpe.

Helgerson, Richard. 1992. "Camões, Hakluyt, and the Voyages of Two Nations." In *Colonialism and Culture,* ed. Nicholas Dirks, 27–64. Ann Arbor: University of Michigan Press.

Helmreich, Stefan. 1992. "Kinship, Nation, and Paul Gilroy's Concept of Diaspora." *Diaspora* 2, no. 2: 243–49.

Hershatter, Gail, and Anna Tsing. 2005. "Civilization." In *New Keywords: A Revised Vocabulary of Culture and Society,* ed. Tony Bennett and Lawrence Grossberg. Malden, MA: Blackwell.

Herzfeld, Michael. 2001. *Anthropology: Theoretical Practice in Culture and Society*. Malden, MA: Blackwell.

Hevia, James. 2001. "World Heritage, National Culture, and the Restoration of Chengde." *positions* 9, no. 1: 219–43.

Hewison, Robert. 1991. "Commerce and Culture." In *Enterprise and Heritage: Cross-Currents of National Culture*, ed. John Corner and Sylvia Harvey, 163–77. London: Routledge.

Hinsley, F. H. 1966. *Sovereignty*. Cambridge: Cambridge University Press.

Hintzen, Geor. 1999. "The Place of Law in the PRC's Culture." *Cultural Dynamics* 11, no. 2: 167–92.

Ho Ping-ti 何炳棣. 1966. *Zhongguo huiguan shilun* 中國會館史論 (A historical survey of *Landsmannschaften* in China). Taipei: Xuesheng shuju.

Honig, Emily. 1992. *Creating Chinese Ethnicity: Subei People in Shanghai, 1850–1980*. New Haven: Yale University Press.

Horsman, Mathew, and Andrew Marshall. 1994. *After the Nation State: Citizens, Tribalism and the New World Disorder*. London: HarperCollins.

Hsia, C. T. 1999. *A History of Modern Chinese Fiction*. 3d ed. Bloomington: Indiana University Press.

Hsia, Tao-tai, and Kathryn A. Haun. 1976. *Peking's Policy Toward the Dual Nationality of the Overseas Chinese: A Survey of Its Development*. Washington, DC: Library of Congress, Law Library.

Hsu, Cho-yun. 1991. "A Reflection on Marginality." *Daedalus* 120, no. 2: 227–29.

Hu Guonian 胡國年. 1994. *Qiantan Aomen jiaoyu zhengce yu ziyuan wenti* 淺探澳門教育政策與資源問題 (On Macau's educational policies and resources). In *Aomen jiaoyu: jueze yu ziyou* 澳門教育：抉擇與自由 (Macau education: continuity and change), ed. Ramsey Koo 古鼎儀 and Ma Qingtang 馬慶堂, 13–23. Macau: Fundação Macau.

Huang Hongzhao 黃鴻釗. 1987. *Aomen shi* 澳門史 (Macau history). Hong Kong: Shangwu yinshuguan.

Huang Qichen 黃啓臣. 1995. "16–19 shiji yi Aomen wei qiao de 'Zhong xue xi jian'" 16–19 世紀以澳門爲橋樑的〈中學西漸〉 (Macau as a bridge for the dissemination of Chinese culture to the West, 16th–19th centuries). In *Aomen jiaoyu, lishi yu wenhua lunwen ji* 澳門教育，歷史與文化論文集 (Essays on Macau education, history and culture), ed. Lu Deqi 盧德祺, 151–71. Guangzhou: Xueshu yanjiu.

———. 1999. *Aomen tong shi: yuangu–1998* 澳門通史：遠古–1998 (General history of Macau: antiquity to 1998). Guangzhou: Guangdong jiaoyu chubanshe.

Hugo-Brunt, Michael. 1954. "An Architectural Survey of the Jesuit Seminary Church of St. Paul's, Macao." *Journal of Oriental Studies* 1, no. 2: 1–21.

Hui, Kwok Fai (Philip), and Lai Man (Helen) Poon. 1999. "Higher Education, Imperialism and Colonial Transition." In *Education and Society in Hong Kong and Macau: Comparative Perspectives on Continuity and Change*, ed. Mark Bray and Ramsey Koo, 99–116. Hong Kong: Comparative Education Research Centre, University of Hong Kong.

Huntington, Samuel. 1993. "The Clash of Civilizations." *Foreign Affairs* 72, no. 3: 22–49.

Ieong, Sylvia. 1994. "Reflections on Language Issues in Macau: Policies, Realities, Prospects." In *Aomen jiaoyu: jueze yu ziyou* 澳門教育: 抉擇與自由 (Macau education: continuity and change), ed. Ramsey Koo 古鼎儀 and Ma Qingtang 馬慶堂. Macau: Fundação Macau.

Ieong Wan Chong, and Chi-sen Ricardo Siu. 1997. *Macau: A Model of Mini-Economy*. Macau: University of Macau Publication Centre.

Instituto Cultural de Macau. 1987. "Editorial." *Revista de cultura* (Portuguese ed.) 2: 5–6.

———. 1998. "Explicação da capa." *Revista de cultura* (Portuguese ed.) 35/36: 2.

Instituto Cultural de Macau, and George Chinnery. 1997. *George Chinnery: Images of Nineteenth Century Macau*. Macau: Instituto Cultural de Macau.

Jesus, C. A. Montalto de. 1902. *Historic Macao*. Hong Kong: Kelly & Walsh.

Jiang Zemin. 2000. Speech by President Jiang Zemin of the People's Republic of China at the Ceremony for the Transfer of Government of Macau Held by the Government of the People's Republic of China and the Government of the Republic of Portugal. In *Aomen lishi yi ke* 澳門歷史一刻 / *The Historic Moment: Macau Handover*, ed. Yiu Ming Poon, 229–31. Hong Kong: Ming Pao.

Jin Guantao. 1988. "The Shadow of History." In *Seeds of Fire: Chinese Voices of Conscience*, ed. Geremie Barmé and John Minford, 133. New York: Hill and Wang

Jing, Jun. 1996. *The Temple of Memories: History, Power, and Morality in a Chinese Village*. Stanford: Stanford University Press.

Jones, Carol A. G., and Jon Vagg. 2007. *Criminal Justice in Hong Kong*. London: Routledge-Cavendish.

Jones, Susan Mann. 1974. "The Ningpo Pang and Financial Power at Shanghai." In *The Chinese City Between Two Worlds*, ed. Mark Elvin and G. W. Skinner, 73–96. Stanford: Stanford University Press.

Jorge, Cecília. 2004. *Macanese Cooking: A Journey Across Generations.* Macau: Associação promotora da instrução dos Macaenses.

Jornal Tribuna de Macau. 1998. *Assembleia popular nacional pronuncia-se sobre a nacionalidade: tudo como dantes.* December 30.

Kalia, N. N. 1980. "Images of Men and Women in Indian Textbooks." *Comparative Education Review* 24: 209–23.

King, Ambrose Yeo-chi 金耀基. 1989. "Renji guanxi zhong de renqing zhi fenxi" 人際關係中人情之分析 (An analysis of *renqing* in interpersonal relationships). In *Zhongguoren de xinli* 中國人的心理 (Chinese psychology), ed. Yang Guoshu 楊國樞, 75–104. Taipei: Guiguan.

———. 1991. "*Kuan-hsi* and Network Building." In *The Living Tree: The Changing Meaning of Being Chinese Today*, ed. Tu Wei-ming, 109–26. Stanford: Stanford University Press.

Kirshenblatt-Gimblett, Barbara. 1998. *Destination Culture: Tourism, Museums, and Heritage.* Berkeley: University of California Press.

Kling, Blair B., and M. N. Pearson. 1979. *The Age of Partnership: Europeans in Asia Before Dominion.* Honolulu: University Press of Hawai'i.

Lam, Agnes. 1998. "Primeiro, sou Macaense." *Ponto final*, July 2, p. 9.

Lamas, Rosmarie Wank-Nolasco. 1998. *History of Macau: A Student's Manual.* Macau: Institute of Tourism Education.

Latham, Robert. 2000. "Social Sovereignty." *Theory, Culture and Society* 17, no. 4: 1–18.

Lazarus-Black, Mindie. 2001. "Law and the Pragmatics of Inclusion: Governing Domestic Violence in Trinidad and Tobago." *American Ethnologist* 28, no. 2: 388–416.

Lazarus-Black, Mindie, and Susan Hirsch, eds. 1994. *Contested States: Law, Hegemony and Resistance.* New York: Routledge.

Leal Senado de Macau. 1992. *Arruamentos da cidade de Macau/Aomen jiedao* 澳門街道. Macau: Leal Senado de Macau.

Lee, Gregory B. 2003. *Chinas Unlimited: Making the Imaginaries of China and Chineseness.* Chinese Worlds. London: RoutledgeCurzon.

Lee, Leo Ou-fan. 1994. "On the Margins of the Chinese Discourse: Some Personal Thoughts on the Cultural Meaning of the Periphery." In *The Living Tree: The Changing Meaning of Being Chinese Today*, ed. Tu Wei-ming, 221–38. Stanford: Stanford University Press.

Lee, Vicky. 2004. *Being Eurasian: Memories Across Racial Divides.* Hong Kong: Hong Kong University Press.

Lei Qiang 雷強 and Zheng Tianxiang 鄭天祥. 1991. "Guanyu Aomen Jiaoyu zhidu jige wenti de tansuo" 關於澳門教育制度幾個問題的探索 (An exploration of some questions about Macau's education system). In

Aomen jiaoyu gaige 澳門教育改革 (Educational reform in Macao)/ *Comunicações do simpósio 'Reforma da educação de Macau,'* ed. Wong Hong Keong 黃漢強, 96–99. Macau: Centro de Estudos de Macau, Universidade da Ásia Oriental.

Levenson, Joseph. 1967. "The Province, the Nation, and the World: The Problem of Chinese Identity." In *Approaches to Modern Chinese History*, ed. R. Murphey, Albert Feuerwerker, and M. C. Wright, 268–89. Berkeley: University of California Press.

Li, Dun Jen, ed. 1969. *China in Transition, 1517–1911*. New York: Van Nostrand Reinhold.

Liao Zixin. 1995. "Modern 'Women's Writing' in Macao." *Revista de cultura*, 2d ser. (English ed.), 5, no. 2: 159–90.

Lilius, Aleko. 1991. *I Sailed with Chinese Pirates*. Hong Kong: Oxford University Press.

Lin Yu-sheng. 1979. *The Crisis of Chinese Consciousness: Radical Antitraditionalism in the May Fourth Era*. Madison: University of Wisconsin Press.

Link, Perry. 1992. *Evening Chats in Beijing: Probing China's Predicament*. New York: W. W. Norton.

Litzinger, Ralph A. 2000. *Other Chinas: The Yao and the Politics of National Belonging*. Durham: Duke University Press.

Liu, Lydia He. 1995. *Translingual Practice: Literature, National Culture, and Translated Modernity—China, 1900–1937*. Stanford: Stanford University Press.

———. 1999a. "Legislating the Universal." In *Tokens of Exchange: The Problem of Translation in Global Circulations*, ed. Lydia He Liu, 127–64. Durham: Duke University Press.

Liu, Lydia He, ed. 1999b. *Tokens of Exchange: The Problem of Translation in Global Circulations*. Durham: Duke University Press.

Liu, Meihui, and Li-Ching Hung. 2002. "Identity Issues in Taiwan's History Curriculum." *International Journal of Educational Research* 37, no. 6–7: 567–86.

Liu, T. M. 2001. *The Hong Kong Triad Societies Before and After the 1997 Change-over*. Hong Kong: Net E-publishing.

Liu, Tao Tao, and David Faure, eds. 1996. *Unity and Diversity: Local Cultures and Identities in China*. Hong Kong: University of Hong Kong Press.

Liu Xianbing 劉羨冰. 1994a. *Shuangyü jingying yu wenhua jiaoliu* 雙語精英與文化交流 (Bilingual elites and cultural exchange). Macau: Fundação Macau.

———. 1994b. *Aomen Sheng Baolu xueyuan lishi jiazhi chu tan* 澳門聖保祿學院歷史價值出探 (On the historical significance of Macau's Colégio de São Paulo). Macau: Instituto Cultural de Macau.

———. 1995. "Di'er ci shijie dazhan qijian de Aomen jiaoyu" 第二次世界大戰期間的澳門教育 (Education in Macau during World War II). In *Jiaoyu zhengwen xuan* 教育徵文選 (Solicited papers on education), ed. Macau Chinese Education Association, 3–17. Macau: Macau Chinese Education Association.

Liu, Xin. 2000. *In One's Own Shadow: An Ethnographic Account of the Condition of Post-Reform Rural China.* Berkeley: University of California Press.

Lo, Jennifer Yiu Chun. 1999. "Curriculum Reform." In *Education and Society in Hong Kong and Macau: Comparative Perspectives on Continuity and Change,* ed. Mark Bray and Ramsey Koo, 135–51. Hong Kong: Comparative Education Research Centre, University of Hong Kong.

Lo, Shiu Hing (Shiu-hing). 1995. *Political Development in Macau.* Hong Kong: Chinese University Press.

———. 2000. "The Politics of the Debate over the Court of Final Appeal in Hong Kong." *China Quarterly,* no. 161: 221–39.

Lopes, Gilberto. 1998. "Grandes empreendimentos para o século XXI." *Revista Macau,* 2d ser., no. 80: 8–35.

Louie, Andrea. 2000. "Re-territorializing Transnationalism: Chinese Americans and the Chinese Motherland." *American Ethnologist* 27, no. 3: 645–69.

———. 2004. *Chineseness Across Borders: Renegotiating Chinese Identities in China and the United States.* Durham: Duke University Press.

Low, Cheryl-Ann, ed. 2002. *Chinese Triads: Perspectives on Histories, Identities, and Spheres of Impact.* Singapore: Singapore History Museum.

Lowenthal, David. 1985. *The Past Is a Foreign Country.* Cambridge: Cambridge University Press.

———. 1994. "Identity, Heritage, and History." In *Commemorations: The Politics of National Identity,* 41–57. Princeton: Princeton University Press.

———. 1998. *Possessed by the Past: The Heritage Crusade and the Spoils of History.* Cambridge: Cambridge University Press.

Lu Deqi 盧德祺, ed. 1995. *Aomen jiaoyu, lishi yu wenhua lunwenji* 澳門教育，歷史與文化論文集 (Essays on Macau education, history, and culture). Guangzhou: Xueshu yanjiu.

Lu, Yu-sun. 1956. *Programs of Communist China for Overseas Chinese.* Communist China Problem Research Series, EC 12. Kowloon, Hong Kong: Union Research Institute.

Lumley, Robert. 1988. *The Museum Time-Machine: Putting Cultures on Display*. London: Routledge.

Ma, Kit-wai. 2001. "Re-advertising Hong Kong: Nostalgia Industry and Popular History." *positions* 9, no. 1: 131–59.

Macau, Equipo do projecto do Museu de, ed. 1998. *Um museu em espaço histórico: a Fortaleza de São Paulo do Monte*. Macau: Museu de Macau.

Macau Government Tourism and Information Bureau. 1979. *Macau: vislumbre de glória / Macau: A Glimpse of Glory*. Hong Kong: Ted Thomas.

Macqueen, Norrie. 1997. *The Decolonization of Portuguese Africa: Metropolitan Revolution and the Dissolution of Empire*. London: Longman.

Magalhães, José Calvet de. 1992. *Macau e a China no após-guerra*. Macau: Instituto português do Oriente.

Mak, Lau-fong. 2002. "The Triads and the Underworld: Solidarity and Change." In *Chinese Triads: Perspectives on Histories, Identities, and Spheres of Impact*, ed. Cheryl-Ann Low. Singapore: Singapore History Museum.

Malkki, Liisa H. 1995. *Purity and Exile: Violence, Memory, and National Cosmology Among Hutu Refugees in Tanzania*. Chicago: University of Chicago Press.

Mamdani, Mahmood. 1996. *Citizen and Subject: Contemporary Africa and the Legacy of Late Colonialism*. Princeton: Princeton University Press.

Manzo, Kathryn. 1996. *Creating Boundaries: The Politics of Race and Nation*. Boulder, CO: Lynne Rienner.

Marreiros, Carlos. 1991. "Traces of Chinese and Portuguese Architecture." In *Macau: City of Commerce and Culture: Continuity and Change*, 2d. ed., ed. R. Cremer, 101–16. Hong Kong: API Press.

———. 1994. "Alliances for the Future." *Revista de Cultura*, 2d ser., no. 20: 162–72.

Maruya, Toyojiro. 1999. "Macroeconomy: Past, Present and Prospects." In *Macao 2000*, ed. J. A. Berlie, 123–44. Hong Kong: Oxford University Press.

Massey, Doreen B. 1994. *Space, Place and Gender*. Cambridge, Eng.: Polity.

Matos, Alice Maria Alvim de. 1990. "Cenários demográficos para Macau." In *Population and City Growth in Macau*, ed. D. Y. Yuan, Wong Hon Keong, and Libânio Martins, 167–83. Macau: Centre of Macau Studies, University of East Asia in association with Macau Census and Statistics Department.

Maurer, Bill. 1996. "Children of Mixed Marriages on Virgin Soil: Citizenship, Descent and Place in the British Virgin Islands." *Political and Legal Anthropology Review* 19, no. 1: 51–58.

————. 1997. *Recharting the Caribbean: Land, Law, and Citizenship in the British Virgin Islands.* Ann Arbor: University of Michigan Press.

Mbembe, Achille. 2003. "Necropolitics." *Public Culture* 15, no. 1: 11–40.

Meagher, Arnold J. 2008. *The Coolie Trade: The Traffic in Chinese Laborers to Latin America, 1847–1874.* Bloomington, IN: Xlibris.

Melville, Herman. 1981. *Moby-Dick.* New York: Bantam Books.

Mendes, Manuel da Silva, ed. 1996. *Manuel da Silva Mendes: a instrução pública em Macau.* Macau: Direcção dos serviços de educação e juventude.

Merry, Sally Engle. 1993. "Legal Vernacularization and Ka Ho'okolokolonui Kanaka Maoli, The People's International Tribunal, Hawai'i 1993." *Political and Legal Anthropology Review* 19, no. 1: 67–82.

————. 2000. *Colonizing Hawai'i: The Cultural Power of Law.* Princeton: Princeton University Press.

Mitchell, Katharyne. 1997. "Transnational Subjects: Constituting the Cultural Citizen in the Era of Pacific Rim Capital." In *Ungrounded Empires: The Cultural Politics of Modern Chinese Transnationalism*, ed. Aihwa Ong and Donald Nonini, 228–58. New York: Routledge.

Mitchell, Timothy. 1988. *Colonising Egypt.* Berkeley: University of California Press.

Miyoshi, Masao. 1993. "A Borderless World? From Colonialism to Transnationalism and the Decline of the Nation State." *Critical Inquiry* 19, no. 4: 726–51.

Mo, Timothy. 1978. *The Monkey King.* London: Abacus.

Moore, Donald. 1998. "Subaltern Struggles and the Politics of Place: Remapping Resistance in Zimbabwe's Eastern Highlands." *Cultural Anthropology* 13, no. 3: 344–81.

————. 2005. *Suffering for Territory: Race, Place, and Power in Zimbabwe.* Durham: Duke University Press.

Moran, Joseph Francis. 1993. *The Japanese and the Jesuits: Alessandro Valignano in Sixteenth-Century Japan.* London: Routledge.

Morbey, Jorge. 1994. "Aspects of the 'Ethnic Identities' of the Macanese." *Revista de cultura*, 2d ser., no. 20: 202–13.

Moreno, Carlos. 1998. "Reutilização da Fortaleza do Monte como museu." In *Um Museu em espaço histórico: a Fortaleza de S. Paulo do Monte*, ed. Museu de Macau, 158–93. Macau: Museu de Macau.

Morrison, Micah. 1998. "The Macau Connection." *Wall Street Journal Interactive Edition* (front section, editorial). http://interactive.wsj.com/edition.../articles/SB888439204883313500.htm.

Mote, F. W. 1973. "A Millennium of Chinese Urban History: Form, Time, and Space Concepts in Soochow." *Rice University Studies* 59, no. 4: 49–53.

Mundy, Peter. 1907. *The Travels of Peter Mundy in Europe and Asia, 1608–1667*. Ed. Richard Carnac Temple and Lavinia Mary Anstey. Works issued by the Hakluyt Society. Cambridge, Eng.: printed for the Hakluyt Society.

Mungello, David E. 1989. *Curious Land: Jesuit Accommodation and the Origins of Sinology*. Honolulu: University of Hawai'i Press.

Murray, Dian H. 1994. *The Origins of the Tiandihui: The Chinese Triads in Legend and History*. Stanford: Stanford University Press.

Ng Lam 伍林. 1997. "Aomen falü bendihua jincheng shuping" 澳門法律本地化進程述評 (Judicial localization in Macau: process and progress). In *Aomen 1997* 澳門 1997 (Macau 1997), ed. Wu et al., 16–21. Macau: Fundação Macau.

Ng, On Cho, and Q. Edward Wang. 2005. *Mirroring the Past: The Writing and Use of History in Imperial China*. Honolulu: University of Hawai'i Press.

Ngai, Gary M. C. 1995. "As perspectivas da preservação e fomento da identidade cultural de Macau no próximo século." *Revista administração* 8, no. 27: 35–48.

———. 1999. "Macau's Identity: The Need for Its Preservation and Development into the Next Century." *Portuguese Studies Review* 7, no. 2: 112–28.

Nogueira, Franco. 1963. *The United Nations and Portugal: A Study of Anti-Colonialism*. London: Sidgwick and Jackson.

———. 1967. *Terceiro mundo*. Lisbon: Ática.

———. 1986. *Um político confessa-se (Diário, 1960–1968)*. Porto: Livraria editora civilização.

Nordstrom, Carolyn. 2000. "Shadows and Sovereigns." *Theory, Culture and Society* 17, no. 4: 35–54.

Oakes, Tim. 2000. "China's Provincial Identities: Reviving Regionalism and Reinventing 'Chineseness.'" *Journal of Asian Studies* 59, no. 3: 667–92.

O'Donnell, Mary Ann. 2001. "Becoming Hong Kong, Razing Baoan, Preserving Xin'an: An Ethnographic Account of Urbanization in the Shenzhen Special Economic Zone." *Cultural Studies* 15, no. 3/4: 419–43.

Ōhmae, Ken'ichi. 1990. *The Borderless World: Power and Strategy in the Interlinked World Economy*. New York: Harper Business.

————. 1995. *The End of the Nation-State: The Rise of Regional Economies.* New York: Free Press.

Ong, Aihwa. 1997. "Chinese Modernities." In *Ungrounded Empires: The Cultural Politics of Modern Chinese Transnationalism,* ed. Aihwa Ong and Donald Nonini. New York: Routledge.

————. 1999. *Flexible Citizenship: The Cultural Logics of Transnationality.* Durham: Duke University Press.

————. 2000. "Graduated Sovereignty in South-East Asia." *Theory, Culture and Society* 17, no. 4: 55–75.

————. 2003. *Buddha Is Hiding: Refugees, Citizenship, the New America.* California Series in Public Anthropology, 5. Berkeley: University of California Press.

————. 2006. *Neoliberalism as Exception: Mutations in Citizenship and Sovereignty.* Durham: Duke University Press.

Ong, Aihwa, and Donald Nonini. 1997. *Ungrounded Empires: The Cultural Politics of Modern Chinese Transnationalism.* New York: Routledge.

Ortet, Luís. 1998. O *Dia seguinte: Macaenses querem continuar Portugueses. Ponto final,* October 30.

Ovalle-Bahamón, Ricardo. 2003. "The Wrinkles of Decolonization and Nationness: White Angolans as *Retornados* in Portugal." In *Europe's Invisible Migrants,* ed. Andrea L Smith, 147–68. Amsterdam: Amsterdam University Press.

Ownby, David. 1996. *Brotherhoods and Secret Societies in Early and Mid-Qing China.* Stanford: Stanford University Press.

Ownby, David, and Mary Heidhues, eds. 1993. *"Secret Societies" Reconsidered: Perspectives on the Social History of Modern South China and Southeast Asia.* Armonk, NY: M. E. Sharpe.

Pearson, M. N. 1987. *The Portuguese in India.* The New Cambridge History of India, vol. 1, pt. 1. Cambridge: Cambridge University Press.

Peerenboom, Randall. 1999. "Ruling the Country in Accordance with the Law: Reflections on the Rule and Role of Law in Contemporary China." *Cultural Dynamics* 11, no. 3: 315–51.

Peixoto, Rui Brito. 1987. "Boat People, Land People: An Approach to the Social Organization of Cultural Differences in South China." *Revista de cultura* (English ed.) 2: 9–19.

Pereira, A. Marques. 1870. *As alfándegas chinesas de Macau.* Macau: Typographia de J. da Silva.

Pereira, Francisco Gonçalves. 1991. "Towards 1999: The Political Status of Macau in the Nineteenth and Twentieth Centuries." In *Macau: City of Commerce and Culture,* ed. R. Cremer, 261–83. Hong Kong: API Press.

Pereira, J. M. Marques. 1995. "O 50° anniversário da morte de João Maria Ferreira do Amaral e da Victoria de Passaleão, 22–25 Agosto de 1849." *Ta-ssi-yang-kuo*, ser. 1, vol. 1–2: 19–30.

Pessoa, Fernando. 1991. *The Book of Disquiet: A Selection.* London: Quartet Books.

Pina-Cabral, João de. 1989. "Sociocultural Differentiation and Regional Identity in Portugal." In *Iberian Identity: Essays on the Nature of Identity in Portugal and Spain*, ed. R. Herr and J. Polt, 3–18. Institute of International Studies Research Series, no. 75. Berkeley: Institute of International Studies, University of California, Berkeley.

———. 1994. "Personal Identity and Ethnic Ambiguity: Naming Practices Among the Eurasians of Macao." *Social Anthropology* 2, no. 2: 115–32.

———. 2002. *Between China and Europe: Person, Culture and Emotion in Macao.* London School of Economics Monographs on Social Anthropology, vol. 74. London: Continuum.

Pina-Cabral, João de, and Nelson Lourenço. 1993. *Em terra de tufões: dinâmicas da etnicidade macaense.* Macau: Instituto Cultural de Macau.

Pinto, Fernão Mendes. 1996. *Peregrinação.* Mem Martins, Portugal: Publicações Europa-América.

Pires, Benjamin Videira. 1988. *Os extremos conciliam-se.* Macau: Instituto Cultural de Macau.

Pittis, Donald, and Susan Henders, eds. 1997. *Macao: Mysterious Decay and Romance.* Hong Kong: Hong Kong University Press.

Porter, Jonathan. 1996. *Macau, the Imaginary City: Culture and Society, 1557 to the Present.* Boulder, CO: Westview Press.

Potter, Pitman B. 1994. "Riding the Tiger: Legitimacy and Legal Culture in Post-Mao China." *China Quarterly*, no. 138: 325–58.

———. 2001. *The Chinese Legal System: Globalization and Local Legal Culture.* Routledge Studies on China in Transition, 11. London: RoutledgeCurzon.

Povinelli, Elizabeth. 1998. "The State of Shame: Australian Multiculturalism and the Crisis of Indigenous Citizenship." *Critical Inquiry* 24, no. 2: 575–610.

Prakash, Gyan. 1992. "Science Gone Native in Colonial India." *Representations* 40: 153–78.

Prescott, Jon, ed. 1993. *Macaensis Momentum—A Fragment of Architecture: A Moment in the History of the Development of Macau.* Macau: Hewell Publications.

Prochaska, David. 1990. *Making Algeria French: Colonialism in Bône, 1870–1920.* Cambridge: Cambridge University Press.

Ptak, Roderich. 1998. "Macau: China's Window to the Latin World?" Paper presented at the International Symposium on the Culture of Metropolis in Macau, September 14–18, 1998, Macau.

Pye, Lucien. 1993. "How China's Nationalism Was Shanghaied." *Australian Journal of Chinese Affairs* 29: 107–33.

Radhakrishnan, R. 1995. "Toward an Eccentric Cosmopolitanism." *positions* 3, no. 3: 814–21.

Raffles, Hugh. 2002. *In Amazonia: A Natural History*. Princeton: Princeton University Press.

Ramírez, Manuel Becerra. 2000. "Nationality in Mexico." In *From Migrants to Citizens: Membership in a Changing World*, ed. Douglas Klusmeyer and T. Alexander Aleinikoff, 312–41. Washington, DC: Carnegie Endowment for International Peace.

Ramos, Rufino, D. Y. Yuan, José Rocha Dinis, and Rex Wilson, eds. 1997. *Macau and Its Neighbors in Transition*. Macau: Faculty of Social Sciences and Humanities, University of Macau.

Rangel, Jorge. 1991. "Prospects and Directions for Education." In *Macau: City of Commerce and Culture*, 2d ed., ed. R. Cremer, 315–22. Hong Kong: API Press.

Reed-Danahay, Deborah. 1996. *Education and Identity in Rural France: The Politics of Schooling*. Cambridge: Cambridge University Press.

Reisman, W. Michael. 1990. "Sovereignty and Human Rights in Contemporary International Law." *American Journal of International Law* 84, no. 4: 866–76.

Ricci, Matteo. 1953. *China in the Sixteenth Century: The Journals of Matthew Ricci, 1583–1610*. New York: Random House.

Riles, Annelise. 2000. *The Network Inside Out*. Ann Arbor: University of Michigan Press.

Rocha, Rui. 1995. "O reconhecimento dos cursos superiores em Macau e a localização da administração." *Revista administração* 8, no. 30: 739–49.

Rofel, Lisa. 1994. "'Yearnings': Televisual Love and Melodramatic Politics in Contemporary China." *American Ethnologist* 21, no. 4: 700–722.

———. 1999. *Other Modernities: Gendered Yearnings in China After Socialism*. Berkeley: University of California Press.

———. 2001. "Discrepant Modernities and Their Discontents." *positions* 9, no. 3: 637–49.

Rosa, Alexandre. 1991. "A situação da educação em Macau e a necessidade da reforma." In *Aomen jiaoyu gaige (yantao hui wenji)* 澳門教育改革(研討會文集)/Comunicações do simpósio "Reforma da Educação de Macau" (Educational reform in Macao [symposium papers]), ed. Wong Hon

Keong, 31–36. Macau: Center for Macau Studies, University of East Asia.

Rosaldo, Renato. 1989. *Culture and Truth: The Remaking of Social Analysis.* Boston: Beacon Press.

Ross, Andrew. 1994. *A Vision Betrayed: The Jesuits in Japan and China, 1542–1742.* Edinburgh: Edinburgh University Press.

Ross, Robert, and Gerard J. Telkamp. 1985. *Colonial Cities.* Dordrecht: Martinus Nijhoff Publishers.

Rotenberg, Robert. 2001. "Metropolitanism and the Transformation of Urban Space in Nineteenth-Century Colonial Metropoles." *American Anthropologist* 103, no. 1: 7–15.

Rouse, Roger. 1995. "Thinking Through Transnationalism." *Public Culture* 7: 403–31.

Rowe, William T. 1984. *Hankow: Commerce and Society in a Chinese City, 1796–1889.* Stanford: Stanford University Press.

Ryckmans, Pierre. 1986. *The Chinese Attitude towards the Past.* The Forty-Seventh George Ernest Morrison Lecture in Ethnology. Canberra: Australian National University.

Sá Cunha, Luís. 1998. "Editorial." *Revista de cultura,* 2d ser., 34: 3–4.

Saldanha, António Vasconcelos de. 1996a. "O problema da interpretação do tratado de 1887 no respeitante à questão da soberania portuguesa em Macau: elementos para uma leitura renovada do n.° 1 do artigo 292.° da constituição da República Portuguesa." *Revista jurídica de Macau* 3, no. 2: 47–90.

———. 1996b. "'Aproximar Portugal e a China num entendimento amistoso': as ofensivas diplomáticas chinesas para a compra de Macau—contributo para o estudo das missões do Zongli Yamen ao Ocidente (1868–1891)." In *Estudos de história do relacionamento luso-chinês, séculos XVI–XIX,* ed. António Vasconcelos de Saldanha and Jorge Manuel dos Santos Alves, 279–397. Colecção memória do Oriente. Macau: Instituto Português do Oriente.

Santos, Boaventura de Sousa, and Conceição Gomes. 1998. *Macau: O pequiníssimo dragão.* Lisbon: Fundação Oriente.

Sassen, Saskia. 1996. *Losing Control? Sovereignty in an Age of Globalization.* University Seminars/Leonard Hastings Schoff Memorial Lectures. New York: Columbia University Press.

Schaub, Jean-Frédéric. 2001. *Portugal na Monarquia Hispânica (1580–1640).* Colecção temas de história de Portugal. Lisbon: Livros horizonte.

Schein, Louisa. 2000. *Minority Rules: The Miao and the Feminine in China's Cultural Politics*. Body, Commodity, Text. Durham: Duke University Press.

Schwarcz, Vera. 1994. "No Solace from Lethe: History, Memory and Cultural Identity in Twentieth-Century China." In *The Living Tree: The Changing Meaning of Being Chinese Today*, ed. Tu Wei-ming, 64–87. Stanford: Stanford University Press.

Scott, Ian. 1989. *Political Change and the Crisis of Legitimacy in Hong Kong*. Honolulu: University of Hawai'i Press.

Scott, James C. 1998. *Seeing Like a State: How Certain Schemes to Improve the Human Condition Have Failed*. Yale ISPS Series. New Haven: Yale University Press.

Scott, Joan. 1991. "The Evidence of Experience." *Critical Inquiry* 17, no. 4: 773–97.

Searle, John. 1989. "How Performatives Work." *Linguistics and Philosophy* 12, no. 5: 535–58.

Segal, Daniel. 2000. "'Western Civ' and the Staging of History in American Higher Education." *American Historical Review* 105, no. 3: 770–805.

———. 2005. "Worlding History." In *Looking Backward and Looking Forward: Perspectives on Social Science History*, ed. Harvey Graff, Leslie Page Moch, and Philip McMichael with Julia Woesthoff, 81–98. Madison: University of Wisconsin Press.

Sharma, Aradhana, and Akhil Gupta, eds. 2006. *The Anthropology of the State: A Reader*. Blackwell Readers in Anthropology, 9. Malden, MA: Blackwell.

Shi, Anbin. 2003. *A Comparative Approach to Redefining Chinese-ness in the Era of Globalization*. Chinese Studies, vol. 28. Lewiston, NY: Edwin Mellen Press.

Shih, Chih-yu. 2002. *Negotiating Ethnicity in China: Citizenship as a Response to the State*. Routledge Studies on China in Transition. London: Routledge.

Shipp, Steve. 1997. *Macau, China: A Political History of the Portuguese Colony's Transition to Chinese Rule*. Jefferson, NC: McFarland.

Silva, Beatriz Basto da. 1986. *Elementos de história de Macau*, vol. 1. Macau: Direcção dos serviços de educação.

———. 1994. *Emigração de cules: dossier Macau, 1851–1894*. Macau: Fundação Oriente.

Silva, F. A. (Jim). 1979. *All Our Yesterdays: The Sons of Macao, Their History and Heritage*. San Francisco: UMA, of California.

Silva, Jorge. 1999. "É e não é." *Jornal tribuna de Macau*, January 19.

Simões, Rui. 1993a. "A língua portuguesa na dinâmica associativa da comunidade macaense." In *Actas do encontro português—língua de cultura*, 217–28. Macau: Instituto português do Oriente.

———. 1993b. "Uma educação para a diáspora: os discursos sobre a instrução em Macau em finais do século XIX." *Administração* 22: 821–29.

Siu, Helen. 1996. "Remade in Hong Kong: Weaving into the Chinese Cultural Tapestry." In *Unity and Diversity: Local Cultures and Identities in China*, ed. Tao Tao Liu and David Faure, 177–96. Hong Kong: Hong Kong University Press.

Siu, Lok. 2001. "Diasporic Cultural Citizenship: Chineseness and Belonging in Central America and Panama." *Social Text* 19, no. 4: 7–28.

Skidmore, Thomas. 1993. *Black into White: Race and Nationality in Brazilian Thought.* Durham: Duke University Press.

Smart, Alan. 2001. "Unruly Places: Urban Governance and the Persistence of Illegality in Hong Kong's Urban Squatter Areas." *American Anthropologist* 103, no. 1: 30–44.

So Chiu Fai 蘇朝暉. 1994. "Aomen de jiaoyu caizheng" 澳門的教育財政 "Educational policies and financial resource allocations in Macau." In *Aomen jiaoyu: jueze yu ziyou* 澳門教育: 抉擇與自由 (Macau education: continuity and change), ed. Ramsey Koo 古鼎儀 and Ma Qingtang 馬慶堂, 1–12. Macau: Fundação Macau.

So, Kwan-wai. 1975. *Japanese Piracy in Ming China During the Sixteenth Century.* East Lansing: Michigan State University Press.

Souza, George Bryan. 1986. *The Survival of Empire: Portuguese Trade and Society in the South China Sea, 1630–1754.* Cambridge: Cambridge University Press.

Spence, Jonathan. 1999. *The Search for Modern China.* 2d ed. New York: Norton.

———. 2001. *Treason by the Book.* New York: Viking.

Spence, Jonathan, and John E. Wills, Jr., eds. 1979. *From Ming to Ch'ing: Conquest, Region, and Continuity in the Seventeenth Century.* New Haven: Yale University Press.

Stewart, Kathleen. 1996. *A Space on the Side of the Road.* Princeton: Princeton University Press.

Stoler, Ann Laura. 2002. *Carnal Knowledge and Imperial Power: Race and the Intimate in Colonial Rule.* Berkeley: University of California Press.

Subrahmanyam, Sanjay. 1993. *The Portuguese Empire in Asia, 1500–1700: A Political and Economic History.* London: Longman.

Tam, Camões 譚志強. 1994. Aomen zhuquan wenti shimo, 1553–1993 澳門主權問題始末, 1553–1993 (Disputes between China and Portugal concerning Macau's sovereignty, 1553–1993). Xueshu yanjiu congshu 5. Taipei: Yong ye.

Tan, Eugene K. B. 2001. "From Sojourners to Citizens: Managing the Ethnic Chinese Minority in Indonesia and Malaysia." *Ethnic and Racial Studies* 24, no. 6: 949–78.

Tan, John Kang. 1993. "History of the History Curriculum Under Colonialism and Decolonization: A Comparison Between Hong Kong and Macau." M.Ed. thesis, University of Hong Kong.

Tang, Fun Hei (Joan), and Keith Morrison. 1998. "When Marketisation Does Not Improve Schooling: The Case of Macau." *Compare* 28, no. 3: 245–62.

Tang Kaijian 湯開建. 1996. "Du Zhen 'Yue-Min xun shi jilüe' zhong de Aomen shiliao yanjiu" 杜臻《粵閩巡視紀略》中的澳門史料研究 (Historical materials on Macau in Du Zhen's "Brief Notes on the Inspection Tour of Guangdong and Fujian"). *Revista de cultura* (Chinese ed.) 27–28: 37–44.

———. 1997. "Tian Shengjin 'An Yue shugao' zhong de Aomen shiliao" 田生金《按粵疏稿》中的澳門史料 (Historical materials on Macau in Tian Shengjin's "Memorial from Guangdong"). *Revista de cultura* (Chinese ed.) 33: 45–53.

Tang, Kwok Chun. 1998. "The Development of Education in Macau." In *Macau and Its Neighbors Towards the 21st Century*, ed. Rufino Ramos, 221–38. Macau: University of Macau and Macau Foundation.

Tao, Chengzhang 陶成章. 1981. "The Evolution of China's Secret Sects and Societies." Trans. Teng Ssu-yu. *Renditions* 15: 80–102.

Taussig, Michael T. 1987. *Shamanism, Colonialism and the Wild Man: A Study in Terror and Healing*. Chicago: University of Chicago Press.

———. 1997. *The Magic of the State*. New York: Routledge.

Taylor, Bruce. 1994. "Planning for High-Concentration Development: Reclamation Areas in Macau." In *Population and Development in Macau*, ed. Rufino Ramos et al., 59–74. Macau: University of Macau and Macau Foundation.

Texieira, Manuel. 1962. "The So-called Slave Trade at Macao." In *Proceedings of the International Association of Historians of Asia, Second Biennial Conference*. Taipei: October 6.

———. 1982. *A Educação em Macau*. Macau: Direcção dos serviços de educação e cultura.

Teixeira, Manuel, and Beatriz Basto da Silva. 1998. "Protagonismo histórico, militar e civil da Fortaleza do Monte." In *Um museu em espaço histórico: a Fortaleza de S. Paulo do Monte*, ed. Equipa do projecto do Museu de Macau, 78–94. Macau: Museu de Macau.

Thongchai, Winichakul. 1994. *Siam Mapped: A History of the Geo-Body of a Nation*. Honolulu: University of Hawai'i Press.

Tölölyan, Khachig. 1991. "The Nation-State and Its Others: In Lieu of a Preface." *Diaspora* 1, no. 1: 3–7.

Ts'ao, Ignatius. 1999. "The Portuguese and the Law in Macau: Past, Present and Future." *Portuguese Studies Review* 7, no. 2: 67–79.

Tse, Hon-Kong. 1990. "Population and Economic Development in Macau." In *Population and City Growth in Macau*, ed. D. Y. Yuan, Wong Hon Keong, and Libânio Martins, 79–102. Macau: Centre of Macau Studies, University of East Asia in association with Macau Census and Statistics Department.

Tse, Raymond Y. C. 1999. "Real Estate and the Housing Market." In *Macau 2000*, ed. Jean Berlie, 145–61. Hong Kong: Oxford University Press.

Tsin, Michael. 1999. *Nation, Governance, and Modernity in China*. Stanford: Stanford University Press.

Tsing, Anna Lowenhaupt. 1993. *In the Realm of the Diamond Queen: Marginality in an Out-of-the-Way Place*. Princeton: Princeton University Press.

———. 2000. "Inside the Economy of Appearances." *Public Culture* 12, no. 1: 115–44.

———. 2004. *Friction: An Ethnography of Global Connection*. Princeton: Princeton University Press.

Tu Weiming (Wei-ming). 1979. "Shifting Perspectives on Text and History: A Reflection on Shelly Errington's Paper." *Journal of Asian Studies* 38, no. 2: 245–51.

———. 1994a. "Cultural China: The Periphery as Center." In *The Living Tree: The Changing Meaning of Being Chinese Today*, ed. Tu Wei-ming, 1–30. Stanford: Stanford University Press.

———. 1996. "Cultural Identity and the Politics of Recognition in Contemporary Taiwan." *China Quarterly*, no. 148 (December): 1115–40.

Tu Wei-ming, ed. 1994b. *The Living Tree: The Changing Meaning of Being Chinese Today*. Stanford: Stanford University Press.

Tuan, Yi-fu. 1996. *Cosmos and Hearth: A Cosmopolite's Viewpoint*. Minneapolis: University of Minnesota Press.

Tuna Macaense. 1994. *Macau sã assi*. Lisbon: Tradisom.

Turner, Victor. 1967. "Betwixt and Between: The Liminal Period in *Rites de Passage*." In *The Forest of Symbols: Aspects of Ndembu Ritual*, 93–111. Ithaca: Cornell University Press.

Unger, Jonathan, ed. 1993. *Using the Past to Serve the Present: Historiography and Politics in Contemporary China*. Armonk, NY: M. E. Sharpe.

Van Ness, Peter. 1970. *Revolution and Chinese Foreign Policy: Peking's Support for Wars of National Liberation*. Berkeley: University of California Press.

Vickers, Edward. 2002. "The Politics of History Education in Hong Kong: The Case of Local History." *International Journal of Educational Research* 37, no. 6–7: 587–602.

———. 2003. *In Search of an Identity: The Politics of History as a School Subject in Hong Kong, 1960s–2002*. East Asia History, Politics, Sociology, Culture. New York: Routledge.

Vieira, Vasco Rocha. 1998. *Discurso de sua excelência o governador de Macau, General Vasco Rocha Vieira, na cerimónia de inauguração do Museu de Macau*. Speech, April 18, 1998. Printed text distributed at opening of the Musuem of Macau.

Wade, Geoff. 1997. "Melaka in Ming Dynasty Texts." *Journal of the Malaysian Branch of the Royal Asiatic Society* 70, no. 1: 31–69.

Wakeman, Frederic. 1972. "The Secret Societies of Kwangtung, 1800–1856." In *Nothing Concealed: Essays in Honor of Liu Yü-Yun*, ed. Frederic Wakeman, 129–60. Chinese Materials and Research Aids Service Center Occasional Series 4. Taipei: Ch'eng wen ch'u pan she.

Waldron, Arthur. 1993. "Representing China: The Great Wall and Cultural Nationalism in the Twentieth Century." In *Cultural Nationalism in East Asia*, ed. Harumi Befu, 36–60. Berkeley: Institute of East Asian Studies, University of California.

Walsh, Kevin. 1992. *The Representation of the Past: Museums and Heritage in a Post-Colonial World*. London: Routledge.

Wang, Edward Q. 2001. *Inventing China Through History: The May Fourth Approach to Historiography*. SUNY Series in Chinese Philosophy and Culture. Albany: State University of New York Press.

Wang, Gungwu. 1981. "On the Origins of Hua-ch'iao." In *Community and Nation: Essays on Southeast Asia and the Chinese*, ed. Wang Gungwu, 118–27. Singapore: Published for the Asian Studies Association of Australia by Heinemann Educational Books (Asia).

———. 1988. "The Study of Chinese Identities in Southeast Asia." In *Changing Identities of the Southeast Asian Chinese Since World War II*, ed. Jennifer Cushman and Wang Gungwu, 1–19. Hong Kong: University of Hong Kong Press.

———. 1991. *The Chineseness of China: Selected Essays*. Hong Kong: Oxford University Press.

———. 1994. "Among Non-Chinese." In *The Living Tree: The Changing Meaning of Being Chinese Today*, ed. Tu Wei-ming, 127–46. Stanford: Stanford University Press.

Wang, Jiangyu. 2001. "China and the Universal Human Rights Standards." *Syracuse Journal of International Law and Commerce* 29: 135–58.

Wang, Jing. 1996. *High Culture Fever: Politics, Aesthetics, and Ideology in Deng's China*. Berkeley: University of California Press.

Watson, James, and Evelyn Rawski, eds. 1988. *Death Ritual in Late Imperial and Modern China*. Berkeley: University of California Press.

Watson, Rubie. 1998. "Tales of Two 'Chinese' History Museums: Taipei and Hong Kong." *Curator* 41, no. 3: 167–77.

———. 2004. "Palaces, Museums, and Squares: Chinese National Spaces." *Museum Anthropology* 19, no. 2: 7–19.

Weller, Robert Paul. 2001. *Alternate Civilities: Democracy and Culture in China and Taiwan*. Westview Press.

Wen Yiduo 聞一多. 2000. *Qi zi zhi ge: Wen Yiduo shi jingxuan* 七子之歌: 聞一多詩精選 (Songs of the seven sons: the best poetry of Wen Yiduo). Taiyuan: Beiyue wenyi.

West, Bob. 1988. "The Making of the English Working Past: A Critical View of the Ironbridge Gorge Museum." In *The Museum Time-Machine: Putting Cultures on Display*, ed. Robert Lumley, 36–62. London: Routledge.

Wheeler, Douglas. 1978. *Republican Portugal: A Political History, 1910–1926*. Madison: University of Wisconsin Press.

Williams, Brackette. 1995. "Classification Systems Revisited." In *Naturalizing Power*, ed. Sylvia Yanagisako and Carol Delaney, 201–36. New York: Routledge.

Williams, Patricia. 1991. *The Alchemy of Race and Rights: Diary of a Law Professor*. Cambridge: Harvard University Press.

Willis, Paul. 1981. *Learning to Labour: How Working Class Kids Get Working Class Jobs*. New York: Columbia University Press.

Wills, John E., Jr. 1979. "Maritime China from Wang Chih to Shih Lang: Themes in Peripheral History." In *From Ming to Ch'ing: Conquest, Region, and Continuity in the Seventeenth Century*, ed. Jonathan Spence and John E. Wills, Jr., 203–38. New Haven: Yale University Press.

Wittgenstein, Ludwig. 1997. *Philosophical Investigations*. Trans. G. E. M. Anscombe. 2d ed. Oxford, Eng.: Blackwell.

Wong Chao Son 黃就順, Deng Hanzeng 鄧漢增, and Huang Junxin 黃鈞燊. 1997. *Aomen ditu ji* 澳門地圖集 / *Atlas de Macau* / *Macau Atlas*. Macau: Fundação Macau.

Wong Hon-keong 黄漢強 and Wu Zhiliang 吳志良, eds. 1996. *Aomen zonglan* 澳門總覽 (Panorama of Macau). 2d ed. Macau: Fundação Macau.

Wong, Shiu-kwan. 1998. "Uma mistura de influências portuguesas e chinesas no património de Macau." *Revista de cultura*, 2d ser., 35/36: 9–75.

Wong Yau Kwan 黄有鈞. 1990. "You Zhonghua renmin gongheguo di Aomen de xin yimin yu xianshi shehui de guanxi" 由中華人民共和國抵澳門的新移民與現時社會的關係 (The new immigrants from the People's Republic of China in Macau). In *Population and City Growth in Macau*, ed. D. Y. Yuan, Wong Hon Keong, and Libânio Martins, 167–83. Macau: Centre of Macau Studies, University of East Asia in association with Macau Census and Statistics Department.

Wu, David Yen-ho. 1994. "The Construction of Chinese and Non-Chinese Identities." In *The Living Tree: The Changing Meaning of Being Chinese Today*, ed. Tu Wei-ming, 148–66. Stanford: Stanford University Press.

Wu Zhiliang 吳志良. 1994. 青年與澳門未來 / *A juventude e o futuro de Macau / Youth and the Future of Macau*. Macau: Fundação Macau.

———. 1996. *Dong-xi jiaohui kan aomen* 東西交匯看澳門 (East meets West in Macau). Macau: Fundação Macau.

Wu Zhiliang 吳志良 and Ieong Wan Chong 楊允中, eds. 1999. *Aomen Baike Quanshu* 澳門百科全書 (Encyclopedia of Macau). Macau: Fundação Macau.

Xinhua she. 1999. "China on State Sovereignty and Human Rights." *People's Daily Online*, http://english.people.com.cn/english/199911/10/eng19991110N161.html.

Xu, Ben. 1998. "'From Modernity to Chineseness': the Rise of Nativist Cultural Theory in Post-1989 China." *positions: east asia cultures critique* 6, no. 1: 203–37.

Xu Jieshun 徐杰舜 and Tang Kaijian 湯開建. 2000. "Guanyu Aomen tusheng Puren wenti de sikao" 關于澳門土生葡人問題的思考 (Some reflections on the Macanese problem). *Minzu yanjiu* 128: 45–53.

Yan, Yunxiang. 1996. "The Culture of Guanxi in a North China Village." *China Journal* 35: 1–25.

Yang, Mayfair Mei-hui. 1994. *Gifts, Favors, and Banquets: The Art of Social Relationships in China*. Ithaca: Cornell University Press.

Yee, Albert H. 1989. *A People Misruled: Hong Kong and the Chinese Stepping Stone Syndrome*. Hong Kong: API Press.

———. 1990. "A Comparative Study of Macau's Education System: Changing Colonial Patronage and Native Self-reliance." *Comparative Education* 26, no. 1: 61–71.

Yee, Herbert S. 1993. "Macau's Civil Service in Transition: The Politics of Localization." *Hong Kong Public Administration* 2, no. 1: 58–70.

———. 1997. "The Eurasians (Macanese) in Macau: The Neglected Minority." *Issues and Studies* 33, no. 6: 113–32.

———. 2001. *Macau in Transition: From Colony to Autonomous Region.* Houndmills, Eng.: Palgrave.

Yen, Ching-Hwang. 1985. *Coolies and Mandarins: China's Protection of Overseas Chinese During the Late Ch'ing Period (1851–1911)*. Singapore: Singapore University Press, National University of Singapore.

Yin Guangren 印光任 and Zhang Rulin 張汝霖. 1992. *Aomen jilüe jiao zhu* 澳門記略校注 (The annotated brief record of Macau), ed. and annot. Zhao Chunchen 趙春晨. Macau: Instituto Cultural de Macau.

Yngvesson, Barbara. 2002. "Placing the 'Gift Child' in Transnational Adoption." *Law and Society Review* 36, no. 2: 227–57.

Young, Robert. 1990. *White Mythologies: Writing History and the West.* London: Routledge.

Yuan Dingzhong 袁定中. 1961. "Tiandihui jiujing shi shenme xingzhi?" 天地會究竟是什么性質? (What is the nature of the Tiandihui?). *Wenhui bao* 文匯報, November 10.

Yuan, D. Y., Wong Hon Keong, and Libânio Martins, eds. 1990. *Population and City Growth in Macau.* Macau: Centre of Macau Studies, University of East Asia in association with Macau Census and Statistics Department.

Zhang, Li. 2001. *Strangers in the City: Reconfigurations of Space, Power, and Social Networks Within China's Floating Population.* Stanford: Stanford University Press.

———. 2002. "Spatiality and Urban Citizenship in Late Socialist China." *Public Culture* 14, no. 2: 311–34.

———. 2006. "Contesting Spatial Modernity in Late-Socialist China." *Current Anthropology* 47, no. 3: 461–84.

Zhang Wenqin 章文欽. 1995. *Aomen yu Zhonghua lishi wenhua* 澳門與中華歷史文化 (Macau and Chinese history and culture). Macau: Fundação Macau.

———. 1999. *Aomen lishi wenhua* 澳門歷史文化 (Macau history and culture). Beijing: Zhonghua shuju.

Zhang Ying 張穎. 2004. "He Houhua: aiguo aixiang wu kui wo xin" 何厚鏵: 愛國愛鄉無愧我心 (Edmund Ho: proud to be *aiguo aixiang*). *NanFang wang/SouthCN.com*. *http://big5.southcn.com/gate/big5/www.southcn.com/news/hktwma/zhuanti/aomwzn/amhuts/200412160620.htm*

Zheng Tianxiang 鄭天祥. 1999. "Aomen wenhua" 澳門文化 (Macau culture). Paper given at the *International Conference on Macao's Reversion to China: Retrospect and Prospects,* May 17, 1999, University of Macau.

Zheng Tianxiang 鄭天祥, Wong Chao Son 黃就順, Zhang Guixia 張桂霞, and Deng Hanzeng 鄧漢增. 1994. *Aomen renkou* 澳門人口 (Population of Macau). Macau: Fundação Macau.

Index

education, in Macau, 27, 29, 79,
166, 342n29; poor quality of, 27,
144, 150, 155, 156; history of,
144–53 *passim*, 159, 160; characteristics of, 153–55, 156, 175,
302–3, 338n3, 342n30; reform
of, 156–57, 159, 160
either-or rhetorics, 9, 46, 100, 109,
125, 131, 141, 181, 298
empire, 10, 67, 150, 152, 212, 241,
313; Chinese, 85, 108, 249; Portuguese, 36–37, 49, 56, 158,
232
Escola Comercial, 171–72,
342n29
Escola Portuguesa 168, 171–73,
344nn44–45
Escola Pui Ching, 161–64, 166,
344n41
Escola Secundária Luso-Chinesa
Luís Gonzaga Gomes (ESLC),
165–68, 174
"Essentials of Macau History"
(textbook), 157–59, 161, 163,
164, 166
Estado da Índia, 37, 320–21n9
ethnicity, 79–80, 110–11, 135,
143, 220, 251, 337n33
Eurasians, *see* Macanese

fado, 262, 357n1
flag (of Macau SAR), 138, 249,
306, 310
flexible citizenship, *see under* citizenship
Fok, K. C., 45
Fong, Henry (film producer), 89,
90
Fortaleza São Paulo do Monte, *see*
Monte Fort

Foucault, Michel, 11, 12, 13,
317n6, 318n9, 318n10
14K triad, 83, 87, 88, 91, 329n12,
330n25
Freyre, Gilberto, 52–54, 55, 56,
58, 325nn38–39, 326n40,
326n42. *See also* luso-
tropicalism
Fujian (province in China), 40,
41, 85, 323n24
Fujianese in Macau, 41, 216,
217–18, 350n39, 351n40

gambling, 3, 72, 90; industry in
Macau 25, 29, 67, 71, 227,
250; inspectors, 69, 70, 83,
93–94. *See also* casinos; Ho,
Stanley; STDM
gaps, 152, 194, 228–29, 248, 251,
258
global, the, 140–45 *passim*, 159,
173–75 *passim*, 182, 280,
339n10, 339n12. *See also under* scale
globalization, 3, 10, 12, 15, 19,
34, 62, 153, 174, 180
Goa, 2, 37, 38, 48, 49, 324n32
Goodman, Bryna, 141
Guangzhou, 40, 48, 74, 87, 92,
162, 207, 232, 321n12,
344n41
Gupta, Akhil, 62

Handler, Richard, 226, 265
handover, the (*huigui*), 21, 29, 36,
60, 65, 80, 131, 249, 298,
305–10; as end of imperialism,
6, 7, 141, 175, 300; as source
of anxiety, 21–22, 25, 111,
113, 160, 173, 203, 199, 219,

296; as deadine for projects, 92–94 *passim*, 185, 208, 225; clock (in Beijing), 6, 59, 199

Haojing, 44, 322nn21–22

He Xin, 57

heritage, 180, 226, 228, 356n36; cultural, 28, 201, 229, 233–39 *passim*, 245–51 *passim*, 255–56, 259–61; architectural, 31, 185, 187, 200, 201–11 *passim*, 245, 265, 286–87, 348n26; in law, 203, 205, 206, 348n29. *See also* UNESCO World Heritage Site

Hershatter, Gail, 145

Hinsley, F. H., 8

history (of Macau), 107, 125, 144–52 *passim*, 259–60, 302, 308, 310; and Macau identity, 2, 3, 5, 14, 29–31, 57, 96, 133, 204, 312; and Chineseness, 17, 33–35, 130, 275–76, 278, 297–98; alternative interpretations of, 36–37, 60, 65–67, 136, 159, 206, 208–9, 212, 298; as colonial, 44, 46, 289–91; and scale, 143–46, 148, 161, 166–67, 174, 175; and place, 188–91, 194–95, 204, 213, 218–19; instruction of, 133–36, 157–70, 172–74; united front on, 159, 164, 298. *See also* past

Ho, Edmund (first chief executive of Macau SAR), 305, 339n14

Ho, Stanley Hung-sun (head of STDM), 26, 71, 75, 103, 310, 331n5

Ho Yin (prominent Macau Chinese in 1960s), 284, 305, 359n16

Hong Kong, 36, 47–51 *passim*, 137, 196, 269–71 *passim*, 280–87 *pas-*sim, 293–95, 338n8; and one country, two systems, 4, 7, 25, 92, 143, 300, 338n9; likened to Macau, 6, 50, 145, 160, 198; contrasted to Macau, 15, 25–27, 30, 40–41, 56–57, 68, 153, 161, 275–78; as model for Macau, 24–25, 153–54, 162, 165, 206; British imperialism in, 30, 41, 46, 56, 57, 66, 79, 107, 115, 169–70; representations of Macau in, 60, 72–73, 82, 87–90, 95, 268; triads in, 74, 81, 83, 86, 92; Eurasians in, 103, 116–17; handover of, 114, 276, 308

huigui, see handover

hybridity: of Macau, 14, 28, 31, 202, 208, 249, 272–73, 278; in lusotropicalism, 53–57 *pas-*sim, 304, 326n40; of Macanese, 106, 248, 333n10

identity: 19–20, 264–65, 297, 302, 357nn2–3; of Macau, 2, 105, 135, 202; government rhetoric of, 3–5, 14, 28–31, 137, 143, 223, 263, 272–73, 282; and Chineseness, 16, 20, 274–75, 295, 303; Macanese, 102, 105, 111–12; alternative views of, 170–71, 229, 256, 274–76, 277

imperialism: and sovereignty, 9, 55, 153, 175; in China, 44, 107, 180, 333n13; Portuguese, 58, 150, 152, 171, 301, 304; in Macau, 158, 234, 298, 311. *See also* colonialism; lusotropicalism

Harvard East Asian Monographs
(*out-of-print)

140. Alexander Barton Woodside, *Vietnam and the Chinese Model: A Comparative Study of Vietnamese and Chinese Government in the First Half of the Nineteenth Century*

*141. George Elison, *Deus Destroyed: The Image of Christianity in Early Modern Japan*

142. William D. Wray, ed., *Managing Industrial Enterprise: Cases from Japan's Prewar Experience*

*143. T'ung-tsu Ch'ü, *Local Government in China Under the Ching*

144. Marie Anchordoguy, *Computers, Inc.: Japan's Challenge to IBM*

145. Barbara Molony, *Technology and Investment: The Prewar Japanese Chemical Industry*

146. Mary Elizabeth Berry, *Hideyoshi*

147. Laura E. Hein, *Fueling Growth: The Energy Revolution and Economic Policy in Postwar Japan*

148. Wen-hsin Yeh, *The Alienated Academy: Culture and Politics in Republican China, 1919–1937*

149. Dru C. Gladney, *Muslim Chinese: Ethnic Nationalism in the People's Republic*

150. Merle Goldman and Paul A. Cohen, eds., *Ideas Across Cultures: Essays on Chinese Thought in Honor of Benjamin I. Schwartz*

151. James M. Polachek, *The Inner Opium War*

152. Gail Lee Bernstein, *Japanese Marxist: A Portrait of Kawakami Hajime, 1879–1946*

*153. Lloyd E. Eastman, *The Abortive Revolution: China Under Nationalist Rule, 1927–1937*

154. Mark Mason, *American Multinationals and Japan: The Political Economy of Japanese Capital Controls, 1899–1980*

155. Richard J. Smith, John K. Fairbank, and Katherine F. Bruner, *Robert Hart and China's Early Modernization: His Journals, 1863–1866*

156. George J. Tanabe, Jr., *Myōe the Dreamkeeper: Fantasy and Knowledge in Kamakura Buddhism*

157. William Wayne Farris, *Heavenly Warriors: The Evolution of Japan's Military, 500–1300*

158. Yu-ming Shaw, *An American Missionary in China: John Leighton Stuart and Chinese-American Relations*

159. James B. Palais, *Politics and Policy in Traditional Korea*

*160. Douglas Reynolds, *China, 1898–1912: The Xinzheng Revolution and Japan*

161. Roger R. Thompson, *China's Local Councils in the Age of Constitutional Reform, 1898–1911*

162. William Johnston, *The Modern Epidemic: History of Tuberculosis in Japan*

163. Constantine Nomikos Vaporis, *Breaking Barriers: Travel and the State in Early Modern Japan*

164. Irmela Hijiya-Kirschnereit, *Rituals of Self-Revelation: Shishōsetsu as Literary Genre and Socio-Cultural Phenomenon*

165. James C. Baxter, *The Meiji Unification Through the Lens of Ishikawa Prefecture*

166. Thomas R. H. Havens, *Architects of Affluence: The Tsutsumi Family and the Seibu-Saison Enterprises in Twentieth-Century Japan*

167. Anthony Hood Chambers, *The Secret Window: Ideal Worlds in Tanizaki's Fiction*

168. Steven J. Ericson, *The Sound of the Whistle: Railroads and the State in Meiji Japan*

169. Andrew Edmund Goble, *Kenmu: Go-Daigo's Revolution*